In Our Backyard

In Our Backyard

Keeyask and the Legacy of Hydroelectric Development

Edited by

AIMÉE CRAFT AND JILL BLAKLEY

UNIVERSITY OF MANITOBA PRESS

In Our Backyard: Keeyask and the Legacy of Hydroelectric Development
© The Authors 2022

26   25   24   23   22   1   2   3   4   5

University of Manitoba Press
Winnipeg, Manitoba, Canada
Treaty 1 Territory
uofmpress.ca

Cataloguing data available from Library and Archives Canada
ISBN 978-0-88755-288-5 (PAPER)
ISBN 978-0-88755-290-8 (PDF)
ISBN 978-0-88755-292-2 (EPUB)
ISBN 978-0-88755-294-6 (BOUND)

Cover design by Vincent Design.
Interior design by Karen Armstrong.
Cover images by KC Adams.

Printed in Canada

This book has been published with the help of a grant from the
Federation for the Humanities and Social Sciences, through the Awards
to Scholarly Publications Program, using funds provided by the
Social Sciences and Humanities Research Council of Canada.

The University of Manitoba Press acknowledges the financial support for
its publication program provided by the Government of Canada through
the Canada Book Fund, the Canada Council for the Arts, the Manitoba
Department of Sport, Culture, and Heritage, the Manitoba Arts Council,
and the Manitoba Book Publishing Tax Credit.

Funded by the Government of Canada | Canada

Names
Ovide Mercredi

I live near a river
It flows by my home
As a child we played together
I, running along its shore
It, rushing by me swiftly
We knew each other by name.

It shared its water with me
For drinking, bathing and swimming
It carried me from place to place
The river still flows by my home
It still knows my name
Even tho it's not the same
A hydro dam came to stop us
I, from living my people's way
It, from flowing freely as before.

I lived near the Misipawistik
A Grand Rapids along the Saskatchewan
Too powerful and great for its own good
Was taken advantage of for progress
Like my people and their culture too.

Now, the Misipawistik is strangely silent
The crackle of electricity replaced its voice
Just as the cackle of Hydro money and bosses
Have drowned our traditional ways and lands.

The river and my people are not the same
Many changes have come in infamy
I cannot drink from the river no more
You cannot hunt on land under water
We both miss the roaring Misipawistik
But, we still know each other's names.

27 December 2006

CONTENTS

FOREWORD

TERRY SARGEANT, FORMER CHAIR OF THE MANITOBA CLEAN ENVIRONMENT COMMISSION

As I begin to write these comments, Canada and the entire world are consumed by the intense struggle to contain the COVID-19 pandemic.

In February 2020, Canada's attention was focused on the blockades of rail lines by those supporting the Wet'suwet'en hereditary chiefs in their opposition to the Coastal GasLink pipeline in northern British Columbia, as well as focused on the Government of Canada's then-pending decision on whether or not to approve Teck Resources' application to build a very large oil sands project in northern Alberta.

At that time, Warren Mabee, in an opinion piece posted on theconversation.com, wrote: "New energy projects have never faced such an uncertain pathway to success." In particular, his piece addressed the changing role of Indigenous peoples in making decisions about resource development in their territories.[1]

This book does the same, in a much more comprehensive way. It looks, in particular, at the experience many of its authors had in respect to the Keeyask Generating Project. It sets the context for this most recent development by reviewing the sixty-plus-year history of hydroelectric resource development in northern Manitoba.

Manitoba Hydro's developments in northern Manitoba began with the Kelsey Generating Station on the Nelson River in the mid-1950s, built to support the nickel mine in Thompson, followed by the Grand Rapids Generating Station on the Saskatchewan River in the 1960s. After that came the start of major development of the lower Nelson, which led to massive rearrangements of waterways throughout the province. These included: the Churchill, Burntwood, and upper Nelson rivers; South Indian Lake; Playgreen Lake; and Lake Winnipeg, among many others.

To say that the impacts of these developments on the human and natural ecology of the region were devastating would be an understatement.

These impacts have been very well documented. Compensation agreements have been negotiated and signed and implemented. Promises to do things differently in the future have been made.

Much damage has been done over those six decades. Tens of thousands of Indigenous people were left to build lives in this much-changed environment. That continues; the damage cannot be undone.

With the backdrop of their Keeyask experiences, the editors and authors of this book have set out to examine the legacy of this development; to examine how and why certain decisions were made by successive governments of Manitoba, Manitoba Hydro, and their agents; to look at the impacts on individuals and communities; and to set out some thoughts on how it might have been done differently. It is their hope that this will lead to better understanding of these impacts, as well as better processes for any future development in northern Manitoba, processes that, at the very least, involve the local Indigenous communities from the very start.

As a Manitoban, I must accept my share in the guilt for this legacy. As an individual, my role has been involved and wide-ranging.

I was an undergrad in university when then-premier Duff Roblin, in a major announcement, introduced the plans for huge hydroelectric development in northern Manitoba. It was to include a number of large generating stations on just about the whole length of the Nelson River, smaller stations on other rivers, including the Burntwood, and significant diversions of other waterways, including the Churchill River.

While policy makers have known about the potential for such development since the early years of the last century, serious planning began in the late 1950s, early 1960s. The plan, as envisaged in the mid-1960s, would have seen as many as eight large generating stations built one after the other, from the upper Nelson, near Cross Lake, to the mouth of Hudson Bay.

One element of this plan involved high-level flooding of South Indian Lake. This would have resulted in the need to move virtually all of the people who lived and worked around this lake. This became a significant issue in the provincial election campaign in June 1969, and contributed to the defeat of the incumbent government.

Also, in June 1969, I took a job at Kettle Rapids and spent six years living and working in Gillam. As such, I was witness to some of the impact of this development on the local Indigenous peoples.

As the Member of Parliament for Selkirk-Interlake in the early 1980s, I represented a number of First Nations communities, two of which—Grand Rapids (now Misipawistik Cree Nation) and Chemawawin Cree Nation at Easterville—experienced significant, negative impacts from the construction of the Grand Rapids Generating Station in the mid-1960s. In visiting those communities, I was told much as to how their lives had been changed by this construction. In the case of Chemawawin, the entire community had been moved from an area rich in fishing and trapping to an area built on rock. This new locale, among other things, made it impossible to install underground water and sewer systems. (However, the houses for the non-Indigenous teachers were serviced by above-ground utilidors, which carried water and sewer.)

This was my first real lesson on the impacts of development in Indigenous territories, with no involvement of the local peoples. I have not forgotten it.

In the later 1980s, I worked for Manitoba Northern Affairs as plans were underway for the construction of the Limestone Generating Station. The Manitoba government and Manitoba Hydro introduced initiatives to enable Indigenous people to work on this project. A major complaint on the projects at Grand Rapids, Kettle, and Long Spruce was that the locals were most often the last hired, first laid-off. And, for the most part, they were relegated to menial, low-skilled jobs.

As an example, in the winter of 1970, of more than 200 employees of the principal contractor at Kettle, there was only one local Indigenous person, a labourer. (As an aside: he continued to work for the contractor, becoming a highly skilled bulldozer operator. With the premier of Manitoba sitting beside him, Noah Massan "turned the sod" for the opening of the Limestone Project in the mid-1980s. Thirty years later, he argued passionately against hydroelectric development at the Keeyask regulatory hearings.)

Perhaps the most important initiative, in the run-up to the Limestone Project, was one to train and support Indigenous workers, so that they wouldn't be restricted to mostly unskilled work. Training programs included everything from bus driving to carpentry to mechanics and, even, professional engineering. As well, there was an on-site support program throughout the project.

With the completion of the Limestone Generating Station in the early 1990s and the abandonment of the Conawapa Project at the same time, there was no new hydro development for over a decade.

The new millennium brought a revitalization of hydro development, with, first, the Wuskwatim Generating Station, near Nelson House; followed by Bipole III, with attendant converter stations at Keewatinook, on the Nelson River, near where Conawapa may or may not be built, and another at Riel, just outside Winnipeg; and the Keeyask Generating Station on the Nelson, near Split Lake.

In this post-2000 era of hydro development, there are two new and very different elements to the process: environmental review, and the involvement of First Nations as equity partners in the projects.

In 1988, Manitoba adopted a new Environment Act. Among its provisions was a redesigned role for the Clean Environment Commission (CEC). While the CEC had been around in different formats and with different names since the 1930s, after 1988, it was charged with conducting reviews of potential impacts to the environment by proposed developments.

In January 2004, I was appointed to be the chair of the CEC and continued in that role until September 2016. Upon appointment, I immediately joined the panel reviewing the proposed Wuskwatim Generating Station. This was the first such review of a hydro project. Since then, Manitoba Hydro has appeared before the commission on a number of occasions, including for Bipole III and Keeyask, and to renew their licence to use Lake Winnipeg as a storage basin.

At the time I left, the commission was engaged in a wide-ranging review of the cumulative effects of all of the hydro development involving the Nelson, Churchill, and related rivers. It was the commission's view that such an assessment could provide a very valuable base for planning any future development in northern Manitoba. While a change in government in 2016 narrowed the scope of this review, the commission, in May 2018, filed a valuable report: *A Review of the Regional Cumulative Effects Assessment for Hydroelectric Developments on the Nelson, Burntwood, and Churchill River Systems.*[2]

Given my role as chair, my views on the CEC review process will be a bit biased. All in all, I think it is a valuable process. During my time with the commission, we expanded the nature of our reviews and, particularly, the role of the public in this work. We travelled throughout the regions germane to the specific review, visiting many towns and First Nations. In those communities, we heard heart-rending stories about past impacts, as well as very reasoned thoughts in respect of the projects under review and their potential impacts.

An important part of the CEC process is a program that makes funding available to groups wishing to be involved in the review processes. This allows community groups, First Nations, consumer groups, and others to engage fully in the process. The funding allows them to hire professionals, to hold community sessions, and to attend the review hearings to present their case and to question the proponents.

It is my firm belief that this "intervener-funding" and stakeholder involvement are essential parts of the review process, leading to a more comprehensive review and, ultimately, to a better result.

It is worth noting that most of the contributors to this book have participated in one or more of the CEC reviews of Manitoba Hydro projects of the past two decades.

Still, the CEC review process is not perfect. It could be improved by granting it more independence and more resources.

Under the Environment Act, the CEC is only an advisory body. The commission gives advice to the minister, who then makes the decision as to whether the project should go ahead. It is also the minister's decision as to whether or not the CEC gets to review any given proposal. And, the minister gets to define the scope of the review.

While I can understand the reason for giving the minister the final say on the go-ahead, I believe that it should not be the minister's decision as to whether or not a specific project is subject to review. Neither should they be the one to set the terms of the review.

In my view, regulations should set out a clearly defined list of project types that would be automatically subject to a review by the commission. It would be up to the commission, with public input, to establish the scope of the review. This would, of course, require some additional resources for the commission. But the result would be very much worth it.

The second "new" element is the involvement of First Nations as equity partners. The Nisichawayasihk Cree Nation in Nelson House is a 30 percent partner in the Wuskwatim Generating Station. Four First

Nations—Tataskweyak Cree Nation, Fox Lake Cree Nation, York Factory First Nation, and War Lake First Nation—have the option to share up to a 25 percent piece of the Keeyask Generating Station.

The concept of equity partnership for First Nations came up for discussion in the later 1980s, as the Limestone Project unfolded. With the pause in hydro development in the 1990s, the idea went nowhere until plans for Wuskwatim became serious and Nisichawayasihk became a partner with Manitoba Hydro. With Hydro's decision to proceed with Keeyask, rather than the much-larger Conawapa Project, it was the First Nations, led by Tataskweyak, that approached Hydro about becoming partners.

While this idea is certainly laudable, the jury is still out as to just how valuable it will turn out to be for the First Nations partners. Some of the arrangements have had to be considerably reworked. Benefits to the communities have not accrued nearly as quickly as anticipated.

There is important discussion on these partnership arrangements in this book.

While this book does focus on experiences surrounding the development of the Keeyask Generating Station, it also reviews many aspects of the history of hydroelectric development in northern Manitoba over the past six-plus decades.

This history is widely known: of widespread, negative impacts to individuals, to communities, to ways of life, to wildlife, and to the environment. These impacts are given further discussion in this book.

There has been much written about this history over many years—books, reports of many inquiries, reviews and studies, academic papers, and so on. There is still a need for a book such as this one. While it incorporates much of the long history, by using Keeyask as its focus, it includes the more recent experiences of the last couple of decades.

This is important, not only because of the development of new projects in the past two decades but also because of a much-changed political context in which to examine these issues. This context includes the much greater attention paid to environmental matters; in particular, climate change, as well as the relatively new era of "reconciliation" in Canada.

I will not go deeply into a discussion of reconciliation, as I am far from being an expert on it. For most Canadians, it is still a new concept.

For the Canada of the future, reconciliation is very important, a concept that will require much work on all sides to define, as well as much action to implement. Within this concept of reconciliation is a recognition that we need to re-examine the rights of Indigenous peoples to determine not only how they live and work in their traditional territories but also how they are fully involved as future resource developments unfold.

This book may be viewed as one of many small steps on the road to reconciliation. While they may not specifically state it, the authors of this book have written their chapters within this political context, with an awareness of the reconciliation process. This will add to its value as a significant contribution to much-needed and ongoing discussions.

At the outset, I quoted a writer who questioned the uncertain future for major energy projects. So, in conclusion, we need to ask whether there will be future hydroelectric development in Manitoba. We know that there is the capacity for much more such development.

Over the last decade or so, a number of observers have written of the end of "big dams." But, as the world moves away from fossil fuels over the next few decades, there is already talk of the need for more hydroelectric power (as well as nuclear) to replace fossil fuel–generated energy.

While we know that the development of hydroelectric power is not nearly as "clean" as many believe, it may prove to be a very difficult fight to convince an energy-abusing world otherwise.

If it does come to that, there will need to be much more consideration given to environmental concerns and much more involvement of the peoples who have lived in their territories for many millennia.

This book, I believe, can play an important role in those discussions.

Notes

1   Warren Mabee, "Teck Aftermath: Ottawa Must Reconcile Big Energy Projects with Climate Policy," https://theconversation.com/teck-aftermath-ottawa-must-reconcile-big-energy-projects-with-climate-policy-132484.

2   Available online at the Manitoba Clean Environment Commission, http://www.cecmanitoba.ca.

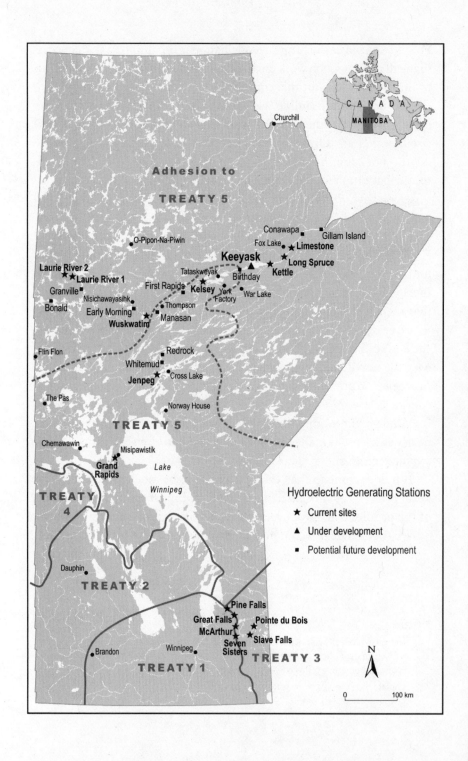

Hydroelectric Generating Stations

★ Current sites

▲ Under development

■ Potential future development

In Our Backyard

" Pimicikamak has many concerns about the impacts of the existing Hydro project and about how Keeyask might alter or add to these impacts. Keeyask will affect Pimicikamak directly and cumulatively with the devastating impacts of existing hydro development, and Pimicikamak just suffers the costs and burdens. The deep impacts we have experienced is what we call genocide."

Darwin Paupanakis, Pimicikamak,
CEC hearings (4 December 2013), 5082

Built on the Back of the Turtle: Reflections on How Hydroelectric Dams Have Changed Landscapes

AIMÉE CRAFT AND JILL BLAKLEY

What once was the pristine landscape of northern Manitoba has been dramatically altered in the last half-century by hydroelectric and other development, including mining and timber extraction. Beginning with the Grand Rapids Dam in the 1960s, a series of projects followed in northern Manitoba. Each of them is part of Manitoba Hydro's integrated power system, which has fractured the landscape, altered watersheds, changed habitat, and deeply affected northern peoples. Development pressures change landscapes and ecosystems, and the significance of the impact should be considered from multiple and cross-cutting perspectives, with an eye to the past and the future, especially when any new development initiatives are contemplated.

The history of hydroelectric development in northern Manitoba is a long and complicated one. There are many competing points of view, but some facts remain. The Nelson River (referred to as "kitchi sipi" or "great big river" by some)[1] has been cut up into segments and fractured by six hydroelectric dams, Keeyask being the most recent. The Churchill River has been diverted to periodically feed the Nelson River and power its dams. New inflow points have been created so that Lake Winnipeg can pour its water into the Nelson at times of the year when its natural flow is reduced. Historic mighty rapids have shrivelled into dried-up riverbeds. Control structures spatter the system to hold back powerful waters and make them move in ways they never did before human intervention. Many of the most directly affected Indigenous residents would tell you that this, far from representing "progress," has caused great sadness.

This collection of works aims to tell a story of the Keeyask[2] hydro-electric dam and accompanying development (including a converter station and major transmission line), from the perspective of Indigenous peoples, directly affected individuals, academics, experts, and regulators. It builds on the rich regulatory environmental and economic evaluation of the Keeyask Dam[3] (currently in its final phase of construction as this book goes to press) as part of a series of regulatory hearings on new development, including the Bipole III transmission line,[4] the Keeyask construction camp,[5] Keewatinohk converter station,[6] and the Needs For and Alternatives To (NFAT) the Hydro preferred plan.[7] It also reflects on other infrastructure in Manitoba as part of a collective legacy and integrated system of hydroelectric generation. Many of the contributors to this book participated in one or more of the hearings, and their voices and writings are assembled here in an effort to continue the conversation beyond the regulatory context. Of particular note here is the importance this book places on Indigenous voices and perspectives.

While the general approach to hydroelectric development has shifted from unconsented destruction of Indigenous lands to new models of consultation and partnership (discussed in chapters in this volume by Joseph Dipple, Jerry Buckland and Melanie O'Gorman, and Aimée Craft), these new approaches may have questionable benefits. They remain problematic in their inherent limitations and inability to address hierarchical structures of power that continue to marginalize groups of people and communities, including primarily Indigenous citizens, as illustrated in the chapter by Buckland and O'Gorman.

In the past and present, hydroelectric power has been generated in northern Manitoba, primarily to meet the needs of the South, including export into the United States. This has benefited Manitobans in the form of the lowest hydro rates in the country for decades and through profits shared with the provincial coffers. However, early hydroelectric development in northern Manitoba was done without regard to the impacts of hydroelectric development on Indigenous peoples, without their consent, which irreparably diminished Indigenous traditional modes of life (see, for example, Chapter 3 in this volume on the impacts of the Churchill Diversion to South Indian Lake). After this first wave, Manitoba First Nations rallied together to speak about their devastating experiences and negotiate the Northern Flood Agreement (NFA), which provided monetary compensation for their losses. This modern Treaty[8] was meant to reset the relationship between Indigenous people in the North and the provincial government, the federal government, and Manitoba Hydro itself.

Yet, after the promises of the NFA and a string of apologies, development that internalizes negative impacts to Indigenous communities continues (see Chapter 6 in this volume by Agnieszka Pawlowska-Mainville with Noah Massan). While governments now prioritize a partnership model with select Indigenous communities—most recently, with four First Nations in the Keeyask area—Manitoba Hydro's goal of generating economic profits in the most expedient way possible has stayed the same.

The chapters in this book argue that the Keeyask development goes far beyond the immediate electric consumption needs of Manitobans and is designed to feed an export market of power supply to the United States' Midwest. As Byron Williams and Will Braun argue, if the production, transmission, and sale of power are to benefit Manitobans, they must take into account a sustainable northern future (including environmental considerations and socio-economic-cultural-human impacts) while keeping costs of electricity in Manitoba low.[9]

If hydro rates are increasing and an already compromised environment is being further impacted, then we should probe Hydro's approach to development in the North. Costs, beyond the proposed and anticipated dollar costs, must be evaluated in the face of shifting economic, social, legal, political, and environmental landscapes. For the first time, a Regional Cumulative Effects Assessment (RCEA) was conducted for the region, but as Jill Blakley points out in Chapter 9 of this volume, the RCEA was limited in scope and the assessment did not include active participation from affected Indigenous people. With a provincial and federal regulatory regime that is struggling to balance development and sustainability, and in light of the inherent rights of Indigenous people to land, livelihoods, and self-determination, this book's contributors highlight the need for purposeful dialogue, principled decision making, and a better legacy of northern development in the future.

In the face of the current climate crisis, people around the world are asking: At what point can money no longer buy what we have lost? Questions like this are why this book is crucial to our contemporary understanding of hydroelectric development practice, not only in Manitoba but as a model of practice that can be understood as relevant to a series of hydro development (and other development) contexts around the world, especially their affected communities.

The following chapters contextualize Keeyask in a broader series of recent developments (like the Wuskwatim Dam) within the Nelson River watershed. They also consider hydroelectric development impacts, past, present, and future, in other regions of Manitoba. However, this book cannot tell the whole story. There is too much to be said in one book, with the impacts—and benefits—of development experienced in different ways by different individuals and groups. There is much yet to be discovered in relation to the outcomes of the Keeyask Project.

It is also impossible for anyone to tell the whole story without having lived the experience or without having seen the destruction in the region or without having been on the land and waters. Environmental assessment processes, including the Manitoba Clean Environment Commission's (CEC) public hearing process into decision making in 2012, have struggled to incorporate Indigenous voices and perspectives. The weight ultimately given to those voices is arguably not as significant as it should be. During those hearings—and as Asfia Gulrukh Kamal, Joseph Dipple, Steve Ducharme, and Leslie Dysart, and Pawlowska-Mainville with Noah Massan illustrate in their chapters—many Indigenous people from the region expressed that without a direct relationship with the land, waters, animals, and others in the territory, one cannot begin to understand the Keeyask Dam's true significance. Robert Spence is a land and resource user from Tataskweyak Cree Nation, one of the four "Keeyask Cree Nations," or KCNs, whose members narrowly voted to join Manitoba Hydro's Keeyask partnership in 2009. As he put it, he "grew up in the shadow of one dam and will die in the shadow of another."[10] Janet McIvor's family has lived in the area for generations; at the CEC hearings, she stated, "There should be constant assessment, evaluation, and traditional knowledge should always be honoured by our visitors. Manitoba Hydro only wants to develop and profit from the land. Our spiritual connection with the land will be lost, yet we sit in front of the Clean Environment Commission to determine the fate of our land, water, animals, and environment. We already see the impacts. Hydro says minimal impacts. It is easy for them to say that, they don't live here, and yet, we are 125 percent affected by the Kelsey, Limestone, Kettle, Long Spruce, Wuskwatim."[11] Eunice Beardy from Split Lake added, "Clean environment to me means the whole environment, the air, the trees, the water. The land, our animals, that is being destroyed by all of these Hydro dams that are developing."[12]

We hope to bring further attention to these voices throughout this volume, through the main chapters themselves and through excerpts from the CEC hearing transcripts, which bring to life the rich community of voices of people who have lived within their lands and territories for generations and care deeply about the future of their territories and relationships with the land. This includes two poems from former Assembly of First Nations National Chief Ovide Mercredi about the loss in Misipiwistik resulting from the Grand Rapids Dam. We have also included statements about attempts at repair and redress by the Province of Manitoba, which shed some light on the tenuous relationships between the Indigenous people affected by hydroelectricity and its proponents.

In this volume, we also hope to bring further attention to the voices of scientists, experts, lawyers, and others who participated in recent public hearings on Manitoba Hydro projects. This cross-disciplinary approach challenges the confines of each discipline and world view to draw knowledge together to assess the full scope of impact of the project. The voices we hear in this book also suggest that we can collectively think of land and water as both place and person—an Indigenous ontological approach to being in relationship with land that requires treating land as not just resources or as social/economic spaces or place but as a relative. By bringing these disciplines into conversation, we suggest that decision making is not about strict application of regulatory regimes or laws—it requires principled decision making that engages partnership in a true sense, including existing relationships between Indigenous peoples and their lands and waters.

This book, *In Our Backyard*, is organized in relation to four important themes, which we hope provide the reader with a wealth of information and perspectives from which to consider hydroelectric development in northern Manitoba, as reflected in the Keeyask experience. This includes sections on the evolution of the development that has taken place in northern Manitoba, with an emphasis on regulatory processes; an analysis of impacts of hydroelectric development and specifically the Keeyask Project; reflections on partnership building for hydroelectric development projects; and perspectives on what constitutes good development and legacy building in northern Manitoba.

In the first part, which probes past and present hydroelectric development in northern Manitoba, we have included an essay by Byron Williams (Chapter 1), a lawyer who has represented public interest groups for more than twenty years in Manitoba, on what happens when politicians' dreams collide with the market analysis relating to the Keeyask Project. Will Braun, a hydro-conscious advocate and analyst, then provides a critique of the overarching narratives of "clean" energy and indefinite growth, and a new approach to Indigenous engagement and social licence. In Chapter 3, Asfia Gulrukh Kamal, Joseph Dipple, Steve Ducharme, and Leslie Dysart provide a thoughtful reflection on how Manitoba Hydro's integrated system has set apart the interests of South Indian Lake from the broader analysis of ongoing and future projects like Keeyask. This section includes a personal narrative by Ramona Neckoway on the experience of Wuskwatim as a precursor to Keeyask that foreshadowed the difficulties that can be incurred when hydroelectric projects do not prove to be as profitable to Indigenous communities as was promised.

Part 2 of the book discusses the existing and experiential impacts of hydroelectric development in northern Manitoba, including on species, communities, and the region, cumulatively, over time. It opens with testimony from Tataskweyak Cree Nation land user Robert Spence, who has lived all his life in Split Lake and shares about the hurt he carries with him because of Manitoba Hydro's activities. In Chapter 4, Jill Blakley and Bram Noble probe the cumulative effects analysis in the Keeyask Environmental Impact Assessment to determine whether we can draw the conclusion from the evidence that there are "no significant cumulative effects" that would result from this project. James Robson in Chapter 5 considers how divergent world views that come together to environmentally assess Keeyask can and should engage different processes and mechanisms that may in turn lead to differing results. In testimony excerpts preceding Chapter 6, Conway Arthurson, a former councillor for Fox Lake Cree Nation, shares his father's stories of working for Manitoba Hydro. Chapter 6, a conversation between Agnieszka

Pawlowska-Mainville and Noah Massan (a Fox Lake citizen), presents the importance of Indigenous narratives in assessing and acknowledging impacts of development on Indigenous territories and people.

In Chapter 7, Annette Luttermann problematizes the effects of river regulation expected from the Keeyask Generation Project on aquatic and riparian habitats and the species they support. James Schaefer, a caribou scientist, invites us in Chapter 8 to listen to what the caribou tell us and to adopt a long and forward-looking view in relation to major developments. Jill Blakley then provides a summary in Chapter 9 of the RCEA that was tabled in 2015 by the Government of Manitoba and Manitoba Hydro following both the Wuskwatim and Bipole III hearing processes. She suggests that there are opportunities to think about and do regional-scale assessments of the total impacts of combined developments better in the future. This section closes with the testimony of the family whose ancestral land is on the Gull Lake Trapline 15 area, and who have been displaced by the Keeyask development.

The third part of the book begins with Aimée Craft's reflections on the unique relationship between Manitoba Hydro, a Crown corporation, with impacted First Nations, which is grounded in the constitutional duty of the Honour of the Crown and which requires a high standard of honourable conduct. Further testimony from Robert Spence talks about his grandfather's lessons on the people with the power to destroy the land. In Chapter 11, Joseph Dipple critiques the partnership approach adopted for the Keeyask Project and asks who stands to benefit from the development of the Keeyask partnership. In the closing chapter of this section, Jerry Buckland and Melanie O'Gorman consider the Keeyask model for community economic development and some of the gaps in the Keeyask approach, including the lack of support for housing and education.

The last section of the book asks the ultimate question: What is good development? It begins with a poem by Ovide Mercredi. Then, in Chapter 13 Aimée Craft analyzes the two-track approach employed to evaluate the Keeyask Project, which attempted to incorporate Cree world views into the environmental impact assessment but missed an opportunity to have it directly influence the final conclusions of the environmental decision-making process. Further testimony from the Trapline 15 family emphasizes their deep connection to the land, and how switching traplines is not a viable option. In Chapter 14, Patricia

Fitzpatrick, Alan Diduck, and James Robson discuss adaptive management and continuous learning as requirements for good development. Chapter 15 then speaks to Kyrke Gaudreau's and Robert Gibson's view on sustainability assessment as an integral component of decision making for long-term, impactful projects like Keeyask.

The conclusion to *In Our Backyard* invites us to think about how we frame northern development moving forward, including the motivations that drive it. It situates us within an evolving context of the Truth and Reconciliation Commission of Canada's critiques of the history of development in Indigenous territories, the compromised historical and legal relationship between Indigenous people and the Crown, and the imperative of reconciliation based on the development of lasting, mutually respectful, and beneficial relationships rooted in the promise of treaties.

The book as a whole centres the Manitoba experience in the wake of recent international recognition of Indigenous peoples' special relationships to lands and territories and their rights of self-determination. More particularly, the United Nations Declaration on the Rights of Indigenous Peoples, to which Canada is a signatory and has promised to fully implement, sets the foundation of all development on the free, prior and informed consent (FPIC) of Indigenous peoples in relation to their territories. This, married with Canadian common law requirements to consult and accommodate Indigenous peoples before the Crown will authorize development that may impact Treaty and Aboriginal rights, requires us to engage deeply with our approaches to development and ensure a more equitable relationship with one another. The Truth and Reconciliation Commission found that, particularly with respect to land use and development, or "economic reconciliation," that "sustainable reconciliation on the land involves realizing the economic potential of Indigenous communities in a fair, just, and equitable manner that respects their right to self-determination. Economic reconciliation involves working in partnership with Indigenous peoples to ensure that lands and resources within their traditional territories are developed in culturally respectful ways that fully recognize Treaty and Aboriginal rights and title."[13]

We are at a unique point in time where we can think critically, strategically, sustainably, and Indigenously about the legacy of hydroelectric development in northern Manitoba and around the world. This includes a deeper, more nuanced understanding of the past, present, and future relationships among the Crown (and its agents), Manitoba Hydro (a Crown corporation), and Indigenous communities in Manitoba. North America as a whole is known as "Turtle Island" by many Indigenous peoples who inhabit it and have long-standing connections with the land and water. Their direct involvement in sustainable decision making is required when dams and other megaprojects are proposed to be built on the Turtle's back.

For many of those involved in the Keeyask experience, the Keeyask Project is a symbol of a seemingly unwavering approach to build more hydroelectric infrastructure in Manitoba, despite myriad signals to pull back or forge a new path. The connection to export markets and the economic drive for further development have proven to date to act as blinders to falling markets, environmental change, and unanticipated costs. In his 2020 report reviewing the Keeyask and Bipole III projects, Commissioner Wall noted that "Keeyask was not necessary at the time of the NFAT to meet the Province's then-anticipated electrical needs in a timely and cost-effective manner" and that its construction "was driven by momentum from previous decisions including reputational risk from export agreements that required new generation when that generation had not been approved, 'sunk costs' of $1.2 billion in infrastructure spending to support the project, and partnership agreements that had already been executed with First Nations after significant effort and good faith on their part."[14]

Like the oversimplified narratives driving human factors, oversimplified approaches to monitoring the Nelson River ecosystem and mitigating for adverse effects may have devastating effects on the plants, birds, fish, animals, and other non-human relations. The future legacy of northern development can be different from that, if we choose.

We owe it to ourselves collectively to ask the question that should have been asked all along, since Manitoba built the first dam in 1900 on the Minnedosa River: Is more development a good thing? There are now fifteen dams, three control structures, five converter stations, and 13,800 kilometres of transmission lines that make up the current integrated Manitoba Hydro system.[15] This system currently generates 6,000 megawatts (MW), with further possible development almost doubling the system's capacity to over 10,000 MW. Whether we really need more development is a relevant question around the world, not only in relation to hydroelectric development but for development generally and within Indigenous territories specifically.

Good development should be good for all Manitobans and should connect to public good. How does our current decision making bridge the potential disconnect between capitalist motivations and the land-based connection of relationship? How does it account for the breakdown of relationships to lands, waters and territories, and amongst people and other beings? Does it provide an opportunity for the re/building of relationships? Is our collective well-being eclipsed by the need to build/expand/exercise power/grow? What is beneficial to Manitobans? Who are Manitobans, if not the people of the North? What is Manitoba, if not Indigenous territory?

Our hope is that this collection of perspectives will support better policy and regional land-use and energy planning decisions in the future, as well as highlight important considerations for future development projects, including Manitoba Hydro's proposed Conawapa Dam[16] and other industry, Crown, and Indigenous partnerships and consent processes relating to use of lands, waters, and resources. We also hope that it will serve as a platform to help educate consumers and citizens of Manitoba (and beyond) about the complexities of hydroelectric development, their corresponding consumption, the economics of exporting power, and the material costs to northern territories and to Indigenous peoples.

Notes

1   Manitoba Public Utilities Board (PUB), Needs For and Alternatives To hearings for the Keeyask Project, 25 April 2014, http://www.pub.gov.mb.ca/nfat/pdf/hearing/april_25_2014.pdf; PUB final report, http://www.pub.gov.mb.ca/nfat/pdf/finalreport_pdp.pdf.

2   Keeyask is the sixteenth generating station built and currently in operation in Manitoba. It is the sixth dam built on the Nelson River and will be the ninth built in northern Manitoba.

3   Manitoba's Clean Environment Commission (CEC) hearings, 24 September 2013–9 January 2013, http://www.cecmanitoba.ca/cecm/hearings/pubs/Keeyask_Generation_Project/Transcripts/Public_Hearing_Sept_24,_2013_-_Gillam.pdf; the Keeyask start date was 16 July 2014, https://keeyask.com/wp-content/uploads/2014/07/07-16-KHLP-News-Release01-Revised.pdf, and is anticipated to be completed in 2021, https://www.hydro.mb.ca/projects/keeyask/.

4   CEC hearings on the Bipole III Project, http://www.cecmanitoba.ca/cecm/ hearings/bipole-iii.html; Bipole III was completed in July 2018, https://www.hydro. mb.ca/regulatory_affairs/projects/bipole3/.

5   Infrastructure construction took place from 2012 to 2014, http://www.pubmanitoba. ca/v1/proceedings-decisions/appl-current/pubs/2017%20mh%20gra/mh%20 exhibits/mh-120%20-%20manitoba%20hydro%27s%20direct%20evidence%20 presentation%20on%20major%20capital%20projects.pdf.

6   First transmission of energy in April 2018, https://www.hydro.mb.ca/corporate/ facilities/converter_stations/.

7   PUB hearings, http://www.pubmanitoba.ca/v1/proceedings-decisions/mh-nfat/ index.html; and final decision, http://www.pub.gov.mb.ca/nfat/pdf/finalreport_pdp. pdf.

8   Eric Robinson, in Government of Manitoba, "News Release," 20 January 2015, https://news.gov.mb.ca/news/index.html?archive=&item=33753; Peter Kulchyski, "A Step Back: The Nisichawayasihk Cree Nation and the Wuskwatim Project," in *Power Struggles: Hydro Development and First Nations in Manitoba and Quebec*, ed. Thibault Martin and Steven Hoffman (Winnipeg: University of Manitoba Press, 2008), 134.

9   In 2017, Manitoba Hydro sought a 7.9 percent rate increase for consumer rates for six years, the highest requested rate increases in a quarter-century. Manitoba consumers indicated that this would result in "rate-shock." The Public Utilities Board approved only a 3.6 percent increase. Order No.59/18 FINAL ORDER WITH RESPECT TO MANITOBA HYDRO'S 2017/18 AND 2018/19 GENERAL RATE APPLICATION., s.1.3 The General Rate Application, 7, http://www. pubmanitoba.ca/v1/proceedings-decisions/orders/pubs/2018%20orders/59-18.pdf.

10 Robert Spence, Manitoba PUB Needs For and Alternatives To hearings, 25 April 2014, 8271.

11 Janet McIvor, CEC hearings, 8 October 2013, 20.

12 Eunice Beardy, CEC hearings, 8 October 2013, 40.

13 Canada, Truth and Reconciliation Commission, *Canada's Residential Schools: Reconciliation*, vol. 6, *The Final Report* (Montreal: McGill-Queen's University Press, 2015), 207.

14 Manitoba, Ministry of Crown Services, *Economic Review of Bipole III and Keeyask*, by Commissioner Brad Wall, vol. 1 (Winnipeg: Economic Review Commission, November 2020), 17.

15 Manitoba Hydro Facilities and Operations; Manitoba Hydro facilities map in this volume.

16 Proposed power production of 1,485 MW in ideal conditions with a peak rating of 1,300 MW in winter. Manitoba Hydro 2010/11 and 2011/12 General Rate Application, https://www.hydro.mb.ca/docs/regulatory_affairs/pdf/gra_2010_2012/ Tab_8.pdf.

PART 1

The Evolution of Hydroelectric Development in Northern Manitoba

" My message is short and simple. We need some kind of mechanism to help record the stories and knowledge of our people, and not in a piecemeal manner. You are in Cree territory. Your activities are impacting our way of life. Respect our culture and respect our way of life, value our knowledge."

Dr. Ramona Neckoway, Nisichawayasihk Cree Nation, CEC hearings (9 December 2013), 5520

CHAPTER 1

When Dreams and Markets Collide: Regulatory Gaps and the Keeyask Generating Station

BYRON WILLIAMS

I can't let go of the dream of building some more hydroelectric power and some more windmills in this province.
— Premier Gary Doer, quoted in the *Globe and Mail*, 20 April 2007[1]

Over the past sixty years, hydroelectric projects in Manitoba have offered a potent but politically combustible trade-off between economic opportunity and social, environmental, and financial risk. Affordable hydroelectric power "at cost" has long been a lodestar of Manitoba's economic and community development strategy, especially when leavened with bright visions of handsome export revenues from the American marketplace.

However, it is impossible to ignore the racialized consequences of Manitoba's commitment to a hydro-driven growth strategy. There is a wealth of evidence demonstrating the significant external consequences of hydroelectric projects, including compromised river systems and social disruption. These costs have been inequitably borne by First Nations and other Indigenous people. Hydroelectric projects have had enduring adverse effects on the way of life of northern Indigenous people within the Nelson and Churchill river watersheds. While public understanding of the traumatic consequences of hydro projects on Indigenous people has slowly evolved,[2] hydro expansion has been viewed by many

Manitobans as a mechanism for vital economic stimulus and the provision of affordable low carbon power.

Emboldened by the success of the Limestone Generating Station
in the early 1990s and by increasingly liberalized access to the U.S.
market in the 1990s and 2000s,[3] Manitoba Hydro initiated plans
for an ambitious series of hydroelectric generation and transmission
projects intended to enhance system reliability and capacity while
capitalizing on increased opportunities for export sales to the U.S. and
to Canadian provinces. During the first decade of the 2000s, Hydro
entered into novel partnerships with Cree First Nations along the
Burntwood and Nelson rivers with the intended purpose of building
and owning the Wuskwatim, Keeyask, and Conawapa hydroelectric
generating stations.

Under Hydro's plan to build new generation before it was required to meet Manitoba needs, the surplus would enable Hydro to
enter into long-term contracts to export "clean, renewable" energy
to utilities in Minnesota and Wisconsin while allaying a significant
portion of upfront capital costs. At the same time, the Bipole III and
U.S. Transmission Interconnection[4] projects would be undertaken to
improve the reliability of the Manitoba grid, enable the transmission
of additional northern power, and significantly enhance access to the
U.S. market.

On paper, Hydro's vision was undoubtedly entrancing. Opportunity
would be created for financially strapped First Nations while improving Manitoba Hydro's somewhat tattered reputation in the North.
Manitoba's economy would benefit, from both the short-term stimulus
of construction and the long-term benefits of higher export revenues
and an increased capacity to produce "low cost, low carbon" hydroelectricity. Consumers would see the expense of hydroelectric projects
mitigated by contributions from the export market.

Meanwhile, the reputation of Manitoba Hydro would be enhanced
by its renewed relationship with First Nations. Environmental decision
making would benefit from the distinctive Cree world view of First
Nation project proponents as well as from Hydro's improved understanding of the implications of its actions.

However, the construction of major capital projects is inherently risky[5] and market realities can be unforgiving of capital-heavy
plans that take more than a decade to execute and that commit

to infrastructure lasting at least 100 years. As early concerns from Manitoba's Public Utilities Board (PUB) went unheeded,[6] dramatic changes in energy supply and demand led to a marked decline in actual and forecast export prices. While the PUB was warning that Manitoba Hydro was building for market conditions that no longer existed, initial cost estimates for projects such as Bipole III and Keeyask were revealed to be highly optimistic.[7]

Both Manitoba Hydro and the Province of Manitoba proved ill-equipped to respond to a sea change in the market. Hydro planners struggled to imagine, much less respond to, market realities that had seemed highly implausible just a few years earlier. At the same time, Hydro's commitment to large-scale, capital-intensive hydroelectric generation led to an undervaluing of flexible demand-side management tools,[8] which had the potential to significantly defer the need date of major capital projects.

Hydro's single-minded megaproject focus was enabled by the Province's fragmented and highly politicized regulatory approval process, which exempted Bipole III from any meaningful alternative analysis while enabling Manitoba Hydro to incur more than $1 billion in sunk costs related to Keeyask and Conawapa before any independent, evidence-based consideration of the Needs For and Alternatives To (NFAT) of these projects was undertaken.[9] Ultimately, while expenditure on the roughly $10.5 billion Conawapa Project was halted, provincial approval was granted for the construction of the Bipole III transmission line (2013)[10] as well as for the Keeyask Generating Station (2014).

By 2017, Manitoba Hydro was faced with capital expenditures for Keeyask and Bipole III that were estimated to be at least $3 billion higher than forecast just three years earlier. Hydro also was claiming it would need rate increases of roughly four times the rate of inflation for six successive years to remain financially self-sufficient. While Hydro's application for a 7.9 percent rate increase in 2018/19 was rejected,[11] a number of Manitobans have expressed regret regarding the decision to build Keeyask and Bipole III.[12]

In response to these significant capital overruns as well as ongoing political controversy, the Province of Manitoba initiated a review of Bipole III and Keeyask as well as proposed legislative changes to Manitoba Hydro's oversight legislation.[13]

Only time will tell whether the investment in Keeyask will deliver sustainable benefits or whether the project will become an onerous burden for its proponents and for Manitobans. What is clear is that the largely unchecked discretion of provincial cabinet members to define the timing, scope, and nature of major review processes denied Manitobans an independent review of alternatives until billions of dollars had already been committed to major Hydro projects.

The history of the Keeyask Project suggests a need for fundamental changes in Hydro's resource planning as well as earlier, independent oversight of major capital expenditures. Meaningful public engagement, including with Indigenous people, ratepayers, and public interest communities, can be a vital and cost-effective mechanism to envision different futures and to assist both resource planning and independent review. But, according to a report by the Canadian Environmental Assessment Agency, "for many Canadians, by the time they are asked to participate, projects are already fully planned with little room for change."[14]

A review of the Keeyask Project's history suggests that Manitoba Hydro and the Province were irreversibly "locked in"[15] to the project well before the public and independent tribunals had an opportunity to examine the merits of the choice and potential alternatives.

Opportunity and Reconciliation

Manitobans have benefited from many decades of inexpensive electricity, in large part because of earlier decisions to develop the province's rich hydraulic resources.

—Manitoba PUB, *A Review of Manitoba Hydro's Preferred Development Plan*, 2014[16]

The Legend of Limestone

Domestic electricity rates in Manitoba are among the lowest in Canada and North America,[17] due in large part to abundant, relatively accessible hydroelectric resources that were developed in an era before modern environmental, labour, and safety regimes.[18]

But historic results from a different regulatory era are no guarantee of future success. Hydroelectric projects are notoriously challenging, given long lead times;[19] forecast risks related to demand, prices, and capital costs;[20] the variability of water flows over time; and the difficulty in matching supply and demand. Large-scale hydro power, by its very nature, is "lumpy" with cost-effective development requiring the addition of large increments of supply, which often outstrip domestic demand when a major project first comes into service.[21] Significant surpluses, at least in the early years of a major project, are the inevitable result.

While Manitoba Hydro's primary duty, as the Manitoba Public Utilities Board has stated, is to ensure that "Manitobans have adequate access to electrical power at all times,"[22] the Crown corporation also has a mandate, according to the Manitoba Hydro Act, "to market and supply [surplus] power to persons outside the province."[23] Between 2002–03 and 2011–12, about a third of Manitoba Hydro's total electricity revenues came from export sales[24] primarily to the Midwestern U.S. market.[25] The export of surplus power made a material contribution to relatively low hydro rates.[26]

Much of that surplus was made possible by the completion of the Limestone Generating Station on the Nelson River in 1992. Limestone, Manitoba Hydro's largest generating station,[27] was completed on time and under budget.[28] Export sales of surplus power in the Limestone era benefited greatly from higher U.S. prices driven by a number of factors, including liberalized access to the "wholesale electricity market."[29] From these robust financial results, the legend of Limestone was born. Limestone became the poster child for those who saw rich vistas of economic opportunity in the U.S.

Figure 1.1, which tracks Hydro export revenues between 1967 and 2013, captures the significant increase in export revenues marked by the confluence of the Limestone surplus and materially increased access to the U.S. market. Annual export revenues (see Figure 1.1) exceeded $200 million for the first time in 1994 and reached a peak of well over $700 million in the halcyon year of 2007.

The financial success of Limestone was clear.[30] Less readily apparent, at least to many southerners,[31] were the traumatic consequences on northern Indigenous people flowing from a series of Hydro projects dating back to the late 1950s.[32]

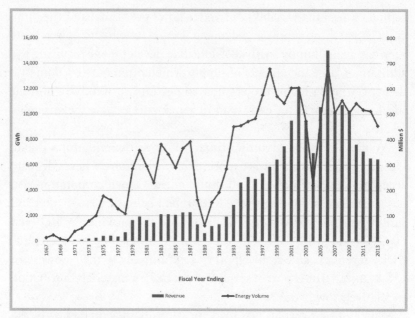

Figure 1.1. Manitoba Hydro Export Sales History, 1967–2013. Source: Manitoba Public Utilities Board, *NFAT*, 96.

Fifty Years of Suffering

In each of the three hydro proceedings, we have heard of a 50-plus year history of pain and suffering.

—Manitoba Clean Environment Commission, *Keeyask Generation Project, Report on Public Hearing*, 2014[33]

The changes in water levels and seasonal flows caused by these major developments negatively affected many individuals and communities in northern Manitoba. This experience continues to influence attitudes and relationships throughout the region and casts a shadow over Manitoba Hydro developments today.

—Manitoba Clean Environment Commission, *Keeyask Generation Project, Report on Public Hearing*, 2014[34]

The economic benefits of hydro development have come at a profound personal, social, and environmental cost for Indigenous persons and communities within hydro-affected watersheds.[35] Consistent with the conclusions of the World Commission on Dams that "the direct adverse impacts of dams have fallen disproportionately" on Indigenous people,[36] recent Manitoba research has characterized these communities as "sacrifice zones" for broader development.[37] Narratives of affected Indigenous people before Manitoba's Clean Environment Commission (CEC) have presented a "50-plus-year history of pain and suffering," leaving the Nelson River "compromised" "while the wealth all goes south."[38]

The enduring conflict between economic opportunity for much of the province and social and environmental costs for affected Indigenous people would have a significant effect on ambitious new plans for hydroelectric development that were emerging in the late 1990s and early 2000s.

Dreams, Opportunity, and Heavy Hearts

By advancing the construction of new hydro plants ahead of domestic needs, Manitoba can both earn additional export revenues and expand valuable interconnection transmission, while also building the plants it will need to meet its own future requirements.

—Manitoba Public Utilities Board, *A Review of Manitoba Hydro's Preferred Development Plan*, 2014[39]

Dating back to the 1990s and with increasing momentum in the early 2000s,[40] Manitoba Hydro and the Province of Manitoba developed a vision for a series of major new generation and transmission projects intended to stimulate economic growth, meet domestic need, achieve reconciliation with Hydro-affected First Nations, enhance domestic reliability, and improve access to export markets, whether in the U.S. or other Canadian provinces.[41]

This "dream" of Manitoba as a major exporter of renewable energy was an important element of public dialogue in the run-up to the 2007 provincial election.[42] Underlying the Province's and Manitoba Hydro's push for projects such as Keeyask was a complex narrative with competing undercurrents of pragmatism and reconciliation. Seeing analogies between Alberta's oil and Manitoba's hydro, Manitoba's premier characterized hydro development as an engine for growth and the means to escape economic mediocrity.[43]

However, unlike prior hydroelectric developments, generating stations such as Wuskwatim, Keeyask, and Conawapa were to be developed with the consent of affected First Nations[44] and in a partnership that mitigated adverse social and environmental effects while promoting economic opportunity.[45] Uniquely, the environmental assessment of the Keeyask Project also would include evaluations carried out by the First Nations project partners and employing a holistic Cree world view.[46]

An important but relatively small[47] first step in the efforts to develop hydroelectricity in concert with First Nations was the completion in 2012 of the 211-megawatt (MW) Wuskwatim Generating Station on behalf of a partnership involving Manitoba Hydro and the Nisichawayasihk Cree Nation.[48] Beyond Wuskwatim, Manitoba Hydro envisioned a further "Decade of Development," which was described in detail by the Manitoba Public Utilities Board (PUB) in a 2012 decision.[49]

Table 1.1 sets out some of the key elements of the "Decade of Development" including the much larger Keeyask and Conawapa generating stations, to be built "in partnership" with a number of Cree First Nations on the Nelson River. Hydro's plans also involved a new interconnection to the U.S. market as well as Bipole III, a major north–south transmission line running from the Nelson River down the west side of the province and then to Winnipeg.[50]

Table 1.1. The Decade of Development (c. 2012)

· 2017/18[a] – the Bipole III transmission line to enhance the ability to reliably bring existing Nelson River power to southern Manitoba while enabling the transmission of the energy generated by Keeyask[b] and Conawapa
· 2019/20 – the Keeyask Generating Station (695 MW)[c] on the Nelson River to be owned in a partnership among Hydro and the Tataskweyak Cree Nation, War Lake First Nation, Fox Lake Cree Nation, and York Factory First Nation (the KCN)
· 2019/20 – a new export/import interconnection with the U.S. market, which would improve the ability to sell surplus Manitoba power to the U.S. market while improving system reliability
· 2023/24 – the Conawapa Generating Station (1,485 MW)[d] on the Nelson River to be owned in a partnership between Hydro and the KCN[e]

Source: Manitoba Public Utilities Board, *Order 5/12*, 7, 33–36 (referring to the 2010–11 Power Resource Plan. The proposed in-service dates for these projects have been amended).

a   Manitoba Public Utilities Board, *Order 5/12*, 125.

b   Kelvin Shepherd, Transcript of Manitoba Public Utilities Board, Manitoba Hydro's 2017/18 and 2018/19 General Rate Application Public Hearing (5 December 2017): 388–89.

c   Manitoba Public Utilities Board, *NFAT*, 47. The estimated capacity of Keeyask in *Order 5/12* was 630 MW. The 695 MW figure is from the Manitoba Public Utilities Board's June 2014 NFAT Final Report.

d   Manitoba Public Utilities Board, *NFAT*, 47. The estimated capacity of Conawapa in *Order 5/12* was 1300 MW. The 1485 MW figure is from Manitoba Public Utilities Board's June 2014 NFAT Final Report.

e   In addition, a north–south transmission upgrade project would be necessary if Conawapa was built.

Intimately linked to the "Decade of Development" were proposed export contracts with utilities in Minnesota and Wisconsin. To "facilitate these projected export contract sales," Hydro planned to bring Keeyask and Conawapa into service before they were needed for domestic purposes.[51] As Hydro explained in 2014, export sales made possible by surpluses in the early years of projects such as Keeyask and Conawapa were seen as a way to "offset a portion of the costs of its proposed new resource needs, mitigate risks for ratepayers, and meet its commitment to sustain low electricity costs."[52]

Representatives of Manitoba Hydro were bullish on the "window of opportunity"[53] in the U.S. market that could be realized by advancing construction of major projects before their domestic need date to sell the surplus to the U.S.[54] Hydro highlighted its assertion that the proposal for enhanced interconnection and transmission to the U.S. market was a "once in a lifetime opportunity"[55] championed by Midwestern U.S. utilities and driven by their demand for low carbon alternatives to coal and other fossil-fired generation.[56]

In contrast to the largely unbridled boosterism of Hydro representatives, the perspective of First Nation individuals living in the KCN communities tended to be considerably more nuanced. As Jerry Buckland and Melanie O'Gorman found, "Many expressed a sense of conflict as they recognised the importance of the potential socio-economic benefits, but also felt 'heavy hearts' because of the impacts of hydro-electric development on the land."[57]

As a number of First Nation community members presciently observed, the assessment of the merits of the Keeyask Generating Station between 2012 and 2014 would be inextricably linked both to the historic legacy of northern hydro development and to Keeyask's role within the larger Hydro development plan. In the face of a review process that gave significant procedural discretion and ultimate decision-making authority to elected officials, provincial and federal review bodies struggled with varying degrees of success to bring evidence-based rigour to the dialogue.

Siloes, Overlap, and Discretion—The Keeyask Approval Regime between 2012 and 2014

The Minister of Conservation and Water Stewardship has the discretion to direct that there be a public hearing to review the [Keeyask] EIS on such terms as the minister determines.

—Manitoba CEC, *Keeyask Generation Project, Report*, 2014[58]

Between 2012 and 2014, the regulatory review processes of Manitoba and Canada would be challenged in trying to reconcile the seemingly inexorable momentum in favour of the Keeyask Project with growing environmental and economic concerns.

Among the important process issues to be addressed were the timing and scope of Keeyask-related projects for approval purposes, the respective responsibility of federal and provincial regulators, and the role to be played by oral public hearings before independent tribunals such as the Manitoba PUB or CEC. A related question was whether it was just the Keeyask projects being approved or was it the wider complex of interrelated Hydro projects including Bipole III, Conawapa, and the U.S. Transmission Interconnection that should be considered as an integrated whole.

Of seminal importance to the ultimate decision was the opportunity for the exercise of bureaucratic and political discretion in terms of the timing and scope of these reviews. It is strongly arguable that Manitoba Hydro and the Province already had irrevocably "locked in" to Keeyask by the time the project came before the CEC and PUB for independent review. It also is patently clear that decisions to narrow the scope of environmental and economic inquiry would have significant consequences for the ultimate recommendations of these tribunals.

Table 1.2 sets out selected elements of the process leading to the approval of the Keeyask project between 2012 and 2014.

Table 1.2. Selected Keeyask Licences, Decisions, and Orders-in-Council

Date	Subject Matter	Licence, Decision or O/C Number
13 April 2012	Infrastructure project authorized: all-weather gravel road, start-up construction camp, first phase main construction camp and waste water treatment facilities	Manitoba Environment Act Licence, 2952R
27 June 2014	Finding that the Keeyask Generation Project is not likely to cause significant environmental effects (Canadian Environmental Assessment Act)	*Environmental Assessment Decision Statement*[a] *Fisheries and Oceans Canada Decision*[b]
2 July 2014	Authorization to develop the Keeyask Generating Station in accordance with the Joint Keeyask Development Agreement (The Manitoba Hydro Act)	Manitoba Order-in-Council, 00291/2014
2 July 2014	Water Power Act and Regulation, Interim Licence for the development of water power resource	Order-in-Council, 00292/2014
2 July 2014	Environmental authorization for Keeyask Generation Project	Environment Act Licence, 3107
10 July 2014	Keeyask Transmission Project authorized	Environment Act Licence, 3106

Source: Manitoba Environment Act Licence No. 3055, Manitoba Conservation, 2013, https://www.gov.mb.ca/sd/eal/registries/5433bipole/3055.pdf.

a Impact Assessment Agency of Canada, Keeyask Generation Project, Environmental *Assessment Decision Statement, 1 March 2019*, https://www.ceaa-acee.gc.ca/050/evaluations/document/99488?culture=en-CA.

b Impact Assessment Agency of Canada, Fisheries and Oceans Canada, Decision, 27 June 2014, https://www.ceaa-acee.gc.ca/050/evaluations/document/99560?culture=en-CA.

Split into Pieces: The Keeyask Project

The Keeyask Project was divided into three categories for environmental approval purposes: (i) the Keeyask Infrastructure Project, which began in 2012 and included an all-weather gravel road, a start-up construction camp, a first phase main construction camp, and waste water treatment facilities for both the start-up and main camp;[59] (ii) the 695 MW generation station to begin in 2014; and, (iii) the Keeyask transmission project beginning in 2014 to provide power for the construction project and to connect Keeyask power to a northern converter station so it could be transmitted to the South.[60] The generation project required both provincial and federal consideration and raised the attendant challenges of multi-jurisdictional reviews.

Provincial and Federal Approvals Required for the Keeyask Generating Station

Notionally, a rigorous and effective review requires effective federal/provincial collaboration. According to the Canadian Environmental Assessment Agency (CEAA), "the Governments of Canada and Manitoba conducted the federal and provincial environmental assessments [of the Keeyask generating station] cooperatively to the fullest extent possible."[61]

At the federal level, potential requirement for approvals under the Fisheries Act and the Navigation Protection Act triggered a "comprehensive study"[62] by CEAA under the former Canadian Environmental Assessment Act.[63] Despite the presence of vulnerable sturgeon in the immediate area of Keeyask and the well-known implications of hydroelectric dams on these populations,[64] Canada did not hold any public hearings relating to Keeyask.[65]

The CEAA report, released in April 2014, concluded that the project was not likely to cause significant adverse environmental effects when the proposed mitigation measures, follow-up program, and necessary federal permits, authorizations, and approvals were taken into account.[66] On 27 June 2014, decision statements by the environment minister and by Fisheries and Oceans Canada (see Table 1.2) echoed these conclusions, leading to the provision of the required *federal* regulatory authorizations and permits.[67]

At the provincial level, the generating station project required Cabinet authorization for Manitoba Hydro to enter into and finance its partnership with First Nations as well as to develop a new power generating station and to supply power to other jurisdictions.[68] Also required was an environmental licence issued by the provincial environment minister[69] and approval by Cabinet to develop the water power resource (interim water power licence).[70] All three approvals were issued on 2 July 2014, shortly after public hearing reports had been issued by Manitoba's CEC and PUB.

Discretion and Public Hearings

Despite the economic scale and geographic scope of intertwined Hydro projects such as Keeyask and Bipole III, there was no mandatory requirement under either provincial or federal law for an oral public hearing regarding these projects before an independent tribunal.[71]

At the federal level, no oral public hearing was undertaken with regard to Keeyask or Bipole III.

At the provincial level, three separate public hearings were held between 2012 and 2014. A hearing took place with regard to the environmental licence for the Bipole III transmission line (CEC in 2013), but the process expressly excluded a Needs For and Alternatives To (NFAT) analysis.[72] The environmental licence for the Keeyask Generating Station was considered in a public hearing (CEC in 2014) but the licensing of the related infrastructure project and transmission project was not part of the review.[73]

In addition, a public hearing was held into the Needs For and Alternatives To Hydro's Preferred Development Plan (PDP), including Keeyask, Conawapa, and the U.S. Transmission Interconnection Project (PUB in 2014). But Bipole III was not considered in the analysis, and over a billion dollars in expenditures related to Keeyask and Conawapa were excluded from the analysis of economic impacts because the money was already spent.[74]

In 2013, and in light of evidence of the highly compromised nature of the Nelson River watershed, the Manitoba Clean Environment Commission also had recommended that: "13.2 Manitoba Hydro, in cooperation with the Manitoba Government, conduct a Regional Cumulative Effects Assessment (RCEA) for all Manitoba Hydro projects and associated infrastructure in the Nelson River sub-watershed; and that this be *undertaken prior to the licensing of any additional projects* in the Nelson River sub-watershed after the Bipole III Project."[75]

While Hydro and Manitoba began the RCEA process in 2014, a CEC report was not issued until 2018, at which time the tribunal was highly critical of the RCEA analysis.[76] Despite the absence of a completed RCEA, the Keeyask Generating Station and transmission line received an environmental licence in July of 2014.[77]

Challenges with the Approval Process

Issues with the timing, nature, and scope of the Keeyask Generating Station approval process resulted in independent tribunals such as the Manitoba CEC and PUB as well as federal government agencies such as CEAA all identifying significant challenges with the process. First, no Needs For and Alternatives To analysis was undertaken for Bipole III,[78] notwithstanding the reality that Keeyask required Bipole III transmission.[79] Second, billions of dollars in expenditures were excluded from the PDP NFAT analysis by virtue of its timing, scope, and prior approvals.[80] Third, environmental analysis for Keeyask was limited by the exclusion of the related infrastructure and transmission projects, which tempered confidence in the cumulative effects assessment.[81] Fourth, the RCEA ultimately undertaken did not include Indigenous participation in creating the document, and the valuable ecological components assessed were incongruent with those identified in the Keeyask environmental review.[82] Fifth, effective environmental analysis of Hydro projects along the Nelson River would have greatly benefited from an earlier and much broader-ranging RCEA that explored more deeply environmental and social limits to change and focused on estimating future conditions in addition to capturing past changes.[83] And, to some degree, the environmental analysis in the PDP NFAT overlapped with prior assessments by the CEC and by CEAA.[84]

While the regulatory requirements for licensing of the Keeyask Project were numerous, the reality remains that important related issues were not examined (no Bipole III NFAT), left too late (RCEA), or significantly immunized from rigorous analysis because of pre-existing sunk costs, which tilted the analysis toward approval of Keeyask (NFAT).[85]

Given gaps and delays in the review process, independent tribunals such as the PUB could only warn of increasing risks while Hydro and the Province proved highly resistant to mounting evidence of disruptive market change.

Markets, Momentum, and Evidence

Once a government is politically committed and construction has begun, the nature of large construction projects makes it extremely hard to change course, even if there are cost overruns, unforeseen negative impacts, or benefits are less than predicted.

—World Commission on Dams, *Dams and Development*, 2000[86]

Optimism bias and strategic misrepresentation are significantly better explanations of project outcomes than previous explanations.

—Flyvbjerg, "What You Should Know About Mega Projects and Why," 2014[87]

Inertia Trumps Analysis: The World Commission on Dams

Challenges identified in the approval process leading to Keeyask stand in unfortunate symmetry with the observations of the World Commission on Dams in its report *Dams and Development* (2000). While noting the significant contribution that dams have made to "human development," the commission observed that "in too many cases an unacceptable and often unnecessary price" has been paid with both the costs and benefits borne unequally.[88]

The commission also noted that early engagement with those who bear the social, economic, or environmental risk of a project is critical to improving project acceptability and effectiveness.[89] The commission identified a number of endemic challenges within the dam industry: comprehensive evaluation of available alternatives was often not undertaken, given that "building large dams was a focal point for the interests and aspirations" of politicians, government, and industry.[90] As well, once a proposed project passed preliminary technical and economic feasibility tests and attracted the attention of government, "the momentum behind the project often prevailed over further assessments."[91]

The commission stated that forecasts that overstate future demand have led "to a perceived need for a large incremental response to meet rapidly growing needs" with the agencies responsible for building supply infrastructure often charged with undertaking demand forecasts.[92] It also found that early political or institutional commitment can override other concerns, "leading subsequent economic analyses to justify a decision that had in fact already been taken."[93]

More recent research on megaprojects from Oxford University in 2014 has flagged similar challenges with premature project "lock-in," weak alternative analysis, optimism bias, and a "norm" of misinformation and misrepresentation.[94] As discussed below, there are uncanny echoes between the findings of the World Commission om Dams, the Oxford research, and the observations of Manitoba's PUB between 2008 and 2013.

Bright Red Flags of Warning: The Public Utilities Board 2008-2013

As set out in Figure 1.1, the 2007 year constituted the high-water mark for Hydro's export sales as it enjoyed high water levels, liberal access to the Midwestern U.S. market,[95] and the relative attractiveness of hydro as a source of supply in the face of extremely high natural gas prices.[96]

However, by 2008, Manitoba's PUB was expressing concerns that Hydro's forecasts of export prices were unduly optimistic.[97] By early 2012, although the PUB did not have the authority to disallow capital projects, it raised a bright red flag of concern that the business cases for Bipole III, Keeyask, and Conawapa were being undermined by "apparently skyrocketing capital costs"[98] and overoptimistic export price forecasts.[99]

In particular, the PUB noted that Hydro's export price expectations could not be reconciled with the economic downturn, resistance to carbon pricing, and the precipitous decline in natural gas prices as a result of the shale gas revolution.[100] Highlighting the importance of a NFAT to test alternatives,[101] the PUB warned, "It greatly concerns the Board that without having had its capital plans reviewed through an NFAT proceeding, and without the US transmission lines required to transmit MH's electricity exports south of the border having been constructed or even been committed to, and without MH having obtained the required regulatory approvals in Canada, MH continues to spend $1–$2 million per day on its currently favoured development plan."[102]

2014: Upheaval in the Energy Marketplace

Wind, solar and energy efficiency technologies, flattening load growth, volatile natural gas prices, climate change and the resulting impacts on water flows, and regulatory changes including the potential for carbon taxes are all creating upheaval in North American energy markets.

—Manitoba PUB, *A Review of Manitoba Hydro's Preferred Development Plan*, 2014[103]

By 2014, the shale gas revolution was not the only market disruption bringing into question the prudence of Hydro's plans. Also of note were the flattening of load growth throughout the U.S.,[104] lower than expected prices, and the increasing adoption of newer competing energy technologies including solar photovoltaic, wind, and ground source heating.[105]

At a more existential level, there was increasing awareness of the risk posed to the existing, highly centralized energy system by alternative sources of supply, storage, and distribution that were threatening to negatively impact U.S. prices and demand (grid parity).[106] These dramatic changes in the marketplace would have direct implications on the business case and risks associated with major new generation projects such as Keeyask and Conawapa.

"Locked in" to Keeyask—the NFAT Narrative

There are realities of the Keeyask Project over which the [NFAT] Panel had no influence. Approximately $1.2 billion has already been spent on the Keeyask Project. The $3.2 billion Bipole III transmission line, which was not subject to the NFAT Review, has already received regulatory approval and will be constructed to carry northern electricity to southern Manitoba. Both of these were treated by Manitoba Hydro as "sunk costs," and therefore excluded from the economic analysis.

–Manitoba PUB, *A Review of Manitoba Hydro's Preferred Development Plan*, 2014[107]

Assessing the Preferred Plan

In February 2014, Manitoba's PUB began oral public hearings into the Needs For and Alternatives To Manitoba Hydro's PDP. This included the 695 MW Keeyask Project (est. $6.5 billion), with a planned in-service date of 2019; the 1,485 MW Conawapa Project (est. $10.7 billion), with a planned in-service date of 2026; the North-South Transmission Upgrade Project (est. $500 million), with an in-service date to coincide with Conawapa; and the 750 MW U.S. Transmission Interconnection Project terminating near Duluth, Minnesota (est. $1 billion).[108]

The PDP also was predicated upon system power sales contracts with Northern State Power, Minnesota Power, and Wisconsin Public Service.[109] In terms of the "needs for," the PUB was asked to determine whether Manitoba Hydro had justified both the need for and timing of the project. Regarding the alternatives analysis, the PUB was asked to consider "whether the Plan is justified as superior to potential alternatives that could fulfill the need."[110]

Consistent with its expertise, a key PUB focus was an analysis from Hydro's perspective of the expected economic value of potential alternative plans as well as a consideration from the ratepayer viewpoint of the potential rate impacts of the plans. The long-term economic and financial analysis also considered the risks associated with various alternatives as well as their implications for Hydro's commercial relationships. Recognizing the work already undertaken by the provincial and federal impact assessments, the PUB undertook a high-level consideration of the relative socio-economic and macro-environmental impacts of the plans.

Two critical questions underpinned the PUB analysis. First, when would new supply be needed to meet domestic needs? Second, was there a business case (from the perspective of both Hydro and ratepayers) to advance construction in advance of domestic needs for the purposes of firm contract sales to the U.S. market?

The alternatives presented in Hydro's initial filing were developed exclusively by Manitoba Hydro. Using a natural gas plan beginning in 2022–23 as a baseline against which all other alternatives were compared, Hydro presented a number of plans for analysis.

In broad terms, plans were distinguished by their mix of energy source, the year in which they came into operation, whether they included a U.S. transmission interconnection, and whether they were linked to contracted export sales to Minnesota and/or Wisconsin. In terms of energy source, some plans were exclusively natural gas; some were exclusively hydro; some had various mixtures of both hydro and natural gas; two plans included some wind.[111]

Kyrke Gaudreau and Robert Gibson's chapter in this volume looks at how these plans could have emphasized other, more sustainable alternatives. However, for a variety of reasons, including the timing of the review, the key alternative to Hydro's Preferred Development Plan (including both Keeyask and Conawapa) was a scaled-down version including Keeyask but not Conawapa.

"Locking out" Alternatives: Bias and Methodological Challenges

By failing to offer an analysis of conservation measures as a stand-alone energy resource competitive with other generation resources, Manitoba Hydro presented an analysis of conservation measures that was neither complete, accurate, thorough, reasonable, nor sound. The NFAT Review demonstrated that DSM measures were not equally weighted with other energy options.

—Manitoba PUB, *A Review of Manitoba Hydro's Preferred Development Plan*, 2014[112]

The PUB analysis of Hydro's PDP was limited by Hydro's failure to robustly examine deferral of the projects as a meaningful alternative and skewed by the monopoly's heavy investment in the Keeyask Project.

Manitoba Hydro's analysis did not allow for a level analytical playing field, especially when it came to the question of whether the domestic need date could be significantly deferred by demand-side activities. While Hydro focused on a variety of supply alternatives including various mixes of natural gas and hydro, it failed to give equal weight to solutions that focused on reducing demand and deferring the need date for new generation. In the words of one expert witness, Manitoba Hydro "de facto excluded the single lowest-cost and lowest-risk re-source option available" and "risks locking itself into a path of new supply that, as a result, will lock out the much less expensive option of more efficient demand."[113]

From the PUB perspective, Hydro's resource planning analysis was found to have unreasonably and unfairly treated demand-side management (DSM) options.[114] In addition, Hydro's economic evaluation was biased in favour of the Keeyask Project by the reality that well over a billion dollars in expenditures on Keeyask were excluded from the economic analysis. This led to a material overstatement of the relative economic value of the plans, which included Keeyask.

Moreover, Manitoba Hydro already was deeply embedded in a number of related commercial arrangements that would be costly both financially and from a reputation perspective to disentangle. As the PUB found, cancelling the Keeyask Project would have material consequences for ratepayers because Hydro would need to recover the $1.4 billion already spent on the project. In addition, arrangements with First Nations would have to be terminated and significant economic opportunities would be lost with potentially adverse consequences for Manitoba Hydro's commercial reputation. The Keeyask general civil contract also would have to be renegotiated and cancellation fees might be payable.[115]

From a methodological perspective, concerns also were expressed by the PUB that Manitoba Hydro's analysis did not model potential long-term market disruptions due to grid parity, which had the potential to reduce demand and suppress prices in Manitoba Hydro's export markets.[116] Independent experts also warned that Manitoba Hydro had "assumed away" the risk of climate change in its analysis.[117]

Taken together, the failure to meaningfully model market disruptions and climate changes suggests that the degree of risk associated with the PDP was understated. This is consistent with the findings of Oxford researchers, suggesting that large capital projects are often overexposed to extreme, complex, or unexpected events.[118]

Risky Bets in a Risky Business: But Not for Government

Decisions cannot be made without taking a view of the future, but the future may prove unwilling to agree with the forecasts made of it.

— Manitoba PUB, *A Review of Manitoba Hydro's Preferred Development Plan*, 2014[119]

The assumption of risk is integral to any long-term capital investment. At a time of rapid market change, capital-intensive hydroelectric projects with lengthy planning and payback periods face the risk that planning assumptions will be overtaken by events.[120]

A fundamental issue raised in the NFAT proceeding was whether the risk of building these large hydroelectric projects before Manitobans needed them was appropriate in light of the Crown corporation's primary role in ensuring reliable domestic supply. In the view of one independent expert, Manitoba Hydro was essentially "acting as a 'merchant' investor, taking substantial market risk based on expectations, or bets, about the future."[121]

Among the fundamental risks related to the Keeyask business case was domestic load uncertainty—with "the biggest short-term uncertainty" being "whether or not 1,700 GWh of new pipeline load w[ould] materialize in Manitoba. This could change the need date for new resources by a *full seven years*."[122] There also was capital cost uncertainty, with "a realistic possibility that the capital cost for the Keeyask Project may reach Manitoba Hydro's 'high' cost scenario of $7.2 billion, with a smaller possibility of total costs increasing beyond that amount."[123] Export sales revenue uncertainty also was a fundamental risk, especially related to the projected $10 billion in opportunity (as opposed to firm contract) sales "if a carbon pricing regime d[id] not materialize."[124] And, fundamental market disruption presented a significant risk—whether in terms of the growth rate of U.S. demand,[125] game-changing technologies for competing supply sources,[126] or the risk to the existing grid of alternative sources of supply, storage, and distribution.[127]

While Hydro and its ratepayers were exposed to serious risks related to Keeyask and the other elements of the PDP, the prospects for the Manitoba government were brighter. The Province was significantly immunized from downside risk due to the assurance of steady revenues from Hydro related to capital taxes, water rentals, and debt-guarantee fees.[128] From the PUB perspective, the expected value to Manitoba of a plan involving "Keeyask and the 750 MW interconnection" "dwarf[ed] the incremental benefits flowing to Manitoba Hydro and its ratepayers."[129]

Keeyask Triumphs over the Preferred Plan

In August 2013, Manitoba Hydro suggested that the PDP would have an incremental Net Present Value of $1.7 billion compared to the All Gas Plan. Since then, based on changed assumptions this advantage has disappeared virtually completely. The incremental Net Present Value is now only $45 million.

—Manitoba PUB, A Review of Manitoba Hydro's
Preferred Development Plan, 2014[130]

There are good reasons to proceed with the Keeyask Project at this time in light of the need for new resources, construction expenditures undertaken to date, the socioeconomic and environmental benefits of the project, and the important commercial relations that Manitoba Hydro has established both with First Nations and through its export contracts. Moreover, there are associated reliability benefits with the 750 MW Transmission Interconnection Project.

—Manitoba PUB, A Review of Manitoba Hydro's
Preferred Development Plan, 2014[131]

The fragility of the PDP became apparent during the NFAT oral hearing when a number of material changes in circumstances[132] led to a collapse of its business case and a recommendation to immediately cease further expenditures on Conawapa.[133]

However, the PUB still recommended proceeding with Keeyask. Relying upon a finding that new supply would be needed by no later than 2024 if forecasts of increased demand for electricity from pipelines materialized, the PUB concluded that there still was a business case to support the advancement of Keeyask to 2019 in order to capitalize on potential export revenue sales.[134]

The PUB determined that plans involving Keeyask and the 750 MW U.S. Transmission Interconnection Project (the Keeyask plan) were superior to the PDP from the perspective of both Hydro economics and ratepayer finances.

Leaving aside the more than $1 billion in sunk costs already spent on Keeyask, the Keeyask plan also had measurable economic benefits and tangible reliability benefits "relative to the All Gas Plan without an interconnection."[135] As compared to the All Gas Plan, the Keeyask plan had a lower GhG (greenhouse gas) impact.[136] In a determination that is likely to be controversial for the certitude in which it is expressed as well as for the term "dissenting voices," the PUB also found that the socio-economic benefits of the Keeyask plan "significantly exceed the benefits of an All Gas Plan, and are to a large extent directed to northern Manitoba, in particular to affected First Nations communities. This is clear from the fact that despite dissenting voices in the community, the Keeyask Cree Nations have unequivocally stated that they support Keeyask being built."[137]

While recommending that Keeyask proceed, the NFAT report was acutely alive to the downside risks of the project as well as to the analytic challenges posed by the heavy Hydro investment in Keeyask and Bipole III that predated the independent review. Within months of provincial regulatory approval being granted in 2014, bad news began to pour in regarding key risk elements such as load forecasts, capital costs, and expected export prices.

A Project Mired in Controversy

The Utility sees the fundamental underlying problem with its financial health as being the major capital expansion and the amount of the debt required to pay for the simultaneous construction of the $8.7 billion Keeyask Generating Station project ("Keeyask") and the $5.0 billion Bipole III Transmission Line project ("Bipole III").

—Manitoba PUB, *Order 59/19*, 2018[138]

By 2015, Manitoba Hydro was reporting a $1.4 billion overrun on Bipole III costs,[139] lower-than-forecast export prices,[140] and a projected pipeline load that was more than 1,000 GWh lower per year than originally forecast at the NFAT.[141] By 2018, Hydro was suggesting that capital costs for Keeyask would be $2.2 billion higher than originally forecast at the NFAT[142] and noting ongoing price challenges in the U.S. market related to low-cost fossil fuels as well as "local options for carbon-free electricity."[143]

In 2018–19, Manitoba Hydro sought an application for a 7.9 percent rate increase and advised that an additional five years of rate increases at four times the rate of inflation would be necessary.[144] Manitoban consumers reacted to this claim with unprecedented vehemence. Over 2,300 Manitobans contacted the PUB to register their views on the rate application. In many cases, these individuals also took the opportunity to share their thoughts and criticisms of capital projects such as Keeyask and Bipole III.[145]

The actual rate increase ordered for 2018–19 was less than half that amount sought by Hydro. In finding that Manitoba Hydro had not justified the rate increases it sought, the PUB expressed concerns about the rapid pace at which Hydro was seeking to meet its financial targets. It also referenced a new export sale to SaskPower as well as factors that might mitigate the need for the rate increase sought by Hydro, including record low interest rates and conservatism in the export revenue forecasts of Manitoba Hydro.[146]

The PUB also responded to the Province's request that it comment upon the status of major capital projects such as Keeyask and Bipole III. Noting the absence of an NFAT process for Bipole III, the PUB found that "Manitoba Hydro undertook unreasonable risk when it developed its $3.28 billion Bipole III cost estimate in 2011."[147] The PUB also concluded that "Manitoba Hydro has been approving projects too early in the process, without sufficient development of scope, design, and engineering."[148]

The complicated legacy of Keeyask continues to be a matter of controversy. In October 2019, the Province of Manitoba announced that former Saskatchewan premier Brad Wall would conduct an economic review of Keeyask and Bipole III as well as make recommendations regarding appropriate oversight and regulatory approvals for future projects. The Wall review was released in February 2021, one week after Keeyask's first of seven units began generating electricity for the first time after nearly seven years of construction. In a report that engendered its own heated response, the Wall review concluded that "the decision history of Bipole III and Keeyask exemplifies errors common to mega-projects around the world with optimism bias, estimating tunneling, and 'locked in' decision making among the contributing factors."[149] The Manitoba government also had introduced legislation that purports to strengthen regulatory oversight over major new capital projects and major new export sales.[150]

As for the project itself, the next six units that make up the Keeyask Generating Station will come online one by one over the next year.

Conclusions

For many Canadians, by the time they are asked to participate, projects are already fully planned with little room for change. As such, the starting point is perceived to be too late for communities, stakeholders and Indigenous Groups to provide input into project design or alternative means by which a project could be realized.

—Canadian Environmental Assessment Agency,
Building Common Ground, 2014[151]

Independent review processes can play an important role in assisting Manitobans to make sustainable business decisions that rigorously consider alternatives, appropriately share benefits and risks, and offer a meaningful voice to the community. Alternatively, they can serve as window dressing for decisions that already have been made.

While adverse developments in the Keeyask business case offer multiple targets for criticism, it is important to recall both the long-lived nature of Hydro assets and the contribution of independent tribunals to the deliberative process. Much of the Keeyask story remains to be written, including an assessment of its impact on its First Nation partners and on vulnerable sturgeon, caribou, and other wildlife populations. The sustainability of the Keeyask business case in a rapidly changing market also remains in the balance with important questions still to be answered about the final cost of the project as well as opportunities for export sales to neighbouring provinces such as Saskatchewan.

In looking at what we know today, the role of Manitoba's PUB in providing an early warning of the risks of Keeyask (2008 to 2012) and in urging the cessation of further expenditures on Conawapa (2014) is notable. Also worthy of recognition is the Clean Environment Commission's call (2013) for a Regional Cumulative Effects Assessment of the Nelson River sub-watershed before further projects were licensed. Manitoba was put on notice that the health of the Nelson River was at a potential tipping point.

Ultimately, Manitoba approved the Bipole III project without conducting a public hearing to examine the business case as compared with alternatives. Manitoba also approved the high-risk Keeyask Project despite being presented with a skewed economic case tainted by over $1 billion in sunk costs and despite the CEC warnings of the highly compromised nature of the Nelson River. Recognizing the challenges of Hydro and Manitoba in major project oversight, there are ample grounds to conclude that initiating an independent review of major capital projects by the Manitoba PUB should not be a matter of Cabinet discretion but a statutory obligation.[152]

Given the health of the Nelson River, there is little reason for confidence that the Province of Manitoba is adequately safeguarding the health of this watershed or that community interests are equally balanced with Hydro imperatives. Much work needs to be done to understand the effects of Hydro activities, to mitigate or reverse the adverse effects of Hydro operations, and to consider ways to democratize environmental oversight to better protect vulnerable communities.

Bright dreams, good planning, and good fortune can build healthy, vibrant communities. But markets are unforgiving of inflexible plans incapable of responding to material changes in circumstances. While independent tribunals played an important role in warning of the economic and environmental risks of building Keeyask, Manitoba's highly politicized regulatory review process ultimately gave the green light to a high-risk project. The current controversy surrounding the Keeyask Project is the inevitable consequence when dreams and markets collide.

Notes

1   Steve Lambert, "NDP Leader Gary Doer," *Globe and Mail*, 20 April 2007.

2   CBC News, "Hydro Projects Left Environmental, Social Scars on Manitoba's North, Report Reveals," 25 August 2018, https://www.cbc.ca/news/canada/manitoba/manitoba-hydro-clean-environment-commission-report-1.4798560.

3   Manitoba Public Utilities Board, *A Final Order With Respect to Manitoba Hydro's Application for Increased 2010/11 and 2011/12 Rates and Other Related Matters, Board Order 5/12*, Winnipeg, 17 January 2012, 66–67, http://www.bipoleiiicoalition.ca/assets/pdfs/5-12.pdf.

4   Manitoba Hydro, *Needs For and Alternatives To, Release History*, August 2013, 2–4, http://www.pubmanitoba.ca/v1/pdf/nfat/nfat_application/nfat_business_case.pdf.

5   Bent Flyvbjerg, "What You Should Know about Megaprojects and Why: An Overview," *Project Management Journal* 45, no. 2 (April 2014): 6, 9, 11, 17.

6   Manitoba Public Utilities Board, *Order 5/12*, 8–10, 69, 76–77, 83.

7   Graham Lane, "How Manitoba's 'Green' Power Dream Became a Nightmare of Runaway Costs," *Financial Post*, 14 April 2016.

8   The term "demand-side management" generally refers to mechanisms that a) assist in reducing consumption of electrical energy to reduce overall energy demand, or b) shift consumer consumption away from peak energy use times and reduce pressure on system capacity. In Manitoba, the term is sometimes used more expansively to include alternatives to hydroelectric energy, which could include, for example, solar photovoltaic.

9   Manitoba Public Utilities Board, *Report on the Needs For and Alternatives To (NFAT): A Review of Manitoba Hydro's Preferred Development Plan*, June 2014, 27, accessed 12 October 2021, http://www.pub.gov.mb.ca/ nfat/pdf/finalreport_pdp.pdf.

10   Manitoba Hydro, 2019–20 Electric Rate Application, 33, https://www.hydro.mb.ca/regulatory_affairs/electric/gra_2019_2020; Kenton Dyck, "Bipole III Transmission Line Has Entered Commercial Service," *SteinbachOnline.com*, 24 July 2018.

11   Manitoba Public Utilities Board, *Final Order with Respect to Manitoba Hydro's 2017/18 and 2018/19 General Rate Application*, Winnipeg, 1 May 2018, 17, http://www.pubmanitoba.ca/v1/proceedings-decisions/orders/pubs/2018%20orders/59-18.pdf.

12   Consumers Coalition, *2,300 Voices: Manitobans Speak Up About Their Manitoba Hydro*, 1 May 2018, http://www.cacmanitoba.ca/data/uploads/pdf/18-02-06_2300_voices_report.pdf.

13   Province of Manitoba, "Manitoba Launches Review of Manitoba Hydro Development of Keeyask, Bipole III Projects," news release, 18 October 2018; Province of Manitoba, Bill 44, The Public Utilities Ratepayer Protection and Regulatory Reform Act (Various Acts Amended), 2nd Sess., 42 Leg., Manitoba, 2019–20.

14   Canadian Environmental Assessment Agency, *Building Common Ground: A New Vision for Impact Assessment in Canada*, York University Digital Library, 2017, 28, https://digital.library.yorku.ca/yul-1120723/building-common-ground-new-vision-impact-assessment-canada.

15   Flyvbjerg, "What You Should Know," 9.

16   Manitoba Public Utilities Board, *NFAT*, 3.

17   Ibid., 163.

18 Ibid., 121.

19 Flyvbjerg, "What You Should Know," 11.

20 For Manitoba Hydro, major forecast risks include domestic market demand, export market demand, export market prices, water flow variability, and capital costs. The implications of climate change add another significant uncertainty, given the long-lived nature of the projects.

21 Manitoba Public Utilities Board, *NFAT*, 97.

22 Ibid., 54–55.

23 The Manitoba Hydro Act, s 2(b), https://web2.gov.mb.ca/laws/statutes/ccsm/h190e.php.

24 Manitoba Public Utilities Board, *NFAT*, 96.

25 Ibid., 99.

26 Ibid., 163.

27 Manitoba Hydro, *Generating Stations*, https://www.hydro.mb.ca/corporate/facilities/generating_stations/.

28 Manitoba Hydro, *Limestone Generating Station*, https://www.hydro.mb.ca/corporate/facilities/generating_stations/#limestone.

29 Manitoba Public Utilities Board, *Order 5/12*, 66–67, 82.

30 Hansard, Manitoba Legislative Assembly, 7th Leg, 3rd Session, No. 19, 24 April 2002, https://www.gov.mb.ca/legislature/hansard/37th_3rd/vol_019/h019.html.

31 Mary Stucky, "Hydropower and the Canadian Cree," *Round Earth Media* (1 October 2000), http://archive.roundearthmedia.org/hydropower-and-the-canadian-cree; CBC News, "Hydro Projects Left Environmental."

32 Manitoba Clean Environment Commission, *Keeyask Generation Project, Report on Public Hearing*, Winnipeg, April 2014, 15–19, http://www.cecmanitoba.ca/cecm/hearings/keeyask.html.

33 Ibid., 162.

34 Ibid., 19.

35 Ibid.

36 World Commission on Dams, *Dams and Development: A New Framework For Decision Making* (London: Earthscan Publications, 2000), 124, accessed 12 October 2021, http://pubs.iied.org/sites/default/files/pdfs/migrate/9126IIED.pdf.

37 Shirley Thompson, *Flooding of First Nations and Environmental Justice in Manitoba: Case Studies of the Impacts of the 2011 Flood and Hydro Development in Manitoba* (Winnipeg: Natural Resources Institute, 2015).

38 Manitoba Clean Environment Commission, *Keeyask Generation Project, Report*, 162.

39 Manitoba Public Utilities Board, *NFAT*, 56.

40 Nisichawayasihk Cree Nation, *Wuskwatim Project History*, 2019, https://www.ncncree.com/business-and-economy/wuskwatim-project; York Factory First Nation, *Kaytesipimotatanwuk Oma Wechaywakantowin: The Way Forward*, 2012, 96, https://keeyask.com/wp-content/uploads/2012/07/Kipekiskwaywinan_Our-Voices_June_2012_Part-6.pdf; Sean Kavanagh, "Pallister Comes under Fire after Province Cancels 2nd Agreement with Manitoba Metis Federation," CBC News, 31 October 2018.

41 Jim Chliboyko, "Ontario, Manitoba May Revisit Power Project," *Business Edge* 1, no. 23 (24 November 2005), http://www.businessedge.ca/archives/article.cfm/

ontario-manitoba-may-revisit-power-project-11296; Manitoba Wildlands and Energy Manitoba, *Hydropower Transmission in Manitoba: Current Status and Future Planning* (Winnipeg: Manitoba Wildlands and Energy Manitoba, 2005), http://www.energymanitoba.org/pdfs/TransOptsMBJan05_.pdf.

42 Lambert, "NDP Leader Gary Doer"; "How Manitoba's 'Green' Power Dream Became a Nightmare of Runaway Costs," *Financial Post*, 14 April 2016.

43 Lambert, "NDP Leader Gary Doer."

44 "Consent" here is used in the Western sense and represents a majority of those choosing to vote in a referendum on the agreement. We offer no opinion on whether this represents consent from an Indigenous world view perspective.

45 Manitoba Clean Environment Commission, *Keeyask Generation Project, Report.*

46 Ibid., xv.

47 Manitoba Hydro, *Generating Stations.*

48 Ibid.

49 Manitoba Public Utilities Board, *Order 5/12*, 7, 33.

50 Manitoba Public Utilities Board, *NFAT*, 47.

51 Manitoba Public Utilities Board, *Order 5/12*, 33.

52 Manitoba Public Utilities Board, *NFAT*, 95.

53 Ibid., 107–8.

54 Ibid., 95.

55 Ibid., 108.

56 Ibid., 107.

57 Jerry Buckland and Melanie O'Gorman, "The Keeyask Hydro Dam Plan in Northern Canada: A Model for Inclusive Indigenous Development?" *Canadian Journal of Development Studies* 38, no. 1 (2017): 72–90, https://doi.org/10.1080/02255 189.2016.1224969.

58 Manitoba Clean Environment Commission, *Keeyask Generation Project, Report*, 8.

59 Manitoba Environment Act Licence No. 2952R, Manitoba Conservation, 2012, https://www.gov.mb.ca/sd/eal/registries/5420keeyask/2952r.pdf; Manitoba Clean Environment Commission, *Keeyask Generation Project, Report*, 25.

60 Manitoba Environment Act Licence No. 3106, Manitoba Conservation, 2014, https://www.gov.mb.ca/sd/eal/registries/5614keeyask_transmission/keeyask3106.pdf.

61 Canadian Environmental Assessment Agency, *Keeyask Generation Project: Comprehensive Study Report,* Ottawa, 2014, 4, https://www.ceaa-acee.gc.ca/050/documents/p64144/99127E.pdf.

62 Ibid.

63 Canadian Environmental Assessment Act, SC1992, c 37; Canadian Environmental Assessment Agency, *Keeyask Generation Project, Comprehensive Study*, iii; Manitoba Clean Environment Commission, *Keeyask Generation Project, Report*, 8.

64 Bruce Owen, "Hydro's Nelson River Sturgeon Plan Problematic: Expert," *Winnipeg Free Press*, 13 November 2013; Committee on the Status of Endangered Wildlife in Canada, *COSEWIC Assessment and Status Report on the Lake Sturgeon (Acipenser Fulvescens), Western Hudson Bay Populations, Saskatchewan-Nelson River Populations, Southern Hudson Bay-James Bay Populations, Great Lakes-Upper St. Lawrence Populations in Canada* (Ottawa: Committee on the Status of Endangered Wildlife in Canada, 2017).

65   The author is not in a position to offer an educated hypothesis on the reasons for the modest federal role or whether it was driven by some combination of a desire to reduce the regulatory barriers to major projects, an opinion that the provincial review process was thorough, or a desire to support the concept of developer/First Nation partnerships.

66   Canadian Environmental Assessment Agency, *Keeyask Generation Project, Comprehensive Study.*

67   Impact Assessment Agency of Canada, *Environmental Assessment Decision Statement*; Canadian Environmental Assessment Agency, *Keeyask Generation Project, Comprehensive Study*; Manitoba Clean Environment Commission, *Keeyask Generation Project, Report*, 8.

68   The Manitoba Hydro Act, ss 2, 15(1.3)(1.5), 16(1)(h)(i.1)(j); Manitoba Public Utilities Board, *NFAT*, 38.

69   Manitoba Environment Act Licence No. 3107, Manitoba Conservation, 2014; The Environment Act, CCSM c E125, Legislative Assembly of Manitoba; Manitoba Clean Environment Commission, *Keeyask Generation Project, Report*, 7, 9.

70   The Water Power Act, CCSM c W60, Legislative Assembly of Manitoba, 14, 18.

71   Manitoba Clean Environment Commission, *Keeyask Generation Project, Report*, 8; Manitoba Public Utilities Board, *NFAT*, 38; Manitoba Clean Environment Commission, *Manitoba-Minnesota Transmission Project: Report on Public Hearing*, 12 September 2017, http://www.cecmanitoba.ca/cecm/hearings/mmtp.html.

72   Manitoba Clean Environment Commission, *Bipole III Transmission Project, Report on Public Hearing*, June 2013, 2, 8, http://www.cecmanitoba.ca/cecm/hearings/bipole-iii.html.

73   Manitoba Clean Environment Commission, *Keeyask Generation Project, Report*, 159.

74   Manitoba Public Utilities Board, *NFAT*, 27.

75   Ibid., 8. Emphasis added.

76   Manitoba Clean Environment Commission, *A Review of the Regional Cumulative Effects Assessment For Hydroelectric Developments on the Nelson, Burntwood, and Churchill River Systems*, Winnipeg, May 2018, 61–65, http://caid.ca/RevCumEffAaaManHyd2018.pdf.

77   Canadian Environmental Assessment Agency, *Keeyask Generation Project, Comprehensive Study*, 140, 160; Manitoba Environment Act Licence No. 3107, Manitoba Conservation, 2014.

78   Manitoba Public Utilities Board, *Order 5/12*, 8–10; Manitoba Public Utilities Board, *NFAT*, 27; Manitoba Public Utilities Board, *Final Order With Respect to Manitoba Hydro's 2017/18 and 2018/19 General Rate Application Order 59/18*, 1 May 2018, 97–98, http://www.pubmanitoba.ca/v1/proceedings-decisions/orders/pubs/2018%20orders/59-18.pdf.

79   Manitoba Public Utilities Board, *NFAT*.

80   Ibid., 27.

81   Manitoba Clean Environment Commission, *Keeyask Generation Project, Report*, 159.

82   Manitoba Clean Environment Commission, *Review of the Regional Cumulative Effects.*

83   Manitoba Clean Environment Commission, *Keeyask Generation Project, Report*, 140; Canadian Environmental Assessment Agency, *Keeyask Generation Project, Comprehensive Study*, 80.

84 Manitoba Public Utilities Board, *NFAT*, 229.

85 The 2017 and 2018 review of the MMTP project by the CEC and NEB might be viewed in a similar light, given the prior multi-billion-dollar commitments to Bipole III and Keeyask.

86 World Commission on Dams, *Dams and Development*, 173.

87 Flyvbjerg, "What You Should Know," 17.

88 World Commission on Dams, *Dams and Development*, xxvii.

89 World Commission on Dams, *Dams and Development*.

90 Ibid., xxxii.

91 Ibid., 168.

92 Ibid., 179.

93 Ibid., 181.

94 Flyvbjerg, "What You Should Know," 9, 17.

95 A key challenge that Hydro faced, especially at peak demand times in the U.S., was limits on the transmission capacity between Manitoba and markets in Minnesota.

96 Manitoba Public Utilities Board, *NFAT*, 197.

97 Manitoba Public Utilities Board, *Order 116/08* as referred to in *Order 5/12*, 83.

98 Manitoba Public Utilities Board, *Order 5/12*, 69.

99 Ibid., 83.

100 Manitoba Public Utilities Board, *Order 5/12*.

101 Ibid., 9.

102 Ibid., 10.

103 Manitoba Public Utilities Board, *NFAT*, 3.

104 Ibid., 195–96.

105 Ibid., 99–100.

106 Manitoba Public Utilities Board, *NFAT*.

107 Ibid., 27.

108 Ibid., 18, 23, 26.

109 Ibid., 23, 26.

110 Ibid., 39.

111 Ibid., 26, 51.

112 Ibid., 91–92.

113 Ibid., 81.

114 Ibid., 91–92.

115 Ibid., 247.

116 Ibid., 69.

117 Ibid., 202.

118 Flyvbjerg, "What You Should Know," 9.

119 Manitoba Public Utilities Board, *NFAT*, 243.

120 Ibid., 157–58.

121 Ibid., 97–98, 114.

122 Ibid., 21. Emphasis added.

123 Ibid., 30, 123.

124 Ibid., 30–31.

125 Ibid., 185–86.

126 Ibid., 196–97.

127 Ibid., 196.

128 Ibid., 206.

129 Ibid., 180–90.

130 Ibid., 160.

131 Ibid., 34.

132 Ibid., 140.

133 Ibid., 206–7.

134 Ibid., 20.

135 Ibid., 160.

136 Ibid., 241–42.

137 Ibid., 227–28.

138 Manitoba Public Utilities Board, *Order 59/18*, 8.

139 Manitoba Public Utilities Board, *Final Order With Respect to Manitoba Hydro's 2014/15 and 2015/2016 General Rate Application Order 73/15*, Winnipeg, July 2015, 4, http://www.pubmanitoba.ca/v1/pdf/15hydro/73-15.pdf; Manitoba Hydro, *Energy Matters* (Winnipeg: Manitoba Hydro, 2018); Manitoba Hydro, 2019/20 Electric Rate Application, 30 November 2018, Appendix 7, 65.

140 Manitoba Public Utilities Board, *Order 73/15*, 4.

141 Ibid., 71.

142 Manitoba Public Utilities Board, *Order 59/18*, 33.

143 Ibid., 123; Manitoba Public Utilities Board, *Order 73/15*, 4.

144 Manitoba Public Utilities Board, *Order 59/18*, 7.

145 Consumers Coalition, *2,300 Voices*, 12.

146 Manitoba Public Utilities Board, *Order 59/18*, 17. For information about the new Systems Participation sale to SaskPower, see the Power Sale Contract table at page 126. The PUB finding on financial targets can be found at pages 63–69. For information about historically low interest rates, see pages 53 and 68. For the PUB findings on the conservatism of export forecast, see pages 128–29.

147 Manitoba Public Utilities Board, *Order 59/18*, 35, 97–98.

148 Ibid., 31–33.

149 Darren Bernhardt, "Hydro Review Slams NDP's Handling of Bipole III, Keeyask but Opposes Privatizing Crown Corp," CBC News, 26 February 2021; Brad Wall, *Economic Review of Bipole III and Keeyask*, November 2020, 12, https://manitoba.ca/asset_library/en/proactive/2020_2021/ERBK-Report-Volume1.PDF.

150 The Public Utilities Ratepayer Protection and Regulatory Reform Act (Various Acts Amended), CCSM c. P280.

151 Canadian Environmental Assessment Agency, *Building Common Ground*, 58.

152 Manitoba Public Utilities Board, *Order 59/18*, 253.

> " I look forward to the day now only a few years off when Keeyask turbines will supply homes and businesses in Manitoba and elsewhere with clean, affordable and reliable energy."

Chief Betsy Kennedy, War Lake First Nation,
CEC hearings (21 October 2013), 106

CHAPTER 2

Concrete Impulse:
A Critique of the Pro-Keeyask Narrative

WILL BRAUN

After an hour by boat up the Nelson River from the Tataskweyak Cree community of Split Lake, the blue cranes come into view, towering in the river where Manitoba Hydro is building the $8.7 billion Keeyask Generating Station. I am travelling with three sisters for whom the area immediately upstream of the dam area has been a seasonal home their whole lives, and we see trees cleared in areas to be flooded.[1] Someone has nailed a Manitoba Hydro hard hat to a tree, as if to stake a claim, where the Kitchekeesik family cabin once stood, a place of refuge and rootedness for them. The dam will flood forty-five square kilometres of the most precious place on the planet to the sisters. The sky is grey; imminent rain and imminent loss gather on the horizon.

The dam being built nearby will rest on a foundation of solid Precambrian granite and unsettling policy premises. These premises, as played out in the driving narrative put forward by Manitoba Hydro and the provincial government, are that: 1) hydropower is clean; 2) demand for electricity will increase indefinitely; and 3) the project will be overwhelmingly positive for hydro-affected Indigenous peoples.

I will consider how the Public Utilities Board's (PUB) 2014 Needs For and Alternatives To (NFAT) hearing and final report on Manitoba Hydro's Preferred Development Plan treated these three foundational arguments. Of course, it mattered little what came of the $9.2 million[2] review process, as Manitoba Hydro had already sunk $1.2 billion into the project[3] and it was clearly intending to proceed. Official government approval followed the NFAT process.

What remains now is to dissect the foundation underlying Keeyask and the process that led to the dam.

What remains for members of the Kitchekeesik family, and others like them, is a lingering story of grief that few Manitobans will hear.

Premise One: "Clean" Power

Manitoba Hydro has fundamentally and permanently altered the five largest rivers in the province, including the Nelson, which is the largest of all and is home to Keeyask (see Table 2.1).

The 1992 final report of the Federal Ecological Monitoring Program summed up the changes to Manitoba's two largest rivers by saying, "The natural regime of the Churchill and Nelson . . . rivers has been dramatically, and perhaps, irrevocably, altered by hydroelectric development."[4]

The provincial utility has also altered, to varying extents, six of Manitoba's twelve largest lakes. These include Lake Winnipeg, Southern Indian Lake, Cedar Lake, Cross Lake, Playgreen Lake, and Sipiwesk Lake.[5] Many smaller bodies of water are affected to varying degrees as well.[6] The operations of Manitoba Hydro significantly compromise the ecological integrity of the majority of Manitoba's key waterways on a permanent basis. This fact is inexplicably absent from the PUB's 306-page final report of the NFAT review.

Any inference that these dramatic changes to lake levels, river flows, and seasonal water fluctuations do not have severe, widespread, and ongoing effects is not supported by the evidence observable by any person travelling affected waterways or by the observations of Indigenous people most intimately acquainted with the bodies of water in question.

Steve Ducharme, president of the South Indian Lake Commercial Fishermen's Association, describes the "drastic" effect of Hydro's Churchill River Diversion (CRD) scheme, which Chapter 3 of this volume explores in depth. Ducharme, who has fished on Southern Indian Lake for decades, says of the Churchill River Diversion project: "More than 800-square-kilometres of land are permanently flooded. Thousands of kilometres of critical shoreline habitat are affected. We see severe shoreline destabilization and erosion. Natural fluctuations of water throughout the seasons—which are essential for the health of shoreline ecosystems—are a thing of the past. The dams to the east

Table 2.1. Hydro-Affected Rivers

River	Average discharge (m3/sec.)	Dams / control structures	Comments
Nelson	2,370[a]	Jenpeg Kelsey Kettle Long Spruce Limestone	Flows on the entire river are artificially regulated. Reservoirs behind Nelson River dams cover 1,091 km sq.[b] About one quarter of the water flowing through dams on the Lower Nelson—including Keeyask—is water diverted from the Churchill.[c]
Churchill	1,200	Missi Falls	About 85 percent of the flow of the river is diverted into the Nelson.[d] Southern Indian Lake—a 140-kilometre-long widening of the Churchill—is flooded by about three metres. The Lower Churchill is seriously dewatered.[e]
Burntwood	863	Notigi Wuskwatim	The Burntwood has become the third-largest river as a result of the diverted water from the Churchill that now flows down it. For the period 1979 to 1988, flows at Thompson were almost ten times what they would have been naturally.[f]
Winnipeg	850	Pointe du Bois Slave Falls Seven Sisters McArthur Great Falls Pine Falls	Flows on the entire river are artificially regulated. (There are two more dams on the Ontario portion of the river.)
Saskatchewan	700	Grand Rapids	The Grand Rapids Dam floods Cedar Lake—part of the Saskatchewan River system—by 115,700 hectares.[g] Roughly half the distance of the Saskatchewan River within Manitoba is impounded and not free flowing.
Red (for size comparison)	236		

Sources: Wikipedia, "List of Longest Rivers in Canada," accessed 18 August 2016, http://en.wikipedia.org/wiki/List_of_longest_rivers_of_Canada; Environment

Canada, *Final Report, Federal Ecological Monitoring Program (FEMP)*, vol. 1 (Ottawa: Environment Canada / Department of Fisheries and Oceans, April 1992), 2–21.

a A bar graph in the *FEMP* shows the discharge of the Nelson River at about 3,250 cubic metres per second. I have used the more conservative number.

b Manitoba Hydro, *Water Power Act Licences: 2013 Annual Water Levels and Flow Report* (Winnipeg: Manitoba Hydro, 22 July 2014), G-3, I-2, J-2, and L-4. Updated data for the Kettle Generating Station was obtained from: Dale Hutchison, Hydraulic Operations Coordinator, Manitoba Hydro, email message to the author, 16 August 2016.

c Dale Hutchison, Hydraulic Operations Coordinator, Manitoba Hydro, email to the author, 15 May 2014.

d R.A. Bodaly et al., "Ecological Effects of Hydroelectric Development in Northern Manitoba, Canada: The Churchill-Nelson River Diversion," in *Effects of Pollutants at the Ecosystem Level,* ed. P.J. Sheehan et al. (Hoboken, NJ: John Wiley and Sons, 1984), 279, accessed 18 August 2016, http://dge.stanford.edu/SCOPE/SCOPE_22/ SCOPE_22_2.6_Bodaly_273-310.pdf.

e Manitoba Hydro, "Churchill River Diversion," accessed 18 August 2016, https:// www.hydro.mb.ca/corporate/water_regimes/churchill_river_diversion.shtml.

f This figure is for mean flows at the city of Thompson for the period from 1976 to 1989.

g Glenn Schneider, Division Manager, Public Affairs, Manitoba Hydro, email message to the author, 18 March 2011.

and south of us prevent natural fish migration. Our lake is sick and dying—the result of 'clean' hydro."[7]

About 25 percent of the water that will flow through Keeyask will be water diverted by means of CRD.[8] The diversion is one of the primary fuel sources of Keeyask. Keeyask is directly connected to the CRD. Yet neither Hydro's main submission to the PUB nor the PUB's NFAT final report even mentions this. Rather than prudently considering upstream impacts linked directly to Keeyask, Hydro narrowed the geographic focus. The PUB, and the government that set the terms of reference for the NFAT process, allowed this. The people who suffer the severe, on-going, and largely unaddressed impacts of the diversion scheme, which will provide a quarter of the water that will flow through Keeyask, were not given even a mention, let alone an impact-benefit arrangement.

Like Ducharme at Southern Indian Lake, traditional land users Ivan Keeper and Robert Spence of Tataskweyak Cree Nation near Keeyask express anguish about hydro impacts: "Our land and water have suffered far too much already from hydro operations. We feel a great sadness and loneliness for what has been lost. Hydro gets "clean" energy, while we don't even have clean water to drink. It hurts us deeply to see irreversible damage to our land and water."[9]

When then premier Greg Selinger visited Pimicikamak on the Nelson River to issue an apology for the effects of the hydropower project in January 2015, Pimicikamak Chief Cathy Merrick responded with a speech in which she said: "It is not possible to capture in words the damage done. Much of the harm is irreparable. It has forever changed our ways of life and our health. For us, hydropower is not clean."[10]

In unrelenting contrast, Manitoba Hydro and provincial government representatives refer to hydropower, as they have for decades, as "clean." While Hydro acknowledges the impacts of its dams, it often mentions these impacts in muted terms and in the past tense, ignoring the ongoing nature of impacts. The dominant narrative remains that of clean power. This forms the cornerstone of the Manitoba Hydro brand. Since climate change has become a matter of public concern, the hydropower industry in Manitoba and around the world has ramped up "clean hydro" communications, seeking to position hydropower as a climate change solution. In a recent report published by the International Hydropower Association (IHA), IHA Chief Executive Richard Taylor and IHA President Ken Adams, who served as senior vice-president, Power Supply, for Manitoba Hydro during development of the Keeyask plan, wrote: "Providing enough clean power for a billion people, hydropower is helping to deliver on the ambition of the Paris Climate Agreement by reducing our reliance on sources with harmful emissions."[11]

The clean energy mantra served as the bedrock of the argument for Keeyask and was generally linked to reducing greenhouse gas (GhG) emissions. During the Clean Environment Commission (CEC) hearing into Keeyask, Ken Adams said: "Keeyask will provide a clean source of renewable, firm energy that will reduce the use of fossil fuels in central North America."[12] Hydro argues that electricity from Keeyask will displace the use of coal-fired energy in the U.S. market since some of the power from the dam is intended for export. Given the urgency of addressing climate change, this rationale merits consideration.

Dams do not reduce GhG emissions per se; they increase energy supply. While one can argue that hydropower exports displace coal use in the U.S. Midwest, one can also argue that powering air conditioners south of the border simply feeds the energy addiction of the most consumptive nation in history. Both arguments contain some truth.

If Keeyask were part of a demonstrated regional emission reduction plan, and if Hydro were candid and honest about hydropower impacts, and if the province had not missed its own legislated GhG reduction targets,[13] then Hydro's climate arguments would seem more convincing and less convenient. Hydropower cannot be part of the solution to climate change if there is no solution. It is possible we could dam every inch of our rivers while regional GhG emission and energy demand would continue to rise.

Plus, since the NFAT hearing and the formal decision to approve Keeyask, serious questions have arisen about export prospects. Manitoba Hydro's single largest customer, Minneapolis-based Xcel Energy, has indicated it expects hydropower to drop from 7 percent of its supply mix in the Upper Midwest in 2015 to only 2 percent in 2030.[14] Of course, this may change.

Xcel is not the only prospective out-of-province customer. According to a 24 March 2021 report in the *Winnipeg Free Press*, Hydro has export contracts worth an estimated $9.4 billion over the next thirty years, including sales to SaskPower. Details of these contracts are not public and the financial future of Keeyask remains uncertain.[15]

A further dent in the clean energy argument is that Hydro earmarked nearly 40 percent of the power from Keeyask for pumping stations on upgraded and new oil pipelines through Manitoba.[16] Manitoba's clean energy will play into the expansion of the controversial oil sands. "Clean" electricity will be used to pump oil, although one of those three pipeline projects—Energy East—has since been cancelled.

A 2010 report issued by the PEW Environment Group[17] exemplifies precisely the sort of nuanced posture missing in Hydro's clean energy narrative. The report about Canada's boreal forest, entitled *A Forest of Blue*, said that, "While it is clear that allowing our societies to be powered by carbon fuels is not sustainable, this does not mean that alternative or renewable energy sources can simply be viewed as having no cost whatsoever," noting that hydropower projects in boreal Canada result in "significant impacts to wildlife habitat, ecological processes and Aboriginal communities."[18] In contrast to Hydro's blinkered narrative, the report continued: "In order to make the best and most informed decisions, we must understand as many of the implications and complexities of the issues as possible and understand that all of our choices—with the exclusion of energy conservation and increased efficiency—involve difficult trade-offs."[19]

To the extent that Manitoba Hydro claims climate concern as a motivator for Keeyask, I would ask: Did the utility start from a desire to address climate change and work its way methodically from there, carefully considering the trade-offs, to a decision to build Keeyask; or did it start with a desire to build a big dam and then work to justify that desire by doubling down on the clean narrative? We must remember that dams themselves are no favour to the environment. The moose and beaver near the Kitchekeesik cabin site do not stand on the shore and applaud as bulldozers rumble and explosives detonate.

At that site, seemingly a million miles from the beige downtown Winnipeg room that is home to PUB hearings, lies a story that clashes harshly with the clean energy narrative. It is a story that would be a footnote, at best, in a regulatory process, perhaps eliciting a sympathetic but fleeting question from a panellist. It is a story that would leave policy wonks and energy market analysts temporarily dumb. But it is a story that should be impossible to ignore. For if we ignore those sacrificed for the sake of "good," we fall short.

Of course, the Kitchekeesiks, like the rest of us, use electricity. That need for energy in a warming world is one of the greatest challenges humanity has ever faced. In the face of such a challenge, can we as a society not be more creative than to respond by reviving a project that has been on the books for decades and involves pouring 870,000 tonnes of cement[20] into a river, affecting some 13,820 hectares,[21] and creating nearly 2,000 kilometres[22] of related transmission corridor?

A silent tear on a soon-to-be-flooded shore will not stop Keeyask. But it calls for greater honesty and creativity in the future.

Premise Two: Indefinite Growth

Even if a project produces power deemed ethically superior, there is still no sense building it unless it is needed. The second piece of the pro-Keeyask discourse to consider is that demand for electricity will continue to grow indefinitely. As Byron Williams explains in the previous chapter in this volume, the stated justification for Keeyask was twofold: the need for the electricity in Manitoba,[23] and lucrative export sales to the United States. A new dam results in a big spike in supply, which does not match the very gradual increase in demand. While Hydro's plan is to sell the excess power in the earlier years, until domestic demand catches up, the stated underlying rationale was still domestic demand. In its August 2013 NFAT filing, Hydro projected that provincial demand would increase, on average, 1.6 percent annually over twenty years.[24] This number is key.

Building new generation capacity is not the only way to address projected demand growth. Industry experience has shown that reducing demand by means of energy efficiency measures is often a less expensive way to address energy needs than construction of new supply. Energy efficiency is a counterintuitive notion from a business perspective. Most businesses do not seek to reduce demand for their product. But an electric utility, particularly a Crown-owned one, is different from those businesses. In the electricity world, energy that is conserved acts as a resource. A megawatt saved is a "negawatt" produced, as some energy gurus like to say. A negawatt has value; it can be exported or used to defer new generation costs. If Manitobans use 1 percent less electricity in a year, that electricity can be exported. Or, to look at it another way, if Manitoba will need 103 new gigawatt hours (GWh) annually to meet projected demand growth, as the utility says,[25] it can build a big dam or save 103 GWh each year. Either way, the lights stay on.

That raises two key questions. How doable would it have been for Manitobans to flatten out the demand curve, thus eliminating the 1.6 percent projected annual demand growth? And how much would such measures cost compared with Keeyask? Remember that the fundamental purpose of Keeyask is to meet domestic demand, with export sales as a vital, though secondary, objective related to the financial viability of the project.

According to the testimony of energy efficiency expert Philippe Dunsky—who has consulted for numerous major utilities in North America, including Manitoba Hydro—at the NFAT hearing, since 1970, 75 percent of demand growth in the U.S. has been supplied by energy efficiency measures.[26] Many jurisdictions in North America are reducing demand by 1.5 to 2 percent annually.[27] Without assuming that the experience of one jurisdiction can translate automatically to another, this at least points to a possibility worth exploring. In a detailed presentation based on in-depth expert analysis, Dunsky said that "a near-flat, long-run demand curve is the most prudent assumption for domestic needs."[28] That would mean Keeyask would serve, he says, "primarily or exclusively [to] serve export opportunities."[29] Or, one could say, that would mean Keeyask—which was widely viewed as highly risky from a financial perspective—did not need to be built to meet provincial growth in demand. A more concerted efficiency plan could have eliminated the need for Keeyask or, at minimum, delayed the project, creating time to further study other options. Dunsky said that application of North American good practice could have delayed the need for Keeyask until 2030 or later.[30]

As for cost, many jurisdictions have found efficiency measures, or "demand-side management" (DSM) as it is called, to be less expensive, sometimes far less expensive, than adding new generation.[31] Dunsky says efficiency measures are generally two to eight times cheaper than new power plants.[32] He estimates that a more aggressive DSM program by Hydro would cost about 3.5 cents per kilowatt hour.[33] For comparison, power from Keeyask will cost about 12 cents per kilowatt hour to produce.[34] In the CEC's 2004 Final Report on the Wuskwatim project (the dam that preceded Keeyask), DSM was the least expensive of nine supply options listed.[35] Though DSM was cheaper than a new dam, Hydro argued it would do both.

In the case of Keeyask, Hydro did not even study a DSM option before deciding on its Preferred Development Plan involving Keeyask. This became clear in the NFAT process. It was also clear from a leaked copy of the confidential version of Hydro's 2010–11 Power Resource Plan. All of the scenarios Hydro considered for this key annual planning document contained the same, very low, levels of DSM. There was no scenario for ramped-up DSM, as there was in the lead-up to Wuskwatim.[36]

In fact, Hydro significantly reduced its commitment to DSM leading up to the NFAT hearing, setting a target of only 0.3 percent annual savings.[37] After facing harsh criticism for this during the early stages of the NFAT process, Hydro significantly revised its DSM planning, though the ambitious DSM targets in the early years of the plan dropped sharply in later years.[38] Still, every form of analysis and modelling it ran pointed in one direction: Keeyask.

Cost savings is not the only potential advantage of DSM. It could have been far less financially risky than a dam. To gain approvals for a dam the size of Keeyask and then build it takes ten to fifteen years. That means the decision to proceed must be made on the basis of predictions of interest rates, export market trends, exchange rates, and energy demand literally decades into the future. The Preferred Development Plan Hydro presented to the PUB included a seventy-eight-year planning period. The PUB concluded that these future projections were "highly speculative and too uncertain."[39] Hydro's argument for its preferred plan leaned heavily on this time frame and on its plan outperforming other options toward the latter part of the seventy-eight-year period.[40] These timelines make Keeyask especially risky, particularly given export market uncertainty.

Energy conservation measures do not entail that risk. A suite of measures can be adopted, adapted, evaluated, and expanded as new technologies arise. Dunsky detailed a number of current options.[41] They require no one-time multi-billion-dollar gamble, and DSM measures do not require cumbersome and costly regulatory processes.

Studies have also shown that jobs created per amount of investment in DSM measures tend to be significantly more than for construction of new generation infrastructure.[42] And the final advantage of DSM is that it is "greener" than pouring concrete in a river, flooding boreal forest, and blazing a transmission corridor through more of that forest.

Instead of seriously considering a ramped-up DSM future scenario, or perhaps a combined DSM-wind-solar scenario, Hydro evidently went with its impulse to build big dams. It assumed that never-ending growth in demand is inevitable. The end game of such a scenario is troubling. Even if new demand is met with low-carbon sources such as hydropower, wind, and solar, what will we do once all the rivers are dammed and the landscape is dotted with wind turbines and solar farms? At some point we—by which I ultimately mean humanity as a whole—will need to make energy conservation our overwhelming priority. The sooner we do so, the better.

The PUB did an admirable job of scrutinizing Hydro's DSM plans—recommending improvements, insisting that a broad range of planning scenarios be considered in the future, and recommending that the government establish an independent body to take over DSM in the province—but it did not recommend Keeyask be put on hold to further study a DSM scenario. Ironically, in its 2017 filings to the Manitoba Public Utilities Board, Manitoba Hydro completely altered its domestic load projections. Instead of the critical 1.6 percent increase, it predicted a drop in domestic load with a recovery to current levels by about 2035.[43] Well before completion of the dam, the utility has negated the fundamental justification for the most expensive project in its history.

Premise Three: "New Era" for Indigenous People

The argument in favour of Keeyask needed to assert the desirability of hydropower as a clean energy source and present a case for the need to meet demand for power. It also needed to address the ethical issues related to hydro-affected Indigenous communities.

Manitoba Hydro's track record with First Nations has been historically turbulent. But by 2009 the utility could boast that five First Nations had become co-proponents in construction of new dams. Nisichawayasihk Cree Nation is a partner in the Wuskwatim Dam, and Tataskweyak Cree Nation, York Factory First Nation, War Lake First Nation, and Fox Lake Cree Nation are co-proponents of Keeyask. As former premier Greg Selinger once told a crowd in Washington DC, those partnerships "yield phenomenal social licence."[44]

That licence is an essential part of Hydro's Keeyask narrative. It is also less solid than it first appears. The centrepiece of the Keeyask partnership is the opportunity for the four Keeyask Cree Nations, as they are called, to purchase a share of up to 25 percent in the dam, and thus reap a quarter of the profits of a presumably lucrative megaproject. The First Nations voted on the deal, known as the Joint Keeyask Development Agreement (JKDA), in 2009 amid glowing visions of the future. At the signing ceremony for the JKDA, Tataskweyak Chief Duke Beardy said Keeyask would provide the community an opportunity to "join the mainstream Manitoba economy" and "build a future of hope that will sustain and provide for all citizens of Tataskweyak Cree Nation."[45]

Today, grandiose claims are heard no more. Talk of a 25 percent share is history. The assumption during the NFAT proceeding was that the four First Nations would end up with a combined ownership stake of somewhere between 1.9 and 2.5 percent.[46] For this lesser ownership, the Keeyask Cree Nations will have to invest approximately $32 million.[47] The 25 percent stake would have cost them in the range of $364 million.[48]

The lower ownership rate, which would come in the form of "preferred shares" instead of "common shares," comes with guaranteed payouts even if the dam loses money, as opposed to the common shares that bring with them the financial risks of the project. Of course, it also means there will be no windfall of the sort implied in communications to Keeyask Cree Nations members prior to the vote. The reduced equity stake is projected to net them about $5 million annually, rising to $6 million in 2028, to be shared amongst the four First Nations.[49] The fact that the Keeyask Cree Nations do not appear to intend to invest in Keeyask in the way that was once presented as the basis of a prosperous future makes it seem as though the co-proponents have lost confidence in their own project.

The JKDA, dated August 2008, is from a different era. Much has changed. First, the projected cost of Keeyask has gone from $3.7 billion to $8.7 billion. Second, the financial projections upon which the JKDA were based could not have factored in the as-yet-unknown extent of the global recession and the fact that U.S. electricity demand did not rebound in step with the economic recovery as analysts expected. Due in part to that, the export market remains questionable. Third, as the communities went to vote on the JKDA in 2009, there was no talk of major annual hydro rate increases, a particularly sensitive matter since hydro bills in these communities are much higher than provincial averages due to cold temperatures, poor housing stock, and no access to natural gas. Thus, expected rate hikes will hit them harder than most Manitobans.

Fourth, no one knew in 2009 that Wuskwatim, which set the model for Keeyask, would fall spectacularly short of its anticipated financial performance. Members of Nisichawayasihk Cree Nation (NCN) were told in 2006 that over the long term the dam was "expected to generate tens of millions of dollars each year in profits," based on projections at the time.[50] These benefits would come from the 33 percent stake NCN obtained in the project.

By 2014 Hydro's projection of NCN's net income over the first ten years of the dam's life was a $134 million loss.[51] The parties have renegotiated the partnership twice in order to avoid NCN having to pay Hydro millions of dollars to cover its share of the losses. Hydro will pay NCN $2.5 million annually for twenty years,[52] unrelated to performance of the dam, to prop up the partnership and salvage the social licence. In terms of long-term employment for the local First

Nation, as of February 2016, only two members of NCN were employed full time at Wuskwatim.[53]

Had the four Keeyask Cree Nations known all this would happen, how would they have voted in 2009? What does the emerging principle of free, prior, and informed consent look like in such a case? Would the spirit of the principle, or the spirit of reconciliation for that matter, suggest that the Keeyask Cree Nations be given an opportunity to renegotiate the agreement in light of the major changes that have occurred since they ratified it? To what extent do these changes and the position in which they put the Keeyask Cree Nations downgrade the social licence derived from the partnerships?

This is to say nothing of the fact that the partnership agreements do not represent best practice in terms of impact benefit agreements in Canada today (though that discussion will be left to others). Other First Nations hosting major resource developments have secured considerably stronger deals.[54] Also worthy of mention are the deep divisions that were created in some of the partnership communities between people who supported the partnerships and those who did not.[55] The pain of these divisions comes through in Agnieszka Pawlowska-Mainville's chapter with Noah Massan, and in many of the community voices included in this book.

In this context, it is perhaps no surprise that Tataskweyak Cree Nation (TCN) Chief Michael Garson, addressing the CEC hearing into Keeyask in 2013, could not speak about the notion of partnership without adding a qualifier: "We're talking about partnership today," he said, "but I call it potential partnership at this moment."[56] After fourteen years of negotiations and approximately $90 million in process and negotiation costs paid to TCN alone,[57] the chief of the lead First Nation partner stumbled over the word "partnership."

Fox Lake Cree Nation councillor Conway Arthurson went further. Noting that he was speaking against the wishes of the band's lawyer, he told the CEC: "[Manitoba Hydro representatives] keep shoving everything down our throat and we are choking." Fox Lake has been "force fed negotiations," he said. Given that, he said he supports Keeyask "by a thread or two."[58]

His message to Hydro was blunt: "We don't trust you." While others from the Keeyask Cree Nations spoke more positively about the partnership, this hesitance and raw frustration speak to the precarious nature of the "phenomenal social licence" to which Premier Selinger referred (see Joseph Dipple, Chapter 11 in this volume).

More recently, leaders of the so-called Keeyask Cree Nations have made public accusations of racism, bullying, and discrimination by Hydro staff and a Hydro vice president.[59] In May 2020, the Keeyask Cree Nations, led by Tataskweyak Cree Nation, blocked access to the Keeyask work site after Hydro announced plans to bring in hundreds of outside workers despite pandemic-related concerns of the Keeyask Cree Nations. With RCMP officers watching and cameras rolling, Chief Doreen Spence of TCN ripped up the court injunction against the blockade and threw the pieces on the ground.[60] It was not a sign of a functional partnership.

Concrete Commitment

As became clear during the NFAT hearing, something other than logic had driven the project, at least in part, from the start. Hydro's approach had not been to start with a diverse range of options, including reducing energy demand, to address energy needs in Manitoba and then systematically weigh the pros and cons of each, something known as Integrated Resource Planning. Instead, Hydro appears to have started with its preferred option—building dams—and selectively constructed a case around that. In its final NFAT report, the PUB panel noted the absence of Integrated Resource Planning and emphasized the vital nature of such a process in the future.[61] A leaked copy of the internal version of Hydro's 2010 Power Resource Plan also demonstrated that Hydro had not seriously considered DSM options.[62] Each of its various future development scenarios all assumed the same level of DSM.

In the end, a rather inexplicable impulse to build dams, bolstered by a narrative of clean, necessary, and Indigenous-licensed energy, prevailed. Manitoba missed its chance to take a bold step in an innovative energy-policy direction. Instead, it made what may have been the largest public policy gamble in the history of the province.

Cranes now stand on the bed of the Nelson River. Concrete is being poured. The water has gone up. What remains to be seen in coming years and decades is: what the final cost will be, what share the First Nations will purchase (they have until after completion of the project to decide), whether the dam will prove financially viable over time, whether there will indeed be a need for Keeyask power, whether Hydro and government officials will adopt a more nuanced narrative, and whether the partnership will survive or succumb to potential First Nation demands for a better deal.

Conclusion

The lessons from the Keeyask process are relatively straightforward. First, the entire commit-first-review-later process must be reversed for any future projects. The public must have a meaningful opportunity for input into the value of and alternatives to prospective projects prior to de facto decisions and major expenditures. Second, government should act as a facilitator of mature, nuanced public discussion rather than pushing a narrow, oversimplified narrative. Creative public policy arises from considered examination of complexities. Third, in relation to any future energy projects, the question must be fundamentally bigger than whether or not to build a project. We as a society must ask instead how we as a province and region can best address energy needs in this age of climate change. We must also ask how, in the context of energy projects, can we best work toward reconciliation with Indigenous peoples? Fourth, a full range of alternative scenarios, including energy conservation, must be considered. Fifth, a current and broad-based social licence must be obtained from First Nations, using the principle of free, prior, and informed consent. Sixth, upstream fuel source impacts, such as those related to the Churchill River Diversion as well as Lake Winnipeg Regulation, must also be addressed. These considerations, rather than an institutional drive to pour concrete into rivers, must be the starting point in any future decision-making process.

Since the final official decision to proceed with Keeyask was made in 2014, the government has changed, the entire board of Manitoba Hydro has changed, the CEO of Hydro has changed, and the Hydro vice-president who took the lead on Keeyask has moved on.[63] Those who made the decisions are gone. Over the next decade or two, they can observe Keeyask's track record, if they choose, from the comfort of cottages and retirement homes. But the people in whose backyard the dam is built, remain.

As I stood with my Cree hosts on land to be flooded by Keeyask, conversation shifted to Conawapa, a proposed dam nearly twice the size of Keeyask that Hydro once planned to build further downstream.

A Cree member of our party said with resignation and anger that he believes Conawapa will be built. "Hydro always gets its way," he said. While market forces appear to have pushed Conawapa off the planning table for the foreseeable future—as the PUB recommended—the comment about Hydro's perceived omnipotence reflects something of the legacy of unofficial bitterness the utility has created in hydro-affected communities. Officially, and according to its own narrative, Manitoba Hydro obtained social licence to construct a dam that Manitoba needed and that would benefit Indigenous peoples. But on the ground just upstream of Keeyask, in the dim light of all that has happened since 64 percent of Tataskweyak Cree Nation members voted in favour of Keeyask in 2009, claims of "clean" energy mean little. The PUB's NFAT report means little. And official "partnership" with Hydro is, for many TCN members, an agonizing irony. Now, this partner has said the dam is not even needed until 2035. Still, it will be built.

Before we got back in our boats to leave the Kitchekeesik cabin site near Keeyask, I noticed a member of our party quietly remove the Hydro hard hat that some company worker had nailed to a tree on the shore. Then we pushed off to continue our tour of a homeland that will soon be a reservoir.

Since this chapter was first written in 2016, the water has gone up behind the Keeyask Generating Station and much of the area where the Kitchekeesik family grew up is flooded. In August 2020, the author again visited the area immediately upstream of Keeyask to join the Kitchekeesik family as they mourned the imminent flooding.[64]

Notes

1   The author travelled to the area on 10 July 2016.
2   Kurt Simonsen, Associate Secretary, Public Utilities Board, email message to the author, 6 May 2016.
3   Regis Gosselin (Panel Chairperson), Richard Bel, Hugh Grant, Marilyn Kapitany, and Larry Soldier, *Report on the Needs For and Alternatives To (NFAT): Review of Manitoba Hydro's Preferred Development Plan* (Winnipeg: Public Utilities Board, 2014), accessed 18 August 2016, 27, http://www.pub.gov.mb.ca/nfat/pdf/finalreport_pdp.pdf [NFAT Final Report].
4   Environment Canada, *Final Report, Federal Ecological Monitoring Program (FEMP)*, vol. 1 (Ottawa: Environment Canada / Department of Fisheries and Oceans, April 1992), 2–21.

5 Lake sizes from "Manitoba—Lake Areas and Elevation," in *The Atlas of Canada*, Natural Resources Canada, accessed 18 August 2016, http://web.archive.org/web/20070410230512/http://atlas.nrcan.gc.ca/site/english/learningresources/facts/lakes.html#saskatchewan.

6 Personal observations of the author from field trips as well as personal communication with dozens of traditional Indigenous resource harvesters from seven hydro-affected First Nations in northern Manitoba between 1998 and the present.

7 Steve Ducharme, "Fighting for a Fishery: The Churchill River Diversion Swamped Lucrative Whitefish Fishery," *Winnipeg Free Press*, 10 December 2013, A9.

8 Dale Hutchison, Hydraulic Operations Coordinator, Manitoba Hydro, email to the author, 15 May 2014.

9 Ivan Keeper and Robert Spence, "Hydro Lacks Authority to Build Bipole," *Winnipeg Free Press*, 20 January 2015, A7.

10 The author, who worked for Pimicikamak at the time of Chief Merrick's speech, was present for the speech and obtained a copy of Chief Merrick's speaking notes. Those notes are also available at https://www.facebook.com/permalink.php?story_fbid=989125991114863&id=929475533746576, accessed 18 August 2016.

11 International Hydropower Association, *Advancing Sustainable Hydropower: Activity and Strategy Report, 2017–18*, Foreword, https://www.hydropower.org/publications/iha-activity-and-strategy-report-2017-2018.

12 Manitoba Clean Environment Commission, *Keeyask Generation Project Public Hearing: Transcript of Proceedings*, vol. 1, 94, accessed 18 August 2016, http://www.cecmanitoba.ca/resource/hearings/39/Transcripts%20-%20Keeyask%20Winnipeg%20Hearing%20Oct%2021,2013.pdf.

13 Bartley Kives, "Province Will Cut GHG Emissions by One-Third by 2030: Selinger," *Winnipeg Free Press*, 3 December 2015.

14 Gavin Bade, "Steel for Fuel: Xcel CEO Ben Fowke on His Utility's Move to a Renewable-centric Grid," *Utility Dive*, 11 July 2017, accessed 13 February 2018, https://www.utilitydive.com/news/steel-for-fuel-xcel-ceo-ben-fowke-on-his-utilitys-move-to-a-renewable-c/446791/.

15 Dan Lett, "Hydro's $5-billion Deals with Saskatchewan 'Deliberately Covered Up,'" *Winnipeg Free Press*, 24 March 2021, https://www.winnipegfreepress.com/local/Manitoba-Hydros-5-billion-deals-with-Saskatchewan-deliberately-covered-up-574052921.html.

16 Total Keeyask output is listed at 4,400 gigawatt hours (GWh) (Gosselin et al., *NFAT*, 47), and expected electricity requires for new pipeline projects is listed at 1,700 GWh (Gosselin et al., *NFAT*, 62). Further to that, Ed Wojczynski of Manitoba Hydro was paraphrased as saying, "The pipelines themselves would require just under 2,000 gigawatt-hours of energy, which is roughly half the dependable energy of Keeyask," *Winnipeg Free Press*, 24 May 2014.

17 PEW Environment Group, *A Forest of Blue: Canada's Boreal* (Seattle: PEW Environment Group, 2011), accessed 18 August 2016, http://www.pewtrusts.org/~/media/legacy/uploadedfiles/peg/publications/report/pegborealwaterreport11march2011pdf.pdf.

18 Ibid., 59, 37.

19 Ibid., 59.

20 This figure is derived from data provided in Keeyask Hydropower Limited Partnership, *Keeyask Generation Project: Environmental Impact Statement, Supporting Volume: Project Description* (Winnipeg: Keeyask Hydropower Limited Partnership, June 2012), 3-11, accessed 18 August 2016, http://keeyask.com/wp-content/uploads/Keeyask_EIS-Project_Description_SV.pdf.

21 Ibid., 2-1.

22 This figure includes Bipole III at 1,384 km, https://www.hydro.mb.ca/projects/bipoleIII/description.shtml; the Manitoba-Minnesota Transmission Line at 213 km, https://www.hydro.mb.ca/projects/mb_mn_transmission/index.shtml; and the Great Northern Transmission Line at "about" 354 km, http://www.greatnortherntransmissionline.com/assets/documents/FinalEIS/FEIS-Chapter02.pdf, 21. All websites accessed 18 August 2016.

23 Manitoba Hydro, *Needs For and Alternatives To (NFAT)* (Winnipeg: Manitoba Hydro, August 2013), primary filing for Manitoba Public Utilities Board Needs For and Alternatives To hearing, Overview, 1–13, accessed 27 October 2021, http://www.pub.gov.mb.ca/nfat/pdf/hydro_application/nfat_business_case__0_overview_meeting_manitobans_electricity_needs.pdf.

24 Ibid., 62.

25 Ibid.

26 Dunsky Energy Consulting, *Manitoba Hydro NFAT Review: Direct Testimony of Philippe Dunsky* (Montreal: Dunsky Energy Consulting, 28 April 2014), slide 8, accessed 18 August 2016, http://www.pub.gov.mb.ca/nfat_hearing/NFAT%20Exhibits/CAC-62.pdf.

27 Manitoba Hydro, *NFAT*, 74. Also, in a presentation to the NFAT hearing, 3 February 2014, Philippe Dunsky noted that some North American jurisdictions have energy-efficiency goals as high as 2.6 percent; see Dunsky Energy Consulting, *The Role and Value of Demand-Side Management in Manitoba Hydro's Resource Planning Process* (Montreal: Dunsky Energy Consulting, 2014), 23, accessed 18 August 2016, http://www.pub.gov.mb.ca/nfat/pdf/demand_side_management_dunsky.pdf.

28 Dunsky Energy Consulting, *NFAT Review: Direct Testimony of Philippe Dunsky*, slide 59.

29 Ibid.

30 Gloria Desorcy and Byron Williams, "What Happened to Hydro's Decade of Returns?" *Winnipeg Free Press*, 25 June 2014, accessed 18 August 2016, http://www.winnipegfreepress.com/opinion/analysis/what-happened-to-hydros-decade-of-returns-264522561.html.

31 Dunsky Energy Consulting, *The Role and Value of Demand-Side Management*, 10–12, 34, http://www.pub.gov.mb.ca/nfat/pdf/demand_side_management_dunsky.pdf.

32 Dunsky Energy Consulting, *NFAT Review: Direct Testimony of Philippe Dunsky*, slide 9.

33 Dunsky, *Role and Value of Demand-Side Management*, 34.

34 Dennis Woodford, "Market Forces Weighing on Hydro Exports," *Winnipeg Free Press*, 5 April 2016, accessed 18 August 2016, http://www.winnipegfreepress.com/opinion/analysis/market-forces-weighing-on-hydro-exports-374574511.html.

35 Gerard Lecuyer (Chairperson) et al., *Report on Public Hearings: Wuskwatim Generation and Transmission Projects* (Winnipeg: Manitoba Clean Environment Commission, September 2004), 55, accessed 18 August 2016, http://www.cecmanitoba.ca/

resource/reports/Commissioned-Reports-2004-2005-Wuskwatim_Generation_
Transmission_Projects_Full_Report.pdf.

36 Ibid., 53.

37 Bruce Owen, "Hydro Conservation Efforts Losing Energy: Expert Tells Public
Utilities Board Power Smart Moving Backward," *Winnipeg Free Press*, 18 January
2013.

38 Bruce Owen, "Too Many Dams and Power Smarter," *Winnipeg Free Press*, 28 April
2014, accessed 18 August 2016, http://www.winnipegfreepress.com/opinion/blogs/
under-the-dome/256997181.html.

39 Manitoba Hydro, *NFAT*, 137 and 18.

40 Ibid., 138–59.

41 Dunsky Energy Consulting, *NFAT Review: Direct Testimony of Philippe Dunsky*,
slides 19–39.

42 Ibid., slide 9.

43 Manitoba Hydro Public Utilities Board, "Rebuttal Evidence of Manitoba Hydro,"
22 November 2017, Fig. 1.6, 7, accessed 13 February 2018, http://www.pubmanitoba.
ca/v1/proceedings-decisions/appl-current/pubs/2017%20mh%20gra/mh%20
exhibits/mh-52%20-%20mh-pub%20-%20rebuttal%20evidence.pdf.

44 Greg Selinger, Speech at the Woodrow Wilson Institute, Washington, D.C., 25
February 2013, http://www.wilsoncenter.org/event/power-partnerships-how-
canada-us-hydroelectric-partnerships-reinforce-america%E2%80%99s-clean-
energy.

45 Manitoba Hydro and Cree Nation Partners, "Manitoba Hydro and Four Cree
Nations Sign Historic Joint Keeyask Development Agreement," news release, 29
May 2009.

46 Manitoba Hydro, *NFAT*, 221; Manitoba Hydro, "Needs For and Alternatives To:
CAC/MH II-006a, Manitoba Hydro," January 2014, accessed 18 August 2016,
http://www.pub.gov.mb.ca/nfat/pdf/ir/CAC-MH%20Round%202.pdf.

47 Scott Powell, Manager, Public Affairs, Manitoba Hydro, email to the author, 7
January 2016.

48 Manitoba Hydro, "Needs For and Alternatives To: CAC/MH II-006a."

49 Ibid.

50 Nisichawayasihk Cree Nation, *Benefits, Risks and Safeguards: Wuskwatim Project
Development Agreement* (Nelson House: NCN Future Development Office, March
2006), 3, accessed 18 August 2016, http://www.ncncree.com/ncn/documents/
PDABenefitsRisksSafeguards.pdf.

51 Manitoba Hydro, "Needs For and Alternatives To: CAC/MH II-006a."

52 Scott Powell, Manager, Public Affairs, Manitoba Hydro, email to the author, 20 June
2014.

53 Scott Powell, Manager, Public Affairs, Manitoba Hydro, email to the author, 16
February 2016.

54 Examples would include the 2002 Paix de Braves agreement between the Grand
Council of the Crees of Quebec (Eeyou Istchee) and the Government of Quebec,
and the 2011 Tshash Petapen (New Dawn) Agreement among the Innu Nation,
Government of Newfoundland and Labrador, and Nalcor Energy.

55 Numerous members of Nisichawayasihk Cree Nation (NCN) and Tataskweyak
Cree Nation spoke with the author of these divisions in many personal conversations

over numerous years. The division was illustrated during the 2004 Clean Environment Commission hearings into the Wuskwatim Project, during which a brother and sister, William Elvis Thomas and Carol Kobliski of NCN, were lined up as the primary NCN proponent and opponent, respectively, of the project.

56 Manitoba Clean Environment Commission, *Keeyask Generation Project Public Hearing: Transcript of Proceedings*, 21 October 2013, 114, accessed 18 August 2016, http://www.cecmanitoba.ca/resource/hearings/39/Transcripts%20-%20 Keeyask%20Winnipeg%20Hearing%20Oct%2021,2013.pdf.

57 Correspondence from Manitoba Hydro to the Canadian Taxpayer's Federation, in response to a request under the Freedom of Information and Protection of Privacy Act, 30 September 2013. Note: TCN accounts for 92.7 percent of Cree Nation Partners.

58 The eleven First Nations are: Chemawawin Cree Nation, Fox Lake Cree Nation, Misipawistik Cree Nation, Mosakahiken Cree Nation, Nisichawayasihk Cree Nation, Norway House Cree Nation, O-Pipon-Na-Piwin Cree Nation, Pimicikamak Nation, Tataskweyak Cree Nation, War Lake First Nation, and York Factory First Nation.

59 Jessica Urbanski-Botelho, "Hydro Bullying, Racism Behind Resignation from Board, Keeyask Partnership VP Says," *Winnipeg Free Press*, 4 September 2018, accessed 13 October 2021, https://www.winnipegfreepress.com/local/hydro-bullying-racism-behind-resignation-from-board-keeyask-partnership-vp-says-492430461.html. See also Alexandra Paul, "York Factory Plans Boycott of Hydro Partnership," *Winnipeg Free Press*, 4 December 2018, https://www.winnipegfreepress.com/local/ york-factory-plans-boycott-of-hydro-partnership-501918641.html. See also Ashley Prest, "Hydro VP Steps Down from Keeyask Partnership: Chief Urges Inquiry into Work Site Allegations," *Winnipeg Free Press*, 7 September 2018, https://www. winnipegfreepress.com/local/hydro-executive-resigns-as-keeyask-partnership-chairman-492720891.html.

60 Rachel Bergen, "Tataskweyak Cree Nation Chief Tears Up Court Injunction at Keeyask Blockade," *CBC News Manitoba*, 21 May 2020, https://www.cbc.ca/ news/canada/manitoba/injunction-ripped-tataskweyak-cree-nation-keeyask-blockade-1.5578625.

61 Gosselin et al., *NFAT*, 33–35.

62 "The 2010/11 Power Resource Plan," Resource Planning and Market Analysis Department, Power Planning Division, Manitoba Hydro, 21 September 2010, 14, 18, 22.

63 On 19 April 2016, the Manitoba Progressive Conservative party, under the leadership of Brian Pallister, defeated the New Democratic Party; the new Manitoba government appointed all new members to the Manitoba Hydro-Electric Board on 4 May 2016; on 7 December 2015, Kelvin Shepherd took over from Scott Thomson as president and CEO of Manitoba Hydro; and Ken Adams, who had been senior vice-president, Power Supply, for the majority of the Keeyask planning period, is no longer with Manitoba Hydro.

64 Will Braun, "Flooded Land, Drowned Memories: Family's Grief, Anger and Sadness Flow along with the Water at Hydro's Keeyask Project," *Winnipeg Free Press*, 19 September 2020, https://www.winnipegfreepress.com/arts-and-life/life/ greenpage/flooded-land-drowned-memories-572453262.html.

"Born into Debt: Wuskwatim"

DR. RAMONA NECKOWAY, NISICHAWAYASIHK CREE NATION

The following text contain excerpts from testimonies given by Ramona Neckoway, citizen of the Nisichawayasihk Cree Nation (NCN), and now assistant professor at University College of the North, during the Clean Environment Commission's (CEC) regulatory hearings for the Wuskwatim and Keeyask projects.

NCN partnered on the Wuskwatim Dam, the first major Hydro project in northern Manitoba, which saw the emergence of "Partnership Agreements" between developers and various Hydro-affected Cree First Nation communities in northern Manitoba; Wuskwatim has been operational since 2012. The first excerpt is from testimony at the CEC hearings held in Thompson, Manitoba, in 2004, and later excerpts are combined testimonies and reflections to Manitoba's CEC and Canada's National Energy Board a decade after the Wuskwatim hearings.

According to Neckoway, the myth of progress has come at great cost, both figuratively and literally. Her testimonies provide critical reflections from a Hydro-affected Cree woman, mother, and grandmother—an often-unexplored narrative lens. The following excerpts offer only a glimpse of this complex and deeply personal lens.

"I Want No Part of It"

Excerpt from the transcript of the Wuskwatim CEC hearings in Thompson, 23 March 2004.

I am here today to voice my opinion about this project and to have my voice, my concerns, publicly recorded for my children and their children so they can look back and see that I was opposed to this [Wuskwatim Dam Project].

I want to begin by stating that I am opposed to this project in its current form. I am opposed to it because I do not trust Manitoba Hydro. And my confidence in their claims for prosperity for my community is non-existent. Many of the dealings Manitoba Hydro has had with the Indigenous peoples of this province have yielded results that are nothing more than empty promises, deception, destruction. One need only look at what has happened in communities such as Cross Lake, South Indian and Nisichawayasihk to see evidence of this. And we've heard evidence of this today.

How can I trust Hydro when they have left a trail of unfulfilled promises and devastation? How can we be expected to trust Hydro when the shiny beads they offer to entice us could end up destroying us again?

Various entities are claiming that the community supports this endeavour and the consultation process has been cited as a part of it. I know for a fact that there are many who are wary of this deal, myself included. For whatever reasons, some have chosen to remain silent and that is their right. If they choose to remain silent, that is their right. It is my right to voice the concerns that I have regarding this project as it has a potential to alter life in my community again as we know it.

It is not only my right to voice my concern, it is also my responsibility. It is my responsibility to my children and their children as well as to those who came before us.

I have a responsibility for my late grandfather whose sweat and blood is on that land, literally. The area where this proposed project is going to be built is adjacent to my grandfather's trapline. My mother grew up in that area. She has memories attached to that land even though she is no longer able to return there. I have a responsibility to her as well as to my grandfathers before us to voice my opposition to this project.

I have seen this term ["consultation"] used excessively and I have some concerns about the supposed consultation process. I am concerned because I have heard and seen this term used redundantly and feel as though I have not been consulted. No one has asked me. No one has asked me what I thought about this, at least not anyone involved with this project who has a fiscally-mandated responsibility to do so.

If consultation means having a package slipped under the door of my home or being handed a book filled with technical jargon which requires degrees of sorts to comprehend in response to my queries, then yes, to that extent, I have been consulted.

But according to the dictionary definition, this is not what consultation is. I would like the Commission to know that I have not been asked my opinion about this project nor have I engaged in any kind of meaningful participation or dialogue with the people involved, despite what has been stated.

I am not opposed to economic development and economic growth and I hope that I am not labelled as opposing economic development in my community. I think that it would be great if we, as a community, could improve our economic and social situation. I am not opposed to new and innovative ideas that will enhance our standard of living.

I am, however, concerned with the current process and mechanisms associated with the Wuskwatim project. I respect what the leadership is trying to do for the community but I am not entirely convinced that this is what is best for us as NCN people. I am wary [of the shiny] beads that are being offered to us.

There are contradictions of sorts associated with Wuskwatim and these contradictions are what made me suspect about this project. One contradiction involves the fiscal responsibility that we, as NCN members, have to assume to be part of this project. How can we invest and buy into something when we have nothing to invest in the first place? Our existing money should be utilized within the community. How can we justify exporting the meagre monies for a project of this magnitude when we have people who are living in destitute conditions? We could be doing other things with the money we save by not buying into this project.

I don't understand how we could sit by and wait 30 odd years to reap monetary benefits from this project. I understand that to fund a portion of this project, NCN will have to come up with about $62 million. And not only that, we will have to come up with $1 million just before the construction begins. I have a couple of questions about this.

As an NCN member, I think I have the right to know where that $1 million is going to come from by the end of this year. According to the SOU summary [the Summary of Understanding agreement, which is non-binding], we will have to come up with a further $21 million. Where will this additional money come from?

I'm wondering if Hydro can tell us, tell me, in simple layman terms how much we are going to have to pay back on the approximately $41 million they are going to lend us. Perhaps they could give us, based on the assumption that we as grassroots NCN people without formal knowledge about interest rates and as such, an estimate of how much we will owe in dollars and cents before the referendum takes place. I also think that we have the right to know where the other $21 million is going to come from.

Together we have to obtain $62 million and I'm concerned about the details. According to the SOU summary, we are going to be borrowing a lot of money for this project which leads me to another question. Why do we have to risk so much? If we must get ourselves involved here, I think that we should just get a percentage of the project. We should get a portion of our monies annually simply because the project is on our land. It is our Aboriginal Right.

Again, I don't see how we can be expected to come up with money that we don't have. I also don't understand how Hydro can ask us to help destroy our own environment, my grandfather's trapline, my mother's memories.

Can we really walk away whenever we want? Will we owe you monies incurred if we choose to back out? Where is this money going to come from for the pre-project business? And will we be responsible for paying back costs incurred with the pre-project phase? I hope that that will not be figured into the millions and millions of dollars we will owe you if this project goes through.

How can a consultation process be of benefit to us as typical everyday grassroots people? Assuming that I have been properly consulted, how can I make sense of the information that is given to me? I possess a university degree and I'm having a hell of a time understanding what is contained in this information. Can you please tell me how my grandmother, who doesn't speak or read English, is to understand what is going on? How can my aunts, uncles and cousins begin to comprehend what is written or even spoken? You need degrees of all sorts to understand what is written down, presuming you can read it in the first place. I also wonder how any pertinent concepts can be effectively translated so that their full implications are relayed and understood.

We are being told what is going on. We need to be asked, not told. I for one am sick of non-Aboriginal entities coming in and telling us what is good for us or that this kind of development will be a benefit to us. Progress does not necessarily mean prosperity.

If this project means destroying the land that my grandfather worked on, lived on and loved, if this project means creating further divisiveness within my own community and divisiveness between my community and other Aboriginal communities, if this project undermines our rights as Aboriginal people, then I want no part of it.

I see this project as another colonial apparatus which will only serve to, and contribute to, the existing tensions in my community and other communities. It is a colonial apparatus that will destroy our autonomy creating further dependence and despair.

Again, I am voicing my concerns about this project because I want my children and their children to know that I did my part to save the land that my grandfather loved. I do not believe that this project is in the best interests of my community, myself or my children.

"You Are in Cree Territory"

Excerpt from the transcript of the Keeyask CEC hearings in Winnipeg, 9 December 2013.

I am still quite young compared to some of the elders that I sit with.... For me to raise issues of culture, as a young woman, I feel, is not my place, and I apologize [to] the elders for having to be the one to come and remind people about our culture and about the importance of our way of life.

But as a woman and as a mother and as a Cree person that lives and is from that territory [in northern Manitoba], I really feel that I have an obligation and responsibility to remind southerners, to remind Manitobans, to remind Manitoba Hydro, and to remind us, even us the Cree, that the knowledge and our way of life and the knowledge of our elders and the way that we lived is important....

[My PhD research is aimed at] record[ing] how hydroelectric development has and is impacting the Cree in the North.... I have had the opportunity to research and visit many Hydro-affected communities, and I [have] spoke[n] with Cree who were and continue to be affected by hydroelectric development. I have heard accounts of racism, segregation, and other forms of abuses that I never would have imagined to be possible here in Canada.... I have gone and done research in Grand Rapids. I have interviewed on both sides of the river.... I spent time in Pimicikamak territory. I have learned about the impacts of Hydro development in that territory. I have also gone and done treaty research which had taken me into communities in the north which were also impacted by hydroelectric development [including Tataskweyak, Fox Lake, and York Landing].

[I'm] looking at this [research in] my role as a mother. I'm [also] a grandmother. My grandson is four years old. As I sit here today, [at] Wuskwatim . . . as far as I [am aware] the rapids are gone . . . That was Grandfather's trapline. As I sit here today, his trapline is gone. My grandson is born into debt . . . because of the [Wuskwatim] project development agreement. He is four years old. So by virtue of that agreement, we are in debt. . . .

Again, compared to the elders beside me and behind me, I am young and I have lots to learn. . . . We have forgotten about what happened to the people. And for me, the goal of my research . . . is to go and document an unfiltered account of what happened to the Cree in my territory.

I agreed to speak here today [at the Keeyask hearings] to serve as a reminder that development is impacting us. By us I mean the Cree in the North. I'm from Nisichawayasihk, but I also have family and kinship connection[s] into Tataskweyak and into Fox Lake. The course of development impacts us all . . .

Do we really need further development? I don't know. I can't answer that.

I was opposed to Wuskwatim because I was really concerned about what was happening to the land, the loss of the traplines. I don't know if people in the South will understand what that really means for us . . .

You can't separate the land from the people. For us as Cree in the North, the land is so important to us. While I'm not a resource user, my chapan, my great-grandmother, instilled [the importance of the land] in me. I saw her working the land. And I hear stories of the old people, [and] what the land meant for them, and the pride and the sense of purpose and the sense of belonging [it created for them]. I don't know how to impart that so that it makes sense. And maybe I don't need to convince you, because we know what it is and how important it is to us. [Through my research] I'm hoping [that] I can record what really happened to the people. . . . You can't forget about what happened to the people. I have heard of atrocities from Grand Rapids all the way up through to some of the bigger dams down on the other end of the Nelson River.

My children may never see the economic benefits promised to them ... I was born into a world that has been and is infected by hydroelectric development activities, and these partnerships have created rifts in some of the communities. I saw it happen in mine. There has been yet to be reconciliation, true reconciliation regarding this earlier wave, rather tsunami of development that happened in the '70s.... We were promised prosperity back when they signed the Northern Flood Agreement. Where is it? ...

It feels like we, the Cree, are entering into these [partnership development] agreements under stress, we want jobs, we want some of the conveniences, we want some access to benefits that the South enjoys as a course of ... your day-to-day. But it seems like we are getting into these agreements and I wonder: do we really know the full impact of what we are getting into? ... For me it seems like through these agreements we are being forced to help destroy and damage our land. And in doing this, it is like we are breaking our own natural laws ...

Some of the interviews that I've done [speak to] the sacredness of the land [and that knowledge and insight] comes clear from the elders ... By being partners in the process we are being forced to break those natural laws ...

How will our children, and our grandchildren know and learn about their land and heritage?

[Wesakejack's] chair, in my territory, they say Wesakejack was there.... There is a land marker there in Footprint Lake that ties back to Wesakejack stories....

Our way of life is not some relic, some way of the past, ... we are still alive, we are still here....

I would ask the [Clean Environment Commission] to recommend that somehow we document unfiltered narratives of what happened to the Cree, and what is happening to the Cree in the territory, and not in a piecemeal manner.... We need to be able to pass some kind of knowledge to our children and our grandchildren ... and leave a record.... Our legacy should be a better one than we have now.

CHAPTER 3

The Augmented Flow Program:
Impacts on South Indian Lake

ASFIA GULRUKH KAMAL, JOSEPH DIPPLE,
STEVE DUCHARME, AND LESLIE DYSART

There is a fundamental fact about the hydroelectric system in northern Manitoba that is often inexplicably absent from regulatory reviews of the area: the importance of interconnection and how deeply current and future generating stations rely on megaprojects of the past. Two of these past projects are the Churchill River Diversion (CRD) and the Lake Winnipeg Regulation Project, both completed in 1976. With each new generating station, the entire system's reliance upon these two projects becomes increasingly necessary, since they control the flow of water through the Nelson River, and thus control the amount of energy produced in the generating stations along this river. These projects have had, and continue to have, devastating impacts on the lakes and rivers they sit on even as they directly contribute to Manitoba Hydro's immense profits.

Manitoba Hydro continues to build the Keeyask Project, which as of early 2021 is in its final year of construction. These decisions directly affect the community of South Indian Lake, home of the O-Pipon-Na-Piwin Cree Nation (OPCN). The Keeyask power will "plug into" the current hydroelectric system of the Nelson River. Approximately four decades ago, Manitoba Hydro constructed the Churchill River Diversion to divert about 75 percent[1] of the water from the Churchill River backwards through Southern Indian Lake, the Rat and Burntwood river systems, and into the Nelson River. As a result, approximately 40 percent of the water running through generating stations along the Nelson River originates from Southern Indian Lake and the Churchill River.[2]

Therefore, the Churchill River Diversion directly affects both the success and profitability of the Keeyask Project, but it was not considered in the federal or provincial environmental assessments for Keeyask. Manitoba Hydro's environmental considerations did not include any areas beyond the "footprint" of the generating station.[3] As a result, impacts on the community of South Indian Lake and their environment were ignored, and there were no mitigation efforts set out to address any possible environmental destruction from the operation of this generating station, let alone impact-benefit agreements. As hydro-conscious advocate Will Braun mentions in the previous chapter in this volume, upstream First Nations like OPCN do not have partnership agreements for Keeyask but will likely suffer the impacts nonetheless. Many within the community who have experienced the destruction of the Churchill River Diversion, as well as the changes in water fluctuations from generating stations along the Nelson River, have deep concerns about what the future holds for their community with yet another hydroelectric dam operating with their water.

Augmented Flow Program: Licence of Power

In order for Manitoba Hydro to use Southern Indian Lake as a reservoir for its battery of generating stations along the Nelson River system, the provincial government granted the Crown corporation a licence under the Water Power Act.[4] This licence prescribes how much the water levels at Southern Indian Lake are allowed to fluctuate, which in turn controls the rest of the Nelson River system. This initial licence allowed Manitoba Hydro to increase or draw down Southern Indian Lake by a maximum of two feet over the course of a twelve-month period. However, shortly after gaining this licence in 1986, the Province gave Manitoba Hydro a temporary licence that gave them further control over the waters of Southern Indian Lake, dubbed the "Augmented Flow Program."[5] Now, Hydro was allowed to increase the lake level by an additional six inches and draw it down by an additional two feet. This has effectively more than doubled the allowable twelve-month fluctuation from 2 feet to 4.5 feet. For almost forty years now, the provincial government grants Manitoba

Hydro's annual request to operate under the Augmented Flow Program. Despite changes to a licence that directly affects those living at Southern Indian Lake, neither the Province nor Manitoba Hydro consulted the community about these changes to the program.[6] Community members have stated that these changes negatively affected their perception of the moral contract the community had with the provincial government.[7]

Now, after decades of the "interim" Water Power Act licence, Manitoba Hydro is applying for a permanent licence to operate the Churchill River Diversion, based on the more lenient flooding and draw-down regulations of the Augmented Flow Program, as confirmed by community members of OPCN.[8] To date there has been no public process to assess this application for a permanent licence.[9] As such, Indigenous people who live around Southern Indian Lake, as well as other concerned Manitobans, do not have an opportunity to challenge this application in the public arena or in environmental hearings.

This is a perfect opportunity to learn from the regulatory gaps and oversimplified narratives explored in the first two chapters of this volume, and do what these authors recommend: hold public hearings on significant hydroelectric projects decisions such as this that offer community members a meaningful opportunity to examine the case and offer alternatives. Granting a permanent licence using the parameters of the Augmented Flow Program instead sanctions a program that has effectively destroyed a stable, sustainable economy in northern Manitoba, through the collapse of North America's second-largest grade-A whitefish fishery.[10]

The Keeyask Project

As has been described in previous chapters in this volume, Manitoba Hydro is constructing the Keeyask Generating Station in partnership with four First Nation communities.[11] Upon completion of the project, much of the energy produced by the Keeyask Generating Station will be sold to Minnesota and Wisconsin.[12] As part of the regulatory process for such a large project, the Clean Environment Commission (CEC) conducted public hearings into the proposal by Keeyask Hydropower Limited Partnership to build the Keeyask Generation Project from September 2013 to January 2014.[13]

Throughout the Clean Environment Commission hearings, it was obvious that the scientific research on environmental effects reviewed

very narrow areas of the Nelson River, predominantly the areas that
would be directly affected during construction and operation.[14] Failures
such as this to view the entire system of Manitoba Hydro's hydroelectric dams as a cohesive whole prevent a nuanced understanding of
the multiple impacts of generating stations. Southern Indian Lake is
one of the reservoirs that powers Manitoba Hydro's arsenal, and any
generating station constructed along the Nelson River affects OPCN.
In particular, Manitoba Hydro can increase energy production at the
generating stations along the Nelson River by releasing water at the
Notigi Control Structure and by preventing water from flowing through
the Missi Falls Control Structure into the Churchill River. As such, the
entire Southern Indian Lake contains a massive amount of potential
energy for times of need—but Manitoba Hydro did not include upstream communities in the Keeyask partnership.

Elder William Dysart of OPCN argues that since the entire boreal
forest river system is interconnected, the damages to the riverine system
are also connected. He said, "The same way when CRD was constructed
many communities, lakes and hunting and fishing areas were affected,
Keeyask is going to either intensify the loss or keep it the same. It is
not going to make things better for us."[15]

While the CEC hearings failed to meaningfully address the full
extent of the anticipated impacts of the Keeyask Project, they become
clear when considered from an OPCN perspective.

Implication of the Keeyask Project: A Community (OPCN) Interpretation

We can truly assess the full extent of the social, cultural, spiritual,
economic, and environmental impacts of the disruption, alteration,
and fragmentation of a natural ecosystem of the rivers and lakes in
northern Manitoba only when we openly acknowledge the destructive
nature of these Hydro projects and the vulnerability of the people who
are exposed to it. As Kuntala Lahiri-Dutt argues, "All the technical
solutions adopted to 'control' rivers curtailed the right of rivers to
move over space, and this not only gave rise to a series of technical
problems, but immense political problems as well. What the river and
its changing moods meant to those who lived in its basin, and to those
who made technology choices for them, must therefore be understood
as a first step."[16]

Indigenous communities in Canada view water and land as sacred, medicinal, and a living entity,[17] an understanding that directly conflicts with a settler interpretation where water and land are considered as material resources that can be owned, wasted, and controlled. For OPCN people, northern Manitoba rivers and ecosystems are integral parts of an interconnected and interdependent human–non-human community. Disregarding the well-being rights of a river means more than losing material resources—it causes a permanent scar to their collective identity, livelihood cycle, and ancestral sovereignty right.

Community members Calvin Baker and Leslie Dysart said the "ecological risk is higher when the entire river system is damaged. The health of water influences weather, food, life cycles and the land quality—damming the river is the easiest way to contaminate the entire cycle of life."[18]

OPCN community members have identified two major indirect impacts Keeyask has had on OPCN: a) its impact on fisheries in all river communities in the Nelson-Churchill river basin, with particular focus on fish migration, and b) the need to acknowledge the Nelson-Churchill region as one river basin and work towards an integrated water management system. Both points carry immense significance for OPCN and all Indigenous communities from a socio-economic and cultural perspective.

Hydroelectric megaprojects on the Nelson River impact the water regime of Lake Winnipeg, the Nelson and Churchill rivers, and connecting channels.[19] Studies consider the hydrologic regime of the Nelson-Churchill River Basin, the third-largest river basin in North America, as a complex one and severely impacted by hydroelectricity generation.[20] The Nelson-Churchill region is very rich with natural resources, with more than 65 percent of the land covered in forested areas and wetlands.[21] According to a 2016 census, the Nelson-Churchill basin is home for 37,041 Indigenous people.[22] According to a report from the International Institution for Sustainable Development (2016), to develop sustainable river basin management strategies, research focus on the Nelson-Churchill hydrologic regime should shift from small-scale impact to the implication on the "whole basin as an integrated system" and long-term objectives.[23]

At present, Lake Winnipeg Regulation increases the Lake Winnipeg discharge capacity by about 50 percent and regulates the discharge for the lower Nelson River.[24] Before Manitoba Hydro built the Churchill River Diversion, water accumulated from rain and snow would flow naturally to the Hudson Bay through both the Churchill and Nelson rivers.[25] Post-diversion, this flow is controlled through the Notigi Control Structure[26] to all generating stations along the Nelson River, including Keeyask. With the construction of the Keeyask Dam, some of the water accumulated in the Southern Indian Lake reservoir might be used to conserve water upstream of Keeyask, which will disturb the interconnected biodiversity of the Nelson-Churchill river basin.

Studies demonstrate that continuously fragmenting river systems through dams, weirs, and control structures can threaten migratory fish populations and increase fish mortality,[27] resulting in the loss of freshwater fish species both upstream and downstream.[28] Dams are also considered one of the greatest threats to freshwater biodiversity worldwide.[29] Development of multiple dams and control structures in China's Mekong River is a well-studied example where thousands of fisher communities experienced a severe loss due to the decline of migratory fish, disturbance in the spawning cycle due to fluctuation of water, and water pollution throughout the river basin.[30]

Concerned for consequences of the Keeyask Dam, Thomas Spence, an Elder and fisherman from OPCN, said,

> We do not see the sturgeon fish anymore in our area. Our Elders used to tell us sturgeon fish can migrate far. They do not come to this side of the water any more. Why? You can say Notigi and Missi seriously affected the movement of big fish such as sturgeon and pike and disturbed the spawning of white fish. If South Indian water is used for Keeyask, this will continue, and I can't imagine how much more damage will happen to our land and water. You tell me, from Missi to Limestone they cut our rivers into so many pieces. It hurts.[31]

Calvin Baker, another fisherman from OPCN, said, "Construction of any dam on the Churchill and Nelson rivers is damaging because it blocks the major route for fish migrations. Most people in this region fish. We are fishers and we harvest from interconnected fisheries."[32]

Another serious concern is how dams cut migratory fish off from their seasonal habitats. A number of OPCN fishermen expressed concerns about the lack of fish passage in the existing control structures.

Elder William Dysart said, "During the construction of control structures in Southern Indian Lake, we discussed the fish passage. Even
though they initially agreed, the plan was not implemented. When
asked, they said lack of budget."[33] As stated in the Conservation and
Water Stewardship Fisheries Branch Manitoba report (2012), "The lack
of upstream fish passage at existing water control facilities is frequently
raised as a concern—for example, there are no specific measures in place
for either up or downstream passage of fish at any of the hydroelectric
generating stations in Manitoba. In addition to the practical limitations
of current techniques to address fish passage issues, the desirability of
providing passage must be considered on a site-by-site basis."[34]

A number of community Elders, including Elder and South Indian
Lake Fishermen's Association President Steve Ducharme, elaborated
on the idea of interconnectedness with the word "kistihtamahwin," a
Cree word meaning "respect for all beings, both living and nonliving."[35]
OPCN perceives and practises its water governance and environmental
stewardship through this lens. The concept is founded on the idea of
one entity—one community that includes both human and non-human beings. Kistihtamahwin is practised by respectful and reciprocal
interaction with nature and taking care of the "one" community.[36] Since
the Nelson-Churchill river basin is interconnected with many water
channels, fragmentation or any kind of disturbance in one area will
disrupt the entire river system's biodiversity, as well as social institutions,
food harvesting, cultural practices, and all forms of relationships within
the community.[37]

As the lands and waters of northern Manitoba will be further affected by the Keeyask Project, so are the Indigenous communities who
have a close relationship with nature and other communities. Late Elder
Vivian Moose said, "We have families living all over north. Who wants
to see the same thing happening to family?"[38] According to the report
released by the federal Canadian Environmental Assessment Agency
in 2014 when they conducted their regulatory review of Keeyask, communities and support groups from across the Nelson-Churchill river
basin, including Pimicikamak Cree Nation, Fox Lake Cree Nation,
Manitoba Metis Federation, Norway House Cree Nation, Shamattawa
First Nation, Tataskweyak Cree Nation, War Lake First Nation, York
Factory First Nation, and OPCN, spoke out about the potential risks
and cumulative effects of the Keeyask Generation Project, particularly

on possible water contamination, the loss of berry and medicinal patches, impacts on health, and access to country food.[39]

Harvesting berries in the late summer and early fall is an important social and cultural practice in Cree communities all over northern Manitoba. However, the erosion of berry patches and medicinal plants is one of the major direct damages that has happened in OPCN territory after flooding, both upstream and downstream of the Churchill and Nelson river systems. Community member Esther Dysart stated, "People do not pick berries from one area only. Besides the flooded land, each year there are new areas that are being affected. There is no balance of how much rain or sun you might get, and these are important factors for growth of berries and medicines."[40] This quote effectively summarizes the importance of having multiple berry patches from which to pick. With water fluctuations, gradually changing climate, and the continuous destruction of berry patches, the number of available patches is decreasing, leading to the inability to harvest berries for fear of overharvesting.

Losing the opportunity to fish or harvest berries and medicines is not merely a nutritional problem. It also hampers communities' ability to continue cultural and collective initiatives that are deeply tied to their relationships with each other. As OPCN community member Shirley Ducharme and Evelyn Montgomery said, "Every year we have to go far or find a new spot for harvesting berries or medicine or go to a different community."[41] Interactions with the environment and family and relatives in other communities while harvesting food and medicine provide community members with opportunities for a healthy lifestyle and the practice of kistihtamahwin. OPCN members worry this will be further disturbed with the Keeyask Project.

Although it is not directly apparent, OPCN community members predict that Keeyask will have a multitude of direct effects on OPCN in the future. According to OPCN Elders, the Churchill River Diversion caused drastic changes in the water system, triggering the massive migrations (such as caribou) and complete extinction of animals in the area (such as porcupine). They expect that further disruption through Keeyask will lead to the extinction of muskrat and reduction of marten populations in their area. Migration of moose and caribou populations and waterfowl is significant in both the Churchill and Nelson river systems. Additionally, Elder Thomas Spence said, "One thing people do not understand is the water quality is not the same anymore. Control of water flow changes the season or the adaptation cycle of everything living in the water, [and] the fish do not taste the same."[42]

Many of the effects described in this section have been observed by community members who have a long-standing history with Manitoba Hydro. When OPCN community members bring forward their concerns, they tell the story of crosscutting issues related to flooding, climate change, food sovereignty, and social and health disparities—a discussion hydrologists and social scientists have been having for decades.

After more than four decades, OPCN is still suffering from the effects of the Churchill River Diversion. A lack of healthy food, fresh drinking water, proper sewage systems, and adequate housing, as well as continuous shoreline erosion, a collapsed fishery, health disparities, and high mortality rates, are some of the worst ongoing impacts of this project, which has been operational since the mid-1970s.[43] OPCN's concerns about the Keeyask Project and the real threats it poses to freshwater biodiversity in the Churchill-Nelson river basin are valid and require immediate attention.

Conclusion

Manitoba Hydro has fundamentally altered the properties of water and how it moves across the land in northern Manitoba by building and maintaining massive hydroelectric generating stations along the Nelson River. This system is interconnected, and all of it is impacted. Through the Churchill River Diversion and Lake Winnipeg Regulation projects, Manitoba Hydro has completely re-engineered the hydrology of the Churchill, Rat, Burntwood, and Nelson rivers and has caused widespread impacts on a vast number of Indigenous communities. Southern Indian Lake, one of the major sources of water flow for the generating stations along the Nelson River and the basis of the Churchill River Diversion, has been affected by each and every generating station constructed along the Nelson River. However, the Indigenous community of South Indian Lake and OPCN has not been consulted or considered in the environmental evaluations of these projects. As a result, the true implications of present and future generating stations are not truly known and the community's expert knowledge has not been recognized.

Because Manitoba Hydro continues to use the Augmented Flow Program, the water systems of Southern Indian Lake and the life they sustain have never been able to recover. The extreme water fluctuation this program allows significantly impacts the Indigenous community that calls it home, and the introduction of new generating stations is expected to cause even more fluctuations on a more regular basis.

Manitoba Hydro is moving forward with plans to develop more generating stations on the Nelson-Churchill river system. Based on what OPCN's knowledge holders have to share, it is evident that Manitoba Hydro is neither concerned about nor considering the negative implication of the Keeyask Project on the entire Nelson-Churchill basin, on OPCN, or on the community of South Indian Lake. As authors Jill Blakley and Bram Noble argue later in this volume, Manitoba Hydro's focus on the footprint of the Keeyask Generating Station fails to account for the broader regional effects that accumulate over time. OPCN members recommend that to avoid large-scale damage, government and Manitoba Hydro decision making needs to include comprehensive assessments of needs, options, and impacts, including cumulative assessments of planned dams that look at the entire river basin. This includes meaningful consultation with communities and consideration for the spirit of kistihtamahwin.

Notes

1   R.A. Bodaly, D.M. Rosenberg, M.N. Gaboury, R.E. Hecky, R.W. Newbury, and K. Patalas, "Ecological Effects of Hydroelectric Development in Northern Manitoba, Canada: The Churchill-Nelson River Diversion," in *Effects of Pollutants at the Ecosystem Level*, ed. P.J. Sheehan, D.R. Miller, G.C. Butler, and Ph. Bourdeau (Chichester, NY: John Wiley and Sons, 1984), 279, http://dge.stanford.edu/SCOPE/SCOPE_22/SCOPE_22_2.6_Bodaly_273-310.pdf.

2   Asfia G. Kamal, Joseph Dipple, Steve Ducharme, and Leslie Dysart, "Learning the Language of the River: Understanding Indigenous Water Governance with O-Pipon-Na-Piwin Cree Nation, Northern Manitoba, Canada," *Case Studies in the Environment* 2, no. 1 (2018): 1–7.

3   Canadian Environment Assessment Agency, *Keeyask Generation Project: Comprehensive Study Report* (Ottawa: Canadian Environment Assessment Agency, April 2014), 14–16, https://www.ceaa-acee.gc.ca/050/documents/p64144/99127E.pdf.

4   Manitoba Hydro, "Churchil River Diversion," accessed 29 April 2021, https://www.hydro.mb.ca/corporate/facilities/water_levels/churchill_river_diversion/.

5   Steve Ducharme, President, South Indian Lake Commercial Fishermen's Association, South Indian Lake, in discussion with Asfia Kamal, September 2014.

6   Steve Ducharme, "Fighting for a Fishery," *Winnipeg Free Press*, 12 October 2013, http://www.winnipegfreepress.com/opinion/analysis/fighting-for-a-fishery-235187641.html.

7   Ducharme, in discussion with Kamal, September 2014.

8   Leslie Dysart, CEO, Community Association of South Indian Lake, in discussion with Asfia Kamal, March 2015.

9   James Beddome, "Say No to Augmented Flow," *Thompson Citizen*, 4 February 2021, https://www.thompsoncitizen.net/opinion/columnists/say-no-to-augmented-flow-1.24277694.

10 Ducharme, "Fighting for a Fishery."

11 Manitoba Hydro, "Keeyask Generating Station Produces First Electricity for Manitoba Grid: Renewable Hydropower from Keeyask Adds to Manitoba's Clean Energy Supply," accessed 20 April 2021, https://www.hydro.mb.ca/articles/2021/02/keeyask_generating_station_produces_first_electricity_for_manitoba_grid/#:~:text=The%20Keeyask%20Generating%20Station%20is,the%20Keeyask%20Hydropower%20Limited%20Partnership.

12 Lynne Fernandez, *Manitoba Hydro—The Long View* (Winnipeg: Canadian Centre for Policy Alternatives, 5 September 2019), https://www.policyalternatives.ca/publications/reports/manitoba-hydro-long-view.

13 Canadian Environment Assessment Agency, *Keeyask Generation Project*, 80.

14 Manitoba Clean Environment Commission, *Keeyask Generation Project, Public Hearings*, 3, Winnipeg, 23 October 2013, 649–50, accessed 29 April 2021, http://www.cecmanitoba.ca/cecm/hearings/keeyask.htm.

15 William Dysart, Elder and fisherman, South Indian Lake, in discussion with Asfia Kamal, August 2015.

16 Kuntala Lahiri-Dutt, "Imagining Rivers," *Economic and Political Weekly* 35, no. 27 (2000): 2396.

17 Nicole Wilson, Leila Harris, Angie Joseph-Rear, Jody Beaumont, and Terre Satterfield, "Water Is Medicine: Reimagining Water Security through Tr'ondëk Hwëch'in Relationships to Treated and Traditional Water Sources in Yukon, Canada," *Water* 11, no. 3 (2019): 624.

18 Leslie Dysart, CEO, Community Association of South Indian Lake, and Calvin Baker, fisherman, South Indian Lake, in discussion with Asfia Kamal, July 2014.

19 Karla Zubrycki, Dimple Roy, Hisham Osman, Kimberly Lewtas, Geoffrey Gunn, and Richard Grosshans, *Large Area Planning in the Nelson-Churchill River Basin (NCRB): Laying a Foundation in Northern Manitoba* (Winnipeg, MB: International Institute for Sustainable Development, 2016), 17, https://www.iisd.org/index.php/system/files/publications/large-area-planning-nelson-churchill-river-basin-full-report.pdf.

20 Ibid., iii.

21 Ibid., 11.

22 Statistics Canada, Aboriginal Population Profile, 2016 Census, accessed 30 April 2021, https://www12.statcan.gc.ca/census-recensement/2016/dp-pd/abpopprof/search-recherche/lst/results-resultats.cfm?Lang=E&G=1&Geo1=&Code1=&GEOCODE=46&SEX_ID=1&AGE_ID=1&RESGEO_ID=1.

23 Zubrycki et al., *Large Area Planning*, 28.

24 Ibid., 17.

25 Joel Edye-Rowntree, "Churchill Residents' Use of the Lower Churchill River in Manitoba," Master's thesis, University of Manitoba, 2007.

26 Ducharme, in discussion with Kamal, September 2014.

27   Phillip Jellyman and John S. Harding, "The Role of Dams in Altering Freshwater
     Fish Communities in New Zealand," *New Zealand Journal of Marine and Freshwater
     Research* 46 (2012): 475–89.

28   Catherine R. Liermann, Christer Nilsson, James Robertson, and Rebecca Y. Ng,
     "Implications of Dam Obstruction 660 for Global Freshwater Fish Diversity,"
     BioScience 62 (2012): 545.

29   Frank Rahel and Robert McLaughlin, "Selective Fragmentation and the
     Management of Fish Movement across Anthropogenic Barriers," *Ecological
     Applications* 28, no. 8 (2018): 2066; World Fish Migration Foundation, "From Sea
     to Source," accessed 12 December 2018, http://kalastajateselts.ee/fail/files_from_
     sea_to_source_2_0.pdf; and C.J. Vörösmarty, P. B. McIntyre, M.O. Gessner, D.
     Dudgeon, A. Prousevich, P. Green, S. Glidden, S.E. Bunn, C.A. Sullivan, C.R.
     Liermann, and P.M. Davies, "Global Threats to Human Water Security and
     River Biodiversity," *Nature* 467 (2010): 555–61, https://www.nature.com/articles/
     nature09440.

30   Guy Ziv, Eric Baran, So Nam, Ignacio Rodriguez-Iturbe, and Simon A. Levin,
     "Trading-Off Fish Biodiversity, Food Security, and Hydropower in the Mekong
     River Basin," *Proceedings of the National Academy of Science* 109, no. 15 (2012):
     5609–14; and Patrick J. Dugan, Chris Barlow, Angelo A. Agostinho, Eric Baran,
     Glenn F. Cada, Daqing Chen, Ian G. Cowx et al., "Fish Migration, Dams, and Loss
     of Ecosystem Services in the Mekong Basin," *Ambio* 39, no. 4 (2010): 344–48.

31   Thomas Spence, Elder, South Indian Lake, in discussion with Asfia Kamal,
     September 2013.

32   Calvin Baker, fisherman, South Indian Lake, in discussion with Asfia Kamal, July
     2015.

33   Dysart, in discussion with Kamal, September 2014.

34   Conservation and Water Stewardship Fisheries Branch Manitoba, "Manitoba
     Lake Sturgeon Management Strategy (Final Draft April 11, 2012)," Government
     of Manitoba, 11 April 2012, 5, accessed 29 April 2021, http://digitalcollection.gov.
     mb.ca/awweb/pdfopener?smd=1&did=25824&md=1.

35   Kamal et al., "Learning the Language of the River," 2.

36   Ibid.

37   Kamal et al., "Learning the Language of the River."

38   Vivian Moose, Elder, South Indian Lake, in discussion with Asfia Kamal, September
     2014.

39   Canadian Environment Assessment Agency, *Keeyask Generation Project:
     Comprehensive Study Report.*

40   Dysart, in discussion with Kamal, September 2013.

41   Shirley Ducharme, Chief, South Indian Lake, and Evelyn Montgomery, Elder,
     South Indian Lake, in discussion with Asfia Kamal, September 2013.

42   Spence, in discussion with Kamal, September 2014.

43   Asfia G. Kamal, Rene Linklater, Shirley Thompson, Joseph Dipple, and Ithinto
     Mechisowin Committee, "A Recipe for Change: Reclamation of Indigenous Food
     Sovereignty in O-Pipon-Na-Piwin Cree Nation for Decolonization, Resource
     Sharing, and Cultural Restoration," *Globalizations* 12, no. 4 (2015): 562.

PART 2

Impacts of Hydroelectric Development in Northern Manitoba

"The Hurt I Carry with Me"

ROBERT SPENCE, LAND AND RESOURCE USER, TATASKWEYAK CREE NATION, CEC HEARING

Excerpt from the transcript of the Keeyask CEC hearing in Winnipeg, 14 November 2013.

Note: Robert Spence testified in both English and Cree. CEC hearing transcripts note when he switches languages with "(Cree spoken)."

(Cree spoken) Some of you that are here know me. (Cree spoken) I'm forty-four years old. (Cree spoken) I have lived my life, my short life on the land in Split Lake where I grew up, where my grandparents brought me up. (Cree spoken) ... It is hard for me to come up here and sit in front of all you here today because what I carry with me, I have carried with me all my life. And I don't know if I can speak enough today, tonight on this occasion to tell you the hurt that I carry within me, that I carried all my life because of Manitoba Hydro.

(Cree spoken) My soul hurts and is dying. I feel as though I'm mourning every day while being on the lake and the land. You can't understand that because you don't want to go past that door. And you can't. I'd like to see you try. To live the life we live as First Nations people being as connected to the water and the land as we are. You killed the land. You killed the water. You killed the fish. You killed the Indian. Ininew. Do you understand that?

I come here with a rage built up inside me for so long that I can't hold it back anymore. (Cree spoken)

CHAPTER 4

The Keeyask Project:
"No Significant Cumulative Effects"?

JILL BLAKLEY AND BRAM NOBLE

One could argue that environmental impacts caused by future hydroelectric developments on the Nelson River are insignificant, given the magnitude of change that has already occurred over the last sixty years. Alternatively, given that environmental impacts on the Nelson River to date have clearly exceeded any past efforts to mitigate them, and the region is now "substantially altered,"[1] one could also argue that the impacts of future development of any kind, including the Keeyask Hydroelectric Generation Project, must immediately be considered significant, given how many other impacts have accumulated to date. If the latter, then additional development should not proceed unless that project's proponents can demonstrate net positive contributions to the sustainability of the Nelson River system and affected Indigenous peoples.

This is more than a philosophical debate: the future of the region hangs in the balance and the two paths forward could not be more different from one another. With more than 5,000 megawatts (MW) in additional hydroelectric development in northern Manitoba that Manitoba Hydro has potentially identified following Keeyask, what is at stake is the ultimate fate of many "valued" yet vulnerable wildlife populations, critical ecosystem services, and Indigenous communities that have been under enduring stress since megaproject development began in the late 1950s.

In this chapter, we discuss the concept of cumulative environmental effects and why assessing these is so critical to effective environmental impact assessments, which are foundational to determining which resource development projects receive the regulatory approvals they need to move forward. Our evaluation focuses on the Keeyask Hydropower Limited Partnership's (KHLP) overall approach to assessing cumulative effects in their Environmental Impact Statement (EIS) submitted to the Clean Environment Commission (CEC). The main purpose of the EIS, beyond securing the Province's regulatory approval for Keeyask, was to evaluate how this new hydroelectric project would impact the environment around it and identify concrete ways to mitigate any "significant adverse effects" (damaging impacts to the water, land, animals, vegetation, and/or local communities nearby) it might cause. However, our review calls into question the soundness of their cumulative effects assessment—particularly their conclusion that the Keeyask Project would result in "no significant cumulative effects" to the surrounding environment. Most importantly, our review is intended to capture the *significance* of the Keeyask decision, and what it means for the future of northern Manitoba.

What Are Cumulative Environmental Effects?

"Cumulative environmental effects" are changes to the environment that are caused by an action in combination with other past, present, and future actions.[2] Each individual disturbance or impact, regardless of its magnitude or its cause, can represent a high marginal cost to the environment. Describing the loss of wetlands along the east coast of the United States between 1950 and 1970, for example, renowned biologist William Odum explains: "No one purposely planned to destroy almost 50% of the existing marshland along the coasts of Connecticut and Massachusetts. . . . However, through hundreds of little decisions and the conversion of hundreds of small tracts of marshland, a major decision in favour of extensive wetlands conversion was made without ever addressing the issue directly."[3]

In other words, cumulative environmental effects can happen by accident through the culmination of many, sometimes small-scale, activities such as building roads and pipelines, seismic lines, river crossings, water diversions,[4] and so on.

People sometimes refer to cumulative effects in other terms such as "progressive nibbling," "death by a thousand cuts," and the "tyranny of small decisions." In particular, the "tyranny of small decisions," a concept originally introduced by economist Alfred Kahn in the 1960s, helps explain how both the insidious process of environmental degradation over time (progressive nibbling) and small but repetitive insults to the same environment component (death by a thousand cuts) can occur simultaneously: a number of separate decisions cumulatively, and often unintentionally, result in a condition that is neither optimal nor desirable.

Fundamental to managing cumulative effects is, therefore, recognizing that a significant adverse effect—which the EIS is ostensibly designed to avoid—can result over time due to the culmination of seemingly small or insignificant actions. The U.S. Council on Environmental Quality,[5] for example, notes that the most devastating environmental effects may result from the combination of individually minor effects of multiple actions over time. Similarly, the BC Forest Practices Board explains: "a series of individually insignificant effects can accumulate to result in a significant overall effect. For example, each water license on a stream may only withdraw a small amount of water, but a large number of small licenses may withdraw enough water to negatively affect fish habitat near the mouth of the stream."[6]

As such, the assessment of cumulative effects must always be approached from the perspective of the environments being impacted, including interconnected ecosystems and Indigenous or other local communities. No project exists in isolation—there is always an environmental and social context that informs the decision about whether or not a new project should proceed. There is also no such thing as a geographical region without people connected to it. Few if any places in the world remain untouched by human activity in some way, and all modern development activities are preceded by Indigenous relationships to land. These are not "property"-based; rather, land means the earth, the water, the air, and all that live within these ecosystems.[7] Treating the effects of a single project as though they do not contribute to the total social, cultural, economic, or environmental effects of preceding projects or disturbances can be a dangerous pitfall in environmental impact assessment, one that cumulative effects assessment (CEA) is meant to avoid.

What Is Cumulative Effects Assessment?

In this context, "cumulative effects assessment" is a process that evaluates the nature and quality of key elements within an environment, and whether the total effects of all stressors in a project's regional environment are acceptable, including the potential additional stress caused by the proposed project. A key aspect of cumulative effects assessment is to identify Valued Ecosystem Components (VECs) according to a set of criteria. These VECs can represent any aspect of the ecosystem that are identified as particularly important or susceptible to adverse effects. This includes at-risk species, such as caribou, lake sturgeon, bald eagles, and native plants, as well as less tangible components, such as ecosystem diversity. The Keeyask EIS identifies aquatic, terrestrial, and socio-economic VECs, including water quality and four species of fish (aquatic), habitat intactness, wetland function, and various species of plants, amphibians, reptiles, birds, and mammals (terrestrial), and employment and training, community health, and culture and spirituality, among others (socio-economic).

The Keeyask EIS states: "The CEA for the project determines the extent to which the project is expected to be incrementally responsible for adversely affecting a Valued Ecosystem Component (VEC) beyond an acceptable point, taking into account the overall suite of stresses on the selected VEC (including stresses from other projects and activities)." This is consistent with our understanding of the general approach to good CEA. The importance of assessing cumulative effects to effective environmental impact reports cannot be overstated: one simply cannot understand the significance of any individual project without considering the total effects of development pressures. In the context of river systems, cumulative effects can result from changes caused by multiple environmental disturbances caused or influenced by humans.[8] Almost all land-use activities in a watershed directly alter environmental parameters, including soil, topography, and vegetation. These, in turn, modify how the river transports water, the organic matter in it, and the pollutants and sediments that accumulate in river systems.[9] As such, the health of a river system is largely a function of the interactions that occur both in the water and on land within the boundary of the watershed.[10] Understanding the significance of the effects of a hydroelectric project requires an understanding of the total effects of other human activities and natural processes that occur within the watershed, such as forestry, mining, linear features such as roads and pipelines, water withdrawal, and other disturbances to aquatic and terrestrial habitat.[11]

Although it is not always reasonable to expect a single project proponent to accurately predict, or manage, the total future development pressures of other projects and disturbances in the regional environment,[12] it is reasonable to expect that a project proponent adopts a sound CEA methodology that analyzes environmental trends and includes, at minimum, the proponent's own history, and future, of regional development activity. In Manitoba Hydro's case, several major hydroelectric development projects precede the Keeyask Project on the Nelson River, including the Jenpeg, Kelsey, Kettle, Longspruce, and Limestone dams, and many more in the Nelson sub-watershed, including the Churchill River Diversion and the Lake Winnipeg Regulation projects.

Cumulative effects assessment methodology typically unfolds in four stages: scoping (i.e., determining which other projects and actions—past, present, and future—will be included in the assessment), retrospective analysis (i.e., looking from the past to the present), prospective analysis (i.e., looking to the future), and management (i.e., identifying appropriate mitigation and monitoring actions) of significant adverse cumulative effects. In the absence of any one of the four components, a CEA should be considered incomplete.

Governments may also undertake a more strategic cumulative effects assessment, to inform regional land-use planning or policy development.[13] As Byron Williams pointed out in Chapter 1 of this volume, the Manitoba Clean Environment Commission recommended this type of regional strategic environmental assessment, or a Regional Cumulative Effects Assessment (RCEA) for all Manitoba Hydro projects in the Nelson River sub-watershed in 2013, before any additional projects (including Keeyask) were approved. This volume's co-editor Jill Blakley does a thorough review of this RCEA, released in 2015, in Chapter 9 of this volume. However, regional CEAs involve a different set of standards from those of project-based CEAs. We do not use RCEA standards in this chapter to evaluate the Keeyask partnership's CEA, as presented in the Keeyask EIS.

Our Approach to the Review

Our review of this particular cumulative effects assessment was based on what can reasonably be expected of a proponent, in this case the Keeyask Hydropower Limited Partnership (KHLP), within the confines of the proposed Keeyask Project. That being said, by definition, cumulative environmental effects are of a scope and nature that require the project proponent to adopt a broad view of the project's environment and of the project's potential interactions with other past, present, and future developments. Our expectations of a reasonable standard of practice for a CEA in a project setting reflect this reality.

Our review criteria are summarized in Table 4.1. The review criteria correspond to each of the four stages of a standard methodology for project-based CEA, as explained above, and are based on well-established principles and standards for CEA. We also refer to previous[14] and more recent[15] reviews of CEA practice and the lessons emerging. Interestingly, we found just three sources drawn from the CEA literature and/or guidance in the Keeyask Project EIS reference list. This effort to connect the Keeyask CEA with established sources outlining good methodology is inadequate in our view.

In undertaking our review, we consulted the relevant chapters and supporting volumes of the Keeyask Project EIS; submitted Information Requests to KHLP regarding cumulative effects; and reviewed responses to our own Information Requests and to Information Requests submitted by others concerning cumulative effects (see Table 4.2).

Key Findings and Observations

When we reviewed the Keeyask Project EIS, and in particular the CEA, we observed that many of the expected elements of a good-practice CEA framework were indeed present. For example, the EIS claimed to adopt an ecosystem perspective (see Chapter 6 and Terrestrial Environment Supporting Volume), which is appropriate for both scoping and analyzing the cumulative effects of the project, given its scale and context. The CEA claimed to examine past conditions, the effects of past projects, and effects of the proposed Keeyask Project, and to examine future conditions with and without Keeyask and in combination with the effects of other future projects and activities.[16] All of this is required for good-practice retrospective and prospective analysis in CEA. Perhaps of greatest significance is the commitment to determine the extent to

Table 4.1. Review Criteria for the Keeyask Project Cumulative Effects Assessment

Cumulative effects assessment component	Guiding criteria for good practice
A. Scoping practices for cumulative effects	The CEA considers all types of activities and stresses (human-induced and natural disturbances) that may interact with the project's effects on Valued Ecosystem Components (VECs)
	The CEA adopts ecologically based scoping
	An explicit rationale is provided for CEA VEC selection
	Spatial boundaries reflect the natural distribution patterns of VECs selected for the CEA
	The CEA adequately captures past development and other certain and reasonably foreseeable future projects and activities
B. Retrospective analysis of cumulative effects	The baseline analysis delineates past and present cumulative effects
	The baseline analysis establishes trends in VEC conditions and known or suspected relationships between changes in VEC conditions and the drivers of change
	Thresholds (e.g., management targets, benchmarks, or ecological limits) are specified against which cumulative change and the significance of effects can be assessed
C. Prospective analysis of cumulative effects	The time scale of cumulative effects predictions is sufficient to capture the scope of impacts associated with the project's life cycle
	There is sufficient analysis/evidence to support conclusions about potential cumulative effects
	The tools and techniques used are capable of capturing cumulative effects pathways and the uncertainties of future developments
	Trends and linkages are established between VEC conditions and disturbances in the baseline analysis and used to inform predictions about cumulative impacts in the future
	Cumulative effects analysis is centred on the total effects on VECs in the project's regional environment, and the project's incremental contributions

D. Cumulative effects management measures	i) Is the significance of a project's cumulative effects measured against a past reference condition and not simply the current, cumulative, or disturbed condition?
	ii) Is the significance of cumulative effects adequately described and justified (e.g., based on regulatory thresholds, environmental policies, expert evaluation, public concerns, etc.) and based on VEC sustainability, defined by a desired or healthy condition or threshold as opposed to the magnitude of the individual project stress on that VEC?
	iii) Are the incremental impacts of the proposed initiative "traded off" against the significance of all other disturbances of activities in the region (i.e., minimized or masked)?
	iv) Are mitigation measures identified that help offset significant cumulative environmental effects and, if so, is consideration is given to multi-stakeholder collaboration to develop joint management measures?
	v) Is adaptive management identified for significant cumulative effects contingent upon future and uncertain developments and impact interactions?

Table 4.2. Keeyask Generation Project Materials Reviewed

EIS Supporting Documentation and Other Reports
Environmental Impact Statement (Response to EIS Guidelines)
Select Environmental Impact Statement project maps and GIS shape files
Physical Environment Supporting Volume
Aquatic Environment Supporting Volume
Terrestrial Environment Supporting Volume
Keeyask Cree Nations Partners Environmental Evaluation
Cumulative Effects Assessment Practitioners Guide (Hegmann et al. 1999)
CEAA Operational Policy Statement (OPS) on cumulative effects (2007)
Select Information Requests and responses focused on cumulative effects (Rounds 1-3)
Keeyask Traditional Plans Workshop Summary (Supplemental Filing # 1)
Updated Caribou Sections (Supplemental Filing # 2)

which the Keeyask Project is incrementally responsible for adversely affecting Valued Ecosystem Components (for
example, caribou or sturgeon) beyond an acceptable point, in relation to the overall suite of stresses on a VEC.[17] Reporting a project's incremental contribution to the total stress on a VEC, including anticipated stress from reasonably foreseeable future projects and activities, is core to good CEA.

Thus, we found that the proponent's *intent* was sound. However, as we read more carefully into the CEA to determine what was actually done, and in reading the Keeyask partnership's conclusions and the evidence they provided to support those conclusions, we found that many of their claims quickly unravelled. Here, we provide a snapshot of the key findings of our review,[18] and offer a number of observations concerning the significance of the decision at hand about whether or not to approve the Keeyask Project.

What in the CEA Was Done Reasonably Well?

The EIS does not dismiss that there will be cumulative effects or interactions with other past, present, and future projects. The EIS, including the CEA chapter, mentions several times that the Keeyask Project will be built in an area that has been significantly altered by development over the past fifty-five years, and that they expect Keeyask will further change the watershed. For example, it is stated: "The aquatic environment of the Nelson River where the Project will be constructed has been *substantially altered* by hydroelectric developments, in particular the Churchill River Diversion (CRD) and Lake Winnipeg Regulation (LWR), and the construction of the Kettle GS [Generating Station]. Effects of the Project will be *super-imposed* on this disrupted environment."[19]

The EIS does contain evidence of the first three basic components of a CEA methodology: scoping, retrospective analysis, and prospective analysis. Regarding scoping, the EIS acknowledges that in addition to past Hydro projects: "past and current linear developments in the region, including upgrades to PR (provincial road) 280, may also overlap with the Project. Other agents of past and current change ... are mining, commercial forestry, commercial fishing of sturgeon and other activities."[20] This is an improvement over previous CEA practices (e.g., Bipole III), where admissions about cumulative effects were almost non-existent. With respect to retrospective analysis, the EIS commits to identifying "trends, conditions, and the major influences of past and present projects and activities"[21] on the local environment. The CEA does a reasonably good job of characterizing the "what was" and "what is" (i.e., past and current conditions) in the local and regional study areas, considering the constraints of available data; however, the futures part of the Keeyask CEA (i.e., predicting, modelling, and evaluating the effects of future activities) is, for many VECs, below an acceptable standard of practice. This is in spite of the fact that the proponent claims: "Ultimately, the focus of the assessment was on the future rather than on the past, i.e., on examining the vulnerability of each VEC today and in the future without the Project (due to whatever factors might affect this vulnerability), in order to help in identifying the extent to which incremental effects on a VEC from additional changes caused by the Project could potentially result in a cumulative significant adverse effect on the VEC."[22]

There is some trends analysis in the CEA, particularly with regard to the effects of future activities on intactness (i.e., habitat). Intactness is presented both spatially and temporally, making it possible to quantify changes over a specific geography and at different periods of time. Changes in intactness are related to risk factors, or vulnerability, to wildlife species—namely, caribou. However, even for intactness, the EIS presents a series of temporal snapshots versus analyzing trends and futures projections per se.

Encouragingly, the EIS recognizes the importance of adopting an ecosystem perspective. Specifically, the EIS adopts local and regional-scale ecological boundaries for the direct effects assessment and adjusts them to the particular VEC being examined. For example, the EIS uses six geographic zones for terrestrial study zones, each successively larger than the last, and study areas "vary between environmental components to appropriately reflect the extent of project effects on that component."[23] Where required, "the study areas extend beyond the zone of impact to provide context for the study."[24] The EIS also applied this practice to VECs considered in the CEA. The Keeyask partnership identified scientific benchmarks or ecological thresholds (i.e., maximum levels of allowable change) for several VECs (or their indicators) but unfortunately (with few exceptions) did not use those thresholds to interpret the significance of the potential cumulative effects of future projects and activities.

The EIS and its supporting volumes by and large did a good job of acknowledging the limitations of the data and of uncertainty in general:

"The assessment where relevant also addresses certainty/uncertainty (i.e., the level of confidence) of the analysis/prediction."[25] That being said, we note that the EIS does not carry forward their discussions of certainty/ uncertainty to inform the CEA chapter in any significant way: in this important section of the EIS, "uncertainty" is mentioned just three times and "certainty" just once. "Confidence intervals," which are a range of values defined such that there is a specified probability that the value of a parameter lies within that range, are not mentioned in the CEA at all.

What Aspects of the CEA Need Significant Improvement?

Scoping

Cumulative effects scoping serves to establish the spatial and temporal boundaries of the assessment. We found that CEA scoping practices in the Keeyask EIS were incomplete in some respects, which then limits the scope of subsequent analysis and the ability to draw defensible con- clusions about the impacts of the project. Simply put, the scoping is too narrow. Although the EIS adopts regional-scale ecological boundaries for the direct effects assessment, the boundaries are project-centred and not broad enough to capture the potential cumulative impacts of other existing and future developments in the region that also contribute to stress on VECs. For example, the Manitoba Clean Environment Commission raises concerns[26] that numerous existing and proposed developments located outside (within sixty kilometres further north- east) of the Study Zone 5 Regional Study Area could also impact upon project VECs but are scoped-out of the CEA. These include a variety of transmission lines, generating stations, converter stations, highways, roads and trails, work sites, communities, and more. Good-practice CEA involves adjusting study boundaries to whatever they need to be to properly assess VEC sustainability. It adopts boundaries that capture both the project's effects and the effects of all other projects and activities that put stress on aspects of the environment we need to protect.

The environmental impact statement also does not scope its CEA broadly enough to address potential cumulative impacts related to certain key past and future Manitoba Hydro projects. The Keeyask Project optimizes the Province's investment in five large, existing hydro generating stations, which together produce 70 percent of energy in Manitoba,[27] and these developments are captured in the analysis of the project's direct effects. But three projects in particular are excluded or not adequately dealt with in the scoping phase of the CEA: the existing Bipole I and II transmission right of way, the Wuskwatim Generating Station (completed in 2012), and the Conawapa Generating Station (since put on hold).

The CEA identifies the Bipole III transmission right-of-way as a relevant future project.[28] It therefore stands to reason that the existing Bipole I and II line should also be scoped in.[29] Understanding the combined effects of all three Bipole lines is necessary to understanding how they may affect species habitat both on land and in the river systems. The EIS does not make this linkage because the Bipole I and II projects are not specifically named in the CEA, and the analysis of habitat intactness, for example, performed earlier in the EIS did not include Bipole III.

The EIS chapter on CEA does consider the Wuskwatim Generation Project a "past or current project." However, in 2013 its three turbines had been in operation only less than two years, with construction having begun in August 2006. As such, its environmental impacts will unfold far into the future. Because the Keeyask partnership categorized it as a "past and current" project, they did not model its future effects, just the effects experienced since construction began to the time the Keeyask EIS was prepared—less than seven years. In our view, this is a scoping error because the future effects of the Wuskwatim Project will unfold over many decades and have not been adequately captured in either the assessment of past and current projects or the assessment of future projects.

The Conawapa Generation Project (including camp) is listed as a future project that could contribute to the cumulative effects of the Keeyask Project.[30] The EIS finds that Conawapa may affect water quality (an aquatic environment VEC),[31] yet the CEA concludes that none of the four fish species named as VECs will likely experience significant adverse effects from the Keeyask Generating Station. In other words, the potential cumulative effects of the Conawapa project are scoped-out of the cumulative effects analysis for fish.[32] Since the future effects of the Wuskwatim Generation Project are largely unknown and the Conawapa Generating Station has yet to be built, it stands to reason that there could be a very significant combined effect on water quality and fish populations, especially given the previous five hydroelectric developments on the Nelson River. This potential interaction is not captured in the Keeyask Project CEA.

Another significant scoping issue in the Keeyask CEA is its failure to clearly identify the temporal scope of analysis. With respect to capturing reasonably foreseeable future activities, the CEA does not clearly specify a time horizon for predictions. Although there is no standard future time frame in CEA, CEA generally uses long-term boundaries in its analysis, where the time horizon extends as long as the environmental impacts do:[33] "the boundary in the future typically ends when pre-action conditions become re-established."[34] Other future temporal limit options for CEA include the end of the operational life of the project, or that time after which project abandonment and reclamation has been complete. A hydroelectric generating station of Keeyask's magnitude implies a distant future time horizon to capture decommissioning and reclamation activities, likely 100 years or more. However, the Keeyask CEA does not state the operational life of the project. If Manitoba Hydro is planning to ever decommission the Keeyask Project, or if they have similar plans for other generating stations on the Nelson River, these activities could cause further (positive or negative) cumulative effects on the region's environment.

Retrospective Analysis

Retrospective analysis is focused on determining baseline conditions to monitor how conditions change over time and how significant those changes are for environmental components of concern. The Keeyask EIS commits to identifying and delineating trends related to the effects of past and present actions.[35] However, we identify two areas of concern about the retrospective analysis (also called a "baseline assessment"): the first relates to how the CEA uses trends to examine baseline conditions; the second concerns the CEA's use (or disuse) of thresholds or benchmarks for interpreting the significance of past and future cumulative effects.

What is weak in the baseline assessment concerning habitat loss and fragmentation is the lack of a trend that can be projected forward, specifically the "rate of loss" and spatial patterns (including feature buffers) of loss or disturbance, from past to present to future, and how VECs have responded and are expected to respond. Focal wildlife species can be adequately assessed by two indicators that track direct and indirect footprint and habitat loss: total area disturbed and total corridor density.[36] We recognize that this approach, typically based on correlations, is characterized by uncertainty, given the complexity of relationships between disturbance and wildlife response, including time lags. However, the objective is to identify trends or patterns over time and across space to indicate whether conditions are "not changing," "getting better," or "getting worse," and what might happen under different future project conditions. This is important to understanding potential future cumulative effects on wildlife populations, including caribou, but was poorly developed in the CEA.

There are some areas where trends in baseline conditions are difficult to discern; some of this is attributed to limited data availability. The EIS reports that technical information is limited regarding Nelson River water quality pre-Hydro development: "methodological differences preclude the analysis of historic data to establish a clear trend of the effects of CRD (Churchill River Diversion) and LWR (Lake Winnipeg Regulation) to the fish communities."[37] We acknowledge that in many cases data are simply not available pre-1950s to establish long-term trends in VEC conditions, particularly for aquatic environments. This problem is not unique to the Nelson River.

However, for aquatic cumulative effects assessments, where data on water quality or aquatic biota indicators are limited, there is the potential to use surrogate indicators to establish trends, such as land-use and land-cover metrics (e.g., riparian zone habitat, stream-crossing density).[38] Landscape metrics can act as indicators of responses by affected systems to cumulative change,[39] and can be used in regression and correlation analyses to provide an indication of cause-and-effect relationships between cumulative change and cumulative effects.[40] Simple regressions are commonly used to describe the effects of landscape and land-use stressors on river system response.[41] The Keeyask EIS could have used any of these techniques to approximate baseline water conditions for its cumulative effects assessment, but it did not.

Thresholds in cumulative effects are typically associated with the degree of change in an indicator. To be useful for cumulative effects management, thresholds also need to be linked to decision-making processes. Few thresholds identified in the EIS are then used in the CEA. The exceptions are habitat thresholds for caribou populations and linear feature benchmarks. Total suspended solids guidelines are noted for water quality, but the threshold is not applied to assess the significance of cumulative effects—perhaps because these levels are reported to be above the Manitoba regulatory guidelines.

We did observe that the EIS presents benchmarks, stated as percentage changes, for priority plants,[42] identifying <1 percent as small magnitude, between 1 percent and 10 percent as moderate magnitude, and >10 percent as high magnitude. One of the citations[43] the EIS provides to support these benchmarks leads the reader to believe that it (a leading CEA practitioner's guide) establishes such benchmarks. However, nowhere in this guidance are there recommended benchmarks for plants of any kind. Also problematic: these benchmarks are not carried forward in the CEA to examine significance.

We acknowledge that thresholds are not available for many ecological receptors. However, stressor-based thresholds that set maximum limits of allowable change or disturbance can be applied—such as in the case of caribou habitat. For example, watershed assessments can rely on indicators of landscape development (e.g., road density, population density, forest cover) as stressor-based thresholds.[44] There is often reluctance to set thresholds or to limit development when our understanding of natural variability and adaptability within the system is poor. For any assessment it is important to have a management target or benchmark against which to assess how much conditions change. Otherwise, it is difficult to determine when to take action and what action to take when undesirable change occurs.

Prospective Analysis

Prospective analysis models future scenarios to assess potential disturbances in the future. We did not review the supporting volumes for all the VECs included in the CEA, so the examples below are not comprehensive of the entire Keeyask EIS. However, we identified three main areas of concern regarding the assessment of the future cumulative effects of the Keeyask projects and activities.

First, we observed that the EIS often simply *describes* the cumulative effects, rather than comprehensively analyzing them. For example, the Terrestrial Environment Supporting Volume states: "As described in the Response to the EIS Guidelines Section 7.2, VECs.... This section provides that assessment." Yet, the total "assessment" of cumulative effects for future projects upon which the EIS CEA is based, and from which conclusions are drawn, is the equivalent of 3.5 pages of a 319-page technical report. To take another couple of brief examples, the Terrestrial Environment Supporting Volume supplies just 3.5 pages describing past and current conditions of plants in a 138-page document, with no reference to any supporting analysis for future effects. The Aquatic Environment Supporting Volume describes past and current conditions and synthesizes water quality and sediment, including trends. But there is little analysis of future effects in combination with other projects and activities. The word "cumulative" does not appear in the water and sediment quality of the Aquatic Environment Supporting Volume at all.

We are not suggesting that "length" is a good measure of the quality of any CEA, but if, as Manitoba Hydro suggests, "ultimately, the focus of the assessment was on the future rather than on the past,"[45] then one would expect to see much more analysis of future conditions to support the CEA's conclusions about future cumulative effects.

Second, we note that many of the claims about cumulative effects with respect to future projects and activities are poorly supported by analysis or reasoned argumentation. To take one example, there are several references to sedimentation (shoreline and instream disturbance) that Keeyask construction and other project-induced shoreline disturbances will cause. The Physical Environment Supporting Volume models critical sheer stress for erosion to assess how it will affect silt deposits as well as gravel downstream of Gull Rapids near the young-of-the-year habitat area for lake sturgeon. This supporting volume expects sedimentation to be "large for all aspects of shoreline erosion."[46] The same volume[47] discusses potential interactions among the Bipole III, Keeyask, and Conawapa projects, and sediment loading as a result of these projects combined with other activities in the watershed (e.g., forestry, access roads, lease sites, etc.). Yet, none of the other activities are considered in any analytical framework or evaluated against water quality guidelines. Roads, trails, river crossings, and cleared areas are a major source of fine sediments to streams in disturbed watersheds.[48] Without assessing the cumulative effect of all sediment-causing activities, the Keeyask EIS's analysis of sedimentation risks is incomplete.

A third area of concern with the prospective analysis is the soundness of the conclusions offered with respect to future cumulative effects. We are not suggesting that it is possible to be "certain" in predicting a given project's cumulative effects on the environment: the future is complex and obviously uncertain in many respects. But many of the Keeyask CEA conclusions present a degree of certainty that is not substantiated by evidence in the EIS. For example, with respect to cumulative impacts on beaver, the Keeyask EIS concluded that "no measurable residual cumulative effects of the project in combination with other future projects are anticipated."[49] Yet, earlier in the chapter, the EIS states that "the magnitude of decline in beaver populations is scientifically uncertain because large comparison rivers that are unaffected by hydroelectric development . . . tend to have fewer beavers."[50] If it is scientifically uncertain or data are lacking or non-existent, then to claim that there are "no measurable" residual cumulative effects is misleading. Making this claim implies that the CEA has adopted some standard of measure and the analysis conducted yielded no statistically or scientifically detectable differenced based on the predicted change. However, this was not the case. We found similarly porous conclusions made with respect to the lack of cumulative impacts involving wetland loss, habitat loss, and sedimentation loading.

Management

Management is designed to identify appropriate mitigation and monitoring actions. In cases where a VEC is already unhealthy, efforts must focus on rectifying or restoring conditions to deliver net positive contributions to regional sustainability.

Following the future-focused prospective analysis of cumulative effects, standard CEA procedure involves two steps: identifying mitigation strategies, followed by evaluating the significance of any residual cumulative effects.[51] Both are absent from the Keeyask CEA. This is likely because the Keeyask partnership does not anticipate any cumulative effects of the project on terrestrial and aquatic VECs. The same claim is ultimately made about socio-economic VECs, following proposed mitigation. The claim of "no cumulative effects" is made in spite of the fact that the CEA also includes statements that suggest not all predicted cumulative effects in the Regional Study Area will be minor, as shown in Table 4.3.

If there is any reason to believe that significant residual cumulative effects may result from the Keeyask Project, the CEA should make additional provisions to manage them. However, with respect to aquatic and terrestrial VECs, there is no management plan proposed beyond mitigating the direct significant adverse effects of the project.

Table 4.3. VECs with Moderate or Significant Predicted Cumulative Effects

VEC	Predicted Cumulative Effect
Ecosystem diversity	"cumulative area losses for all priority habitat types are predicted to remain in the small to *moderate* magnitude range"
Priority plant species	"cumulative losses are predicted to remain in the nil to *moderate* range, depending on the species"
Fish	"the technical analysis indicates that there are no adverse effects of the Project on fish populations" but that "Members of the KCNs [Keeyask Cree Nations] … have stated that they *expect a larger spatial and temporal extent of effects* than indicated in the technical analysis." "As with water quality, Members of the KCNs at workshops to discuss Project effects and mitigation have stated that they expect a decline in the numbers and health of most fish species as a result of the Keeyask Project and that *adverse effects will extend to Split Lake*."

Source: Keeyask Hydropower Limited Partnership, *Keeyask Environmental Impact Statement*, ch. 7, 7-32; 7-33; 7-23; 7-20. Emphasis added.

What Is the Significance of the Keeyask Decision?

Preceding and inspiring our review of the Keeyask CEA was the Manitoba Clean Environment Commission's 2013 recommendation (emerging from its report on the Bipole III project) that "Manitoba Hydro, in cooperation with the Manitoba Government, conduct a Regional Cumulative Effects Assessment for all Manitoba Hydro projects and associated infrastructure in the Nelson River sub-watershed; and that this be undertaken prior to the licensing of any additional projects in the Nelson River sub-watershed after the Bipole III Project."[52]

Manitoba Hydro did undertake a regional CEA beginning in 2014, which is the subject of Chapter 9 in this volume. However, in our view, undertaking a regional CEA in the Nelson River sub-watershed that considers the potential cumulative effects of all Manitoba Hydro projects and associated infrastructure is a prerequisite to an effective CEA and to managing the potential cumulative effects of hydroelectric development in the region—including the most recent major hydroelectric project: Keeyask. The fifty-plus-year history of incremental hydro development on the Nelson River unquestionably warrants it.

Interestingly, the EIS attributes some of the limitations of Manitoba Hydro's Keeyask Project CEA to inadequacies in the Bipole III EIS. For example, the Keeyask supporting volumes note several times that the lack of information available concerning the potential effects of Bipole III on certain VECs is problematic. But both the Keeyask and Bipole III projects are Manitoba Hydro projects, and both have been preceded by numerous other Manitoba Hydro projects in the region. The lack of connection from one project to the next suggests that the incremental, cumulative effects of development are likely being missed, and underscores how important it should have been to have a regional CEA completed before the Keeyask CEA. That being said, neither the presence nor absence of a regional CEA is a valid excuse for any proponent not to conduct a good-practice CEA as part of assessing the environmental impacts of their project(s); in fact, information from previous project environmental impact assessments should potentially inform subsequent project assessments—both streamlining and enriching each new CEA exercise. In essence, this systematic "learning as you go" approach is the basis for adaptive management, explored more thoroughly in Chapter 14 in this volume.

The focus of our analysis was not on whether the cumulative effects of the Keeyask Project are significant per se, but on whether or not the overall methodological approach to the CEA meets a reasonable standard of practice. After reviewing the CEA, various sections of the EIS, selected technical reports, and a large number of information requests and responses, we offer the following observations concerning the significance of the Keeyask Project with respect to cumulative environmental effects in the Nelson River sub-watershed.

The EIS states several times that the local and regional environment in which the Keeyask Project is proposed has already been "substantially" altered. For example:

> The aquatic environment in the lower Nelson River, including the area to be affected by the Project, has been *substantially altered* by past hydroelectric development and *continues to experience* those effects today.[53]

> The terrestrial environment in the area to be affected by the Project has been *substantially altered* by past hydroelectric

developments, linear developments (including transmission lines, highways, and rail lines), forestry and mining exploration, and other agents of change, and *continues to experience* those effects today.[54]

The socio-economic environment in the area to be affected by the Project has been *substantially changed* by past hydroelectric developments, linear developments (including transmission lines, highways, and rail lines), forestry and mining exploration, and other agents of change, and *continues to experience* those effects today.[55]

Particularly influential have been the construction and operation of the four generating stations and the substantial water management projects of the LWR and CRD noted above, which taken together, have *substantially adversely affected* the land, water and traditional way of life of the KCNs.[56]

Further, the EIS reports that:

Priority habitat types that tend to occur along the Nelson River were also disproportionately affected by hydroelectric development, which flooded some reaches of the Nelson River and altered water regimes along its remaining length.[57]

[The Keeyask Project] will affect open water levels for about 41 km upstream ... [and] about 45 km^2 of initial flooding is predicted. This inundation, along with ongoing erosion, will affect water quality and terrestrial aquatic habitat.[58]

From the late 1950s to the present, more than 35 major generation, conversion and transmission projects have been undertaken by Manitoba Hydro in northeastern Manitoba affecting the traditional territories of the KCNs, their communities and members.[59]

The most detailed information is provided for the hydroelectric development era between 1957 and the present in order to depict how the construction and operation of these northern hydroelectric projects resulted in life-altering changes to the water, land and traditional way of life for First Nations members living in the Keeyask area.[60]

A sizeable portion of CNP's [Cree Nation Partners] major waterways in their homeland ecosystem are no longer able to sustain their traditional ways due to alterations from hydro-electric development.[61]

Based on the regulatory assessment ... adverse effects of the Keeyask Project are expected for all terrestrial VECs, and these adverse effects are also expected to overlap with the other future projects or activities.[62]

Given these statements in the EIS, it is clear that the regional environment in which the Keeyask is proposed *has already been substantially altered by past development*; and the Keeyask Project will be *superimposed on this disrupted environment*. It is puzzling, then, that the cumulative effects of the Keeyask Project in combination with the effects of past, current, and future projects are determined to be "not significant." The EIS states: "Overall ... review of other projects that could overlap with the effects of the Keeyask Project does not indicate any with the potential to result in cumulative adverse effects that require further mitigation for the Keeyask Project or would alter the conclusion with respect to the regulatory significance."[63]

Technical and procedural analyses aside, the above conclusion seems contradictory to the series of statements made in the EIS indicating that the area to be affected by the Keeyask Project has already "been substantially altered." If a region has already been "substantially altered" (i.e., significantly affected), then must not any additional effect, no matter how small or incremental in nature, be considered cumulatively significant? For example, the EIS Executive Summary states: "The Project is located close to communities that have been greatly affected by past hydroelectric and other developments. Each of the Keeyask Cree Nations has documented the history of its people, and the profound effect that hydroelectric development over the past 55 years has had on its relationships with the environment, changing its way of life and culture."[64]

The Cree Nation Partners "concluded that, like previous hydroelectric developments, the Project will have certain major unavoidable effects,"[65] and "the Keeyask Cree Nations know that the effects of past development cannot be undone."[66] (For more on the discrepancies between the Keeyask EIS and the Cree Environmental Evaluations, see Aimée Craft, Chapter 13.) In other words, current environmental and socio-economic conditions in the region, which form the development context for the Keeyask Project, are in fact the present-day expression of the cumulative effects of past developments. The Keeyask Hydropower Limited Partnership clearly agrees that they are significant and substantial.

However, the EIS still concludes that *there will be no significant adverse cumulative effects attributable to the Keeyask Project*.[67] The rationalization often presented in the CEA is that any additional cumulative effects on the already stressed environment are insignificant because: a) they are either local and thus insignificant on a larger (regional) scale, or b) they are insignificant in comparison with the magnitude of change that has already occurred. With regard to intactness, the EIS states: "Overall, the likely residual Project effects on regional intactness are expected to be adverse but small because the Project Footprint is located in an area where intactness is already low due to past human activities."[68]

Conclusion

There is no "scientific" answer, but the question of the significance of the Keeyask decision is more than philosophical—it is *fundamental* to determining whether the additional effects caused by the Keeyask Project and projects like it in the future, in an already significantly altered environment, are acceptable to affected Indigenous communities and the citizens of Manitoba. Given the magnitude of the potential future Conawapa Hydroelectric Generation Project and other projects possibly to come in the Nelson sub-watershed region, the Keeyask Project represents a critical decision point in the future of hydroelectric development and sustainability in northern Manitoba and in the province as a whole.

Peter Duinker and Lorne Greig perhaps put it best: "continuing the kinds and qualities of CEA currently undertaken may be doing more harm than good."[69] Looking back on the Keeyask EIS five, ten, fifty, or 100 years from now, the quality of the CEA will not be judged by the number of maps or volumes of information produced but by whether it supported a sound decision about the overall significance of the Keeyask Project in the broader Nelson River sub-watershed. Will the Keeyask decision confirm the legacy of this region as a resource hinterland, permanently locked into dependency as so many provincial hinterlands are, or can it spark conversation that leads to a different and better legacy of development in the North?

Notes

1 Keeyask Hydropower Limited Partnership, *Keeyask Environmental Impact Statement*, 2012, accessed 27 May 2021, https://keeyask.com/project-timeline/environment-assessment-process/environmental-licensing-process/.

2 G. Hegmann, C. Cocklin, R. Creasey, S. Dupuis, A. Kennedy, L. Kingsley, W. Ross, H. Spaling, and D. Stalker, *Cumulative Effects Assessment Practitioner's Guide* (Ottawa: Minister of Public Works and Government Services Canada, 1999).

3 William Odum, "Environmental Degradation and the Tyranny of Small Decisions," *BioScience* 32, no. 9 (1982): 728.

4 Bram Noble, *Introduction to Environmental Impact Assessment: A Guide to Principles and Practice* (Don Mills: Oxford University Press, 2010).

5 United States Council on Environmental Quality [US CEQ], *Environmental Quality Along the American River: The 1996 Report of the Council on Environmental Quality* (Washington, DC: n.p., 1996).

6 BC Forest Practices Board, *Cumulative Effects: From Assessment Towards Management*, Special report FPB/SR/39 (Victoria: n.p., 2011), 4.

7 See: https://indigenousfoundations.arts.ubc.ca/land__rights/, accessed 12 December 2018.

8 Keeyask Hydropower Limited Partnership, *Keeyask Environmental Impact Statement*; Leslie Reid, "Cumulative Watershed Effects and Watershed Analysis," in *River Ecology and Management: Lessons from the Pacific Coastal Ecoregion*, ed. R. Naiman and R. Bilby (New York: Springer-Verlag, 1998), 476–501.

9 Lucinda Johnson, Carl Richards, George Host, and John Arthur, "Landscape Influences on Water Chemistry in Midwestern Stream Ecosystems," *Freshwater Biology* 37 (1999): 193–208; and David Schindler, "The Cumulative Effects of Climate Warming and Other Human Stresses on Canadian Freshwaters in the New Millennium," *Canadian Journal of Fish and Aquatic Science* 58 (2001): 18–29.

10 Nicole Seitz, Cherie Westbrook, and Bram Noble, "Bringing Science into River Systems Cumulative Effects Assessment Practice," *Environmental Impact Assessment Review* 31 (2011): 180–86.

11 See George Xian, Mike Crane, and Junshan Su, "An Analysis of Urban Development and Its Environmental Impact on the Tampa Bay Watershed," *Journal of Environmental Management* 85 (2007): 965–76; Garry Scrimgeour and Patricia Chambers, "Cumulative Effects of Pulp Mill and Municipal Effluents on Epilithic Biomass and Nutrient Limitation in a Large Northern River Ecosystem," *Canadian Journal of Fish and Aquatic Science* 57 (2000): 1342–54; and Erin Kelly, David Schindler, Peter Hodson, Jeffrey Short, Roseanna Radmanovich, and Charlene Nielsen, "Oil Sands Development Contributes Elements Toxic at Low Concentrations to the Athabasca River and Its Tributaries," *Proceedings of the National Academy of Sciences USA* 107 (2010): 16178–83.

12 Hegmann et al., *Cumulative Effects Assessment*.

13 For example, Canadian Council of Ministers of the Environment, *Regional Strategic Environmental Assessment in Canada: Principles and Guidance* (Winnipeg: Canadian Council of Ministers of the Environment, 2009); and Jill Gunn and Bram Noble, "A Conceptual Basis and Methodological Framework for Regional Strategic Environmental Assessment (R-SEA)," *Impact Assessment and Project Appraisal* 27, no. 4 (2009): 258–70.

14 For example, Wanda Baxter, William Ross, and Harry Spaling, "Improving the Practice of Cumulative Effects Assessment in Canada," *Impact Assessment and Project Appraisal* 19, no. 4 (2001): 253–62.

15 For example, Larry Canter and Bill Ross, "State of Practice of Cumulative Effects Assessment and Management: The Good, the Bad and the Ugly," *Impact Assessment and Project Appraisal* 28, no. 4 (2010): 261–68.

16 Keeyask Hydropower Limited Partnership, *Keeyask Environmental Impact Statement*, ch. 5, 5-3; ch. 7, 7-1.

17 Ibid., ch. 7, 7-2.

18 See Bram Noble and Jill Gunn, *Review of KHLP's Approach to the Keeyask Generation Project Cumulative Effects Assessment* (Winnipeg: Manitoba Public Interest Law Centre, 2013).

19 Keeyask Hydropower Limited Partnership, *Keeyask Environmental Impact Statement*, ch. 6, 6-54. Emphasis added.

20 Ibid., ch. 7, 7-4.

21 Ibid., sec. 5.3.1, 5-5.

22 Ibid., Response to CEC Rd 1 CAC-0012, 3.

23 Ibid., ch. 5, 5-4.

24 Ibid.

25 Ibid., ch. 5, 5-14.

26 Ibid., CEC Rd 2 CEC-0103a.

27 Ibid., Executive Summary, 7.

28 Ibid., ch. 7, 7-7.

29 Ibid., ch. 7, 7-5.

30 Ibid., ch. 7, 7-7.

31 Ibid., ch. 7, Table 7-3.

32 Ibid., see Table 7-3, 7-12.

33 Hegmann et al., *Cumulative Effects Assessment*.

34 Ibid., 15.

35 Keeyask Hydropower Limited Partnership, *Keeyask Environmental Impact Statement*, sec. 5.3.1, 5-5.

36 Salmo Consulting Incorporated, Diversified Environmental Services, Gaia Consulting Incorporated, Forem Technologies, and AXYS Environmental Consulting Ltd., *Cumulative Effects Indicators, Thresholds and Case Studies Final Report*, Cumulative Effects Management for Northeast BC, Volume 2, 2003, https://reviewboard.ca/upload/project_document/EA0506-007_Cumulative_Effects_Indicators__Thresholds__and_Case_Studies.pdf; Terry Antoniuk, Steve Kennett, Craig Aumann, Marian Weber, Susan Davis Schuetz, Rob McManus, Kathryn McKinnon, and Karen Manuel, "Valued Component Thresholds (Management Objectives) Project," in *Environmental Studies Research Funds Report No. 172*, Calgary, AB, 2009, https://www.yumpu.com/en/document/view/48581221/valued-component-thresholds-le-fonds-pour-lactude-de-l-.

37 Keeyask Hydropower Limited Partnership, *Keeyask Environmental Impact Statement*, Aquatic Environment Supporting Volume, sec 5.3.

38 Murray Ball, Gila Somers, Julie Wilson, Rajiv Tanna, Cecilia Chung, Dennis Duro, and Nicole Seitz, "Scale, Assessment Components, and Reference Conditions:

Issues for Cumulative Effects Assessment in Canadian Watersheds," *Integrated Environmental Assessment and Management* (2012), DOI: 10.1002/ieam.1332.

39 Seitz, Westbrook, and Noble, "Bringing Science."

40 See Johnson et al., "Landscape Influences on Water Chemistry."

41 Seitz, Westbrook, and Noble, "Bringing Science."

42 Keeyask Hydropower Limited Partnership, *Keeyask Environmental Impact Statement*, ch. 6, sec. 6.5.4.2.1, 6-331–6-332.

43 Hegmann et al., *Cumulative Effects Assessment*.

44 Allison Squires and Monique Dubé, "Development of an Effects-Based Approach for Watershed Scale Aquatic Cumulative Effects Assessment," *Integrated Environmental Assessment and Management* (2012), DOI: 10.1002/ieam.1352.

45 Keeyask Hydropower Limited Partnership, *Keeyask Environmental Impact Statement*, CEC Rd 1 CAC-0012, 3.

46 Ibid., ch. 6, sec 6.4, and AE-SV sec. 2.

47 Ibid., sec. 7.4.5.

48 Cornel Yarmoloy and Brad Stelfox, *An Assessment of the Cumulative Effects of Land Uses within the Ghost River Watershed, Alberta, Canada*, 2011, https://www.ghostwatershed.ca/GWAS/ewExternalFiles/2011-GhostReport-web.pdf.

49 Keeyask Hydropower Limited Partnership, *Keeyask Environmental Impact Statement*, ch. 7, 7-36.

50 Ibid., ch. 7, 7-27.

51 Hegmann et al., *Cumulative Effects Assessment*.

52 Manitoba Clean Environmental Commission, *Bipole III Transmission Project, Report on Public Hearing*, June 2013, 126.

53 Keeyask Hydropower Limited Partnership, *Keeyask Environmental Impact Statement*, ch. 7, 7-16. Emphasis added.

54 Ibid., ch. 7, 7-23. Emphasis added.

55 Ibid. Emphasis added.

56 Keeyask Hydropower Limited Partnership, *Keeyask Environmental Impact Statement*, ch. 6, 6-13. Emphasis added.

57 Ibid., ch. 7, 7-23 and 7-24.

58 Ibid., ch. 7, 7-4.

59 Ibid., ch. 6, sec 6.2.2.3, 6-12.

60 Ibid., ch. 6, 6-7.

61 Ibid., ch. 6, 6-20.

62 Ibid., ch. 7, 7.31–7.32.

63 Ibid., ch. 7, sec. 7.5.2.3.

64 Ibid., Executive Summary, 37.

65 Ibid., Executive Summary, 15.

66 Ibid., Executive Summary, 15.

67 Ibid., Executive Summary, 36; ch. 7, 7-21.

68 Ibid., ch. 7, 7-28.

69 Peter Duinker and Lorne Greig, "The Impotence of Cumulative Effects Assessment in Canada: Ailments and Ideas for Redeployment," *Environmental Management* 37, no. 2 (2006): 153.

" As a people we are inseparable from our relationships with Mother Earth, relationships that are developed over thousands of years. Our relationship with Mother Earth on the basis of our language, history, spirituality and our culture. This is the foundation of our worldview and it is key to our survival."

Robert Flett, Tataskweyak Cree Nation, Cree Nations Presentation at CEC hearings (6 November 2013), 2406

CHAPTER 5

Divergent World Views and Environmental Assessment

JAMES P. ROBSON

Almost thirty years ago, Catherine Shapcott wrote a critical appraisal of environmental assessment (EA) in Canada, pointing to the misfit between EA and the beliefs and values of Indigenous peoples.[1] She concluded that EA did not make sense in an Indigenous context, and quoted an excerpt from a 1987 interview with William Rees, who argued that because EA was "structured by people of a particular world-view," it was "procedurally biased." Despite legislative reforms to involve Indigenous peoples and communities in environmental assessment, more recent commentaries still point to an epistemological Western bias,[2] with, as Shapcott says, assessment processes still couched in the "language of the technocratic fixers; of rigorous, rational inquiry; of a worldview which holds the economic as the highest value,"[3] and guided by the values, structures, and policies of a dominant Eurocentric society.[4]

These concerns, among others, have led Indigenous peoples in Canada to negotiate not only greater control over resources but management decisions that better reflect their world views, including the knowledge they possess about land and water.[5] Examples abound of Indigenous groups in Canada—from the Anishinaabeg (Ojibway) of Pikangikum in northwestern Ontario to the Kanien:keha'ka (Mohawks) of Kahnawake in Quebec, the Gitksan Wet'suwet'en Nation in northern British Columbia, and the Okanagan people in southern

British Columbia[6]—looking for ways to meet, on their own terms, the demands of living in a Canadian society dominated by Eurocentrism.[7]

Such an intent featured strongly in the decisions of the four First Nations communities in northern Manitoba (Tataskweyak Cree Nation, War Lake First Nation, Fox Lake Cree Nation, York Factory First Nation) to join Manitoba Hydro's Keeyask Hydropower Limited Partnership (KHLP). The KHLP constitutes an Indigenous-Industry-Government partnership—an emergent model in Canada[8] and one that potentially marked a new direction for how large-scale development and resource extraction projects are planned and implemented.[9] It shifts the goalposts of Indigenous participation in environmental assessment from one of consultation and engagement, already institutionalized in Canadian and international EA systems,[10] to a scenario where Indigenous communities play a leading role in shaping such processes.[11]

Joint ventures of this kind, however, present several challenges; not least is the need to accommodate divergent world views and navigate the communication, conceptual, or political barriers that come with multiple values, practices, and contexts that often conflict with each other. As illustrated in this volume so far, environmental assessment in Canada occurs at the intersection of complex economic, social, legal, political, and ecological issues, and can evoke deeply held beliefs about the nature of community, the definition of the "good life," and the meaning of the relationship between humans and nature.[12] While previous research stresses the need to better understand, learn from, and accommodate Indigenous world views,[13] there is little in the way of a blueprint, or comprehensive set of guiding principles, to help achieve this.[14]

In this chapter, Keeyask acts as a test case for assessing how well EA processes function within the context of Indigenous-Industry-Government partnerships that are framed by Eurocentric legal and political structures, and to identify areas of concern. Through an extensive review of the Keeyask Environmental Impact Statement (EIS),[15] I analyze the performance of Keeyask's environmental licensing process against scholarly and practitioner recommendations for accommodating Indigenous world views.

Understanding World Views and Their Importance to EA in Canada

No matter how dominant a worldview is, there are always other ways of interpreting the world. . . . If we are to understand why Aboriginal and Eurocentric worldviews clash, we need to understand how the philosophies, values and customs of Aboriginal cultures differ from those of Eurocentric cultures. Understanding the differences in worldviews gives us a starting point for moving forward.

–Leroy Little Bear, "Jagged Worldviews Colliding," 2000[16]

Indigenous and non-Indigenous people construct their knowledge of the world differently from each other.[17] This can create fertile ground for "worldview conflicts"[18] that result from "different criteria for evaluating ideas or behaviour," "exclusive intrinsically valuable goals" or "different ways of life, ideology, or religion." World views have been variously described as mental lenses for perceiving the world around us, or the cognitive and perceptual maps people use to make sense of the social landscape and find their way to whatever goals they seek.[19] While an Indigenous world view is not synonymous with the Indigenous knowledge that is shaped by it (see Aimée Craft, Chapter 13 in this volume), our world views shape the decisions we make and actions we take on a daily basis.

If those involved in partnership share similar world views, they draw on roughly similar "cognitive maps."[20] If there is overlap in their world views but also some difference, they may have to navigate a more complex situation that results in dissent but perhaps also common ground upon which differences can be accommodated.[21] Where individuals or groups share little commonality in their world views, however, common ground is harder to reach and conflict much more likely. This is a concern for cross-cultural EA processes. Indigenous peoples in Canada traditionally hold a holistic (or cosmocentric) view of the world,[22] which emphasizes the importance of the universe or nature. A broad Eurocentric world view, which strongly emphasizes humankind as the most important element of existence, would appear not only antithetical to Indigenous world views but potentially hostile—with prevailing Eurocentric ideologies clearly separating human and non-human worlds and allowing hierarchy, competition, and centralized authority to thrive.[23]

Efforts to integrate Indigenous knowledge systems into EA provide an example of such difficulties. Traditional Ecological Knowledge (TEK), while understood to represent Indigenous peoples, has been (largely) conceived and constructed by non-Indigenous researchers, academics, and development professionals.[24] While these groups view TEK as a body of factual, specific observations,[25] which are compatible to a degree with the knowledge understood by resource managers and bureaucrats,[26] for Indigenous peoples "knowledge" is action-oriented and based on the *relationships* among knowledge, people, and all of Creation.[27] Context thus becomes critical for understanding and communicating knowledge in Indigenous societies, which poses problems of comprehension between "high-context" (Indigenous) and "low-context" (Eurocentric) societies.[28] The misinterpretation and poor application of TEK in environmental assessment processes have been a major reason why Indigenous peoples in Canada have advocated for their ways of knowing to be solely directed by Elders and their own political leaderships.[29]

As Leanne Simpson argues, Canada's Indigenous peoples have the right to be "at the table using the knowledge inside of ourselves to make decisions that impact our people, our communities, the plants, the animals and our lands . . . we do not want scientists interpreting our knowledge, when it has been removed from the values and spiritual foundations that give it meaning."[30] Yet, how Indigenous and Eurocentric world views should inform EA, and how to best navigate their differences, is far from clear. The potential to misrepresent or misuse Indigenous perspectives and knowledge, especially by those who do not understand or appreciate the world view in which they are embedded, remains a constant possibility. As Mark Stevenson notes, Western perspectives are "not inimical to Aboriginal worldviews, but the potential for incongruence is considerable."[31] Even if non-Indigenous partners are able to put aside their initial assumptions about how the world works to co-construct new models, Indigenous peoples are at risk of losing what sets them apart and gives them authority in co-management processes if their perspectives are misused.

Assessing Keeyask from a World View Perspective

During the Clean Environment Commission's public hearings on the Keeyask Generating Station, we learnt that the Cree world view is very different from the Eurocentric or Western world view.[32] The four Keeyask Cree Nations, or KCNs, that joined the Keeyask Hydropower Limited Partnership made clear that there is no singular Cree world view. Rather, the variants that circulate among these communities and their members are all founded on human-human and human-environment relationships that have, as their goal, mino-pimatisiwin, or, as Michael Hart defines it, "the good-life, or life in the fullest, healthiest sense."[33] This contrasts with a Western world view that places emphasis on individual values and notions of property (including capital and profit).

Given these differences, the rationale for allowing Cree perspectives and knowledge to influence Keeyask planning, design, and implementation is sound. The Keeyask Cree Nations shared a number of statements in the Environmental Impact Statement about who they are, how they live, and what is true to them, pointing to a common set of core values and a powerful argument for their involvement in the EA process. Yet, the KCNs, as partners in the KHLP, were faced with participating in a process that remains bound by Eurocentric frameworks, with an industry partner whose corporate culture and large numbers of its staff understand the world in a different way from the KCNs. As Byron Williams, Aimée Craft, and Joëlle Sala note, such differences may be hard to reconcile.[34]

Unfortunately, the Environmental Impact Statement fails to provide any detail as to how the partnership addressed the challenge of accommodating divergent world views throughout the process. Rather, discussion is limited to the (albeit very important) decision to instigate a two-track approach that gave equal weighting to the KCNs' environmental evaluations, based on their Cree world view, and the conventional environmental assessment, based on "technical science."[35] In Chapter 13 of this volume, Craft assesses how successful this "equal weighting" truly was and provides a critique of the Keeyask report's false distinction between Western science and Cree world view. However, even before exploring the final result, it should be noted that the EIS does not include any text or sections that explicitly deal with the issue of differences in world view as they set out this approach, including how they affected decision making, or how common ground was sought—including, for example, how EA findings were interpreted and implemented as part of the final EIS.

In the absence of clear information of this type, it is important to assess how well the stated actions of the Keeyask partnership match up to best practices when formalizing Indigenous participation and addressing divergent world views within EA processes. Table 5.1 provides a summary of such an assessment, based on the author's extensive review of the EIS, two rounds of Information Requests, and the public hearings presided over by the Manitoba Clean Environment Commission.

Stevenson notes that Indigenous concerns about EA, as implemented in Canada, derive from three main sources: their knowledge and world view concerning ecosystem relationships and appropriate behaviours; past experience with northern industrial developments; and the lack of information about proposed developments and how these affect their lands and lifestyles.[36] Recognizing such concerns and engaging in subsequent dialogue are a prerequisite to full Indigenous participation in EA. The Keeyask partnership does an excellent job of accomplishing this. First, because the KCNs compiled their own evaluation reports, community members were able to explain, in their own words, the (expected) environmental, social, and economic impacts of the project. Second, the partnership allowed the KCNs to incorporate "Aboriginal Traditional Knowledge" (ATK)[37] into the proposed environmental monitoring and management programs.

Adopting a two-track approach kept the knowledge of the KCNs—and how it is collected, interpreted, and used—in Cree hands, and gave the KCNs an important level of authority. By opting to carry out their own assessments, their traditional knowledge remains under the exclusive control of each community, who decided how best to document this knowledge and share it with outside interest groups. As Chapter 2 of the EIS points out, the decision to "determine and present their own evaluation of the environmental impacts of the Project [on their respective communities]" was made because of "the implications of [holding a] different worldview."[38] This avoids the situation of Manitoba Hydro's taking Cree knowledge out of context, with little understanding of Indigenous cultures, realities, or knowledge systems. It also does not place the KCNs in the position of having to communicate their concepts and understandings of the environment (and their place in it) in the language of a dominant Eurocentric ideology. This means that knowledge that local Cree possess, not just their ecological knowledge, can potentially be brought to bear on EA as part of the Keeyask process.

Table 5.1. Recommended EA Practices for Dealing with Divergent World Views

Recommended Practice	Adopted by Keeyask?
Partnerships and Power Sharing	
The cooperation of Indigenous people is re-quired to identify and adequately address so-cial and ecological concerns about proposed developments, and best achieved through partnerships that ensure a true balance of power in decision making and the contribu-tion of knowledge, especially in regard to identifying impacts and devising solutions for their mitigation.[a]	YES
Involvement of Indigenous people begins with communities most directly affected by proposed development.[b]	YES
Partnership recognizes the legal standing, interests and expertise of Indigenous part-ners.[c]	YES, with caveat.[f] There is no evidence that the partner-ship intended to apply a Cree law framework for decision making.
Partnership provides for a balance of power and ownership that communities, agencies, and councils are comfortable with.[d]	YES
Partnership is equitable, open, and honest, with level of trust established and main-tained such that Indigenous ways of knowing and seeing are not only shared but also treated with dignity and respect. To occur through increased communication at all levels and a concerted effort at relationship building.[e]	UNCLEAR because of a lack of detailed information in the EIS. Requires follow-up with partners.

Partner Involvement	
Partner communities are involved from the initial stages of decision-making processes.[g]	YES
Indigenous participation covers not only the impact assessments for the project, but also takes place in the strategic planning phase when multiple futures are still possible.[h]	YES
Community members are able to express their key concerns regarding the proposed development, including a desire to participate directly and effectively in impact prediction and assessment and for that to be based on what people know, what they have experienced, or what they fear might happen in the future.	YES
Each affected Aboriginal community is able to express connection to, and value of, the environment, language, the consumption of country food, life on the land, identity, and cultural survival as part of the assessment process, thus affirming their identity as a coherent cultural whole located within the land for which they claim responsibility.[i]	YES
Aboriginal involvement goes beyond processes designed to determine whether a project should proceed, to continue into the project's operational phase.[j]	YES

Use of Indigenous Knowledge	
Traditional knowledge is enshrined as part of the initiative, and guides the process,[k] with mechanisms in place to protect Indigenous control over how their knowledge is collected, represented, and controlled.[l]	YES
Indigenous knowledge forms an essential component of environmental management governance structure (e.g., is included in the principles of operation).[m]	YES
Traditional knowledge contributions are considered upon their own terms as valid for discussion and debate, arising as they do from an independently viable system of knowledge and unique way of life.[n]	YES (Two-track approach, Executive Summary)
Indigenous knowledge is recognized and respected on an equal footing with Western science as a valid source of knowledge to be applied in environmental governance and management.	UNCLEAR[o]—while the KCNs' evaluation reports are evidence of this, interventions from members of Fox Lake and York Factory during the public hearings questioned whether equal footing had been afforded
Identification of VECs	
TEK to be given key role in identifying VECs, impacts on these VECs, or knowledge gaps relevant to these VECs.[p]	UNCLEAR due to lack of detailed information[q]
Process to start with the identification of VECs from an Indigenous perspective, through community consultations and then a direct exchange of information between developers and with target groups and individuals selected by the community members themselves.	UNCLEAR—It is not clear if the VEC selection process started with KCN input
While the needs and interests of government and industry carry some weight, the ranking of VECs and mitigation priorities are determined by those most directly affected by development (in this case, the KCNs).	NO

Appropriate Communication Methodologies	
Include ceremonies as a means to developing insight and connection.[r]	YES
Maintain throughout the key values of sharing and respect.[s]	YES
Allow Indigenous partners to maintain a degree of control over the decision-making process, by rooting it in the local culture, with decisions based on dialogue and consensus. Elders are to be involved in every aspect of the planning process.[t]	YES
Establish procedures that are flexible enough to allow communities to hold unstructured and informal hearings, not the usually "intimidating environment" of formal EA hearings.	UNCLEAR because of a lack of detailed information in the EIS. Requires follow-up with partners.
Establish processes and technologies that facilitate communication with and among Indigenous people, and apply time frames that are consistent with Indigenous decision-making practices.[u]	YES, with caveat. The main public hearings were held in Winnipeg, Manitoba, and followed Eurocentric traditions
Monitoring	
A monitoring program involves Indigenous people, knowledge, and expertise fully and meaningfully. Aboriginal representatives should determine the extent of their own participation and the inclusion of their knowledge and expertise in this phase.[v]	YES
Reporting	
Frequent reporting reaches all partners,[w] and provides sufficient time for Indigenous community meetings and inputs into the project, as well as ensures that concerns/issues are identified, mitigated, and addressed in the EA rather than post-submission.	YES, with caveat. Concern in Fox Lake and York Factory that not enough time provided ahead of community vote

Cumulative Effects	
These incorporate the knowledge and insights of Indigenous people who have already experienced the impacts of mining and other industrial activities in order to predict, assess, and manage specific and cumulative impacts.	YES—evident in the KCN assessment reports

a   Marc G. Stevenson, "Indigenous Knowledge in Environmental Assessment," *Arctic* (1996): 278–91.

b   Anne N. Glucker, P.P. Driessen, Arend Kolhoff, and Hens Runhaar, "Public Participation in Environmental Impact Assessment: Why, Who and How?," *Environmental Impact Assessment Review* 43 (2013): 104–111; Aniekan Udofia, Bram Noble, and Greg Poelzer, "Meaningful and Efficient? Enduring Challenges to Aboriginal Participation in Environmental Assessment," *Environmental Impact Assessment Review* 65 (2017): 164–74.

c   Elmar Plate, Malcolm Foy, and Rick Krehbiel, *Best Practices for First Nation Involvement in Environmental Assessment Reviews of Development Projects in British Columbia* (West Vancouver: New Relationship Trust, 2009).

d   Joan Eamer, "Keep it Simple and be Relevant: The First Nine Years of the Arctic Borderlands Ecological Knowledge Co-op," in *Bridging Scales and Knowledge Systems: Concepts and Applications*, ed., Walter Reid, Fikret Berkes, Thomas Wilbanks, and Doris Capistrano (Washington: Island Press, 2006), 185–206.

e   Deborah McGregor, "Linking Traditional Knowledge and Environmental Practice in Ontario," *Journal of Canadian Studies* 43, no. 3 (2009): 69–100.

f   A series of IRs (CEC Rd 1 CAC-0095, 0096, 0098) asked whether Cree/Ineniwak Legal Traditions are considered part of the EA process. The responses provided little in the way of an answer, making reference to the KCNs' individual evaluation reports that do not provide detailed information about role of Indigenous Legal Traditions. No inclusion of Cree law principles into terms and conditions of licences.

g   Nicolas Houde, "The Six Faces of Traditional Ecological Knowledge: Challenges and Opportunities for Canadian Co-management Arrangements," *Ecology and Society* 12, no. 2 (2007); Glucker et al., "Public Participation."

h   Plate, Foy, and Krehbiel, *Best Practices for First Nation Involvement.*

i   Ibid.

j   Ciaran O'Faircheallaigh and Tony Corbett, "Indigenous Participation in Environmental Management of Mining Projects: The Role of Negotiated Agreements," *Environmental Politics* 14, no. 5 (2005): 629–47.

k   McGregor, "Linking Traditional Knowledge."

l   Assembly of First Nations (Environment Division), "The Feasibility of Representing Traditional Indigenous Knowledge in Cartographic, Pictorial or Textual Forms," Draft Final Report, 1995; Stevenson, "Indigenous Knowledge in Environmental Assessment."

m   McGregor, "Linking Traditional Knowledge."

n   Ibid.

o   Several IRs (CEC Rd 1 CAC-0099: CEC Rd 1 CAC-0101, 0102, 0103, 0104, 0105, 0106; CEC Rd 1 KK-0005, 0006, 0007a, CEC Rd 2 KK-0014, 0015) sought but failed to elicit a clear answer to this question.

p   Stevenson, "Indigenous Knowledge in Environmental Assessment."

q   Information Request CEC Rd 1 CAC-0055a and its follow-up (CEC Rd 2 CAC-0141) sought to determine the nature and extent of discussions between the KCNs and Manitoba Hydro around the identification of VECs. The responses did not provide any details (i.e., content) beyond the fact that meetings took place.

r   Killulark Arngna'naaq, Heather Bourassa, Don Couturier, Kaviq Kaluraq, and Kelly Panchyshyn, *Realizing Indigenous Law in Co-Management* (Toronto: The Gordon Foundation, n.d.), https://gordonfoundation.ca/wp-content/uploads/2020/04/JGNF_2018-2019_Realizing-Indigenous-Law-in-Co-Management.

s   Michael Hart, *Seeking Mino-pimatisiwin: An Aboriginal Approach to Helping* (Halifax: Fernwood Books, 2002).

t   McGregor, "Linking Traditional Knowledge."

u   Ciaran O'Faircheallaigh, "Environmental Agreements, EIA Follow-up and Aboriginal Participation in Environmental Management: The Canadian Experience," *Environmental Impact Assessment Review 27*, no. 4 (2007): 319–42.

v   McGregor, "Linking Traditional Knowledge."

w   Eamer, "Keep it Simple and Be Relevant."

In summary, the partnership model provided a solid foundation for the accommodation of the Cree world view in project planning, implementation, and operation. The recognition of difference became the first critical step towards accommodation and acceptance, and a foundation for co-existence and sustainability.

A detailed review of the EIS, however, still raises concerns about whether the EA process, as it is structured and regulated, remains consistent with Cree values and beliefs throughout. In particular, there is a concern that the Keeyask EIS's extensive use of conventional Valued Ecosystem Components (VECs) as its framework appears to run counter to the claim that Keeyask adopts an "*integrated* and *collaborative* approach" that gives "*equal consideration* to both technical-scientific studies and ATK."[39]

As Deborah McGregor notes (as do Asfia Gulrukh Kamal, Joseph Dipple, Steve Ducharme, and Leslie Dysart in Chapter 3 of this volume), one key difference between Indigenous and non-Indigenous world views is that, in the former, people, knowledge, and land are viewed as a single, integrated whole, and thus regarded as inseparable.[40] Chapter 2 of the EIS, along with the KCN evaluation reports, all point to the interdependent relationships that KCN members hold with Askiy (the land or world) and all of Creation—assuming the responsibilities given to them by the Creator to maintain and enhance those relationships, based on the reinforcing principles of harmony and respect. An environmental assessment that remains predominantly structured around identifying and testing individual VECs runs the risk of reducing Askiy to prioritized components. This was of particular concern to two of the four KCNs, with Fox Lake Cree Nation finding the VEC process very difficult to accept because it "ignores the inter-relatedness of people, animals, water, landscape and plants."[41] Similarly, members of York Factory First Nation drew on prior experience with hydroelectric development to argue unequivocally that Keeyask would change "[our] respectful relationships with the land, water, plants and animals that have sustained our people, our culture and that are entrusted to us to pass on to future generations."[42]

A possible mismatch between project rhetoric and EA implementation is not only apparent with the use of VECs. At the heart of the project's Adverse Effects Agreements (AEA), signed by Manitoba Hydro and each of the KCNs, are a number of offsetting programs designed to provide appropriate replacements, substitutions, or opportunities to offset "unavoidable adverse effects on the practices, customs and traditions integral to the First Nations' distinctive cultural identity."[43] These offsetting programs were said to be "aligned with the Cree worldview," and co-developed with each community. Yet offsetting—compensating for losses at an impact site by generating equivalent gains elsewhere—involves trading places, which makes whatever is being offset "fungible," with the value of "place" pushed to the periphery. KCN members' testimony at the Clean Environment Commission (CEC) hearings stressed the restorative benefits of their (cultural) landscapes as places for spiritual renewal, which form the basis for an "Aboriginal sense of place," feeling of home and of identity.[44] With their knowledge rooted in place,[45] offsetting landscapes to a process of commodification rather than stewardship is disassociated from Cree perspectives on Askiy.

The EIS also points to an existing discrepancy regarding the appropriate time frames for analyzing the environmental and social impacts of Keeyask. As previous chapters in this volume have explored, the project is located in a region that has been greatly altered over the past six decades. The EIS states that the monitoring of changes and impacts will be measured against current conditions (i.e., prior to construction and operation of the Keeyask Dam and Generating Station), which contradicted the beliefs of multiple members from Fox Lake Cree Nation and York Factory First Nation. They argued in their respective evaluation reports that baseline conditions should be taken as those that existed prior to the construction of the first dam in the late 1950s, in recognition of the broader context of development to have impacted the region. As Jill Blakely and Bram Noble establish in Chapter 4 of this volume, this is consistent with best practices in cumulative effects assessment. To monitor projects such as the Keeyask Dam and Generating Station only against current conditions runs the risk of inadequately assessing the project's true effects on its environment.

While the EA process would appear to have met many of the recommended practices set out in Table 5.1, there were still a number for which it was possible to designate only an "Unclear" or "Yes, with caveat" response, largely because of the lack of specific information available in the EIS. This may point to unresolved issues, a less than transparent EA process, or the need for further consultation and follow-up[46] with the partners.

Effective Follow-up and Institutional Learning

Understanding how well collaboration of this kind has worked (or even what "worked" means) is as difficult as understanding the cultural nuances of the process itself. Only limited insights are forthcoming following a review of the EIS. Arguably, the more valuable lessons to be learned would require the partners to self-reflect and report on their experiences. This would help identify the differences (and similarities) that exist between the philosophies, values, and customs held and practised by each of them. Keeyask has the potential to develop institutional structures and management processes specifically designed to facilitate follow-up and learning over the whole of project life.[47] Instead of competing with the KCNs' knowledge, or having one dominate the other, the partners could choose to focus attention on a mutual exchange of information, based on the principles of co-existence, cooperation, and respect.

From an outsider's perspective, it is unclear whether the Keeyask partners have undertaken such a systematic follow-up. Indeed, it is not clear that the partners would consider such efforts valuable or worthwhile—to take the time to think about how they make sense of the world, make judgments about the "right" and "proper" things to do, and question whether such beliefs limit their ability to design better ways of doing things. In the case of Fox Lake Cree Nation and York Factory First Nation, individual testimonials of community members featured heavily in the evaluation reports and public hearings. In contrast, the EIS provided no personal insights on the part of Manitoba Hydro staff. This suggests that follow-up and learning have not been formalized as part of the Keeyask partnership process.

Table 5.2 lays out some of the possible questions that Manitoba Hydro and the KCNs could respond to as part of a process of self-assessment. This could help the partnership determine how well their interactions match the ideals of cross-cultural collaboration, and to evaluate the prospects for true collaboration.[48]

It is only through effective follow-up and learning that Indigenous and non-Indigenous partners can identify those rationales that transcend cultural factors and those that cannot, because their world views overlap only partially or not at all. At the same time, it is important to focus on similarities also, since tensions will likely persist if only the perceived and real differences between the two are stressed.[49] Has the Keeyask process "made sense" to each of the partners, and, if not, what is needed for that to change in the future? For Manitoba Hydro, asking such questions, according to Leanne Simpson, would enable its staff to "spend time looking inside themselves, uncovering their own biases and privileges and [identify willingness] to learn from our people—not about Aboriginal peoples, but about themselves and their place in the cosmos."[50] This is important not only for their dealings with the KCNs but also for the longevity and sustainability of other similar partnerships in the future.

Collaboration of this kind could see shared experiences lead to new knowledge being used to make collective judgments about actions to take in the name of responsible and sustainable improvements. World view perspectives are capable of evolution and development, as reflected in transformations of basic value and belief assumptions, which are achieved through "higher order" cognitive processing and captured in the notion of *epistemic development*.[51] Indigenous partners may have a key role to play here, given their ability to bridge world views, with most members having experienced both traditional and non-traditional realities and lifestyles.

Table 5.2. Sample of Questions for Keeyask Partners to Guide Self-Reflection

Questions about what has been learnt (for representatives from all partners)

Has decision-making power been structured in a way that provides all partners with equal voice?

In what way have the technical scientists and Cree land users become interested in each other's kind of information/knowledge, and did this lead to a reciprocal knowledge-exchange protocol?

How did the partnership avoid or overcome dialogue problems between science and traditional knowledge as hampered by fundamental differences in concept and language?

What was learnt about how partner meetings were planned and conducted? What was learnt about how the hearings and other regulatory meetings were planned and conducted?

What are the similarities in world view shared by the partners?

What has changed in the partners' practices, processes, and goals since the partnership began?

Questions about what has been learnt (for staff and representatives of Manitoba Hydro)

In extensive dealings with the KCNs, were they aware of the nature and significance of their own individual and corporate world view (as expressed by the board of directors or in company policy documents) or epistemic perspectives? Were their world views expressed collectively as a prevailing and pervasive set of shared beliefs, values, and assumptions that characterize Western culture?

What did staff learn from listening to the stories and testimonials provided by the KCNs, through the evaluation reports, during negotiations, and working together, and in the public hearings?

Questions about what has been been learnt (for members of each KCN) (adapted from Hart 2002)

To what degree did the EA process afford respect for your community and individual members?

To what degree did Manitoba Hydro, as a partner, understand the values of reciprocity and responsibility, demonstrated by the ways in which its proponents would relate and act within your community, and share and present ideas with the intent of supporting your community?

To what degree did Manitoba Hydro honour respect and safety, which made community members feel safe in the process, including confidentiality in a manner desired by the community and its members?

In meetings, to what degree did Manitoba Hydro remain quietly aware and watch without interfering with individual and community processes?

To what degree did Manitoba Hydro listen and hear with more than their ears, paying attention to how their sense of being is emotionally and spiritually moved?

Divergent World Views and Canada's EA Regulatory Framework

Giuliana Casimirri noted that even if a planning process looks participatory, it can still be "disempowering" when the framework used to structure that planning is based on the supremacy of Western ways of knowing and systems.[52] The values of the dominant culture can be so embedded in EA processes that alternative values struggle for consideration. The Keeyask partnership is significant because it provides an opportunity for ongoing assessment of environmental performance and modification of management systems throughout the life of the project, yet its potential as a model of cross-cultural EA is constrained not only by differences in world view among its proponents but by the federal regulatory framework it adheres to.

Cree Elders' assertion that they have a responsibility as stewards of Mother Earth is in direct conflict with legislation and regulatory agencies, which have been assigned the responsibility "for the good of all" to determine the most effective and efficient use of resources. In round one of the information requests, the Keeyask partners were asked "to describe the nature and extent of the efforts made to bridge the gap between what the regulations required and their synergy (or lack thereof) with the beliefs and views of the KCN Partners." No response was forthcoming.[53] In a subsequent information request, the partners were asked if discussions took place "about making 'value' a designation of significance, in order to better reflect Cree perspectives of the Keeyask homeland ecosystem."[54] The partnership responded that, "In accordance with related regulatory guidance, the Partnership did not consider making 'value' a criterion for designation of significance . . . regulatory guidance is clear that the determination of regulatory significance regarding effects of a project on a VEC must be limited to questions related to scientific analysis and interpretation."[55]

The partnership's response suggests that what matters in environmental assessment testing, at least from a regulatory standpoint, are things that can be counted or quantified. The kind of qualitative assessments based on world views, and the knowledge, values, and customs these are tied to, struggle to find a place within the test for significance, which remains the principal mechanism by which environmental impacts are assessed and upon which the decision whether or not to approve licences is often made.

Keeyask, by providing voice to an alternative (i.e., non-Western) knowledge system, shows it is incumbent for government and industry to abandon old concepts and explore new ways to incorporate Indigenous peoples' perspectives and values into the EA process. Government regulations appear increasingly inadequate once viewed through the lens of a cross-cultural assessment process, since Western scientific knowledge continues to take precedence over Indigenous ways of knowing. This calls into question how well provincial and federal governments can appropriately regulate an EA process in twenty-first-century Canada, which states that not only equal consideration but also equal weight[56] will be given to Indigenous as well as non-Indigenous world views and knowledge systems.

While the partnership affords, on paper, authority and rights to the KCNs, KCN participation does not, in any of the agreements signed, extend to the exercise of regulatory powers. Government maintains control of this area. The KCNs may participate "fully" in an EA process, but, like that of other Indigenous peoples in Canada, their participation takes place within the confines of a Western, Eurocentric tradition.[57] In my mind, Keeyask thus falls short of constituting a First Nations environmental assessment process, given that their participation remains couched within a larger regulatory process driven by non-Indigenous world views. In the absence of control over the environmental licensing process, what can we say is the true extent of the KCNs' influence over what happened with the Keeyask decision-making process? And can this change as long as the federal Canadian Environmental Assessment Agency's "Principles," despite the incorporation of "traditional ecological knowledge" and "community consultation" as policy requirements for environmental assessment and resource management in Canada's North, fail to provide specific instructions in guidance documents, operating procedures, or judgments on how to implement this requirement? I believe that until changes are made in this regard, the potential for successful outcomes is constrained.

This is perhaps why learning from the Keeyask process could prove so useful, particularly if Manitoba Hydro and the KCNs provide feedback on their experiences, not only in terms of working with one another but also in how this has played out within the context of overarching legislation and regulatory frameworks. It could help identify opportunities for "decentralized decision making" for learning and adaptation, which the regulatory framework does not promote. There are examples of partnerships in Canada that may offer some guidance, including the cultural landscape model seen in Quebec—the concept of *forêt habitée* (inhabited forest) as applied to land-use planning[58]—and forest management in Ontario.[59] Such a perspective embodies traditional narratives and spiritual meaning, as well as economic use,[60] and would integrate Indigenous concerns into initial planning by projecting into the future what the land would look like under different management scenarios and finding the one that best matches the needs of those who live there.

Conclusion

Beyond a broad need for greater public participation, the active involvement of Indigenous governments and communities in EA processes is critical.[61] This is not only because Indigenous communities are often the most directly and severely impacted by resource development activities but also because their participation gives environmental assessment the necessary knowledge and context to improve assessment planning and outcomes.[62] In Canada, Indigenous governments and communities have been given (on paper at least) a greater role in both provincial and federal environmental decision-making arenas,[63] particularly where proposed activities may infringe on Treaty rights.[64] However, while Indigenous participation is now an accepted component of EA best practice, the specific role that their participation plays in furthering the goals of environmental assessment, and sustainable development more broadly, is wholly contingent upon the way such processes are envisioned, structured, and implemented.[65]

In this way, it is less about whether participation takes place and much more about how participation is structured and unfolds over the life cycle of a project. The number of Canadian environmental assessments that bring industry, government, and Indigenous peoples together is increasing, with partnerships among these sectors an important form of organization in the movement towards sustainability, including agreement on the impacts and benefits of planned developments.[66] This trend coincides with a growing desire at a broad societal level to see Indigenous knowledge inform the decision making that impacts Indigenous lives and lands, and for Indigenous peoples to maintain ownership over that knowledge, the right to practise what

"they know and hold to be true," and the ability to participate in decisions that affect their future.[67]

For non-Indigenous actors, such partnerships require creative systems
of working with Indigenous communities and forms of governance that
recognize Indigenous peoples as distinct and unique.[68] Keeyask created
for the first time in Manitoba Hydro's history a limited partnership with
four Cree Nations, and the opportunity to fully incorporate Indigenous
perspectives into resource development and planning. Keeyask does a
number of things very well. Not least, it enables the Cree Nations most
impacted by the proposed development to be involved throughout the
life of the project (from planning to implementation to operation)
in a stated commitment to respectful, appropriate, and meaningful
Indigenous participation. It is a partnership that lays the foundation
for more equitable working relations between Indigenous peoples and
industry players in the future and should be applauded.

Yet, upon review of the EIS, one is still struck by the differences between Cree and Eurocentric ways of seeing and doing (knowing), and
a realization that any proper evaluation of EA in a Canadian context
must critically examine how these partnerships strive to accommodate
often divergent world views. This would encourage more sensitive
and responsible practices, minimize the adversarial and technocratic
orientation of EA, and build cooperative links between people for environmental governance. In the case of Keeyask, a number of concerns
emerge. First, the regulatory test for significance and the use of valued
environmental components sit awkwardly with a relational Indigenous
world view, as does the use of offsetting programs that undermine the
importance of place to local people. Second, the partnership's apparent
failure to institute a process of individual and collective learning limits
the potential for Manitoba Hydro and the KCNs to follow up on their
experiences and feed information back into decision-making structures.
This would help determine whether Indigenous partners have been
empowered through their involvement, or whether empowerment is
undermined by the needs, expectations, and regulatory demands of
industry and government actors.

This is particularly important to explore, given the tenuous nature of
the relationships between Manitoba Hydro and KCN community members evident at the Clean Environmental Commission's hearings, four
years after the KHLP was formally agreed to. As Will Braun, Agnieszka

Pawlowska-Mainville, and Joseph Dipple argue in this volume, those who still supported Keeyask did so despite deep internal conflict. And as evidenced in the Community Voices sections of this book, that support was in no way unanimous across the four First Nations.

While Keeyask was ultimately approved and construction on the project is almost complete, the partnership itself between Manitoba Hydro and the KCNs will continue for many decades yet as the generating station creates power and, presumably, profit. Thus, it is not too late for the partners to offer an honest appraisal of the partnership process to date, to express in their own words what worked well and what barriers or obstacles remain. This self-reflection may begin to erode the power imbalances that no doubt exist between Indigenous and non-Indigenous players in EA processes.

EA regulations and policies advocate for Indigenous participation. However, if power remains concentrated in Euro-Canadian bureaucratic structures, then Euro-Canadian values will remain the primary basis for action. It is difficult to see how Canada's current regulatory and legislative framework can match the needs and realities of partnerships like Keeyask in Canada's North. As a way of integrating Indigenous values and concerns, the process adopted by the KCNs makes a great deal of sense. Yet, without significant structural change, current government-regulated processes run the risk of performing no more than a legitimization function: that is, serving to mitigate against damage created by capitalist development and consumption. These are the structural obstacles that limit the potential of models such as Keeyask and suggest that "fixing" environmental assessment in cross-cultural settings will have less to do with improving techniques for integrating knowledge, or tweaking the structures of particular planning regimes, and much more to do with restructuring the very institutions, practices, and underlying assumptions of environmental assessment itself.

I would like to acknowledge that the Keeyask Project is built in Treaty 5 territory. This manuscript was drafted in Treaty 1 and finalized in Treaty 6 territories. I would like to thank the Public Interest Law Centre, and the Consumers Association of Manitoba, who supported my efforts to provide an independent analysis of how divergent world views shaped the environmental assessment process for the Keeyask project. I also thank Aimée Craft and Jill Blakley for their work to bring this important case study forward.

Notes

1   Catherine Shapcott, "Environmental Impact Assessment and Resource Management, a Haida Case Study: Implications for Native People of the North," *Canadian Journal of Native Studies* 9, no. 1 (1989): 55–83.

2   Deborah McGregor, "Linking Traditional Knowledge and Environmental Practice in Ontario," *Journal of Canadian Studies* 43, no. 3 (2009): 69–100; Leanne Simpson, "Aboriginal Peoples and Knowledge: Decolonizing Our Processes," *Canadian Journal of Native Studies* 21, no. 1 (2001): 137–48.

3   Shapcott, "Environmental Impact Assessment," 78.

4   Ciaran O'Faircheallaigh, "Environmental Agreements, EIA Follow-up and Aboriginal Participation in Environmental Management: The Canadian Experience," *Environmental Impact Assessment Review* 27, no. 4 (2007): 319–42; Chris Paci, Ann Tobin, and Peter Robb, "Reconsidering the Canadian Environmental Impact Assessment Act: A Place for Traditional Environmental Knowledge," *Environmental Impact Assessment Review* 22, no. 2 (2002): 111–27.

5   Nicolas Houde, "The Six Faces of Traditional Ecological Knowledge: Challenges and Opportunities for Canadian Co-management Arrangements," *Ecology and Society* 12, no. 2 (2007), http://www.ecologyandsociety.org/vol12/iss2/art34/.

6   Simpson, "Aboriginal Peoples and Knowledge"; R. Michael O'Flaherty, Iain J. Davidson-Hunt, and Micheline Manseau, "Indigenous Knowledge and Values in Planning for Sustainable Forestry: Pikangikum First Nation and the Whitefeather Forest Initiative," *Ecology and Society* 13, no. 1 (2008), http://www.ecologyandsociety.org/vol13/iss1/art6/; Matthew Sparke, "A Map That Roared and an Original Atlas: Canada, Cartography, and the Narration of Nation," *Annals of the Association of American Geographers* 88, no. 3 (1998): 463–95; Christopher Alcantara, "To Treaty or Not to Treaty? Aboriginal Peoples and Comprehensive Land Claims Negotiations in Canada," *Publius: The Journal of Federalism* 38, no. 2 (2008): 343–69.

7   Thomas R. Berger, *Northern Frontier, Northern Homeland*, vol. 1 (Toronto: J. Lorimer and Company, 1977); Stephen Bocking, "Thomas Berger's Unfinished Revolution," *Alternatives Journal* 33, no. 2–3 (2007): 50–52; John Ralston Saul, *A Fair Country: Telling Truths about Canada* (Toronto: Penguin, 2009).

8   Ciaran O'Faircheallaigh, *Negotiations in the Indigenous World: Aboriginal Peoples and the Extractive Industry in Australia and Canada* (New York: Routledge, 2015).

9   William J. Couch, "Strategic Resolution of Policy, Environmental and Socio-economic Impacts in Canadian Arctic Diamond Mining: BHP's NWT Diamond Project," *Impact Assessment and Project Appraisal* 20, no. 4 (2002): 265–78; Annie L. Booth and Norman W. Skelton, "Improving First Nations' Participation in Environmental Assessment Processes: Recommendations from the Field," *Impact Assessment and Project Appraisal* 29, no. 1 (2011): 49–58; Richard Missens, Leo Paul Dana, and Robert Anderson, "Aboriginal Partnerships in Canada: Focus on the Diavik Diamond Mine," *Journal of Enterprising Communities: People and Places in the Global Economy* 1, no. 1 (2007): 54–76; Ciaran O'Faircheallaigh, "Public Participation and Environmental Impact Assessment: Purposes, Implications, and Lessons for Public Policy Making," *Environmental Impact Assessment Review* 30, no. 1 (2010): 19–27; Ciaran O'Faircheallaigh, "Community Development Agreements in the Mining Industry: An Emerging Global Phenomenon," *Community Development* 44, no. 2 (2013): 222–38.

10 Aniekan Udofia, Bram Noble, and Greg Poelzer, "Meaningful and Efficient? Enduring Challenges to Aboriginal Participation in Environmental

Assessment," *Environmental Impact Assessment Review* 65 (2017): 164–74; A. John Sinclair and Alan P. Diduck, "Public Participation in Canadian Environmental Assessment: Enduring Challenges and Future Directions," in *Environmental Impact Assessment: Practice and Participation*, 3rd ed., ed. K.S. Hanna (London: Oxford University Press, 2016), 65–95; Diane Ruwhiu and Lynette Carter, "Negotiating 'Meaningful Participation' for Indigenous Peoples in the Context of Mining," *Corporate Governance* 16, no. 4 (2016): 641–54; Philippe Hanna, Frank Vanclay, Esther Jean Langdon, and Jos Arts, "Improving the Effectiveness of Impact Assessment Pertaining to Indigenous Peoples in the Brazilian Environmental Licensing Procedure," *Environmental Impact Assessment Review* 46 (2014): 58–67.

11   O'Faircheallaigh, *Negotiations in the Indigenous World*.

12   After Frank Blechman, Jarle Crocker, Jayne Docherty, and Steve Garon, "Finding Meaning in a Complex Environmental Policy Dialogue: Research into Worldviews in the Northern Forest Lands Council Dialogue, 1990–94," Working Paper No. 14 (Fairfax, VA: Institute for Conflict Analysis and Resolution, George Mason University, 2000). See also York Factory First Nation, *KIPEKISKWEWINAN: Our Voices* (York Factory First Nation, 2012); and Fox Lake Cree Nation, *Fox Lake Environmental Evaluation Report* (Fox Lake Cree Nation, 2012), https://keeyask. com/project-timeline/environment-assessment-process/activites/keeyask-cree-nations-enviro-evaluation-reports/.

13   Leroy Little Bear, "Jagged Worldviews Colliding," in *Reclaiming Indigenous Voice and Vision*, ed. Marie Battiste (Vancouver: University of British Columbia Press, 2000), 77–85; Simpson, "Aboriginal Peoples and Knowledge."

14   Jerry H. Gill, *Native American Worldviews: An Introduction* (Amherst, NY: Humanity Books, 2002).

15   The EIS for Keeyask consisted of four separate environmental assessments: (i) the Response to EIS Guidelines (provided by the proponent, Manitoba Hydro); (ii) the Cree Nation Partners' Keeyask Environmental Evaluation Report (January 2012, 181 pp); (iii) York Factory First Nation's *KIPEKISKWEWINAN: Our Voices* report (July 2012; 158 pp); and (iv) Fox Lake Cree Nation's *Fox Lake Environmental Evaluation Report* (September 2012, 111 pp). As such, the partner KCNs conducted their own assessments of the proposed project. Two of the communities—Tataskweyak Cree Nation (TCN) and War Lake First Nation (WLFN)—joined forces to form their own partnership within the KHLP—the Cree Nation Partners (CNP)—because of a "shared interest in future hydroelectric development" on traditional lands.

16   Little Bear, "Jagged Worldviews Colliding," 77.

17   Deborah McGregor, "Coming Full Circle: Indigenous Knowledge, Environment, and Our Future," *American Indian Quarterly* 28, no. 3/4 (2004): 385–410.

18   Blechman et al., "Finding Meaning."

19   Richard Bawden, "Messy Issues, Worldviews and Systemic Competencies," in *Social Learning Systems and Communities of Practice*, ed. Chris Blackwell (London: Springer, 2010), 89–101; Michael Anthony Hart, *Seeking Mino-Pimatisiwin: An Aboriginal Approach to Healing* (Winnipeg: Fernwood Publishing, 2002).

20   Blechman et al., "Finding Meaning."

21   Christine Byrch, Kate Kearins, Markus Milne, and Richard Morgan, "Sustainable 'What'? A Cognitive Approach to Understanding Sustainable Development," *Qualitative Research in Accounting and Management* 4 (2007): 26–52.

22   Brian Rice, *Seeing the World with Aboriginal Eyes* (Winnipeg: Aboriginal Issues Press, 2005); Mark G. Stevenson, "Indigenous Knowledge in Environmental

Assessment," *Arctic* 49, no. 3 (1996): 278–91; Simpson, "Aboriginal Peoples and Knowledge."

23 Marie Battiste, ed., *Reclaiming Indigenous Voice and Vision* (Vancouver: University of British Columbia Press, 2000).

24 Marie Battiste and James (Sa'ke'j) Youngblood Henderson, *Protecting Indigenous Knowledge and Heritage: A Global Challenge* (Vancouver: Purich Publishing, 2000); McGregor "Linking Traditional Knowledge"; Simpson, "Aboriginal Peoples and Knowledge."

25 Houde, "Six Faces of Traditional Ecological Knowledge."

26 Paul Nadasdy, "Reevaluating the Co-management Success Story," *Arctic* 56, no. 4 (December 2003): 367–80.

27 Battiste and Henderson, *Protecting Indigenous Knowledge.*

28 Edward T. Hall, *Beyond Culture*, 2nd ed. (NY: Anchor, 1989).

29 McGregor, "Coming Full Circle"; O'Faircheallaigh, "Environmental Agreements."

30 Simpson, "Aboriginal Peoples and Knowledge," 140.

31 Stevenson, "Indigenous Knowledge in Environmental Assessment," 289.

32 Byron Williams, Aimée Craft, and Joëlle Pastora Sala, "Keeyask—A Watershed Decision: Closing Arguments" (Winnipeg: Consumers' Association of Canada [Manitoba], 2014). Submitted to the CEC on 14 January 2014.

33 Hart, *Seeking Mino-Pimatisiwin.*

34 Williams, Craft, and Sala, "Keeyask—A Watershed Decision."

35 Keeyask Hydropower Limited Partnership [KHLP], *Keeyask Generation Project Environmental Impact Study: Executive Summary [EIS Executive Summary]*, June 2012, 3, https://keeyask.com/project-timeline/environment-assessment-process/environmental-licensing-process/executive-summary/.

36 Stevenson, "Indigenous Knowledge in Environmental Assessment."

37 ATK is grounded in the Cree world view and a method of communicating Indigenous know-how about particular environmental and social phenomena, based on intergenerational learning and experience, and is seen as being of vital importance to assessment processes because it constitutes the baseline information that technical science can struggle to provide; see Williams, Craft, and Sala, "Keeyask—A Watershed Decision."

38 Keeyask Hydropower Limited Partnership [KHLP], *Keeyask Generation Project Environmental Impact Study* [EIS], ch. 2, page 7, https://keeyask.com/project-timeline/environment-assessment-process/environmental-licensing-process/.

39 KHLP, *EIS Executive Summary*, 6 and 42. Emphasis in original.

40 McGregor, "Coming Full Circle."

41 Fox Lake Cree Nation, *Environmental Evaluation Report*, 18.

42 York Factory First Nation, *KIPEKISKWEWINAN*, 26.

43 Manitoba Hydro, "Preferred Development Plan Facilities," Chapter 2, p. 5, http://www.pubmanitoba.ca/nfat/pdf/hydro_application/nfat_business_case_chapter_02_manitoba_hydros_preferred_development_plan_facilities.pdf.

44 Frank Duerden and Richard G. Kuhn, "Scale, Context, and Application of Traditional Knowledge of the Canadian North," *Polar Record* 34, no. 188 (1998): 31–38; Susan Buggey, "An Approach to Aboriginal Cultural Landscapes in Canada," in *Northern Ethnographic Landscapes: Perspectives from Circumpolar Nations*, ed. Igor Krupnik, Rachel Mason, and Tonia W. Horton (Washington: National Museum of

Natural History, 2004), 17–44; D.G. Callaway, "Landscapes of Tradition, Landscapes of Resistance," in *Northern Ethnographic Landscapes: Perspectives from Circumpolar Nations,* eds. Igor Krupnik, Rachel Mason, and Tonia W. Horton (Washington: National Musuem of Natural History, 2004), 177–201.

45 Gregory Cajete, *Look to the Mountain: An Ecology of Indigenous Education* (Durango, CO: Kivaki Press, 1994); Little Bear, "Jagged Worldviews Colliding."

46 Here, "follow-up" is used differently from how the Canadian Environmental Assessment Agency understands the term (which uses it to verify the accuracy of the environmental assessment of a project, or to determine the effectiveness of any measures taken to mitigate the adverse environmental effects of said project). Rather, "follow-up" refers in the context of this chapter to a process of self-reflection that partners can embark upon in order to generate lessons that can strengthen existing or future partnerships.

47 After Houde, "Six Faces of Traditional Ecological Knowledge."

48 Paul Nadasdy, "The Politics of TEK: Power and the 'Integration' of Knowledge," *Arctic Anthropology* 36, no. ½ (1999): 1–18; O'Faircheallaigh, "Environmental Agreements."

49 Leonard J.S. Tsuji and Elise Ho, "Traditional Environmental Knowledge and Western Science: In Search of Common Ground," *Canadian Journal of Native Studies* 22, no. 2 (2002): 327–60.

50 Simpson, "Aboriginal Peoples and Knowledge."

51 Bawden, "Messy Issues"; Michael A. Hart, "Indigenous Worldviews, Knowledge, and Research: The Development of an Indigenous Research Paradigm," *Journal of Indigenous Social Development* 1, no. 1A (2010): 1–16.

52 Giuliana Casimirri, "Problems with Integrating Traditional Ecological Knowledge into Contemporary Resource Management," paper presented at the 12th World Forestry Congress, Quebec City, September 2003.

53 Clean Environment Commission (CEC), *Keeyask Generation Project Environmental Impact Statement, Responses to Information Requests,* CEC, Round 1 CAC-0054, https://keeyask.com/wp-content/uploads/2013/07/CEC-Round-1-Web-Version-July-31-2-pm.pdf.

54 Ibid., CEC, Round 1 CAC-0055b.

55 Ibid. The Canadian Environmental Assessment Agency Reference Guide, *Determining Whether a Project Is Likely to Cause Significant Adverse Environmental Effects* (Ottawa: Federal Environmental Assessment Review Office, November 1994), 186, notes that "public input into the determination of significant adverse environmental effects must limit itself to questions related to scientific analysis and interpretation. Issues that are not directly linked to the scientific (including traditional ecological knowledge) analysis of environmental effects . . . cannot be introduced into the determination at this step."

56 The term "equal consideration" is used in the more prominent sections of the EIS (the *Executive Summary,* for example) and there are question marks over whether "equal consideration" can be understood as being synonymous with "equal weight." However, the term "equal weight" is used at least once in the EIS, in Chapter 2, where the first "Common Principle" regarding inclusion of ATK in the Keeyask EA is written as: "Giving Equal Weight—the EA process honours and respects ATK and the Cree worldview. The EA aims to give equal weight to ATK and western science." It is a principle that was quoted at a session (24 October 2013) of the Keeyask Public Hearings, by Manitoba Hydro employee Vicky Cole. See lines 11–17, page 687, of the following transcript: http://www.cecmanitoba.ca/resource/

hearings/39/Transcripts%20-%20Keeyask%20Winnipeg%20Hearing%20Oct%20 24,2013.pdf.

57 Duerden and Kuhn, "Scale, Context, and Application"; Simpson, "Aboriginal Peoples and Knowledge."

58 Luc Bouthillier and Dionne Hugues, *La forêt à habiter: La notion de "forêt habitée" et ses critères de mise en œuvre. Rapport final au Service canadien des forêts-Québec* (Quebec: Université Laval, 1995).

59 McGregor, "Linking Traditional Knowledge."

60 Buggey, "Approach to Aboriginal Cultural Landscapes."

61 See O'Faircheallaigh, "Environmental Agreements"; Assembly of First Nations (Environment Division), "The Feasibility of Representing Traditional Indigenous Knowledge in Cartographic, Pictorial or Textual Forms," Draft Final Report, 1995; Denis Kirchhoff, Holly L. Gardner, and Leonard JS Tsuji, "The Canadian Environmental Assessment Act, 2012, and Associated Policy: Implications for Aboriginal Peoples," *International Indigenous Policy Journal* 4, no. 3 (2013): 1–15.

62 James P. Robson and Patricia Fitzpatrick, *A Critical Analysis of the L3RP Aboriginal Engagement Process* (Winnipeg: Public Interest Law Centre, 2015); Stevenson, "Indigenous Knowledge in Environmental Assessment."

63 O'Faircheallaigh, "Public Participation"; O'Faircheallaigh, *Negotiations in the Indigenous World.*

64 Peter J. Usher, "Traditional Ecological Knowledge in Environmental Assessment and Management," *Arctic* 53, no. 2 (June 2000): 183–93.

65 Robson and Fitzpatrick, "A Critical Analysis of the L3RP."

66 O'Faircheallaigh, *Negotiations in the Indigenous World*; Frank Vanclay, Ana Maria Esteves, Ilse Aucamp, and Daniel M. Franks, *Social Impact Assessment: Guidance for Assessing and Managing the Social Impacts of Projects* (Fargo, ND: International Association for Impact Assessment, 2015); Michael Hitch and Courtney Riley Fidler, "Impact and Benefit Agreements: A Contentious Issue for Environmental and Aboriginal Justice," *Environments Journal* 35, no. 2 (2007): 45–69.

67 Stevenson, "Indigenous Knowledge in Environmental Assessment."

68 McGregor, "Coming Full Circle."

"What Happened in Fox Lake"

CONWAY ARTHURSON, FORMER COUNCILLOR, FOX LAKE CREE NATION

Excerpt from the transcript of the Keeyask CEC hearing at Split Lake, 8 October 2013.

I want to talk a little bit about the past. What happened to us in Fox Lake. Some of the things that I heard, some of the things that my dad has told me. And, I know we signed a settlement agreement in 2004, forgiving Hydro for the past, but I need to let you guys know some of the things that have happened to our people. . . .

There was a cabin that was in the way of that surveyor's line, by about three feet. And, my dad went to his boss, and said we have to move that line a little bit over because the house is in the way. His boss said no, give that lady five minutes to get her stuff out of there. And my dad went in to protect her. And, that lady—and my dad was very emotional when he was telling me this. And I am very emotional now, because I sensed and I felt what he felt.

He told that lady, you have five minutes to get your stuff together, because we are going to move your house. And she put her stuff in the blanket, put it over her shoulder, and walked a few feet, and dropped it and started crying and the bulldozer came, and moved it out of the way.

Another story I heard, was a trapper, he went to check his traps in the morning. He came back, all he found were cat tracks, up to the bush, and a pile of wood which used to be his house. Never been compensated for things like that.

Although, as I said, we forgive Hydro for that past. We will never forget.

Another story my dad told me, when he was surveying the hospital, a hospital, the corner of the hospital there was a grave right in the corner of it, and again my dad went to his boss, and said, we have to move that hospital about two feet over, because there is a grave there. His boss says, dig up that grave, and move that grave, my dad did that by himself. And it was, that casket, he said, wasn't even bigger than this table. It was a little baby, or child.

And those are the kind of things that I think about, when we talk about hope. Another thing, what our people went through growing up in Gillam, were beatings, rapes, sometimes murders that weren't even investigated. . . .

But those are the kind of things that we have to live with in the past. And, it is hard for me to move forward in a good way when I see a lot of these things happening right now.

CHAPTER 6

"The Flooders" and "the Cree": Challenging the Hydro Metanarrative Using Achimowinak "Stories"

AGNIESZKA PAWLOWSKA-MAINVILLE IN
CONVERSATION WITH NOAH MASSAN

"They are always lying to me. Hydro's always lying to me." With these words, Noah, an Elder and harvester from Makeso Sakahican or Fox Lake Cree Nation, and I end our conversation about Keeyask. It has been almost five years since the Keeyask Clean Environment Commission hearings and its decision to approve the project, and the experience still resonates with us. We are driving across Noah's trapline, weaving in and out on dirt roads outside of Gillam and occasionally stopping to take photos of the newest generating station. Naturally, our conversation turns to Hydro; it is an inescapable narrative as Keeyask's infrastructure is located largely on Noah's trapline, including access roads, traffic, and flooding from the dam itself. Noah tells me that there is nothing to trap, as Hydro pushed out all the animals. As we talk further, Noah shares with me other stories of how hydro development has damaged his trapline and his community in northern Manitoba: "Hydro. Clean energy they say . . . there's nothing clean about the shorelines here." Noah has seen the profound changes hydroelectric development has had and continues to have on the sturgeon populations, on moose populations, on caribou and geese migration patterns, on the populations of the local woodlands caribou herds, and on medicines obtained from the land. He has lived through the construction of all four dams on the Nelson River, and his story tells us that it is trappers like Noah who carry the burden of this sixty-year-old growing energy need.

Noah Massan,[1] an Inninu trapper, has harvested most of his life. Keeyask and all other hydro development in the area directly impact Noah's trapline: his cabin was first flooded with the Kettle and Long Spruce generating stations in the 1970s, and more of this land will be destroyed with the Keeyask Project. At over seventy years old, he continues to go out on his land and check his traps regularly—only now, he goes out to monitor the damage done by Manitoba's newest generating station.

Keeyask, meaning "gull" in Inniumowin (Cree) is a seven-generator hydroelectric dam that is meant to be part of a solution to reducing greenhouse gas emissions in Manitoba.[2] Manitoba Hydro is building the dam over the beautiful Keeyask Rapids at Kichi Sipi (Nelson River), where endangered sturgeon spawn. "No more rapids there, eh, no more sturgeon," shares Noah as we head towards the site.

Noah and I met during my employment at the Fox Lake Cree Nation Negotiations Office two years before the Manitoba Clean Environment Commission's (CEC) public hearings on whether or not to recommend that the Province of Manitoba issue an environmental licence to the Keeyask Hydropower Limited Partnership (KHLP), which included Fox Lake. Noah and I became friends, which led to our subsequent application for participant status at the CEC hearings to present Noah's concerns over the Keeyask Project. With $200,000 in funding from the CEC funding, we established the Concerned Fox Lake Grassroots Citizens (CFLGC). Assisted by academic experts, Inninuwak Elders, and other grassroots community members, we carried out fieldwork, gathered information, conducted interviews, and created videos that were used as the basis of our testimonies and Expert Witness reports at the hearings in Winnipeg in 2013 and 2014 (please see the CEC website for copies of the Expert Witness reports, http://www.cecmanitoba.ca/hearings/).

As Jill Blakley and Bram Noble detail in Chapter 4 in this volume, the Environmental Impact Statement (EIS) that the Keeyask partnership presented to the CEC stated that there will be "no significant effects" from the proposed megaproject. However, our collective argued that there *will* be significant and profound adverse effects to Noah's trapline, the land and the river, and his community—the entire

Makeso Sakahican landscape. Whereas Manitoba Hydro had data and experts affirming the EIS scientific findings that this project is "clean and green," our group had achimowinak, "stories [seen as facts]," that articulated the Inninuwak lived experience of hydro development. As the proceedings went on, it became evident that there were two distinct faces of the same project. As such, "truth" was presented in two opposing narratives.

One side, the intervenors (including CFLGC) shared their achimowinak through multiple voices, each of them experiencing hydro development differently and yet all expressing the feeling of collective loss and trauma associated with each Hydro project. The proponents, including the First Nations partners, acknowledged this historical trauma, but nevertheless supported the broader position of "moving forward" and the need to build the Keeyask Dam. Many of the participant Inninuwak presented a series of experiences and "on the ground" stories; the proponents constructed a metanarrative that ignored community stories that didn't fit their message. As such, this chapter will discuss the two sides to Keeyask: one taken from the discourse of the niskipaowuk, "the flooders," and the other from the perspective of the Inninuwak (the Cree). In discussing the niskipaowuk metanarrative and the Makeso Sakahican Inninuwak achimowinak that were presented at the CEC Keeyask hearings, we illustrate the conflicting stories of hydro development in Canada. And, while recognizing the multiplicity of truths surrounding "clean and green" development, in the case of Keeyask, granting a licence for yet another generating station on Inninuwak territory ultimately legitimized what is considered *the* truth about adverse effects from dams.

Creating Space for "Little Stories"

Even though it is publicly available, the almost thirty-volume EIS, couched in highly technical language, remains largely inaccessible to these land-based kitayatsuk, "harvesters"—despite the proponents' promises of business and employment opportunities, as well as environmental impacts, stemming from the project.

Many Elders from Makeso Sakahican, Fox Lake, were eager to share their stories with us because they felt as though their voices, opinions, and knowledges were not being heard by Manitoba Hydro. The CFLGC provided them with a venue through which to tell their achimowinak, "stories [seen as facts]/ personal narratives," detailing their experiences with three dams already (the Kettle, Long Spruce, and Limestone dams), and now with Keeyask as the fourth.

Currently, Noah's trapline is experiencing much of the construction for Keeyask. Together with the access road, dynamite explosions, constant flow of traffic, and the associated noise, all have decimated animal populations from the area. "There is nothing there anymore, all the animals are gone," shares Noah as we stand overlooking the enormous pit of metal "bones" protruding from the concrete landscape. Amidst the boreal forest landscape that can be seen from the flight to northern Manitoba, the barren area around Keeyask looks like a big muddy desert with the trees cleared out, growing in the centre of that eerie landscape. It is not until one sees this view that the term "raping the land" has any meaning.[3] As we overlook the tremendous size of the project, Noah's voice tells me he managed to catch one wolf and one lynx on his trapline last year. "That's probably the last of them," he says.

Although Fox Lake Cree Nation is a partner in the Keeyask Project, numerous Makeso Sakahican harvesters decided to speak to us because they felt that their concerns were not acknowledged and, in some cases, were even ignored by Manitoba Hydro and their consultants. Although hope for economic opportunities reinforced the community's resolve in signing onto Keeyask, more and more Elders, harvesters, and community members became hesitant about, if not outright opposed to, the proponent's findings as the project developed further. Ranging from the frustrations with the Valued Ecosystem Components (VEC), many of which overlook culturally relevant species such as whisky jack and sage, to Hydro's insistence that the endangered woodland caribou will not be affected as they are no longer in the area, Elders regard the EIS process as vastly unsound. As we sit at the CEC hearings, listening to Hydro's experts emphasize "valued" species like sturgeon, moose, and caribou, Noah leans over and asks, "What about the squirrels?" Later, as we deliberate on the presentations, Noah continues, "What about all those rabbits floating dead in the water? We tell them we want to know about the squirrels or the whisky jack, and they say they don't know. What do they know? Yeah, they don't listen to First Nations people."

Similarly, when harvesters voiced their concerns over the noise from the generating stations affecting caribou ears, and of saving fish from being shred to pieces by the turbines, Hydro consultants have continually told Elders that this is not their area of expertise. In mentioning the need for top executives to see the effects of the dams for themselves, Noah says, "They got so many people working over there and no one knows anything. I like to come early to watch them get ready [for consultations] and everything, and I always stay until the end, but they never talk to us about what we want to know."

Indeed, as the CEC hearings progressed, an increasing number of people came forward to voice their concerns over the Keeyask Project. A growing amount of Fox Lake community members became more opposed to the project itself as time went on and they often came up to us during the hearings to share their own frustrations at the presentations made by Manitoba Hydro experts. Many people just came to shake Noah's hand for running the CFLGC and speaking to Hydro "bosses" directly. Other Inninuwak from Nisichawayasihk Cree Nation, Tataskweyak Cree Nation, and Pimicikamak Cree Nation also shared, both in their roles as intervenors at the hearing as well as informally during the breaks, about their fears of losing their traditional way of life, their culture, and their language, and about more destruction to lands and waters. Many supported the CFLGC and indicated that their own experiences were similar to the Makeso Sakahican Inninuwak narratives. Many of these community members came to these hearings with the hope that people in the South, including decision makers, would hear some of these fears. In that sense, they saw the CEC process as the only way to get their stories heard directly.

In responding to my question as to why the CFLGC's presence at the hearings was so important for all these people, Noah affirms that it is because he could speak to them [the commissioners and Hydro] directly: "I could just talk to them, me. Don't want those Hydro people twisting my words around. I could just tell them all the stuff that is happening on my [trap]line. People are scared to talk, they don't wanna talk. But they just saw me doin' it, talking to them. They [community members] didn't believe it [could be possible]." Laughing, Noah adds, "Now I have professors working for me." Undeniably, he very much appreciated having the support of academics and other experts who could support his narratives and help him fight "within the system" against further destruction of his trapline. Having a platform from which to speak directly to Hydro, to "look them in the eyes and tell them what I think," as Noah states, was immensely valuable and empowering. The

CFLGC would often invite the harvesters themselves to speak to the commissioners directly at the hearings, because members were eager to speak for themselves—not in Gillam, where their voices and their stories were already known, but in Winnipeg. Many felt that what they had been saying for years already had been filtered out of consultants' reporting. Therefore, they wanted to be sure that they could "tell their stories," right in Winnipeg, to the people in the South.[4]

It's also important to note that not only were Inninuwak voices heard, they were also *welcomed* to present their achimowinak. Being invited to the hearings to communicate their narratives directly before the commissioners was one form of legitimizing Inninuwak lived experiences. Being provided with the space to counter-argue Manitoba Hydro's metanarrative empowered many Inninuwak to finally share their own achimowinak of the adverse effects experienced in the region.

Metanarratives and Achimowinak

A "metanarrative" can be characterized as a grand narrative that is common to all: the master idea. The term was brought into prominence by Jean-François Lyotard (1984), who voiced in *The Postmodern Condition* his apprehension about certain grand narratives like "progress." Lyotard writes that truth has a value in the discourse that occupies a certain place in our society. Arguing against totalitarian or unifying theory—the metanarrative—Lyotard pressed for the urgency of *petits récits,* or "little narratives."[5] These little narratives, rather than assenting to the universal truth or agreeing to a consensus, can destabilize existing metanarratives that obliterate all counter-positions.[6]

At the CEC hearings, individual proponent voices within Keeyask Hydro Limited Partnership seemed to consolidate into one overarching metanarrative. As participants in the hearings, we heard narratives like "hydroelectric development is 'progress' as no greenhouse gases are emitted," "dams are 'clean energy,'" "the local economy will improve," and "the quality of life will be better for Manitobans as science, new technology, modern infrastructure and sustainable development were guiding the development of Keeyask." In describing how the project is about "moving forward," the Keeyask Hydro Limited Partnership stated that mitigation measures would counter any negative effects: "[The] Partnership has or will mitigate, remediate and compensate for these [adverse] effects using past experience, Aboriginal Traditional Knowledge and state-of-the-art scientific and engineering techniques. . . . The project provides many benefits for the Partner First Nations, specifically business opportunities, employment, training and income. The result has been a thoughtful, carefully planned and designed project."[7]

As Will Braun outlined in Chapter 2 in this volume, the EIS (and the proponents, more generally) continuously reiterated the grand narrative surrounding the benefits of "clean" energy sources like the Keeyask Generating Station through the privileged discourse of "truth" and "progressive enlightenment." For a dam—the huge wall of concrete that will forever block the natural flow of the river and flood the surrounding watershed—to have "minimal" impacts on the environment is a tactical narrative whose validity is limited to the specific context in which it appears. Manitoba Hydro's metanarrative of "clean and green" progress reflects its own political and historical discourse—for example, politicians' dreams of a "Decade of Development" for hydroelectricity in Manitoba, as Byron Williams describes in Chapter 1 in this volume. It is then justified through specific scientific prescriptions. For Lyotard, information is a commodity the metanarrative sells: science, as the discourse that legitimizes certain facts over others, was used at the hearings to separate personal experiences from "objective" knowledge. In this way, hegemonic capitalist discourse powers the metanarrative of the "economic necessity" for the subsequent dams in northern Manitoba.

In the context of the Keeyask hearings, the Cree achimowinak not only offered legitimization of Cree aski keskentamowin, "land knowledge," they also challenged the dominant idea of non-renewable resource development as "progress." Grassroots voices illustrated Inninuwak lived experience of loss, trauma, and socio-environmental destruction caused by hydro development. These achimowinak, "regular stories" and/or "stories [seen as facts]/personal narratives," constituted their lived experience of "progress" in the North. Jack and Christine Massan, who were part of our CFLGC discussions, illustrate this by articulating how hydro development damaged their ability to harvest medicines:

> The elder elders, the ones that are older than us and have lived through all those years, say the other dams did a real, did a lot of damage on the Cree here. And they're afraid that if they go through one more, that'll be the end of them. And I

think they're speaking out, [not] just lives, but also culturally. Our environment is, is not very clean anymore. You know, a number of our elders still use plants for medicinal uses. So Hydro will come and ask, where do you get your plants and we won't go in that area. Like, do you always go in the same spot to pick things? Do you go to the same shopping centre to buy whatever? . . . you used to go in a place and pick. And now you gotta go further and further. (CLFGC 2013)

Ivan Moose, one of the Inninu (Cree) presenters from Fox Lake speaking for CFLGC, similarly affirms a different face of Keeyask: "Fox Lake knows, singularly, the drastic adverse effects of hydro development. Regardless of what supporters of the Keeyask project may say, Manitoba Hydro, at the end of the day, will not understand our plight. . . . We will witness the compete destruction of what little is left of Fox Lake's social, cultural and moral fabric."[8]

The multiplicity of achimowinak shared by Inninuwak as well as by other interveners, participants, and the public serves to confront Hydro's hegemonic discourse with personal experiences of injustice, poverty, and the socio-environmental effects associated with hydro development. Because Inninuwak achimowinak and lived experience remain largely unacknowledged, they occupy a space outside of the hegemonic discourse about hydro development. Consequently, they explicitly confront the metanarrative of non-renewable resource exploitation as "progress."

The Metanarrative of the Niskipaowuk (the Flooders)

Keeyask represents an invaluable enrichment of our human capacity.

–Councillor George Neepin, CEC hearings, 2014[9]

Manitoba Hydro, the Crown corporation, goes by many names in the community of Makeso Sakahican. Some Inninuwak refer to them as "destroyers," "liars," or as the niskipaowuk, "the flooders." Ivan Moose states, "We have many names for hydro in the community: *kakinaskisuk, niskipaowuk, kaniskipaowuk, nachistawuk,* and *oniskipochokeo. Kipahekun*—blocking the highway or the river—is what we also refer to them as. The Nelson was traditionally used as a highway for our people."[10]

The word "dam" in Inninumowin, for example, is based on the Inninuwak understanding of the feature: that which blocks the highway but differs from the beaver dam. Now, the niskipaowuk are partnering with the community. In 2012, when the project's Environmental Impact Statement was publicly filed, Manitoba Hydro presented Keeyask as a precedent-setting business opportunity for the Inninuwak. Opportunities for employment and business ventures were presented, as were protection and mitigation measures for ensuring the dam will not damage the landscape. Despite seven generators and forty-five square kilometres of flooding, the proponents concluded that the effects on the terrestrial and aquatic environments were neutral or, in many cases, none—and therefore, mitigation measures are limited. Expert consultants insinuated that the alarmingly low lake sturgeon populations, which many parties were concerned over, was due to First Nation overharvesting[11]—insinuations community members said was a lie.[12]

The most surprising outcome of the research on nameo, lake sturgeon, presented at the hearings was the confidence that this low lake sturgeon population is expected to increase in some regions due to stocking.[13] In other words, the proponents argued that the Keeyask Dam will actually *increase* imperilled fish populations! Certainly, as the Fisheries and Oceans Canada 2010 assessment for lake sturgeon indicates, the most important current threats to survival and recovery of lake sturgeon on the Nelson River are "habitat degradation or loss resulting from the presence of dams/impoundments and other barriers."[14]

Likewise, the proponents argued that the caribou calving grounds on which some of the caribou go to have their young will not be adversely affected by the project, its construction, or its infrastructure, because inundating the land will create islands that caribou can calve on. The interpretation that the Keeyask Project will actually *better* the environment, as caribou calving grounds will be enhanced, was met with groans and exasperation from community members in the room. The protected woodlands caribou will apparently not be significantly adversely impacted either—this is because the scientists argued that the animals do not frequent the area and no evidence of their presence around Keeyasko Powistik (Gull Rapids, where the dam has been built) could be found.

This claim directly challenged the testimonies of the local Inninuwak, who maintained that they always hunted caribou in those areas. The issue of caribou is a sensitive and frustrating issue for the local Inninuwak like Noah, who identified that noschimik atikuk (woodland caribou) were indeed present in the area. Noah's nephew has actually harvested one. Not willing to acknowledge the presence of this caribou species on the project site, the Hydro-employed scientists have instead referred to these seemingly unidentifiable animals as the "summer residents" of the barren land species herd, which warrants extra precautions but represents no concerns for the possible extirpation of the species. Noah, visibly angry at the insistence that the animals in question are not woodland caribou, strongly exclaimed in his testimony that he would go and kill a woodland caribou and put it at Manitoba Hydro's lawyer's doorstep for proof. This caused the entire room to be filled with applause and laughter at the hearings. Responding to the cross-examining lawyer, Noah stated: "Because as a user, I get to see stuff there, you know. So you can't prove—you have to be there to see these things. But next time I kill a caribou, I'm going to bring it to you [the Hydro cross-examining lawyer], if you are around. I will take pictures of it."[15]

Arguments directly challenging the lived experience of harvesters and Elders like Noah, any of whom have spent most of their lives hunting, trapping, and fishing, make up the foundation of the Hydro metanarrative. Core elements—denying the existence of woodland caribou and any damage this dam could have on endangered sturgeon populations—not only uphold the metanarrative of "clean and green" with scientific progress, they outright delegitimize voices and data that exist through Inninuwak aski keskentamowin, "land knowledge." Local land knowledge takes into account "everything, even the little squirrels and the whisky jacks," Noah explains.

This is not to say that no Inninuwak supported the project and the Hydro metanarrative. Fox Lake Cree Nation Councillor Neepin argued that it would "take days to present every benefit we see as forthcoming from the project. All of which cumulatively outweigh what we see as negative effects."[16] For Elder William Beardy from Tataskweyak Cree Nation, the Keeyask Project, through "these waters and their power," was regarded as "once again help[ing] to provide for our people."[17] Claiming that Keeyask will bring jobs, business opportunities, training, and numerous social, economic, and harvesting benefits for the local Inninuwak, Manitoba Hydro experts put up graphs and data to support this view. However, many Elders did not see these promises as long-term solutions to the poverty and inequality that exist in Hydro-affected communities.

As we drive around the Town of Gillam (nicknamed "Hydro-town" by local Inninuwak) in 2018, Noah points to the beautiful townhouses of Hydro workers. "Hydro pays for their heat," he says. "How come we don't get that? Those guys there, they have their heat blasting in their garage all winter. They don't have to pay for it, that's why." We continue driving around, and Noah points to the lovely single-detached homes and the "fancy boats" the workers use to harvest without a licence: "Those guys take everything from the water. We know not to take from this water. I've seen them catch sturgeon, too. Half of those guys don't even have their licences. They even go hunting too [points to the bush], and they leave the animals just lyin' there."

We then drive into the area of Gillam where most First Nations people live. The view is vastly different from the townhouses, with trailer homes, some of them run down, closely placed together; even the boats are not as elaborate as the ones owned by Hydro workers. When I ask Noah what he thinks about all the job opportunities at Keeyask that were promised at the hearings, he waves his hands and says: "All these promises of all these jobs. Hydro has no control over the [sub]contracts [the people they hire]. And the contractors, they bring people in from the south, from Quebec. They hire and then fire people from here." Our visit to the Keeyask campsite confirms Noah's perception that the workforce is largely non-Inninuwak, where we are shown around by a nice Quebecker with a thick French accent. Noah confirms that "once those guys from the South leave with all that money," opportunities for local people will be limited. Undeniably, one of the biggest concerns that the Inninuwak shared with us during the CEC hearings were that once Keeyask is complete, the local workforce will no longer be needed. Any future employment opportunities would present themselves only with another dam built in Fox Lake territory.

These few examples paint a very different picture of the metanarrative of hydroelectric development in Manitoba's North from that indicated by Manitoba Hydro. Undeniably, the proponents sought to present Keeyask as an isolated, stand-alone project that would nonetheless provide much-needed "clean energy" for the South and opportunities for the North. However, members of CFLGC have taken into account their entire history of the impacts of hydroelectric dams to date and expressed their apprehensions over the impacts yet another project will have on the already fragile social, cultural, and economic fabric of the Makeso Sakahican Inninuwak. They challenged the Manitoba Hydro totalizing metanarrative and publicly shared their accounts so that others would learn that exploiting natural resources in Manitoba's North comes at the expense of the Inninuwak.

The Achimowinak of the Inninuwak

The Keeyask Project will greatly impact on traditional uses by our First Nation. The total effects of the dams that Keeyask will add to will only pollute further our streams and local environments and further attempt to silence our voices of concerns in regards to this project.

-Fox Lake Nation member, CFLGC, 2013[18]

The CEC hearings presented First Nations members with the opportunity to recount their experiences with hydro development. Ranging from the Makeso Sakahican in the Gillam area through to Tataskweyak and Pimicikamak Cree Nations and all the way to Peguis First Nation, one by one, these communities illustrated the ramifications of each generating station at the local level. Located as far as 700 kilometres from the proposed Keeyask site, Peguis First Nation argued that previous projects and the fluctuating waters of Lake Winnipeg already affect its people. Pimicikamak Cree Nation likewise suffers from water level inconsistencies caused by the Jenpeg Generating Station; the images demonstrating how the ebb and flow of local waters exposes the bones of ancestors and scatters them across the disturbed riverbanks[19] was difficult to watch for some people present in the CEC room. The Hydro-controlled water levels continue to interrupt the natural flow of the water, unpredictably changing locals' knowledge of the river environments they grew up in: "I know people that have drowned," shares Noah. "They go on the river, but the ice gives up under them. That [one family] fell in the water along with their skidoos."[20]

In our work comparing the two distinct interpretations of Keeyask's effects, we have concluded that numerous short- and long-term adverse effects will profoundly change the environment and the social, economic, and cultural well-being of the local Inninuwak communities. The data presented in the EIS and at the Clean Environment Commission hearings do not reflect the true nature of the negative effects and of the current situation experienced by the kitayatsuk, the harvesters. When effective mitigation and rehabilitation plans are not developed, as they were not at the time of the hearings,[21] impacts are difficult to neutralize. To this day, hydro development continues to represent the largest form of destruction of Inninuwak values, history, and local mino-pimatisiwin (well-being) many people have ever seen—the historical disruption that has forever ingrained itself into the Inninuwak world. Tom Nepetaypo, one of the CFLGC members who testified at the hearings, states:

> Oh, the land was beautiful here, here where it is called Stephen[s] Lake now. We used to trap all around there too, for muskrats, beaver. Oh, there were a lot of beavers when we went there. But when they build the dam, oh, the lake was empty, everything drowned; they drowned right away, all the animals, the beaver—everything.... We didn't know how much Hydro had destroyed. No one knew how much Hydro had destroyed, and it only became known as time passed, as we travelled around by boat and saw the extent of the damage. The trees were under the water we travelled over. And we lost our nets, eh, our sturgeon nets that we were using to fish.[22]

The aesthetic of the land was directly tied to local livelihoods, and the destruction of that source of income was unimaginable for many. Noah recognizes this narrative of complete destruction of local liveli-hoods, as he has experienced the decline of the Inninuwak way of life, including their diet. While Noah and I prepare for his testimony, he acknowledges that after hydro development, "there was no caribou in our area. They were all gone. Hydro destroyed their lands and destroyed our [way of] life. This is my life. The old people used to tell stories about lots of caribou crossing the river. But after Hydro came, there was no caribou. Hunting, that is my life. And caribou. . . . What will happen to the caribou on my trapline after Keeyask? Where will all the caribou go?"[23]

The Elders are worried about the loss of animals and its effects on their entire hunting and trapping economy, as well as on their individ-ual livelihoods. Dependence on caribou for meat has been drastically affected since the Kettle Dam was built in the 1960s, one of the first

to flood the Fox Lake area (see James Schaefer, Chapter 8 in this volume, for more on caribou throughout northern Manitoba). Elders and
community members fear that the caribou will continue to disappear
with yet another dam; they are also very sensitive to caribou deaths, and
seeing all the caribou bodies floating in the newly formed lake was very
painful to watch for many Elders. Since that first flooding in Gillam, the
Inninuwak food system has been highly impacted as sturgeon, mariah,
and other fish as well as caribou and berries were almost extinguished.
Prior to the mid-1960s, according to the *Fox Lake Environmental Report*,
"there used to be berries growing here [in Gillam] long ago, blueberries
and those other kinds, raspberries. [Now] there's not one kind. It used to
be beautiful here with lots of berries."[24] Additionally, mercury, dust, and
other contamination as well as an increase in disturbance and harvesting
restrictions continue to affect traditional food systems.

Indeed, as local narratives indicate, hydro development destroys the
land and the animals; these are very significant and real adverse effects
of generating stations. Unlike the metanarrative that Keeyask will be
"clean," local achimowinak point to the fact that access to local environment gets "put on hold" for the construction of dams. For example,
Jack Massan and his wife, Christine, talk about Hydro-imposed "No
Trespassing" signs—and the way they resist these restrictions in their
access to the resources:

> *Christine:* We take them off. . . .
>
> *Jack:* And then there's that first one just on top of the
> Limestone River. There's a No Trespassing; you just go down
> there, that's where you go to fish. . . . I've been telling that guy
> that looks after, like the trappers and that, I've been telling
> him, how come they've been putting no trespassing signs on
> my trapline?
>
> *Christine:* He's a Hydro employee.[25]

Noah also confirms that he often goes past the "no access" signs: "This
is my trapline," he says. "I am more authorized to be here than they are.
I don't need a visitor's pass—they tell us to get a visitor's pass now. . . .
This is *my* land." Certainly, the fact that access to the traplines will be
limited, temporarily or otherwise, is rarely discussed as an impact of
hydro development. Given that federal and provincial governments have

already pushed Indigenous peoples off traditional territories, Hydro-controlled restrictions or "pass systems" to traditional lands damages local livelihoods and knowledge transmission. For many Elders, access to certain sites for cultural reasons or for resources is important for mino-pimatisiwin. Nancy Beardy, another Elder from Fox Lake Cree Nation, also spoke to CFLGC about her traditional life, reflecting on the cultural value system of food sharing and her personal memory of having seen a big sturgeon catch: "My dad was a hunter for our family, whoever wanted things, eh. That's the kind of life we had, we lived off the land. And whoever came and got something, it's, if they wanted something, like if we were short of lard or something. Whatever, you know. Whatever. If we had fish, they'd come and ask if we had fish. They killed a, a sturgeon one time. Got a big sturgeon ... holy was he long."[26]

For Nancy, these values and harvesting skills have a symbolic meaning embedded in the culture she is from. Seeing big sturgeon in the water is more than just a sign of food; it is also a sign that the Inninuwak looked after the fish and allowed the sturgeon to grow big and to reproduce. Once, while we participated in a fishing study, Noah pulled out a small whitefish. We were sitting in the boat together and Noah gently took the "little guy," as he called it, kissed it, and let it go, insisting that he still needs to grow. Thinking into the future by giving up a present source of food is part of the Inninuwak kitayatsuk responsibility to care for the land and waters at Makeso Sakahican.

Part of Keeyask's proposed solution to restricting community members' access to traplines is to relocate the harvesters so they can continue their traditional ways on areas not impacted by the construction of the Keeyask Dam. The four Keeyask Cree Nations approved this "offsetting program" within the Adverse Effects Agreement in 2009, but many of the harvesters were skeptical of the associated "benefits." At the CEC hearings, Jack Massan and his wife, Christine, laughed at the inappropriateness of the idea to relocate traditional harvesters to other territories:

CFLGC interviewer: [Manitoba Hydro said] we could move, we could move your trap, trappers to a different [area].

Christine: Elsewhere (laughs).

Jack: Elsewhere. And I said no way (laughs). . . .

Christine: Why should we move? Why don't they move?

Jack: See, that's another thing, what we're saying. What are we gonna do to help the animals? Like, gotta help the Caribou. How can we help them? Well the best way to help them is, don't do anymore damage to the bush.

Christine: Yep.

Jack: You know, just, just leave everything, what's, how it looked before, eh. You can't. That's the best way to help the animals. Yea, you don't, uh, just forget about all the construction that's going, that's going on in the bush.[27]

The Alternative Resource Use Program was a three-year, $300,000 program to temporarily move harvesters to other areas in Manitoba so they can hunt, fish, trap, and pick medicines or blueberries. However, very few harvesters from Fox Lake actually knew of the program, and fewer still had even the slightest idea how the program operated. In 2018, five years after the program was discussed at the CEC hearings, few, if any, Makeso Sakahican Elders and harvesters had taken advantage of this "opportunity."[28]

While the program was perhaps a good idea at the start, the short lifespan and unclear mechanics of this program, plus the added bureaucracy, may not only be daunting for harvesters, but it will not safeguard against what Ivan Moose calls the "continued state of poverty [the Innunuwak] live in."

Additionally, flying (or driving?) out Elders and harvesters from their own traplines to an unfamiliar—and most likely an already occupied—landscape is culturally unacceptable. Relocating people to other areas dis-members them from their homeland and from the regular access to resources that are encompassed with living mino-pimatisiwin. For many traditional harvesters, offsetting programs will do precisely that: offset, or cancel out, the relationship between trapline holders and their lines. For them, the land and land-knowledge are an extension of their heritage. Relocation to other territories causes a crisis of cosmology;[29] it upsets the local systems of knowledge and symbols that the Inninuwak have written into the landscape. The cultural practice of passing down a trapline from one member of the family to another, and the associations to specific places and spaces within this landscape, are irreplaceable.

Likewise, the way of life and security that come with a harvester's knowledge of and access to his own trapline, the intellectual and economic freedom to follow the paths of the previous generations, cannot be replaced. A harvester can choose the day to go hunting, he can select his own hours, he can set traps where he knows the animals will be; he can continue to validate his knowledge of the land through recurring visits; and he can pass on that knowledge, his skills, and aski achimowinak, "land stories," to future harvesters. Relocating harvesters to other areas of the province as part of the Alternative Resource Use Program indicates only how little Manitoba Hydro actually heard of the Inninuwak achimowinak.

With saddened voices, Elders and harvesters at the CEC hearings also voiced their fears that the traplines that are so important to the survival of Inninuwak heritage would become irrelevant with the negative effects from Keeyask. If animals will no longer be there, if trappers are not harvesting, who will pass on the culture, the skills, the language, and the stories of the landscape? The narratives of loss are minimized in the Hydro metanarrative of "clean energy" and progress. Although Inninuwak achimowinak illustrate that numerous intangible elements of culture will be impacted—elements such as language, the harvesting diet, community values like mino-pimatisiwin, and even the cultural sense of responsibility towards the land and waters, the Keeyask EIS makes no mention of how these will be impacted. Very little, if any, mention was made of the Inninuwak cultural expressions that are anchored to specific places and that serve as the foundation of the community's identity, or even to the oral [hi]stories—the atunogawinak—that are embedded within the cultural landscape that will once again be flooded out and submerged.

Jack and Christine Massan, two Makeso Sakahican Elders, share both their joy at transmitting their way of life and their sadness at the inability of young people to experience that life at Gull Rapids, where Keeyask will be.

> [Our granddaughter] wants to learn how to trap, she's great
> at fishing, she's been fishing since she was just tiny. I know
> we used to go fishing at the Gull Rapids area. Used to put
> her on the side when she was sleeping when she was just a
> little baby (laughs). Like a rock. Yea, she just loves to be out

there. She's got it in her, in her blood. She can cast better than we do. Just go. She made a book, she made a book, she won a prize, about her and grandpa fishing, and used some of the pictures we have. Cute little thing. She created it. But there are a lot of kids that don't get that opportunity, eh? And it's kind of sad.[30]

Similarly, Nancy Beardy, another Makeso Sakahican Elder, recognizes the Inninuwak sense of community that exists when families are out harvesting on the land: "And the thing that I miss too is when we used to go pick berries, like it was a family thing. And my late mum, and my grandma and all like the family would take pans and stuff with them to make bannock out in the bush and make tea and we'd pick berries and we'd make the jam outside and it was like a family picnic thing. That's what I miss too."[31]

Culture is a living presence; it is a way of life that goes beyond knowledge and use of the local environment.[32] There is not always evidence of cultural value on a landscape, but when someone is talking to local community members, culture is unveiled. Embodied through people, numerous elements of culture represent the forms of expressions such as language, songs, skills, and narratives as well as practices that connect Indigenous people to each other. It is important to extend knowledge of how the relationship to place is affected by the understanding of social relationships within a space, specifically, the *living* heritage. Although largely intangible, these elements of cultural heritage are also affected by each dam. Consequently, they are essential components that must be included as part of an environmental assessment process or any other project affecting an Indigenous community.[33] This was perhaps one of the biggest flaws in the Keeyask Environmental Impact Statement: the lack of discussion (or even mention) of the impact this generating station will have on Inninuwak elements of cultural heritage. Although the lengthy document did take into account tangible heritage such as archaeological sites, burial grounds, and sacred places that will be affected by Keeyask, a significant gap exists in the way that cultural heritage was understood and approached.[34] The one-page focus on cultural practices as merely a by-product of the environment was lost in the 400-page Supporting Volume page on Socio-Economic Environment, Resource Use and Heritage Resources.

Although in existence within the heritage discourse since 2003, the notion of "intangible cultural heritage" as interpreted by UNESCO's Convention for the Safeguarding of the Intangible Cultural Heritage was mentioned only once in the Keeyask Environmental Impact Statement and not one reference was made to the framework at the CEC hearings. Given that culture is transmitted through people, the narrow focus on the physical archaeological sites-as-culture renders the Keeyask EIS inadequate. While including cultural heritage in environmental regulations requires policy change at the federal level, it is important to point out that Manitoba Hydro can take (and should have taken) a proactive approach to understanding "heritage impacts," and enlarged its scope beyond just environmental impacts on the Inninuwak cultural landscape.

Without a doubt, Hydro development forever impacts the larger Inninuwak community, with little regard for the stories of those they are impacting. Our interviews with Elders tell of Hydro workers who take snowmobiles and chase after animals, use moose and bears as target practice, and fish for "everything and anything" they could get.[35] Noah, who worked for Manitoba Hydro once, shared stories of fish left to die in the drained pools of water prior to a dam's operation, of equipment and other construction garbage being buried rather than properly disposed of, and of an uncontrollable influx of workers from outside the community who exploited Inninuwak women. Expressing the fact that "Hydro people, they have no respect for First Nations," Noah shows me a photo in 2014 of a white stuffed teddy bear that a Hydro worker put in his trap. Frustrated at these behaviours, Noah shares with me the "side effects" of having a temporary labour force in the area: "Hunting is my life. It is what I eat. I take care of my family with my land. You know, we hunt caribou, and sometimes you see caribou in the dump there. People have seen the caribou there. Those Hydro people just throw away the caribou. Us people, we never disrespect the animals like that."[36]

With an angry voice and five years later, Noah admits that Hydro does not have control of its workers. He exclaims that "those guys, they just go under all the power lines with their skidoos into my trapline. They just take everything." The frustration is valid, as few Hydro workers seem to know anything about Inninuwak land tenure systems; despite being "guests" on Noah's trapline, even the presence of Hydro security suggests that ensuring Hydro interest is the foremost goal. Recalling the time that a security guard stopped him a few kilometres past a No Trespassing sign on his trapline, Noah reveals that the man proceeded to question him about who he was and what he was doing: "He kept telling me that this is private property," recounts Noah, "that there is no access here." Essentially telling the security guard to "eff off," as Noah explains to me, the anecdote illustrates how little knowledge Hydro workers have of the local people. To this day, these achimowinak represent "invisible data" generated in the cycle of adverse effects local community members experience on a daily basis with each successive Hydro project.

Conclusion

At the 2013 Clean Environment Commission hearings, Manitoba Hydro argued that the fragile woodlands caribou populations will not be endangered because science cannot claim with certainty that they exist in the area; that the endangered lake sturgeon populations are more likely better off with the dam because habitats and passages will be created for them. The proponents were certain that appropriate mitigation measures would be applied to address concerns over these and other sensitive species when necessary, and pushed their narrative of sustainability by arguing that Keeyask "will produce a fraction of the greenhouse gas emissions produced by a natural gas or coal station of the equivalent size."[37] While many Elders and harvesters like Noah reject Hydro's metanarrative, the Keeyask CEC hearings served as a worthwhile process for Inninuwak achimowinak to be heard, and to challenge many of Hydro's "scientific" findings within the EIS. Since a significant portion of the lands and waters they have been using since time immemorial will *again* be damaged by Hydro development, this was immensely important.

The metanarrative of Manitoba Hydro is that "only" forty-five square kilometres will be flooded with the Keeyask Generating Station. However, Inninuwak achimowinak tell us that the additional infrastructure needed for Keeyask, including access roads, transmission lines, diverse power, converter and grounding stations, and numerous others will all significantly impact larger amounts of land and the Inninuwak way of life. Perhaps within the imagination of Canada's North, forty-five square kilometres may not seem like much. However, with the surrounding area also affected, it is at least forty-five square kilometres of knowledge, experience, cultural embeddedness, wildlife habitat, and the Inninuwak homeland that is forever lost—for the purpose of selling energy to U.S. markets. It is important to emphasize that cultural knowledge specific to this area cannot be found anywhere else in the world; one cannot ever cross another set of rapids exactly like the Keeyask Rapids or affiliate the Inninuwak oral histories to these spaces. Almost in a whisper, Noah recalls the time he went fishing on the Nelson River with his partner; they were travelling towards Gull Rapids to set out nets: "We were going with our boats and then we felt something soft. It was soft. Underwater. We didn't see nothing. We looked back behind us, and we saw a whirlpool. Something had dived. So I said to my partner there, 'maybe we'll catch it in the nets.' We were setting a 300 by 2 net. . . . There are stories of the Misopisew [the Large Water Lynx] in the water. . . . But, there are no more rapids at Keeyask there now."[38]

Certainly, it took generations to learn the landscape around the Keeyask Rapids; and it will take a lot of new history to learn to navigate another landscape after this area is flooded. Once the environment of the area is lost, the knowledge of the area is lost as well. No one will ever be able to access the knowledge of the area in the same way it took generations to learn about it through an interdependent relationship. The young people—the future this project is being built for—will never have the chance to relive what was there. Due to the immense loss of knowledge, then, the Keeyask Project is not about progressing forward, but about being set back; new history must now be relearned and recreated in a Manitoba Hydro–controlled space.

With a broken voice and a heavy heart, Noah frequently acknowledges his "complicity" in the eradication of the local landscape. As we discuss the damage Hydro had done in his community, Noah, sitting in his wheelchair and with his eyes mostly covered by his baseball cap, repeats solemnly, "I worked for Hydro, me. I helped destroy my community." Sadly, the guilt of some of those Inninuwak employed at Hydro comes out occasionally; during our time together at the Fox Lake Cree Nation Negotiations Office and as part of CFLGC, Noah and I have sporadically seen both: the sorrowful expressions, and the tormented, alcohol-influenced statements of remorse from Inninuwak members receiving "Hydro money."

Indeed, as local narratives illustrate, hydro development continues to erode the mino-pimatisiwin of the Inninuwak in northern Manitoba. But one has to come to the North and see the damage done at the source of Manitoba's "clean and green" energy. In the meantime, the only evidence of the "on the ground" effects of hydro development are the Inninuwak achimowinak. And, if listened to, these narratives can tell the broader public that "clean, green, and renewable" hydro energy is, in fact, devastating the Inninuwak, their culture, their way of life, and their economy—in addition to significantly impacting aquatic and terrestrial environments. People in the South must acknowledge the burden that northern Manitoba's Indigenous people carry with each dam. In voicing the local realities of Hydro's mantras at the Keeyask CEC hearings, these small, local narratives—the achimowinak—have already, albeit slowly, began the process of deconstructing and maybe even reconstructing Hydro's metanarrative of progress.

Ni pahiten kita achimowina ekwa ki nanas komit tinawaw kiskisno-hamowina. *To all the CFLGC members and Inninuwak affected by hydro development: we thank you for sharing your stories and we acknowledge your voices. This chapter would not be complete without the invaluable work of our esteemed CFLGC colleagues Ivan Moose, Peter Kulchyski, Steph McLachlan, Jack and Christine Massan, Johnny Spence, Nancy Beardy, Ramona Neckoway, Judy DaSilva, and Thomas Nepetaybo. Insight gained from our work at the Fox Lake Negotiations Office helped us find a collective CFLGC voice. We thank the commissioners at the Keeyask hearings for providing us with the funding for this project and allowing Inninu achimowinak to be heard.*

Notes

1   A note to the readers: Linguistic structure made this co-authored article challenging to write as "we." Our options were to have APM as a single author with significant acknowledgement to Noah for providing the information, or to write in a collective voice. However, while only Noah has the lived experience of hydro development in the North, this piece could not occur without Agnieszka, who helps Noah articulates those experiences in writing beyond the Hydro meetings. As such, Agnieszka could not be part of the "we" of hydro impacts and excluding Noah as co-author was not an option. Therefore, because Noah is both a co-author and an "informant" and Agnieszka more of a "narrator," the chapter is written in a dialogical format with

Noah identified in the third person. All discussions unless otherwise stated were taken between 2012 and 2018.

2   Manitoba, n.d., "Green and Growing: Manitoba's Commitment to Green Jobs," accessed 20 June 2018, https://www.gov.mb.ca/sd/annual-reports/sdif/green_ growing.pdf/.

3   Andrea Smith, *Conquest* (Cambridge: South End Press, 2005).

4   "Agnieszka Pawlowska-Mainville: Opening Statement for CFLGC," Transcripts, volume 1, 21 October 2013, http://www.cecmanitoba.ca/hearings/.

5   Steven Best and Douglas Kellner, *Postmodern Theory* (New York: the Guilford Press, 1991), 147.

6   Ibid., 166.

7   "KHLP Presentation: Introduction to the Project," Transcripts, 21 October 2013, pages 15 and 17–19, accessed on 25 December 2013, http://www.cecmanitoba.ca/ hearings/#3.

8   "CFLGC Presentation to the CEC," Transcripts, accessed on 27 December 2014, http://www.cecmanitoba.ca/hearings/.

9   "KHLP Presentation to the CEC," Transcripts, CEC K-volume 16, 3536, accessed on 27 December 2014, http://www.cecmanitoba.ca/hearings/.

10   CFLGC, Interviews, 2013.

11   "KHLP Presentation on Aquatic and Terrestrial Environment Panel," Transcripts, 29 October 2013, p. 1235, accessed 17 December 2013, http://www.cecmanitoba. ca/resource/hearings/39/KHLP-041%20Aquatic%20&%20Terrestrial%20 Environment%20-20Part%201%20for%20print2.pdf.

12   "Robert Spence Presentation to the CEC," Transcripts, volume 15, 2013, 3363, accessed on 16 January 2013, http://www.cecmanitoba.ca/hearings/.

13   "KHLP Presentation on Aquatic and Terrestrial Effects," Transcripts, 25 October 2013, p. 68, accessed 14 August 2016, http://www.cecmanitoba.ca/resource/ hearings/39/KHLP-041%20Aquatic%20&%20Terrestrial%20Environment%20 -20Part%201%20for%20print2.pdf.

14   Fisheries and Oceans Canada, "Document Presented at the Clean Environment Commission hearings for Keeyask as CAC-002," 2014, http://www.cecmanitoba. ca/resource/hearings/39/CAC-002%20Recovery%20Potential%20Assessment%20 of%20Lake%20Sturgeon-Nelson%20River.pdf (accessed 15 January 2016).

15   "CFLGC and Noah Massan cross-examination at the CEC Keeyask Hearings," Transcripts, 10 November 2013, volume 25, 5824, accessed 30 August 2016, http:// www.cecmanitoba.ca/hearings/.

16   "Councillor Neepin, Opening Statement," Transcripts, volume 1, 21 October 2013, accessed 28 August 2016, http://www.cecmanitoba.ca/hearings/.

17   "KHLP Closing Arguments," Transcripts, accessed on 15 January 2014, http://www. cecmanitoba.ca/hearings/#3.

18   Fox Lake Cree Nation member. CFLGC, Interviews, 2013.

19   "Pimicikamak Cree Nation CEC Presentation," Transcripts, volume 22, 5071–72, 4 December 2013, accessed January 2016, http://www.cecmanitoba.ca/hearings/.

20   Noah Massan, personal communication, 2013.

21   "Stephane McLachlan Testimony," Transcripts, 10 December 2013, volume 25, 5675–78, accessed 17 January 2014, http://www.cecmanitoba.ca/hearings/.

22 Fox Lake Cree Nation, *Ninan*, Draft (Fox Lake Cree Nation, 2012), 310–12.

23 CFLGC, Interviews, 2013.

24 Fox Lake Cree Nation, *Fox Lake Environmental Report* (Fox Lake Cree Nation, 2012), 48.

25 CFLGC, Interviews, 2013.

26 Ibid.

27 Ibid.

28 In my conversation with Noah in Gillam on 10 July 2018, he indicated that neither he nor the other Elders have received any further knowledge about the Alternative Resource Use Program.

29 J.T. Carson, "Ethnography and the Native American Past," *Ethnohistory* 49, no. 4 (Fall 2002): 769–88.

30 CFLGC, Interviews, 2013.

31 Ibid.

32 Agnieszka Pawlowska-Mainville, "Stored in Bones," unpublished manuscript, 2022.

33 Ibid.

34 Ibid.

35 CFLGC, Interviews, 2013.

36 Pawlowska-Mainville, "Stored in Bones."

37 Keeyask EIS, *Environmental Impact Statement: Executive Summary* (Winnipeg: Manitoba Hydro, 2012), 7.

38 CFLGC, Interviews, 2013 and 2018.

"What about the Sturgeon?"

ROBERT SPENCE, LAND AND RESOURCE USER, TATASKWEYAK CREE NATION

Excerpt from the transcript of the Keeyask CEC hearing in Winnipeg, 14 November 2013.

Note: Robert Spence testified in both English and Cree. CEC hearing transcripts note when he switches languages with "(Cree spoken)."

What about the sturgeon? (Cree spoken) The Churchill River, the sturgeon are getting wiped out. The only place where we harvest sturgeon is at the mouth of the confluence of the little Churchill River because they have a river there that they can survive from. The Churchill little River from Fidler to Billard. No sturgeon there no more.

Yet twenty years ago is the last time anybody has harvested a sturgeon from Fidler Lake from TCN. But today there's none. Why is that? Thirty years ago, I'm guessing commercial fishing on Billard. What happened to them? Split Lake never went there in thirty years and yet fifteen years ago there was sturgeon there.

Redhead Rapids, ten, twelve years ago, there was sturgeon there, they are gone. And I heard a so-called expert say that it was overharvest[ing], it was due in part of overharvesting by First Nations people. That was a lie. Whoever said that and whoever is repeating that is also lying. Those are strong words, especially [in] my culture. Maybe in yours, too.

Same thing happening on the Nelson River. Sturgeon are dying. I fed my mama sturgeon. My dad told me when I went and fed the sturgeon to my mom (Cree spoken) I gave her that sturgeon. Boy she was happy. But my dad told me later on, Robert, that sturgeon had no taste. It's like the water. Your mom had to put ketchup on it just to give it flavour.

That's when we noticed about a lot of the fish on the Nelson River. We have tagged sturgeon there too. And as for (Cree spoken) no evidence of sturgeon spawning at Gull Rapids (Cree spoken). I thought that's crazy.

I was part of a study that went to Gull Rapids. . . . The province was part of it. When we picked up some of the sturgeon that we were tagging, they were molting. I didn't know what it was at first. They were molting which meant they were ready to spawn. A lot of the females that we caught you can tell they were females because some of the eggs were coming out. That would only happen when they are ready to spawn.

How is it that you guys are getting away with saying there's no evidence of sturgeon spawning there? (Cree spoken)

CHAPTER 7

Beavers, Sturgeon, and Terns: How River Regulation Can Affect Aquatic and Riparian Ecosystems in Northern Manitoba

ANNETTE LUTTERMANN

As earlier chapters have established, proponents of new hydroelectric generating opportunities frequently cite climate change as a reason to support dam development in the Canadian North. These projects will reduce greenhouse gas emissions and benefit the environment, the reasoning goes. However, manipulation of the seasonal cycles of water flow has numerous consequences for the health and integrity of northern river ecosystems. There is extensive habitat change related to building and operating large hydroelectric facilities. This is in addition to the fossil fuel use that does accompany these major developments throughout the planning, construction, and operations phases. We must factor these effects into the decisions we make as a society regarding our collective energy production and consumption.

The Keeyask Project is the latest dam and generating station complex to significantly alter the Nelson River. The northern Manitoba hydroelectric system has converted the Nelson, Churchill, Rat, and Burntwood rivers into a series of artificially controlled reservoirs and river channels. This chapter discusses a few of the ways the Keeyask Project can affect aquatic and riparian (shoreline) habitats and the species they support. In particular, it focuses on how changes in daily and seasonal patterns of flow caused by hydroelectric regulation can influence shoreline vegetation communities, aquatic mammals including beaver and muskrat, water birds, and fish species that are adapted to natural river flow patterns for different parts of their life cycle.

Boreal plants and animals have evolved within the context of extreme seasonal cycles of temperature and precipitation that create relatively harsh environmental conditions. Many of the birds are migratory, and those that reside in boreal regions year-round are quite resilient. The fact that there are few if any endemic[1] species in northern regions often leads decision makers to accept arguments that adverse effects on wildlife from large industrial projects are not significant, since boreal habitats and species are widespread. The Keeyask Environmental Impact Statement (EIS) reached this conclusion for many of the project's predicted effects on wildlife habitat. In other words, the reasoning says, there is plenty of habitat for moose, beavers, and ducks, so we don't have to worry about them too much.

Nonetheless, we must understand that many boreal species require large regions of suitable habitat to persist over time. The fact that these animals are resilient does not make them immune to the effects of large hydroelectric projects, especially as the overall network of dams and generating stations in addition to other industrial land uses continues to grow. Long-term Indigenous harvesters have observed numerous changes in wildlife populations since the construction of large dams began: "I stopped trapping about ten years go. The water keeps going up and down—the slush comes. There are hardly any muskrat on the river. There are some beavers—there used to be lots. Even on the trapline there is nothing. There used to be lots of geese, but over the past five years, there are not enough" (Floyd Ross, Pimicikamak trapper, Cross Lake, 17 September 2013).

As illustrated in the quote above, the human cultures that evolved in these environments have relied on the ability to harvest wildlife over wide regions. We cannot disregard the fact that the habitat degradation that results from these projects is extensive and most directly affects the Indigenous peoples in whose traditional territory these projects are located.

Seasonal Flow Changes under Hydroelectric Regulation

Dams influence aquatic and riparian ecosystems in various ways, depending on the characteristics of the river environment and the specific infrastructure and operations.[2] Direct habitat loss results not only at the site of the dams but also throughout the entire construction "footprint" of the facilities, including generating stations, dikes, access roads, transmission lines, transformer stations, and construction camps. These effects are relatively easy to assess. It is more complex to evaluate the longer-term responses of habitats and species that are subjected to modified patterns of water flow over time.

The seasonal patterns of flowing water are one of the most influential physical processes that shape the ecological characteristics of boreal river shoreline and instream habitats. Typically, northern rivers experience rising water levels during spring floods, followed by declining flows during the growing season, periodic smaller increases during heavy rain or snowfall events, and fairly stable flows under ice cover throughout the winter. During the spring melt channels will open up in the river, and often shore ice stays attached and melts in place. In some areas ice floes may build up and scour the banks and riverbed. High-energy rapids may stay open all winter and provide important staging areas for migrating birds in early spring. The life cycles of boreal plants and animals have coevolved with these seasonal patterns.

A central objective of hydroelectric dam engineering is to change and control natural water levels and flow patterns to maximize energy production capacity at any one site. This may involve flooding or diverting river channels, wetlands, and lakes. The resulting reservoirs and the downstream reaches below dams usually have radically different daily and seasonal patterns of flow than under natural conditions.

Prior to the Keeyask Project, the Nelson River had already been altered by several large dams, which dramatically changed the patterns of river flow. The Churchill River Diversion and Lake Winnipeg Regulation significantly increased the maximum flows in the Nelson River. As an example, Figure 7.1 shows two years of pre-hydroelectric development data for Split Lake in the lower Nelson River. Split Lake had a typical pattern of spring flooding followed by a gradual decline in water levels. Post-development water levels are more variable depending on whether it is a dry or wet year in the region.

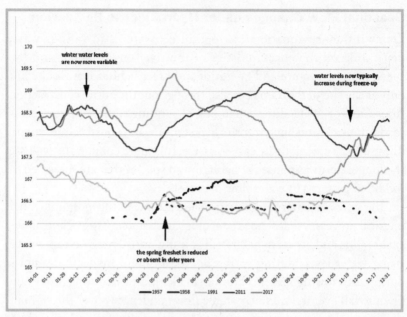

Figure 7.1. Nelson River Water Levels at Split Lake Two Years Pre- and Four Years Post-Hydroelectric Development (masl). The pre-development data are very limited but suggest the typical pattern of spring flooding followed by a gradual decline in water levels through the summer. Post-development water levels are variable depending on whether it is a dry or wet year in the region. Data extracted from the Water Survey of Canada website, https://wateroffice.ec.gc.ca/mainmenu/historical_data_index_e.html (accessed 25 October 2018).

The operation of a reservoir depends on factors such as how much water it can store and for how long, the characteristics of the hydroelectric generation station, how the system is designed to meet the demand for electricity, and any constraints placed on operations by regulators. Some reservoirs are large enough to capture the spring runoff from snow melt and higher spring rains and store this water to be used the next winter, or even the following year. Such storage reservoirs typically experience water levels that continue to rise throughout the summer during the growing season and then are drawn down over the winter. This can create wide shorelines that are unproductive for plants. Shore nesting birds may be flooded out. Increased rates of shoreline erosion in vulnerable areas and more dangerous ice conditions can result. This is the situation in the Southern Indian Lake reservoir, discussed in Chapter 3 in this volume.

Figure 7.2. Eroding Clay and Silt Banks on the Nelson River at Stephens Lake, Downstream of the Keeyask Site, in 2014. Photo: A Luttermann.

The Keeyask environmental assessment documents explained that the project's reservoir design is "run-of-river" and is one of the least damaging possible. The *Executive Summary* stated that the project will operate within a one-metre reservoir range. While a relatively small fluctuation in reservoir water levels may be preferable to a storage reservoir that has a large winter draw-down zone, this is not necessarily a good thing from an ecological perspective. A more stable water regime does not support the seasonal flooding that creates the habitat diversity typical of a large northern boreal river system. These reaches of the river will not experience the long-term ecological benefits of spring freshets in the flood plain, greatly reducing the extent and diversity of productive riverside habitats. This type of operation is typical of a "control reservoir," as illustrated in Figure 7.3. The reservoir shores will also be subject to long-term erosion as flooded upland soils and peat layers are exposed to wave action. Many areas of the Nelson River are already experiencing increased rates of erosion due to hydroelectric regulation (Figure 7.2).

Shoreline and Wetland Vegetation Communities

Any resource development project that regulates the flow of water on a large river will directly change that river's riparian and wetland habitats.[3] Hydroelectric reservoirs in which water levels are kept more stable throughout the year are sometimes described as similar to a natural lake. However, stable water levels are also not a natural characteristic of boreal rivers or lake expansions on large rivers. Many plant species that grow on river shorelines and nearby wetlands are adapted to water levels that vary with the season. In boreal regions under natural conditions, a distinct vertical zonation of plant communities, ranging from forest to shrub to herbs, sedges, and grasses, to aquatics, tends to form on the banks of lakes and large rivers (Figure 7.3).[4]

River shorelines are dynamic environments. They develop a wide variety of characteristics in response to water flow and sediment transport, especially during flood events. Eroding riverbanks in high-energy areas deposit sediments in other areas downstream, creating a constantly shifting mosaic of diverse habitats along the shoreline that provides excellent food for wildlife. Spring floods bring nutrients from the water up onto the banks of the river and deposit fine silts and sands, creating places for seeds to germinate as floodwaters slowly recede early in the growing season. For example, several species of willows and herbs such as wild mint are adapted to grow on the margins of riverbanks that are flooded in the spring and exposed as the water levels drop over the summer. Aquatic plants grow in the shallow water areas (littoral zones). These are essential habitats for many species.

River reaches with slower flow, and low areas that are flooded during high water periods, typically develop rich marsh habitats. Marsh wetlands and shrub/rich herb zones in the floodplain would not exist without the regular disturbance of spring floods.[5]

The amount of riparian habitat depends to a large extent on the difference in water levels between the highest floods in spring and the summer low-water period.[6] Peak flows from extreme flood events that may occur several years apart can also have a significant longer-term influence on the floodplain vegetation over a much wider area. Despite reassurance by the Keeyask proponent that this is the least damaging reservoir design, it should be understood that the limited active riparian zone characteristic of a "run-of-river" reservoir with narrow water level

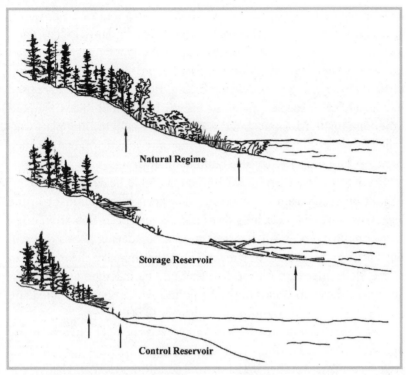

Figure 7.3. Riparian Zones Under Various Seasonal Water Level Regimes. Riparian zones that are formed under natural flow patterns with high spring floods and lower water during the growing season typically have richer vegetation communities. Storage reservoirs that are flooded during the growing season may have wide barren shores when drawn down. "Run-of-river" reservoirs with a narrow range of water levels will also have less diverse riparian zones. The arrows show a conceptual range of high and low water levels. Illustration: A Luttermann.

fluctuations will typically produce much less species-rich shorelines compared with a free-flowing river system (Figure 7.3).

Aquatic Mammals—Beaver and Muskrat

Human harvesters have long valued beaver and muskrat for their fur and meat, and they are important prey for other species. Beaver and muskrat also alter natural wetland and shoreline environments in ways that increase overall biodiversity at local and regional scales.[7]

These species are primarily herbivorous and require water bodies with good aquatic and riparian vegetation development. They both eat

aquatic plants in great quantities, which creates a mosaic of vegetation patches. In smaller streams, beavers construct dams, lodges, bank
burrows, and canals by harvesting deciduous woody vegetation and
excavating large quantities of mud, clay, and peat. They increase habitat
diversity by creating ponds, wetlands, and rich meadows that are used
by a host of other species, including insects, birds, amphibians, fish, and
other mammals. Muskrats build smaller lodges and feeding platforms
called "push-ups" in shallow water using only aquatic vegetation such
as rushes and sedges. They also build bank burrows.[8]

Prior to hydroelectric development, suitable beaver and muskrat
habitat on the Nelson River would have been most abundant in the
back bays, side channels, lee side of islands, and in smaller tributaries.
Beaver build dams on smaller streams to create deeper ponds that will
not freeze to the bottom in winter. Along the shores of the main stem
of the Nelson River, both species also build bank lodges and burrows
anywhere they can excavate the bank and where there are adequate
shrubs, rushes, grasses, and sedges adjacent to water.

The unseasonal fluctuations in water levels created by hydroelectric
operations can cause direct mortality to beaver and muscrat year after
year. As explained earlier, under natural conditions river and lake water
levels tend to slowly drop in winter or stay relatively stable after ice cover
forms in fall. Beaver and muskrat do not hibernate but spend most of
the winter actively feeding under the ice. They require water levels high
enough to maintain access to their underwater lodge entrances and to
stay protected from land predators such as wolves.[9]

The sections of northern river systems that are subject to significant,
artificial, winter water-level fluctuations may be long-term population "sinks" for beaver and muskrat. Beaver colonies will periodically
abandon sites and move if they run out of food. Also, each year, young
beaver and muskrat will disperse from their natal homes to form new
colonies or join others that do not have a mating pair. If they disperse
to regulated water bodies, depending on the existing water regime,
their chances of surviving the winter may be much lower than under
natural conditions.

In spring and summer when water levels are lower, many beaver
and muskrat have been observed moving into areas that are within the
zone of influence of hydroelectric reservoirs and downstream reaches of

Figure 7.4. A Tributary Marsh on the Upper Nelson River at Cross Lake. This marsh is isolated from the effects of regulation by causeway. Diverse vegetation will develop if water levels are suitable, providing excellent habitat for aquatic mammals, birds, fish, and others. Photo: A. Luttermann, 2016.

Figure 7.5. Beaver Lodge in the Upper Nelson River. This beaver lodge at Cross Lake was reoccupied in the summer of 2017 and then abandoned again in the fall. Water levels were very low due to regulation upstream at the Jenpeg Dam, exposing the lodge entrance and canals. Wolf tracks were abundant as beavers are vulnerable to predation when lodge entrances are exposed. Photo: A. Luttermann, 2017.

dams. There they may build new burrows, lodges, and push-ups in the late summer and early fall. These can be constructed very quickly, which means that if water levels appear suitable over a week, for example, the animals may decide to settle. In some river reaches, water levels may be drawn down in spring and summer to store water upstream, or in mid-fall to allow ice cover to form on an upstream reservoir. If water levels then rise with winter releases from hydroelectric dams after ice has formed, beaver and muskrat are frequently flooded out of their lodges, and often freeze to death into the slush ice that can form under these conditions. Forced out in the open without the protection of the lodge and ice cover in winter, they are extremely vulnerable to a host of predators, to the weather, and to starvation.

The environmental assessment report for the Keeyask Project estimated that about twenty to thirty existing beaver colonies would be directly affected by the construction, and about 5 percent of the habitat in the larger study area would be made unsuitable for beaver due to fluctuating water levels in the reservoir. The new reservoir would flood existing tributary creeks and small ponds near the Nelson River that previously hosted good beaver and muskrat habitat. The assessment concluded that the effects on beaver populations are small, since beaver are plentiful, and they can in theory populate other areas instead. In fact, the animals can relocate only if other habitat is not already occupied, so mortality would most certainly be high for the flooded-out colonies.

Mitigation measures therefore included trapping out the beavers before Manitoba Hydro cleared and filled the reservoir.[10] The beaver carcasses are distributed among local Indigenous communities and are therefore not wasted in terms of human use. This is a typical measure employed during hydroelectric reservoir development all over northern Canada. Hydro proponents argue that this harvest prevents useless mortality of beavers when they are flooded out of their homes.

Of course, these mitigation measures address the fate of only the current generation of existing beavers during construction. The overall effect of additional river regulation is a cumulative loss of suitable habitat, which will reduce the number of beaver and muskrat within the region over the long term. Because their dams and burrows help create ponds, wetlands, and rich habitat for other species, this contributes to a permanent reduction in wetland and riparian biodiversity in these riverine systems.

Avian Species—Colonial Water Birds

Existing dams and generating stations along the Nelson and Churchill rivers have almost certainly altered the distribution and abundance of breeding colonial water birds due to habitat loss and degradation. The Keeyask EIS predicted that it would cause additional loss of foraging and breeding habitat for colonial birds, including ring-billed gull, herring gull, common tern, Bonaparte's gull, and Caspian tern. These fish-eating birds typically nest in large groups on islands in rapids where there is plenty of food nearby and protection from many ground predators.

The Manitoba government has permitted the Keeyask Project to move forward under the conditions that active nests are not disturbed during construction and that there will be habitat-enhancement efforts to compensate for lost nesting grounds. Construction will make rocky islands and reefs in the middle of the river unsuitable for nesting, and the new reservoir will flood or otherwise permanently destroy several large existing nesting sites. Breeding birds may also avoid some habitat due to noise and light disturbance.

Since environmental permits for the Keeyask Project did not allow construction near active nests, a key part of the environmental protection strategy has been to use human-controlled falcons and hawks to haze gulls and terns away from the active construction sites to prevent nesting each year at most of the traditional nesting islands in the area. This is also done to protect worker safety at the site, as large numbers of birds in an area can present a hazard to helicopters, for example. The assumption is that the falcons and hawks will simply chase the water birds to other areas nearby where they may be able to successfully nest.

Monitoring the effects of Keeyask construction on colonial water birds started in 2014, using helicopters and drones to observe where the displaced birds went to nest and whether their nesting was successful. The results so far are unclear. For example, while a decreased abundance of nesting colonial water birds was evident in 2017 over 2016, reports attributed this to high water levels in 2017 that scoured some habitat rather than to construction activity.[11]

Manitoba Hydro attempted to build artificial nesting platforms for gulls and terns. As of 2019, these had not been observed to be used and therefore the program was discontinued.[12] Habitat replacement efforts will be monitored over the coming years and, if not successful, perhaps new innovations will be created that are more effective. Monitoring after reservoir filling in summer of 2020 will provide more information about the response of these populations. The net result will likely be a reduction in colonial water bird productivity in this area.

Fish and Fish Habitat—Lake Sturgeon

Lake sturgeon, or nameo, is a unique long-lived species that has considerable cultural significance to local Indigenous peoples. Previously abundant in many large rivers in North America, their populations declined due to overexploitation by commercial fisheries throughout the late 1800s to the mid-1900s.[13] Commercial and subsistence harvesting has been limited since that time, but populations have not recovered to previous levels in any major river system.

In recent years considerable research effort has been put into gaining a better understanding of lake sturgeon life history, habitat use, and threats to reproduction and survival.[14] Although progress is being made, there is still much to be learned about the combined effects of multiple hydroelectric dams on sturgeon population recovery. Habitat loss, alteration, and degradation due to hydroelectric dams in all the major rivers in Manitoba are thought to inhibit the long-term recovery of lake sturgeon.[15]

Natural recruitment (the number of young fish added to the population each year) in many parts of the Nelson River is currently very low. This may be due to the small number of adults of spawning age in many segments of the river system. Possible dam-related physical factors that may influence spawning include seasonal and daily changes in water flow, loss of former spawning habitat, degradation of rearing habitat, blockage of upstream passage by dams, and mortality of small fish that are transported through turbines. However, the fact that there is habitat that appears to be suitable but currently has very few spawning lake sturgeon may also suggest that hydroelectric dams themselves are not the only thing that is limiting population growth.[16]

Sturgeon typically spawn in swift water near the base of large rapids and falls. After spawning, whether the eggs successfully hatch depends on well-oxygenated flowing water. Larvae then settle down under sand or gravel in the riverbed. Once sufficiently developed, they disperse by drifting downstream with the flow of water. In their first year of life sturgeon may depend on sandy river bottoms for feeding effectively, where they are vulnerable to predation by many other species. Older fish use a variety of habitats for feeding on bottom-dwelling creatures, and so their survival may not be as affected by habitat alteration caused by dams.[17]

Dam construction and reservoir creation have already destroyed numerous natural falls and rapids in regulated rivers throughout Manitoba. Each new dam contributes to the cumulative loss and degradation of pre-existing spawning habitat for sturgeon and several other aquatic species. The Keeyask Generating Station reservoir has flooded two large sets of rapids that previously supported sturgeon spawning. The hope is that sturgeon will be able to spawn at the base of the new Keeyask Generating Station in the future. There are plans to monitor sturgeon spawning at the site and possibly operate the spillway to try to increase spawning success.

In 2006 the Committee on the Status of Endangered Wildlife in Canada recommended that several populations of lake sturgeon, including the Nelson River populations, be listed as "Endangered" under the federal Species at Risk Act.[18] That status report stated that overexploitation and dams were the primary historical threats, and that currently dams probably present the most important threat to recovery. In 2017 an updated status report explained that there is increased evidence to suggest that lake sturgeon can spawn in rapids below some dams; that growth rates in some reservoirs are good; and that both wild-bred and stocked young sturgeon are surviving in regulated sections of northern Manitoba rivers.[19]

Research in other river systems has provided some evidence that lake sturgeon are most negatively affected by river regulation, as compared with other stressors such as water contamination.[20] For example, in the Ottawa River lake sturgeon were found to be more abundant in unflooded reaches. The faster growth observed in reservoirs was thought to be related to the lower density of fish in those bodies of water, which increases the relative amount of available food.[21]

The Saskatchewan–Nelson river populations as a whole are still considered to be endangered. However, the federal government has not made a decision regarding listing these populations under the Species at Risk Act. Part of the reason for this is that habitat for this species is ostensibly protected under the federal Fisheries Act. Nevertheless, federal and provincial governments continue to permit new megaprojects such as Keeyask as long as there are commitments to monitor fish communities and implement mitigation works to try to compensate for the destruction of additional critical habitat. The drive to build more hydroelectric generating stations on the Nelson River is a major incentive to support this work.

Fish communities are receiving more research and monitoring attention than many other environmental components of affected river systems. However, there is a significant lack of pre- and post-hydroelectric development data on fish habitat characteristics and fish populations in Manitoba. Mitigation planning intended to compensate for the additional destruction of sturgeon-spawning habitat at the Keeyask Project is still largely experimental in nature, since rivers are unique and little previous habitat-enhancement work has been attempted for sturgeon or other fish species in these northern rivers.

In order to attempt to increase wild populations, Manitoba has implemented a stocking program in the Nelson River.[22] Stocking young fish from a hatchery in Grand Rapids operated by Manitoba Hydro is one of the major mitigation programs intended to offset the habitat loss from existing and new dams. This effort is showing potential for enhancing wild populations, as some released hatchery fish have been recaught later, demonstrating survival and growth in regulated environments. However, it remains to be seen whether stocking fish in these northern regulated environments will in fact lead to self-sustaining populations.[23] Male fish reach reproductive age in twelve to twenty years. For females it may take as long as fifteen to thirty years to reach maturity, and they will then spawn only once every three to seven years.[24] Monitoring the potential reproductive success of hatchery fish will require long-term effort.

Lake sturgeon habitat compensation is a major condition of environmental licensing for the Keeyask project. Manitoba Hydro is monitoring adult fish movement during construction, and considerable effort was made to rescue several species of stranded fish as sections of the river were drained.[25] Mitigation efforts will continue, including attempts to recreate effective spawning and rearing habitat. Nevertheless, each new major development on the Nelson River arguably makes it increasingly difficult to support the long-term goal of self-sustaining lake sturgeon populations in these river systems.

Large-Scale Hydroelectric Development— A Solution to Climate Change?

The acknowledged need to radically decrease the rate at which we burn fossil fuels is lending more support to the corporate and political drive to develop additional large hydroelectric projects in northern Canada.[26] It is indisputable that widespread burning of fossil fuels is creating changes in our global climate that will inevitably lead to many harmful consequences for ecosystems and human communities. This is one of the largest global threats that we are facing, partly because it affects everyone on the planet.[27]

Climate change risks include declines in biodiversity, loss of habitat, changes in the distribution and abundance of wildlife and plant species, and fluctuations in precipitation and weather patterns that alter water flows in rivers, leading to more extreme floods and droughts.[28] Regulating the flow of large rivers creates many similar changes at local and regional scales. Unusual patterns in water levels degrade habitats for aquatic and riparian species, and impede people's traditional and current use of the land and waterways. Altering the distribution and abundance of fish and wildlife affects local Indigenous livelihoods and food security.

Hydroelectricity has long been marketed to the general public as "green" power. Water recirculates in a global cycle, constantly returning to rivers, and thus hydroelectricity is described as "renewable" compared with burning fossil fuels. It is true that hydroelectric power has much lower greenhouse gas emissions than burning coal or oil per unit of energy generated. Initiatives focused on the electrification of modes of transportation, for example, are important and worthy to pursue. However, it is also essential to acknowledge the direct, widespread, and long-term negative ecological and social justice consequences that are related to river regulation, and to consider this in the context of our total energy production and consumption.

In our search for solutions to reduce the risks associated with climate change, we cannot ignore the numerous adverse effects of hydroelectric development. The cumulative effects of all forms of industrial energy use and production at a global scale are significant. It is reasonable to argue that we need to work much more diligently towards reducing our per capita consumption of all forms of industrially generated energy, rather than focusing on producing ever larger quantities of marketable power. As others have pointed out, this form of restraint is a hard sell politically since energy production is very big business.

Due to more rigorous provincial and federal environmental assessment and licensing requirements, the level of effort invested in pre-development data collection, analysis, and post-development monitoring commitments has increased substantially for the more recently initiated hydroelectric projects in Canada, including Wuskwatim, Keeyask, and Bipole III.[29] However, provincial and federal regulators have deemed the myriad effects of each new project to be "acceptable." There is still a serious lack of detailed long-term baseline data needed to inform robust cumulative effects assessment.[30]

From the perspective of many Indigenous peoples in northern Canadian communities, hydroelectric development produces a number of effects on a local and regional scale that are similar to many of the predicted threats of climate change. The claim that more large-scale hydroelectric projects are necessary to combat climate change is alarming at the very least. As each one of these projects is developed, concern over the ongoing incremental degradation of major river systems increases.

Exacerbating this concern is the fact that some of the proposed mitigation efforts to protect wetlands and vegetation, beaver and muskrat, gulls and terns, and at-risk fish communities like lake sturgeon are experimental in nature and will not likely offset many of the adverse effects at a meaningful scale. Ecosystems are complex; it is difficult to predict exactly how specific efforts will affect the whole. Early mitigation results are mixed and will require long-term monitoring to determine whether they are successful. New strategies may need to be developed using adaptive management and sustainability criteria, as explored in the final section of this book. In the meantime, what is certain is the overall detrimental effect of large projects such as Keeyask on aquatic and riparian ecosystems, and the life they support: "Studies should be done here and all the places where the wetlands have been affected already. There are not many ducks in our marshlands compared to before. There are few water creatures compared to before, like water striders, crayfish, and even caddis flies. The animals move around and there are large areas on the Nelson, Churchill and Burntwood rivers where the marshlands are not like they were" (Danny Halcrow, Interview with the author, Cross Lake, 14 September 2013).

There is much more to be learned about the state of wildlife habitat in northern Manitoba associated with the extensive flow manipulation of large-scale hydroelectric facilities. It is necessary to increase efforts to mitigate the adverse effects of existing dams in close collaboration with all affected Indigenous peoples.

Notes

1   Endemic species are those that are exclusively found in particular locations rather than being widely distributed across a landscape.
2   R.M. Baxter, "Environmental Effects of Dams and Impoundments," *Annual Review of Ecology and Systematics* 8 (1977): 255–83; David Rosenberg, M. Fikret

Berkes, Richard A. (Drew) Bodaly, Robert E. Hecky, C.A. Kelly, and John Rudd, "Large-Scale Impacts of Hydroelectric Development," *Environmental Reviews* 5, no. 1 (1997): 27–54; Christer Nilsson, Catherine Reidy, Matts Dynesius, and Carmen Revenga, "Fragmentation and Flow Regulation of the World's Large River Systems," *Science* 308, no. 5720 (2005): 405–08.

3   Christer Nilsson and Magnus Svedmark, "Basic Principles and Ecological Consequences of Changing Water Regimes: Riparian Plant Communities," *Environmental Management* 30, no. 4 (2002): 468–80.

4   Alison M. Fox, "Macrophytes" in *The Rivers Handbook: Hydrological and Ecological Principles*, vol. 1., ed., P. Calow and G.E. Petts (Oxford: Blackwell Scientific Publications, 1992); George P. Malanson, *Riparian Landscapes* (Cambridge: Cambridge University Press, 1993).

5   Beth Middleton, *Wetland Restoration, Flood Pulsing, and Disturbance Dynamics* (New York: John Wiley and Sons, 1999).

6   Christer Nilsson and Paul A. Keddy, "Predictability of Change in Shoreline Vegetation in a Hydroelectric Reservoir, Northern Sweden," *Canadian Journal of Fisheries and Aquatic Sciences* 45 (1988): 1896–1904; Christer Nilsson and Magnus Svedmark, "Basic Principles and Ecological Consequences of Changing Water Regimes: Riparian Plant Communities," *Environmental Management* 30, no. 4 (2002): 468–80; Roland Jansson, Christer Nilsson, Mats Dynesius, and Elisabet Andersson, "Effects of River Regulation on River-margin Vegetation: A Comparison of Eight Boreal Rivers," *Ecological Applications* 10, no. 1 (2000): 201–24.

7   Michael Pollock, Robert Naiman, Heather Erickson, Carol Johnston, John Pastor, and Gilles Pinay, "Beaver As Engineers: Influences on Biotic and Abiotic Characteristics of Drainage Basins," in *Linking Species and Ecosystems*, ed. C.G. Jones and J.H. Lawton (New York: Chapman and Hall, 1995), 117–26; Justin Wright, Clive Jones, and Alexander Flecker, "An Ecosystem Engineer, the Beaver, Increases Species Richness at the Landscape Scale," *Oecologia* 132 (2002): 96–101; Amanda Little, Glenn Guntenspergen, and Timothy Allen, "Wetland Vegetation Dynamics in Response to Beaver (*Castor Canadensis*) Activity at Multiple Scales," *EcoScience* 19, no. 3 (2012): 246–57; Carol Johnston, *Beavers: Boreal Ecosystem Engineers* (Cham: Springer, 2017); Moez Touihri, Julie Labbé, Louis Imbeau, and Marcel Darveau, "North American Beaver (*Castor Canadensis* Kuhl) Key Habitat Characteristics: Review of the Relative Effects of Geomorphology, Food Availability and Anthropogenic Infrastructure," *Ecoscience* 25, no. 1 (2018): 9–23.

8   William Clark, "Ecology of Muskrats in Prairie Wetlands," in *Prairie Wetland Ecology: The Contribution of the Marsh Ecology Research Program*, ed. H.R. Murkin, A.G. van der Valk, and William R. Clark (Ames: Iowa State Press, 2000), 287–313; François Messier and John Virgl, "Differential Use of Bank Burrows and Lodges by Muskrats (Ondatra Zibethicus) in a Northern Marsh Environment," *Canadian Journal of Zoology* 70, no. 6 (1992): 1180–84.

9   Michael Ervin, "Population Characteristics and Habitat Selection of Muskrats (Ondatra Zibethicus) in Response to Water Level Management at the Summerberry Marsh Complex, The Pas, Manitoba, Canada," M.Sc. thesis, Iowa State University, 2011.

10   Manitoba Clean Environment Commission, *Report on Public Hearing: Keeyask Generation Project*, Winnipeg, April 2014, http://www.cecmanitoba.ca/resource/Reports/Keeyask%20WEB%20FINAL2.pdf; Wildlife Resource Consulting Services, *Keeyask Generation Project Terrestrial Effects Monitoring Plan Report*

#TEMP-2018-19: Beaver Habitat Effects and Mortality 2016 to 2018, report prepared for Manitoba Hydro, Winnipeg, June 2018. https://keeyask.com/wp-content/uploads/2018/06/TEMP-2018-19-Beaver-Habitat-Effects-and-Mortality-Monitoring.pdf.

11   Wildlife Resource Consulting Services, *Keeyask Generation Project Terrestrial Effects Monitoring Plan Report #TEMP-2018-09: Colonial Waterbird Habitat Enhancement Monitoring 2017*, report prepared for Manitoba Hydro, Winnipeg, June 2018, https://keeyask.com/wp-content/uploads/2018/06/TEMP-2018-09-Colonial-Waterbird-Habitat-Enhancement-Monitoring.pdf; Wildlife Resource Consulting Services, *Keeyask Generation Project, Beaver Habitat Effects and Mortality 2016 to 2018*.

12   Wildlife Resource Consulting Services, *Keeyask Generation Project Terrestrial Effects Monitoring Plan Report #TEMP-2019-08: Colonial Waterbird Habitat Effects Monitoring 2019*, report prepared for Manitoba Hydro, Winnipeg, June 2019, https://keeyask.com/wp-content/uploads/2019/07/TEMP-2019-08-Colonial-Waterbird-Habitat-Effects-Monitoring.pdf.

13   Kenneth Stewart and Douglas Watkinson, *The Freshwater Fishes of Manitoba* (Winnipeg: University of Manitoba Press, 2004).

14   See, for example, Darcy Pisiak, L.T. Dolce Blanchard, and Don MacDonell, *Results of the 2010 Fish Community Investigations Focusing on Lake Sturgeon in the Conawapa Study Area*, report prepared for Manitoba Hydro by North/South Consultants, Winnipeg, 2011; Claire Hrenchuk and Cam Barth, *Adult Lake Sturgeon Investigations in the Keeyask Study Area, 2012*, report prepared for Manitoba Hydro by North/South Consultants, Winnipeg, 2013; Craig McDougall, Paul Blanchfield, and Gary Anderson, "Linking Movements of Lake Sturgeon (Acipenser Fulvescens Rafinesque, 1817) in a Small Hydroelectric Reservoir to Abiotic Variables," *Journal of Applied Ichthyology* 30, no. 6 (2014): 1149–59; Craig McDougall, Steve Peake, and Gary Anderson, "Downstream Passage of Lake Sturgeon through a Hydroelectric Generating Station: Passage Route Determination, Survival, and Fine-scale Movements," *North American Journal of Fisheries Management* 34, no. 3 (2014): 546–58; Manitoba Hydro, *Lake Sturgeon in Manitoba: A Summary of Current Knowledge*, Winnipeg, 2016, https://www.hydro.mb.ca/environment/pdf/lake_sturgeon_summary.pdf; Trent Sutton and Craig McDougall, *Assessment of Lake Sturgeon Spawning Habitat Suitability below the Kettle Generating Station*, a Lake Sturgeon Stewardship and Enhancement Program report prepared for Manitoba Hydro by North/South Consultants, Winnipeg, 2016.

15   Committee on the Status of Endangered Wildlife in Canada (COSEWIC), *COSEWIC Assessment and Status Report on the Lake Sturgeon Acipenser Fulvescens, Western Hudson Bay Populations, Saskatchewan-Nelson River Populations, Southern Hudson Bay-James Bay Populations and Great Lakes-Upper St. Lawrence Populations in Canada* (Ottawa: COSEWIC, 2017), https://www.registrelep-sararegistry.gc.ca/default.asp?lang=En&n=25C7260C-1&printfullpage=true.

16   Manitoba Hydro, *Lake Sturgeon Stewardship & Enhancement Program Annual Report*, Winnipeg, 2016, https://www.hydro.mb.ca/environment/pdf/lake_sturgeon_annual_report_2016.pdf.

17   Manitoba Hydro, *Lake Sturgeon in Manitoba: A Summary of Current Knowledge*, https://www.hydro.mb.ca/environment/pdf/lake_sturgeon_summary.pdf.

18   The purpose of the Species at Risk Act is to prevent wildlife species in Canada from disappearing; to provide for the recovery of species that are extirpated (no

longer exist in the wild in Canada), endangered, or threatened as a result of human activity; and to manage species of special concern to prevent them from becoming endangered or threatened. Committee on the Status of Endangered Wildlife in Canada, *COSEWIC Assessment and Update Status Report on the Lake Sturgeon Acipenser Fulvescens in Canada* (Ottawa: COSEWIC, 2006), www.sararegistry.gc.ca/status/status_e.cfm.

19 COSEWIC, *Assessment and Status Report* (2017).

20 Tim Haxton, Mike Friday, T. Cano, and Charles Hendry, "Assessing the Magnitude of Effect of Hydroelectric Production on Lake Sturgeon Abundance in Ontario," *North American Journal of Fisheries Management* 35 (2015): 930–41; Tim Haxton and Scott Findlay, "Variation in Lake Sturgeon (Acipenser Fulvescens) Abundance and Growth among River Reaches in a Large Regulated River," *Canadian Journal of Fisheries and Aquatic Sciences* 65 (2008): 645–57.

21 Moira Ferguson and George Duckworth, "The Status and Distribution of Lake Sturgeon, Acipenser Fulvescens, in the Canadian Provinces of Manitoba, Ontario, and Québec: A Genetic Perspective," *Environmental Biology of Fishes* 48, no. 1–4 (1997): 299–309; David C. Caroffino, Trent M. Sutton, Robert F. Elliott, and Michael C. Donofrio, "Early Life Stage Mortality Rates of Lake Sturgeon in the Peshtigo River, Wisconsin," *North American Journal of Fisheries Management* 30, no. 1 (2010): 295–304.

22 Cheryl Klassen, Yhana Michaluk, Laura Groening, and Meagan Alexander, *Lake Sturgeon Production and Stocking Summary for Birthday Rapids and Burntwood River Populations, October 2015 to September 2016: Year 3 Construction*, Keeyask Generation Project Fisheries Off-Setting and Mitigation Report #FOMP-2017-01 (Winnipeg: Manitoba Hydro, June 2017).

23 A.L. Smith and D. Hobden, *Lake Sturgeon (Acipenser Fulvescens) Stocking in North America* (Peterborough, ON: Fish and Wildlife Branch, Ontario Ministry of Natural Resources, 2009).

24 COSEWIC, *Assessment and Status Report* (2017).

25 Claire Hrenchuk, Christine Lacho, and Cam Barth, *Adult Lake Sturgeon Movement Monitoring in the Nelson River between Clark Lake and the Limestone Generating Station, October 2016 to October 2017: Year 4 Construction*, Keeyask Generation Project Aquatic Effects Monitoring Plan Report #AEMP-2018-03, report prepared for Manitoba Hydro by North/South Consultants, Winnipeg, June 2018.

26 Elizabeth Ingram, "Canadian PM Announces Federal System for Price on Carbon Pollution to Be in Place in 2019," *Hydro Review* (25 October 2018).

27 Nick Watts et al., "The 2018 Report of the Lancet Countdown on Health and Climate Change: Shaping the Health of Nations for Centuries to Come," *The Lancet* 392, no. 10163 (28 November 2018): 2479–514.

28 Intergovernmental Panel on Climate Change, "Summary for Policymakers," in *Global Warming of 1.5°C: An IPCC Special Report* (Geneva: World Meteorological Organization, 2018): 7–10. https://www.ipcc.ch/site/assets/uploads/sites/2/2019/05/SR15_SPM_version_report_LR.pdf.

29 Coordinated Aquatic Monitoring Program, *Three Year Summary Report (2008–2010)*, report prepared for the Manitoba Hydro MOU Working Group by North/South Consultants, Winnipeg, 2014.

30 Michel Bérubé, "Cumulative Effects Assessments at Hydro-Québec: What Have We Learned?" *Impact Assessment and Project Appraisal* 25, no. 2 (2007): 101–09;

Peter Duinker, Erin Burbidge, Samantha Boardley, and Lorne Greig, "Scientific Dimensions of Cumulative Effects Assessment: Toward Improvements in Guidance for Practice," *Environmental Reviews* 21 (2013): 40–52; Manitoba Hydro, *Regional Cumulative Effects Assessment for Hydroelectric Developments on the Churchill, Burntwood and Nelson River Systems*, Phase II Report, Winnipeg, 2015, https://www.hydro.mb.ca/regulatory_affairs/regional_cumulative_effects_assessment.shtml; Manitoba Hydro, *Regional Cumulative Effects Assessment for Hydroelectric Developments on the Churchill, Burntwood and Nelson River Systems: Integrated Summary Report*, Winnipeg, 2017, https://www.hydro.mb.ca/regulatory_affairs/pdf/rcea/rcea_integrated_summary.pdf; Manitoba Clean Environment Commission, *A Review of the Regional Cumulative Effects Assessment for Hydroelectric Developments on the Nelson, Burntwood, and Churchill River Systems*, Winnipeg, May 2018, http://www.cecmanitoba.ca/resource/hearings/42/RCEA%20Design%20Web%20Accessible%20May24.pdf.

" You destroy the essence of our lives, the spirit of it, and that we are connected to this land. . . . We are the Pimicikamak people. We believe we are the land. . . . We are part of the animals. . . . We gather berries, we heal our bodies, we gather medicines to heal our bodies. We are one with this land, we are one with the water, we are one with these animals. We are also one with the very fibre of such ecological destruction that's happened to us. So we die inside."

Tommy Monias, Pimicikamak,
CEC hearings (9 October 2013), 25

CHAPTER 8

The Conservation of Caribou: Matters of Space, Time, and Scale

JAMES A. SCHAEFER

They represent some of the most mobile pedestrians on the planet. Among terrestrial animals, they exhibit the longest migrations[1] and the largest home ranges.[2] They are among nature's most efficient walkers, expending about half of the energy expected for a 100-kilogram ungulate.[3] They have been key to the survival of people at least since the emergence of modern humans.[4] Today, they likely represent the most daunting conservation challenge in Canada.[5]

They are caribou (*Rangifer tarandus*), a species that often commands disproportionate attention and scrutiny. In northern environmental assessments, including the Keeyask hydroelectric project, caribou are frequently singled out as a valued ecosystem component. Indigenous people have maintained a special relationship with caribou, made clear by the frequent concerns and intimate knowledge expressed by the four Keeyask Cree Nations, Concerned Fox Lake Grassroots Citizens, Kaweechiwasihk Kay-Tay-A-Ti-Suk, and the Manitoba Métis Federation.[6] Even this edited volume (with just one chapter devoted to a single terrestrial species) is testament to caribou as an important and charismatic animal.

This attention is likely deserved. Among mammals, largebodied species are more prone to decline[7] and extinction.[8] Large-bodied animals are also valuable to conservation. Because of their demands for space, such animals may serve as umbrella species. That is, by conserving caribou, we might enhance the conservation of other boreal species, including small mammals, birds, beetles, and ants.[9] Caribou are also recognized as an indicator of the connectedness of the boreal forest,[10] perhaps embodying the Cree concept of "kistihtamahwin," the deep respect for all interconnected beings, taught to us by Elder Steve Ducharme in Chapter 3 of this volume. The conservation of caribou, therefore, is likely to further the conservation of biodiversity on a broad front.

Charisma, however, does not guarantee conservation. Many of the best-known wildlife species in the world are declining; some are likely headed for extinction.[11] For caribou, too, recent numerical and geographic patterns underscore their circumpolar decline. Without a change in this trajectory, the prospects for caribou—especially forest-dwelling caribou—are bleak.[12] We can be confident about one matter: the issue of caribou conservation is likely only to rise in the coming decades.

Here, I explore the essentials of caribou ecology and conservation. Using Keeyask as a platform, I focus on the challenges and opportunities of conserving caribou in Canada's North. To keep caribou on the landscape—a long-lived animal of nearly unparalleled mobility—is to grapple with vast spatial and temporal scales. As a starting point, projects like Keeyask need to be assessed on scales that are on par with the biology of this animal.

The Conservation of Two Ecotypes

At its heart, wildlife conservation is about detecting, diagnosing, and reversing declines.[13] This means identifying population limiting factors—the variables that govern the rate of population growth.[14] For this reason, it is essential to differentiate two ecotypes of caribou: the migratory ecotype and the sedentary ecotype.[15] While biologists generally agree on these ecotypic designations, the labels may vary. Migratory caribou are sometimes called "barren-ground" or "forest-tundra" caribou. Sedentary caribou are often referred to as "woodland," "forest-dwelling," or "boreal" caribou. In the Keeyask area, too, Cree Nations distinguish a small number of local caribou (Mistikoskaw utikuk—"caribou of a wooded area") from smaller-bodied, migratory caribou (Puskwaw utikosisak—"small caribou of a barren land") and coastal caribou (Namowin atikok—"caribou from the north east").[16]

Indigenous knowledge seems to mirror scientists' designations of two ecotypes.

In recent decades across the circumpolar North, most caribou populations have been declining.[17] For sedentary caribou, nearly half (seventeen of thirty-six) of boreal forest populations in Canada whose numerical trend was known have been decreasing.[18] This is the reiteration of a global trend.[19] Many migratory herds are declining, too.[20] In the vicinity of the Keeyask Project, this includes the migratory Beverly Qamanirjuaq herd[21] and Pen Islands herd. For the Pen Islands herd, although the exact numerical trends are not well understood, the population recently shifted its calving grounds.[22] Such a shift often signals a decline in numbers.[23] Scientific and Indigenous knowledge agree on these trends. Cree Nations, too, report decreases in caribou of all types in the Keeyask region since the 1950s.[24]

Geographic evidence retells these declines. In North America by the beginning of the twenty-first century, caribou had disappeared from 24 percent of their historic range[25] and woodland caribou (the threatened "boreal" population) vanished from 40 percent of their range,[26] leaving a broad zone of extirpation at the southern portion of their former distribution. This range loss reflects patterns of endangered species worldwide. A species' decline is often in one geographic direction; any remnant populations tend to persist at the range margin, away from the detrimental sweep of humans.[27] Caribou exemplify this pattern. Their range collapse coincides with the expanding northward reach of industrial activities into the boreal forest.[28] Remaining populations may persist in islands of intact habitat. Isolated, they are still at risk of extinction, even inside national and provincial parks.[29] Such areas have been generally insufficient in size to ensure viable populations. (See "Matters of Space," below.)

Why these declines? The distinction between ecotypes is crucial here, because migratory and sedentary caribou differ demographically. For sedentary caribou, the immediate limiting factor is often predation, although the ultimate cause can usually be traced to habitat disturbances. Citing more than a dozen studies, Callaghan and colleagues wrote: "There is wide agreement that the primary proximate limiting factor for boreal caribou populations is predation, driven by human-induced or natural landscape changes that favour early seral stages and higher densities of alternative prey."[30] Those predators are often wolves (*Canis lupus*)[31] and black bears (*Ursus americanus*).[32] In addition, invading white-tailed deer may transmit the meningeal worm (*Parelaphostrongylus tenuis*), a parasite lethal to caribou.[33]

How we define "habitat" is crucial. For caribou, the definition must encompass habitat in its broad sense—not merely vegetation, topography, and other easily mapped features but predators and their alternate prey. For the persistence of forest-dwelling caribou, refugia from disturbances are pivotal.[34]

The two ecotypes differ in abundance, too. The population densities of sedentary caribou are typically low and unchanging—a median density across North America of 0.066 animals per square kilometre.[35] This stands in contrast to their migratory counterparts where, in a few decades, herds may show 100-fold changes in numbers, sometimes reaching densities of more than one animal per square kilometre.[36] For barrenground caribou (although wolf predation is important),[37] food tends to be the principal limiting agent, especially when their populations reach high numbers.[38] There is mounting evidence that these swings in abundance may ultimately be governed by oscillations in climate.[39] (This underscores the seriousness of regional-scale, cumulative effects assessments, like the one studied in the next chapter in this volume, that fail to gauge the impending effects of climate change.)

If there are detrimental effects of industrial developments like Keeyask, therefore, they likely exacerbate these limiting factors—i.e., heightened predation on woodland caribou, and compromised food sources for barrenground caribou. These direct effects are likely to be exacerbated by the disruptive, indirect effects of climate change, which are still only partially understood.[40]

Matters of Space

Underlying our understanding of caribou is their single most striking feature: use of space. Indeed, the two ecotypes are distinguished on how they use space—in particular, on how females distribute themselves at calving time.[41] In the spring, females typically either band together to give birth (the migratory ecotype) or they spread apart (the sedentary ecotype). Both are interpreted as strategies to minimize predation risk.[42] Both appear to be ingrained in female caribou. Switches in this behaviour between ecotypes, if they occur at all, are exceedingly rare.[43]

This implies that the two ecotypes are distinct and that one cannot readily substitute for the other.

Virtually all caribou have immense requirements for space. A useful and common metric is the home range—the area traversed by an animal in one year. Home ranges of sedentary caribou tend to be in the hundreds or thousands of square kilometres—for example, in northern Ontario, roughly 3,600 to 5,300 square kilometres for an adult female.[44] Migratory caribou are renowned for their mobility. Home range sizes of females are typically 23,000 to 98,000 square kilometres for the Pen Island herd[45] and 160,000 to 208,000 square kilometres for the Beverly Qamanirjuaq herd.[46]

This poses a conceptual problem. Such scales, whether expressed in thousands of square kilometres or millions of hectares, tend to outstrip our comprehension. To make them more understandable, I find it useful to apply a more familiar geographic unit—say, the area of Prince Edward Island (PEI). Converted into those units, the area of these home ranges is nearly one PEI for sedentary caribou, and thirty-three PEIs for migratory caribou. The practical problem of caribou conservation becomes clear. Even some of the largest protected areas in the country fail to match these scales. Pukaskwa National Park (0.33 PEI), Quetico Provincial Park (0.82 PEI), and Banff National Park (1.17 PEI) have all lost their caribou populations.[47]

Especially for sedentary caribou, the need for space is most acute during the calving and postcalving periods (generally from late May until midsummer). During this time, in the words of Tom Bergerud, sedentary caribou females "space out," such that they occupy their entire population range as they disperse into the boreal forest and peatlands. Migratory caribou "space away," exemplified by their long migration to calving grounds on the tundra, north of the treeline, where they distance themselves from wolves and gather to give birth.[48]

Female caribou show strong site fidelity, too—a tendency to return to their previous calving and postcalving locations. For woodland caribou, a female may return to precisely the same spot each year.[49] Such behaviour is adaptive; more pronounced site fidelity is correlated with higher survival of the calf.[50] Migratory caribou show less site tenacity; their annual return to traditional calving grounds may shift somewhat each year.[51] Both ecotypes show little fidelity to winter locations, often separated by tens or hundreds of kilometres, one year to the next.[52] This, too, appears adaptive. Female woodland caribou survive better when they show lower fidelity to winter locations.[53] Space is pivotal to survival.

Not surprisingly, confining caribou can have detrimental effects. Where habitat becomes disturbed, female caribou tend to move less;[54] they contract the size of their home ranges[55] and, consequently, they appear to show stronger range fidelity.[56] The effects can be both physiological (heightened stress hormones)[57] and, as noted above, demographic (heightened mortality).[58]

Nearly two decades ago, Chris Johnson and colleagues concluded that "there is a large body of compelling evidence to support the assertion that caribou have a negative response to human disturbances."[59] Conserving space is key to conserving caribou.

Of course, in ecology, we are interested in cause and effect. To pinpoint the reasons for a decline, the most compelling signal is often demographic: impairments to survival or reproduction. An important milestone for conserving woodland caribou, therefore, are the comprehensive analyses linking population condition to habitat condition—in particular, the work spearheaded by Environment Canada in 2011 and by Cheryl Johnson and colleagues in 2020.[60] By marshalling studies from across the species' distribution in Canada, these analyses revealed lower caribou recruitment (i.e., fewer additions to the adult population) and lower caribou survival on more disturbed ranges, especially when altered by humans. This is a clear example of cumulative effects assessment. The approach demands that all forms of disturbance, both human caused and natural, are considered in aggregate, rather than in isolation. The implications are clear. To assess such projects as Keeyask, we must understand the broad ecological context. For caribou, the consequences of a piecemeal approach to managing boreal forest habitat are obvious.[61]

These studies also provide a definition of critical habitat. To meet conservation objectives, we can surmise that roughly two-thirds of woodland caribou range must be in undisturbed condition.[62] Although it is tantalizing to use this relationship as a threshold,[63] we must be cautious.[64] "The challenge to management of any wild resource," noted Paul Dayton in *Science*, "is to provide a buffer for uncertainties."[65]

Two forms of uncertainty are noteworthy. One form stems from variation in the relationship between recruitment and disturbance itself. Indeed, there is still much variation unaccounted for in this relationship;

circumstances unique to each caribou population could result in dramatically different outcomes.[66] The other form of uncertainty stems from chance events—natural disturbances like wind, insects, and fire. Indeed, in the Keeyask region, fire is a recurrent if unpredictable occurrence.[67] Manitoba Hydro's Keeyask Environmental Impact Statement was frank: "A single large and/or severe fire could substantially alter habitat composition over the long term, which could alter many of the terrestrial environment predictions."[68] A margin of security against both types of uncertainties is essential—especially given the prolonged and uncertain recovery of habitat (see "Matters of Time," below). When the effects may be irreversible, wisely managing forests means not foreclosing on options.[69]

Matters of Time

Time can complicate our understanding of caribou; it can obscure the path toward conservation. Such complications arise from the vast temporal scales of ecological processes in the North—often decades or longer.

The boreal forest is a dynamic, fire-prone ecosystem. Woodland caribou generally require old forests, and areas burned less than forty to fifty years ago are unsuitable.[70] Although caribou eventually reinhabit areas disturbed by fire (after all, the whole boreal forest has burned at one time or another), a major uncertainty remains: Will caribou reoccupy forests disturbed by logging or other industrial activities? At this point, we have only cursory observations, and only at small spatial scales.[71] We have not witnessed recovery of habitat, once disturbed by industry and once caribou have disappeared, at the scale of a whole population.[72] This may be due to one of two reasons: either such habitat has not had enough time to recover, or it will not recover. The distinction is critical. The outcome will have immense bearing on how we manage boreal forest habitat for caribou survival in the long term.

The answer, too, will take time. Indeed, the forty-to-fifty-year "rule of thumb" for caribou habitat recovery may prove insufficient in some circumstances. Seismic lines, for example, are a pernicious disturbance on many caribou ranges in western Canada. For the Little Smoky herd in Alberta, for instance, Justina Ray described a range "blanketed by 11,277 km of linear features that include seismic lines, pipelines, well sites and other features."[73] Linear features are not just pernicious but persistent. Philip Lee and Stan Boutin reported, after thirty-five years, that two-thirds of seismic lines had recovered only to herbaceous vegetation.[74] Complete recovery was projected at 112 years.

Time also complicates our understanding of the link between habitat condition and caribou response. The disappearance of woodland caribou typically unfolds over decades—a slow tumbling of dominoes that starts with forest disturbance, followed by influxes of other deer species (like white-tailed deer and moose), sometimes more parasites (like the meningeal worm), or more predators (like black bears and wolves), along with greater access of predators (sometimes hunters) into caribou range. The pace of these processes is incompletely understood. Expectation and evidence suggest a delay of roughly two decades between disturbance and caribou disappearance.[75] This is the "extinction debt"—a scenario where an existing population is destined to disappear, even after the cessation of habitat loss. Such lags may be further complicated by forest productivity, which can influence the speed of habitat recovery.[76]

Time is important in the dynamics of migratory caribou, too. Dramatic changes in the size of migratory herds are likely the norm; fluctuations may unfold over decades or centuries.[77] These populations may exhibit cycles in abundance, perhaps on the order of a century.[78] Science may be capable of spanning vast spaces, but it is too young to fully grasp this ecological complexity. Indigenous knowledge, on the other hand, is often deep in time. This suggests that to improve our ecological understanding, the two knowledge systems can serve as complements.[79]

Matters of Scale

The scales of caribou biology can be surprising. There are many examples of caribou avoiding areas well beyond the precise bounds of landscape alterations. Diminished occupancy by distances of one to ten kilometres is common,[80] including around hydroelectric developments.[81] This extent of avoidance is comparable to the critical distance (four kilometres from unimproved roads) predicting the local extinction of woodland caribou in Ontario.[82] Caribou, therefore, give new meaning to the concept of "edge effects." Often construed as a few hundred metres beyond the precise bounds of habitat change—likely because this distance is close to our own perceptions—edge effects exist at a much broader scale for caribou. Without grasping such scales, we risk vastly underestimating the loss of caribou habitat due to Keeyask and other industrial developments.

The scales of caribou biology can be deceiving, too. In the Keeyask Environmental Impact Statement, for instance, habitat was denoted as "the place where an organism or population lives."[83] Perhaps because of this restrictive definition, the impact statement repeatedly inferred that habitat for resident caribou "does not appear to be limiting to summer cows and calves" and "appears to be underutilized";[84] that more habitat was available than used; accordingly, if displaced, "caribou ... will most likely find suitable habitat elsewhere."[85] Indeed, surveys showed that just 5 to 10 percent of lake islands and peatland islands were inhabited. Thus, concluded the impact statement, "not all suitable calving islands are occupied."[86]

Such conclusions fall into the trap of human-centric scales. They ignore the importance of space itself as habitat. Low densities of sedentary caribou, especially during calving and postcalving, are crucial to calf survival. Bergerud argued that rareness is key—that a density of 0.06 caribou per square kilometre represents a stabilizing density, above which sedentary caribou populations decline.[87] If this density is exceeded, the space shrinks between calving females, conceivably improving the search efficiency of predators, leading to lower survival of calves.[88] The loss of undisturbed space—even apparently "unused" space—represents the loss of habitat.

We can also note that temporal and spatial scales of habitat use are linked. Habitat can be construed at several scales: fine scales, such as an ephemeral feeding site for one caribou; and broad scales, such as a landscape suitable for the long-term persistence of caribou populations and the species. These scales are not just matters of size but significance.[89] Because slower ecological processes may constrain faster ones, habitat at broad scales represents the key constraints.[90] Consider lichens, an important food source to which caribou are uniquely adapted. In the southern boreal forest, where caribou have largely disappeared, there are plenty of small-scale lichen stands, but these stands occur in fragmented forests.[91] They are unsuitable for caribou survival. In other words, fine-scale, stand-level features like lichens may be necessary, but they are insufficient when in the midst of roads and industrial disturbances.[92] Broad-scale landscape features, like the intactness of the forest, are key to the persistence of caribou.

This hierarchy of scales implies a continuum of ways to manage caribou habitat in the boreal forest. At one end are fast interventions, such as controlling predators or other deer species. At the other end are slow interventions, such as the recovery of the forest. As noted by Elizabeth Wilman and Elspeth Wilman, "management interventions for fast variables are necessary complements to interventions for slow variables, but cannot replace them."[93] Conservation demands a focus on the long-term goal of habitat planning, not just short-term, halfway measures.[94] For conserving of species like caribou, scale helps to clarify what is sufficient and what is necessary.

Keeyask and Caribou Conservation

The Keeyask Project represents another test case in resource development: the opportunity to reconcile economic desires with ecological reality, to mobilize multiple forms of knowledge, and to acknowledge the evidence and the uncertainties in conservation. Viewed through the lens of caribou biology, however, Keeyask reveals that such environmental assessments are still beset with optimism and nearsightedness.

Residual effects of the Keeyask Generation Project on caribou were anticipated to be "adverse" but "small" to "medium" in extent; "long term" in duration but "small" in magnitude. These assessments were considered to have moderate to high degree of certainty, even "high confidence" with respect to habitat availability, core areas, and regional intactness.[95] Yet, during the public hearings, Indigenous residents, scientists, and even the Environmental Impact Statement itself pointed to Keeyask's substantial cumulative impacts. Assessment of the project effects was plagued by uncertainty. Studies of caribou in the project area—trail cameras, track and winter surveys—were small in extent and short in duration. As means to reduce these uncertainties, they were destined to fail.

One key uncertainty pertained to the designation of "summer resident" caribou. Given that boreal woodland caribou are deemed threatened both provincially and federally, and that habitat loss has been the chief driver of their decline, the designation is important. The weight of the evidence in the project area—the low density of caribou, the dispersed calving distribution, the presence of woodland caribou in adjacent northern Ontario, even the antler shape of resident caribou—implied that, more likely than not, boreal caribou occupied the project area. Compounding this uncertainty was the projection of future habitat conditions. Although the Keeyask Project was acknowledged to potentially exacerbate habitat loss in a "greatly altered region"[96] "where intactness is already low,"[97] habitat is likely to be disturbed further by additional industrial projects and forest fires. In aggregate, such alterations could diminish the undisturbed portion of caribou range below the acceptable level of 65 percent.

In its report, Manitoba Clean Environment Commission did find that the combination of past, present, and future projects in the region created the potential for significant cumulative effects on caribou.[98] The commission did cite habitat disturbance to resident caribou in the project area as a potential concern, and it did admonish Manitoba Hydro's partnership group for not estimating the likely area of future fire disturbance, which "would have greatly added to the evaluation in the EIS."[99] It did find that the Keeyask partnership placed a great deal of confidence in the success of its mitigation measures. Indeed, the major effects of industrial development on caribou cannot be mitigated at fine scales. Typical mitigative measures—like avoiding calving areas or minimizing blasting during the calving season[100]—are too narrow in space or time to secure the conservation of this mobile animal. Such fine-scale measures confuse what is necessary with what is sufficient.

Conclusions

Wildlife conservation, I have learned, is as simple—and as difficult—as taking the long view. Caribou epitomize the challenge. Conserving this animal is often regarded as tantamount to stymying the economy, especially for northern communities and northern development.[101] To some, caribou stand in the way of projects like Keeyask and their promise of jobs. This apparent tension, however, can be distilled as a matter of scale. Jane Lubchenco wrote: "The false assertion that society must choose between the economy and the environment is often made. In reality, this 'jobs versus the environment' choice is a false dichotomy: the real choice is between short-term gain and long-term, sustained prosperity."[102]

Caribou are an invitation to accept the long view. Their biology demands it. To conserve this species, we must consider more than the short term and the immediate: we must embrace whole landscapes and multiple decades. Caribou conservation entails a rethinking of scales—a reassessment of the duration and scope of our desires, plans, and actions. In practice, it begins with identifying each local caribou population and understanding the habitat and demographic conditions at this scale. What is necessary is to view the population as the practical unit for conserving the species.[103]

Caribou are a call to something even bigger. More than just a conservation challenge, caribou are an opportunity to adopt a broader view of how we gauge success. They are an invitation to a world view that is expansive, forward-looking, and hopeful. In the end, the outcome of the Keeyask Project—and many others, planned or present, in the North—can be evaluated only on big scales. Caribou stand as a mark of our real accomplishments. We simply need to scale up our thinking to match their biology.

Notes

1   Andrew M. Hein, Chen Hou, and James F. Gillooly, "Energetic and Biomechanical Constraints on Animal Migration Distance," *Ecology Letters* 15, no. 2 (2012): 104–10; Kyle Joly et al., "Longest Terrestrial Migrations and Movements Around the World," *Scientific Reports* 9, no. 1 (2019), article no. 15333.

2   Douglas A. Kelt and Dirk H. Van Vuren, "The Ecology and Macroecology of Mammalian Home Range Area," *The American Naturalist* 157, no. 6 (2001): 637–45.

3   Stephen G. Fancy and Robert G. White, "Energy Expenditures for Locomotion by Barren-Ground Caribou," *Canadian Journal of Zoology* 65, no. 1 (1987): 122–28.

4   Eugene Morin, "Evidence for Declines in Human Population Densities During the Early Upper Paleolithic in Western Europe," *Proceedings of the National Academy of Sciences* 105, no. 1 (2008): 48.

5   Marco Festa-Bianchet, Justina C. Ray, Stan Boutin, Steeve D. Côté, and Anne Gunn, "Conservation of Caribou (*Rangifer tarandus*) in Canada: An Uncertain Future," *Canadian Journal of Zoology* 89, no. 5 (2011): 419–34; Mark Hebblewhite, "Billion Dollar Boreal Woodland Caribou and the Biodiversity Impacts of the Global Oil and Gas Industry," *Biological Conservation* 206 (2017): 102–11; James A. Schaefer, "Long-Term Range Recession and the Persistence of Caribou in the Taiga," *Conservation Biology* 17 (2003): 1435–39.

6   Clean Environment Commission, Manitoba [CEC], *Report on Public Hearings, Keeyask Generation Project*, 2014, http://www.cecmanitoba.ca/cecm/archive/pubs/commission%20reports/keeyask%20web%20final2.pdf.

7   M. Di Marco, L. Boitani, D. Mallon, M. Hoffmann, A. Iacucci, E. Meijaard, P. Visconti, J. Schipper, and C. Rondinini, "A Retrospective Evaluation of the Global Decline of Carnivores and Ungulates," *Conservation Biology* 28, no. 4 (2014): 1109–18.

8   Marcel Cardillo and Lindell Bromham, "Body Size and Risk of Extinction in Australian Mammals," *Conservation Biology* 15, no. 5 (2001): 1435–40; Ana D.

Davidson, Marcus J. Hamilton, Alison G. Boyer, James H. Brown, and Gerardo Ceballos, "Multiple Ecological Pathways to Extinction in Mammals," *Proceedings of the National Academy of Sciences* 106, no. 26 (2009): 10702–05.

9   Orphé Bichet, Angélique Dupuch, Christian Hébert, Hélène Le Borgne, and Daniel Fortin, "Maintaining Animal Assemblages Through Single-Species Management: The Case of Threatened Caribou in Boreal Forest," *Ecological Applications* 26, no. 2 (2016): 612–23; cf. Yolanda F. Wiersma and Darren J. H. Sleep, "The Effect of Target Setting on Conservation in Canada's Boreal: What Is the Right Amount of Area to Protect?" *Biodiversity and Conservation* 27, no. 3 (2018): 733–48.

10   Canadian Council of Forest Ministers, *Criteria and Indicators of Sustainable Forest Management in Canada, National Status 2000* (Ottawa: Canadian Council of Forest Ministers, 2000).

11   Franck Courchamp, Ivan Jaric, Céline Albert, Yves Meinard, William J. Ripple, and Guillaume Chapron, "The Paradoxical Extinction of the Most Charismatic Animals," *PLOS Biology* 16, no. 4 (2018): e2003997.

12   Hebblewhite, "Billion Dollar Boreal Woodland Caribou," 102; Dennis L. Murray, Yasmine N. Majchrzak, Michael J.L. Peers, Morgan Wehtje, Catarina Ferreira, Rob S.A. Pickles, Jeffrey R. Row, and Daniel H. Thornton, "Potential Pitfalls of Private Initiatives in Conservation Planning: A Case Study from Canada's Boreal Forest," *Biological Conservation* 192 (2015): 174–80; Schaefer, "Long-Term Range Recession," 1435.

13   Graeme Caughley and Anne Gunn, *Conservation Biology in Theory and Practice* (Cambridge: Blackwell Science, 1995).

14   Charles J. Krebs, "Beyond Population Regulation and Limitation," *Wildlife Research* 29 (2002): 1–10.

15   Arthur T. Bergerud, "Caribou, Wolves and Man," *Trends in Ecology and Evolution* 3, no. 3 (1988): 68–72; Arthur T. Bergerud, Stuart N. Luttich, and Lodewijk Camps, *The Return of Caribou to Ungava* (Montreal: McGill-Queen's University Press, 2008); Bruce A. Pond, Glen S. Brown, Kaitlin S. Wilson, and James A. Schaefer, "Drawing Lines: Spatial Behaviours Reveal Two Ecotypes of Woodland Caribou," *Biological Conservation* 194 (2016): 139–48.

16   Keeyask Hydropower Limited Partnership, *Keeyask Generation Project: Environmental Impact Statement, Supporting Volume, Terrestrial Environment, Section 7, Mammals* (June 2012), https://keeyask.com/wp-content/uploads/2012/07/TE-SV-7.0-Mammals-web-version-text-only.pdf.

17   C. Callaghan, S. Virc, and J. Duffe, "Woodland Caribou, Boreal Population, Trends in Canada. Canadian Biodiversity: Ecosystem Status And Trends 2010," Technical Thematic Report No. 11 (Ottawa: Canadian Councils of Resource Ministers, 2011); Festa-Bianchet et al., "Conservation of Caribou," 419; D. Hervieux, M. Hebblewhite, N.J. DeCesare, M. Russell, K. Smith, S. Robertson, and S. Boutin, "Widespread Declines in Woodland Caribou (*Rangifer tarandus caribou*) Continue in Alberta," *Canadian Journal of Zoology* 91, no. 12 (2013): 872–82; Liv S. Vors and Mark S. Boyce, "Global Declines of Caribou and Reindeer," *Global Change Biology* 15, no. 11 (2009): 2626–33.

18   Callaghan, Virc, and Duffe, "Woodland Caribou, Boreal Population."

19   Frank F. Mallory and Tracy L. Hillis, "Demographic Characteristics of Circumpolar Caribou Populations: Ecotypes, Ecological Constraints, Releases, and Population Dynamics," special issue, *Rangifer* 10 (1998): 49–60.

20 A. Gunn, D. Russell, and J. Eamer, *Northern Caribou Population Trends in Canada 2010. Canadian Biodiversity: Ecosystem Status and Trends 2010,* Technical Thematic Report No. 10. (Ottawa: Canadian Councils of Resource Ministers, 2011); James A. Schaefer and Shane P. Mahoney, "Spatial Dynamics of the Rise and Fall of Caribou (*Rangifer tarandus*) in Newfoundland," *Canadian Journal of Zoology* 91, no. 11 (2013): 767–74.

21 Gunn et al., *Northern Caribou Population Trends.*

22 Erica J. Newton et al., "Causes and Consequences of Broad-Scale Changes in the Distribution of Migratory Caribou (*Rangifer tarandus*) of Southern Hudson Bay," *Arctic* 68 (2015): 472–85.

23 Schaefer and Mahoney, "Spatial Dynamics," 767.

24 CEC, *Report on Public Hearings, Keeyask Generation Project,* April 2014, http://www.cecmanitoba.ca/cec/archive/pubs/commission%20reports/keeyask%20web%20final2.pdf.

25 Andrea S. Laliberte and William J. Ripple, "Range Contractions of North American Carnivores and Ungulates," *BioScience* 54, no. 2 (2004): 123–38.

26 Kaitlin S. Wilson, Bruce A. Pond, Glen S. Brown, and James A. Schaefer, "The Biogeography of Home Range Size of Woodland Caribou *Rangifer tarandus caribou,*" *Diversity and Distributions* 25, no. 2 (2019): 205–16.

27 Rob Channell and Mark V. Lomolino, "Trajectories to Extinction: Spatial Dynamics of the Contraction of Geographical Ranges," *Journal of Biogeography* 27, no. 1 (2000): 169–79.

28 Schaefer, "Long-Term Range Recession," 1435; Liv S. Vors, James Schaefer, Bruce A. Pond, Arthur R. Rodgers, and Brent R. Patterson, "Woodland Caribou Extirpation and Anthropogenic Landscape Disturbance in Ontario," *Journal of Wildlife Management* 71, no. 4 (2007): 1249–56; Wilson et al., "The Biogeography of Home Range Size," 205.

29 Arthur T. Bergerud, Brian E. McLaren, Ludvik Krysl, Keith Wade, and William Wyett, "Losing the Predator-Prey Space Race Leads to Extirpation of Woodland Caribou from Pukaskwa National Park," *Ecoscience* 21, no. 3–4 (2014): 374–86; and M. Hebblewhite, C. White, and M. Musiani, "Revisiting Extinction in National Parks: Mountain Caribou in Banff," *Conservation Biology* 24, no. 1 (2010): 341–44.

30 Callaghan, Virc, and Duffe, "Woodland Caribou, Boreal Population," 16.

31 Arthur (Tom) T. Bergerud, "Decline of Caribou in North America Following Settlement," *Journal of Wildlife Management* 38 (1974): 757–70; Bergerud et al., *Return of Caribou;* W. James Rettie and François Messier, "Dynamics of Woodland Caribou Populations at the Southern Limit of Their Range in Saskatchewan," *Canadian Journal of Zoology* 76 (1998): 251–59; James A. Schaefer, Alasdair M. Veitch, Fred H. Harrington, W. Kent Brown, John B. Theberge, and Stuart N. Luttich, "Demography of Decline of the Red Wine Mountains Caribou Herd," *Journal of Wildlife Management* 63, no. 2 (1999): 580–87; Dale R. Seip and Deborah B. Cichowski, "Population Ecology of Caribou in British Columbia," special issue, *Rangifer* 9 (1996): 73–80.

32 Guillaume Bastille-Rousseau, Daniel Fortin, Christian Dussault, Réhaume Courtois, and Jean-Pierre Ouellet, "Foraging Strategies by Omnivores: Are Black Bears Actively Searching for Ungulate Neonates or Are They Simply Opportunistic Predators?" *Ecography* 34, no. 4 (2011): 588–96; A. David Latham, M. Cecilia Latham, Nicole A. McCutchen, and Stan Boutin, "Invading White-Tailed Deer Change Wolf-Caribou Dynamics in Northeastern Alberta," *The Journal of Wildlife*

Management 75, no. 1 (2011): 204–12; Mathieu Leblond, Christian Dussault, Jean-Pierre Ouellet, and Martin Hugues St-Laurent, "Caribou Avoiding Wolves Face Increased Predation by Bears—Caught Between Scylla and Charybdis," *Journal of Applied Ecology* 53, no. 4 (2016): 1078–87.

33   Roy C. Anderson, "The Ecological Relationships of Meningeal Worm and Native Cervids in North America," *Journal of Wildlife Diseases* 8, no. 4 (1972): 304–10.

34   Arthur T. Bergerud, "Evolving Perspectives on Caribou Population Dynamics, Have We Got It Right Yet?" special issue, *Rangifer* 9 (1996): 95–116; H.G. Cumming, D.B. Beange, and G. Lavoie, "Habitat Partitioning Between Woodland Caribou and Moose in Ontario: The Potential Role of Shared Predation Risk," special issue, *Rangifer* 9 (1996): 81–94; Rettie and Messier, "Dynamics of Woodland Caribou," 251; W. James Rettie and François Messier, "Hierarchical Habitat Selection by Woodland Caribou: Its Relationship to Limiting Factors," *Ecography* 23 (2000): 466–78.

35   James A. Schaefer and Shane P. Mahoney, "Spatial and Temporal Scaling of Population Density and Animal Movement: A Power Law Approach," *Ecoscience* 10 (2003): 496–501.

36   Bergerud, "Evolving Perspectives on Caribou Population," 95; Serge Couturier, Robert D. Otto, Steve D. Côté, Glenn Luther, and Shane P. Mahoney, "Body Size Variations in Caribou Ecotypes and Relationships with Demography," *Journal of Wildlife Management* 74, no. 3 (2010): 395–404; Schaefer and Mahoney, "Spatial and Temporal Scaling," 496.

37   Bergerud, "Evolving Perspectives on Caribou Population," 95; B.J. Hearn, S.N. Luttich, M. Crête, and M.B. Berger, "Survival of Radio-Collared Caribou (*Rangifer tarandus caribou*) from the George River Herd, Nouveau-Quebec—Labrador," *Canadian Journal of Zoology* 68 (1990): 276–83.

38   Couturier et al., "Body Size Variations," 395; Shane P. Mahoney and James A. Schaefer, "Long-Term Changes in Demography and Migration of Newfoundland Caribou," *Journal of Mammalogy* 83 (2002): 957–63; F. Messier, J. Huot, D. Le Hénaff, and S. Luttich, "Demography of the George River Caribou Herd: Evidence of Population Regulation by Forage Exploitation and Range Expansion," *Arctic* 41 (1988): 279–87; James A. Schaefer, Shane P. Mahoney, Jackie N. Weir, J. Glenn Luther, and Colleen E. Soulliere, "Decades of Habitat Use Reveal Food Limitation of Newfoundland Caribou," *Journal of Mammalogy* 97, no. 2 (2016): 386–93.

39   Guillaume Bastille-Rousseau, James A. Schaefer, Shane P. Mahoney, and Dennis L. Murray, "Population Decline in Semi-Migratory Caribou (*Rangifer tarandus*): Intrinsic or Extrinsic Drivers?" *Canadian Journal of Zoology* 91, no. 11 (2013): 820–28; Shane P. Mahoney, Jackie N. Weir, Glenn Luther, James A. Schaefer, and Shawn F. Morrison, "Morphological Change in Newfoundland Caribou: Effects of Abundance and Climate," *Rangifer* 31 (2011): 21–34; Conor D. Mallory, Mitch W. Campbell, and Mark S. Boyce, "Climate Influences Body Condition and Synchrony of Barren-Ground Caribou Abundance in Northern Canada," *Polar Biology* 41, no. 5 (2018): 855–64.

40   Eric Post and Mads C. Forchhammer, "Climate Change Reduces Reproductive Success of an Arctic Herbivore Through Trophic Mismatch," *Philosophical Transactions of the Royal Society B: Biological Sciences* 363, no. 1501 (2008): 2367–73; Dennis L. Murray, Michael J.L. Peers, Yasmine N. Majchrzak, Morgan Wehtje, Catarina Ferreira, Rob S.A. Pickles, Jeffrey R. Row, and Daniel H. Thornton, "Continental Divide: Predicting Climate-Mediated Fragmentation and Biodiversity Loss in the Boreal Forest," *PLoS ONE* 12, no. 5 (2017): e0176706.

41 Bergerud, "Caribou, Wolves and Man," 68; Pond et al., "Drawing Lines," 139.

42 Bergerud et al., *Return of Caribou.*

43 Pond et al., "Drawing Lines," 139.

44 Kaitlin S. Wilson, "Temporal and Spatial Variation in Home Range Size for Two Woodland Caribou Ecotypes in Ontario," MSc thesis, Trent University, 2013; Wilson et al., "Biogeography of Home Range," 205.

45 Wilson, "Temporal and Spatial Variation."

46 John A. Nagy, Deborah L. Johnson, Nicholas C. Larter, Mitch W. Campbell, Andrew E. Derocher, Allicia Kelly, Mathieu Dumond, Danny Allaire, and Bruno Croft, "Subpopulation Structure of Caribou (*Rangifer tarandus* L.) in Arctic and Subarctic Canada," *Ecological Applications* 21, no. 6 (2011): 2334–48.

47 Bergerud et al., "Losing the Predator-Prey Space," 374; Hebblewhite et al., "Revisiting Extinction in National Parks," 341; Vors et al., "Woodland Caribou Extirpation," 1249.

48 Bergerud, "Evolving Perspectives on Caribou Population," 95; Bergerud et al., *Return of Caribou.*

49 James A. Schaefer, Carita M. Bergman, and Stuart N. Luttich, "Site Fidelity of Female Caribou at Multiple Spatial Scales," *Landscape Ecology* 15, no. 8 (2000): 731–39.

50 Alexandre Lafontaine, Pierre Drapeau, Daniel Fortin, and Martin Hugues St-Laurent, "Many Places Called Home: The Adaptive Value of Seasonal Adjustments in Range Fidelity," *Journal of Animal Ecology* 86, no. 3 (2017): 624–33.

51 Schaefer and Mahoney, "Spatial Dynamics," 767; Joëlle Taillon, Marco Festa-Bianchet, and Steeve D. Côté, "Shifting Targets in the Tundra: Protection of Migratory Caribou Calving Grounds Must Account for Spatial Changes over Time," *Biological Conservation* 147, no. 1 (2012): 163–73.

52 S.H. Ferguson and P.C. Elkie, "Seasonal Movement Patterns of Woodland Caribou (*Rangifer Tarandus Caribou*)," *Journal of Zoology* 262, no. 2 (2004): 125–34; Jesse N. Popp, James A. Schaefer, and Frank F. Mallory, "Female Site Fidelity of the Mealy Mountain Caribou Herd (*Rangifer Tarandus Caribou*) in Labrador," special issue, *Rangifer* 19 (2011): 87–95; Schaefer et al., "Site Fidelity of Female Caribou," 731; Schaefer and Mahoney, "Spatial Dynamics," 767.

53 Lafontaine et al., "Many Places Called Home," 624.

54 Maria L. Arlt and Micheline Manseau, "Historical Changes in Caribou Distribution and Land Cover in and Around Prince Albert National Park: Land Management Implications," *Rangifer* 31 (2011): 17–31; Simon J. Dyer, Jack P. O'Neill, Shawn M. Wasel, and Stan Boutin, "Quantifying Barrier Effects of Roads and Seismic Lines on Movements of Female Woodland Caribou in Northeastern Alberta," *Canadian Journal of Zoology* 80, no. 5 (2002): 839–45; Alexandre L. Vignault Rasiulis, Isabelle Schmelzer, and Christian G. Wright, "The Effect of Temporal Sampling Regime on the Characterization of Home Range for Female Boreal Woodland Caribou (*Rangifer tarandus caribou*) in Labrador, Canada," *Rangifer* 32, no. 2 (2012): 227–39.

55 David Beauchesne, Jochen A.G. Jaeger, and Martin Hugues St-Laurent, "Thresholds in the Capacity of Boreal Caribou to Cope with Cumulative Disturbances: Evidence from Space Use Patterns," *Biological Conservation* 172 (2014): 190–99; Victoria M. Donovan, Glen S. Brown, and Frank F. Mallory, "The Impacts of Forest Management Strategies for Woodland Caribou Vary Across Biogeographic Gradients," *PLoS ONE* 12, no. 2 (2017): e0170759; Michelle V.A. Ewacha, James D. Roth, W. Gary Anderson, Dennis C. Brannen, and Daniel L.J. Dupont, "Disturbance and Chronic Levels of Cortisol in Boreal Woodland Caribou," *The Journal of Wildlife Management*

81, no. 7 (2017): 1266–75; Doug MacNearney, Karine Pigeon, Gordon Stenhouse, Wiebe Nijland, Nicholas C. Coops, and Laura Finnegan, "Heading for the Hills? Evaluating Spatial Distribution of Woodland Caribou in Response to a Growing Anthropogenic Disturbance Footprint," *Ecology and Evolution* 6, no. 18 (2016): 6484–6509; Kirby G. Smith, E. Janet Ficht, David Hobson, Troy C. Sorensen, and David Hervieux, "Winter Distribution of Woodland Caribou in Relation to Clear-Cut Logging in West-Central Alberta," *Canadian Journal of Zoology* 78 (2000): 1433–40; Wilson et al., "Biogeography of Home Range," 205.

56   Geneviève Faille, Christian Dussault, Jean-Pierre Ouellet, Daniel Fortin, Réhaume Courtois, Martin Hugues St-Laurent, and Claude Dussault, "Range Fidelity: The Missing Link Between Caribou Decline and Habitat Alteration?" *Biological Conservation* 143, no. 11 (2010): 2840–50; Lafontaine et al., "Many Places Called Home," 624.

57   Ewacha et al., "Disturbance and Chronic Levels," 1266.

58   Lafontaine et al., "Many Places Called Home," 624.

59   Chris J. Johnson, Mark S. Boyce, Ray L. Case, H. Dean Cluff, Robert J. Gau, Anne Gunn, and Robert Mulders, "Cumulative Effects of Human Developments on Arctic Wildlife," *Wildlife Monographs* 160, no. 1 (2005): 26.

60   Environment Canada, "Scientific Assessment to Inform the Identification of Critical Habitat for Woodland Caribou (*Rangifer tarandus caribou*), Boreal Population, in Canada: 2011 Update," Ottawa, 2011, https://www.registrelep-sararegistry.gc.ca/document/doc2248p/sec4_st_caribou_e.cfm; Cheryl A. Johnson, Glenn D. Sutherland, Erin Neave, Mathieu Leblond, Patrick Kirby, Clara Superbie, and Philip D. McLoughlin, "Science to Inform Policy: Linking Population Dynamics to Habitat for a Threatened Species in Canada," *Journal of Applied Ecology* 57, no. 7 (2020): 1314–27.

61   Roger Suffling, Vince Crichton, Justina C. Ray, James A. Schaefer, and Ian D. Thompson, *Report of the Ontario Woodland Caribou Science Review Panel: The Path Forward* (Toronto: Ontario Ministry of Natural Resources, 2008); Vors et al., "Woodland Caribou Extirpation," 1249.

62   Johnson et al., "Science to Inform Policy," 1314.

63   Cathryn Clarke Murray, Janson Wong, Gerald G. Singh, Megan Mach, Jackie Lerner, Bernardo Ranieri, Guillaume Peterson St-Laurent, Alice Guimaraes, and Kai M.A. Chan, "The Insignificance of Thresholds in Environmental Impact Assessment: An Illustrative Case Study in Canada," *Environmental Management* 61, no. 6 (2018): 1062–71.

64   Chris J. Johnson, "Identifying Ecological Thresholds for Regulating Human Activity: Effective Conservation or Wishful Thinking?" *Biological Conservation* 168 (2013): 57–65.

65   Paul K. Dayton, "Reversal of the Burden of Proof in Fisheries Management," *Science* 279 (1998): 821.

66   Justina C. Ray, "Defining Habitat Restoration for Boreal Caribou in the Context of National Recovery: A Discussion Paper," Toronto, Ontario, Canada, 2014, accessed 3 May 2021, https://www.cclmportal.ca/resource/defining-habitat-restoration-boreal-caribou-context-national-recovery-discussion-paper; Johnson et al., "Science to Inform Policy," 1314.

67   Glen W. Armstrong, "A Stochastic Characterisation of the Natural Disturbance Regime of the Boreal Mixedwood Forest with Implications for Sustainable Forest Management," *Canadian Journal of Forest Research* 29, no. 4 (1999): 424–33.

68 Keeyask Hydropower Limited Partnership, *Keeyask Generation Project: Environmental Impact Statement, Supporting Volume, Terrestrial Environment, Section 2, Habitats and Ecosystems* (June 2012), 13.

69 Suffling et al., *Report of the Ontario Woodland Caribou.*

70 Caroline Hins, Jean-Pierre Ouellet, Claude Dussault, and Martin Hugues St-Laurent, "Habitat Selection by Forest-Dwelling Caribou in Managed Boreal Forest of Eastern Canada: Evidence of a Landscape Configuration Effect," *Forest Ecology and Management* 257, no. 2 (2009): 636–43; James A. Schaefer and William O. Pruitt, Jr., "Fire and Woodland Caribou in Southeastern Manitoba," *Wildlife Monographs* 116 (1991): 1–39; Eliot L. Terry, Bruce N. McLellan, and Glen S. Watts, "Winter Habitat Ecology of Mountain Caribou in Relation to Forest Management," *Journal of Applied Ecology* 37, no. 4 (2000): 589–602.

71 M.A. Rose and G.D. Racey, *Caribou in the New Forest: Lessons from South Allely Lake and 20 Years of Caribou Habitat Management on the English River Forest,* Technical Report TR-145 (Thunder Bay: Ontario Ministry of Natural Resources, 2011).

72 Ray, "Defining Habitat Restoration."

73 Ibid., 3.

74 Philip Lee and Stan Boutin, "Persistence and Developmental Transition of Wide Seismic Lines in the Western Boreal Plains of Canada," *Journal of Environmental Management* 78, no. 3 (2006): 240–50.

75 Vors et al., "Woodland Caribou Extirpation," 1249.

76 Daniel Fortin, Florian Barnier, Pierre Drapeau, Thierry Duchesne, Claude Dussault, Sandra Heppell, Marie Caroline Prima, Martin Hugues St-Laurent, and Guillaume Szo, "Forest Productivity Mitigates Human Disturbance Effects on Late-Seral Prey Exposed to Apparent Competitors and Predators," *Scientific Reports* 7, no. 1 (2017): 6370.

77 Gunn et al., *Northern Caribou Population Trends.*

78 Messier et al., "Demography of the George River Caribou," 279.

79 Micheline Manseau, ed., "Traditional and Western Scientific Environmental Knowledge," *Terra Borealis* 1 (1998): 1–62.

80 John Boulanger, Kim G. Poole, Anne Gunn, and Jack Wierzchowski, "Estimating the Zone of Influence of Industrial Developments on Wildlife: A Migratory Caribou *Rangifer tarandus groenlandicus* and Diamond Mine Case Study," *Wildlife Biology* 18, no. 2 (2012): 164–79; Daniel Fortin, Pietro-Luciano Buono, André Fortin, Nicolas Courbin, Christian Tye Gingras, Paul R. Moorcroft, Rhéaume Courtois, and Claude Dussault, "Movement Responses of Caribou to Human-Induced Habitat Edges Lead to Their Aggregation Near Anthropogenic Features," *The American Naturalist* 181, no. 6 (2013): 827–36; Newton et al., "Causes and Consequences," 472; Jackie N. Weir, Shane P. Mahoney, Brian McLaren, and Steven H. Ferguson, "Effects of Mine Development on Woodland Caribou *Rangifer tarandus* Distribution," *Wildlife Biology* 13, no. 1 (2007): 66–74.

81 Shane P. Mahoney and James A. Schaefer, "Hydroelectric Development and the Disruption of Migration in Caribou," *Biological Conservation* 107 (2002): 147–53; C. Nellemann, I. Vistnes, P. Jordhøy, and O. Strand, "Winter Distribution of Wild Reindeer in Relation to Power Lines, Roads and Resorts," *Biological Conservation* 101, no. 3 (2001): 351–60.

82 Vors et al., "Woodland Caribou Extirpation," 1249.

83   Keeyask Hydropower Limited Partnership, *Keeyask Generation Project: Environmental Impact Statement, Response to EIS Guidelines,* Chapter 6, "Environmental Effects Assessment" (June 2012), 6-85, https://keeyask.com/wp-content/uploads/Keeyask-SV-EIS.pdf.

84   Keeyask Hydropower Limited Partnership, *Keeyask Generation Project: Environmental Impact Statement, Response to EIS Guidelines,* Chapter 7, "Cumulative Effects Assessment" (June 2012), 7-26, https://keeyask.com/wp-content/uploads/Keeyask-SV-EIS.pdf.

85   Keeyask Hydropower Limited Partnership, *Response to EIS Guidelines,* Chapter 6, 6-369.

86   Keeyask Hydropower Limited Partnership, *Keeyask Generation Project: Environmental Impact Statement, Responses to Information Requests — CEC, Round 1* (July 2013): [CEC Rd 1 CEC-0037a], 14, https://keeyask.com/wp-content/uploads/2013/07/CEC-Round-1-Web-Version-July-31-2-pm.pdf.

87   Arthur T. Bergerud, "Rareness as an Antipredator Strategy to Reduce Predation Risk for Moose and Caribou," in *Wildlife 2001: Populations,* ed. D.R. McCullough and R.H. Barrett (London: Elsevier, 1992), 1008–21; Bergerud et al., *Return of Caribou.*

88   Bergerud et al., *Return of Caribou.*

89   Rettie and Messier, "Hierarchical Habitat Selection," 466.

90   Stephen J. Mayor, David C. Schneider, James A. Schaefer, and Shane P. Mahoney, "Habitat Selection at Multiple Scales," *Ecoscience* 16, no. 2 (2009): 238–47.

91   David W. Schindler and Peter G. Lee, "Comprehensive Conservation Planning to Protect Biodiversity and Ecosystem Services in Canadian Boreal Regions Under a Warming Climate and Increasing Exploitation," *Biological Conservation* 143, no. 7 (2010): 1571–86.

92   Rettie and Messier, "Hierarchical Habitat Selection," 466; Vors et al., "Woodland Caribou Extirpation," 1249.

93   Elizabeth A. Wilman and Elspeth N. Wilman, "Fast, Slow, and Adaptive Management of Habitat Modification-Invasion Interactions: Woodland Caribou (*Rangifer tarandus*)," *Ecosphere* 8, no. 10, article e01970 (2017): 12.

94   Nat B. Frazer, "Sea Turtle Conservation and Halfway Technology," *Conservation Biology* 6, no. 2 (1992): 179–84.

95   Keeyask Hydropower Limited Partnership, *Response to EIS Guidelines,* Chapter 6.

96   Keeyask Hydropower Limited Partnership, *Environmental Impact Statement,* Section 7.

97   Keeyask Hydropower Limited Partnership, *Response to EIS Guidelines,* Chapter 6.

98   CEC, *Report on Public Hearings, Keeyask Generation Project.*

99   Ibid., 94.

100   CEC, *Report on Public Hearings, Keeyask Generation Project.*

101   Ian Dunn, "Forestry Industry Also Committed to Protecting Caribou," *Toronto Star,* 22 February 2018, www.thestar.com/opinion/contributors/2018/02/22/forestry-industry-also- committed-to-protecting-caribou.html.

102   Jane Lubchenco, "Entering the Century of the Environment: A New Social Contract for Science," *Science* 279, no. 5350 (1998): 491.

103   Caughley and Gunn, *Conservation Biology in Theory and Practice.*

" My umbilical cord is tied to the land that we walk on every day. I come here to speak the truth, that what Manitoba Hydro is doing is killing our mother. Every day we watch what Manitoba Hydro is doing. You go out and you watch your mother die of cancer [every] day. You watch her die over and over and over and over again. Every day, you watch her die."

Robert Spence, Tataskweyak Cree Nation,
PUB hearings (25 April 2014), 8224–25

CHAPTER 9

Connections and Disconnections: A Review of the Regional Cumulative Effects Assessment in Northern Manitoba

JILL BLAKLEY

The increased pace and intensity of resource development in many regions of the world combined with increased concern for environmental protection has brought Regional Cumulative Effects Assessment (RCEA) into focus in recent years. At the top of many research and policy agendas across Canada and elsewhere is developing innovative means to address cumulative effects issues such as global warming, worsening air quality, freshwater shortages, deforestation, noise and light pollution, and wildlife habitat fragmentation. Other examples particularly relevant to Manitoba include the incremental loss of prairie wetlands;[1] acid rain created by electricity generation, factories, and vehicles;[2] and access roads and fly-in/fly-out programs introduced in northern development regions, leading to significant strains on community health and infrastructure.[3]

In 2017, a federally convened Expert Panel endorsed regional-scale impact assessment as a core component of "next generation" environmental impact assessment practice, signalling Canada's intention to assess the collective impacts of development on a regional basis.[4] In Manitoba, the Clean Environment Commission (CEC) called for a Regional Cumulative Effects Assessment at the close of both the Wuskwatim (2004) and Bipole III (2013) environmental assessment public hearings, based on mounting concern for the cumulative effects of all Manitoba Hydro projects and associated infrastructure in the Nelson River sub-watershed.[5] Numerous other provincial and federal government departments, non-government organizations, and industries in Canada have also initiated or called for regional impact assessments independently over the past decade or so, including: Fisheries and Oceans Canada; the Saskatchewan Ministry of the Environment; Alberta Environment and Parks; Parks Canada Agency; Teck Resources Limited; Aboriginal Affairs and Northern Development Canada (in partnership with the energy industry, Inuvialuit, and other regional stakeholders); the Canadian branch of the World Wildlife Federation; the Wildlife Conservation Society of Canada and Ecojustice; and ConocoPhillips,[6] among others.

While the Keeyask Environmental Impact Statement (EIS) issued in 2012 did include a cumulative effects assessment—which Chapter 4 of this volume examines closely—it was limited to a defined footprint around the Keeyask Project and did not look at the entire affected region. Despite the fact that the CEC recommended that an RCEA be completed before any additional projects were approved after Bipole III, the Clean Environment Commission nonetheless recommended that the Keeyask Project move forward in April 2014. The RCEA process began in the same year, and in December 2015, the Manitoba provincial government and Manitoba Hydro completed a Regional Cumulative Effects Assessment for the Churchill, Burntwood, and Nelson river systems. This chapter explores the Province's and Manitoba Hydro's approach to their assessment of regional cumulative environmental effects.

The Importance of Regional Cumulative Effects Assessment in Northern Manitoba

The importance of initiating an RCEA exercise in northern Manitoba is clear. Following nearly six decades of hydroelectric development and other intensive development such as mining and forestry, significant cumulative change to the environment, including social and cultural impacts to Indigenous and non-Indigenous communities in the region, is undeniable. As explained in Chapter 4, more than thirty-five major generation, conversion, and transmission projects have been undertaken by Manitoba Hydro in northeastern Manitoba, affecting the traditional territories of numerous Indigenous communities.[7] Rivers have been diverted, wildlife killed, reserve land flooded, and communities relocated, with many key decisions in the first two decades of development (1960 to 1977) being rushed and Indigenous communities faced with decisions unlike anything with which they had ever been confronted.[8]

In 1979, a Commission of Inquiry into Manitoba Hydro (the "Tritschler Report") found that by 1972, Manitoba and Manitoba Hydro did not have a compensation scheme for the impacts of this development, that various government departments failed to cooperate in the areas of compensation and mitigation, and that they adopted a confrontational, hostile stance toward the affected Indigenous communities.[9] In 1977, the Province of Manitoba, Manitoba Hydro, and the federal government signed the Northern Flood Agreement (NFA), which was ratified by First Nations leaders,[10] to address mitigation and management deficiencies (see Chapter 11 in this volume). Between 1978 and 1992, Manitoba Hydro and the Province made a number of major efforts to implement the agreement, including land use studies, ecological monitoring programs, and community infrastructure upgrades. However, First Nations were generally discontented with the way implementation and compensation were handled, leading to Manitoba Hydro's signing major implementation settlement agreements between 1992 and 1997. Additional supplemental agreements with NFA communities were signed between 2004 and 2015. At issue were ongoing concerns such as flooding of land and damage to shorelines by the Churchill River Diversion and Lake Winnipeg Regulation projects, compensation for adverse high-water events that occurred between 1977 and 2016, and provision of alternative employment opportunities.

The 2004 Wuskwatim environmental assessment hearing marked the Clean Environment Commission's first formal statement of concern about cumulative effects in northern Manitoba. It recommended that the government of Manitoba should undertake a regional planning initiative in northern Manitoba and on the east side of Lake Winnipeg to address existing and future hydroelectric and other developments. The commission noted the potential for a strategic environmental assessment approach to future development in northern Manitoba, including hydroelectric, mining, transportation, infrastructure, and related projects. Later evaluations of both the Bipole III and Keeyask project environmental impact assessments revealed a tendency to downplay the significance of cumulative effects, dismissing the cumulative effects of the project in combination with the effects of other development activities, whether hydro-related or otherwise. In other words, project impacts were often "compared with" the effects of other actions, versus considered "in addition to" any past changes in valued ecosystem component (VEC) conditions and "in addition to" the effects of other current and future actions.[11]

In light of these recommendations, and in light of the current Canadian national policy agenda on Truth and Reconciliation, the window for policy change and a better legacy of development in northern Manitoba remains open. The Province of Manitoba, by enacting the Path to Reconciliation Act in 2016, has committed to "engage with Indigenous Nations and peoples to develop a strategic path forward."[12] Looking ahead, there are over 4,000 megawatts (MW) of additional potential hydroelectric generating capacity that Manitoba Hydro is considering developing in the region[13]—nearly as much as the 5,000-plus MW already developed or in development. Many more important decisions about hydroelectric development in northern Manitoba are still to come. A robust RCEA initiative can help define issues that need to be on the provincial policy agenda and increase policy makers' knowledge of the concerns of northern residents that have persisted over the past half-century. Most importantly, RCEA can serve as a means to proactively address regional cumulative effects issues, as well as inform and strengthen policy initiatives such as the Manitoba Clean Energy Strategy, the Growing Our Watersheds initiative, and, potentially, a widely endorsed vision for development in the North.

What Is Regional Cumulative Effects Assessment?

As explained in Chapter 4 in this volume, cumulative environmental effects are changes in the environment caused by multiple interactions among human activities and natural processes that accumulate across space and time.[14] Not surprisingly, a regional-scale analysis is typically necessary to effectively capture cumulative effects. This is because many impacts ultimately occur beyond a project's physical footprint. For example, if a new rail spur and unloading facility were to be built outside a town to collect oil from a new pipeline, noise could carry beyond the physical boundary of the project to disturb neighbouring communities. Depending on how much other noise is generated by other industry operations in the area, community members may perceive the noise added by the new rail development as "too much." RCEA is premised on the idea that each individual disturbance, regardless of its magnitude, can represent a high marginal cost to the environment and/or society when all other development is taken into account.

Regional cumulative effects assessment is ideally future-focused or "strategic," meaning that decision makers can use this information to inform and explore alternative future development scenarios for the region. Once a preferred development scenario that describes the desired nature and pace of change is selected, that preferred scenario is used as a reference to inform all subsequent development decisions and project assessments in the region. Regional cumulative effects assessment without a future-focused, strategic aspect is still potentially very useful in that it can serve as a basis for monitoring future changes by establishing existing baseline conditions, but it stops well short of its potential to proactively chart a course to the future we want, as opposed to the future we accidentally or unintentionally end up with. In the case of northern Manitoba, there has never been a public process to collectively select and endorse a desired state of the region now profoundly affected by hydro development, or to chart a course to achieving that desired state.

Instead, the region—by default—has been treated as a northern energy storehouse that services on-demand a largely southern and increasingly international population. This is the shared fate of many northern and rural hinterlands and Indigenous traditional territories, explained in part by Canadian historian Harold Adam Innis, who, according to James Careless, developed a theory of social and economic development that describes "how economically advanced societies, through trade and colonialism, distort and retard economic development of less developed societies and regions."[15] Strategic regional cumulative effects assessment can help break the bonds of past legacies in hinterland regions such as northern Manitoba by viewing them as more than simply a storehouse of natural resources.

Taking a strategic approach to regional cumulative effects assessment means that the assessment is proactive and objectives-led, designed to influence development policies, plans, or programs at the highest level and earliest opportunity possible. It involves assessing the impacts of either a single sector (such as forestry, mining, or energy) or multiple development sectors.[16] Potential benefits of a strategic approach include establishing a common, long-term framework for decision making, analyzing impacts that aren't otherwise captured in project-specific assessments, and contributing to meaningful discussions about sustainable development.[17] Procedurally, engaging in an RCEA can also improve regional databases, information sharing, and state-of-the-art environmental monitoring; save time and resources that would have gone into mitigation by avoiding environmental impacts altogether; and involve the public in regional environmental issues. In 2009, the Canadian Council of Ministers of the Environment issued a number of core and methodological principles for a strategic approach to regional cumulative environmental assessment, which will be discussed in more depth at the end of this chapter.[18] They also recommended three phases in the assessment process. In Phase 1, the pre-assessment phase, the lead actors develop a reference framework, assemble regional baseline information, and identify regional stressors and trends. Phase 2, the assessment phase, identifies alternative development scenarios for the region; assesses the cumulative effects for each scenario; and identifies a preferred scenario or development path forward. Following this is a post-assessment phase, Phase 3, which consists of identifying mitigation needs and management actions; developing a regional follow-up and monitoring strategy; and implementing that strategy.[19]

The cumulative effects assessment portion of the RCEA process (undertaken in Phase 2) includes the same four basic steps as does project-based assessment—i.e., cumulative effects scoping, retrospective analysis, prospective analysis, and management—with the slight difference that the analysis is adjusted as needed to appropriately capture the effects of multiple projects and initiatives, rather than primarily focusing on the direct effects of a single project.

Approach to Cumulative Effects Assessment

Scope

Scoping a cumulative effects assessment involves deciding what and who to include in the assessment. This includes the appropriate spatial scope (geographic extent) of the assessment, the temporal scope (how far into the future and past the analysis of trends will extend); the scope of Regional Study Components, or RSCs (more commonly known in project environmental assessment as "Valued Ecosystem Components," or VECs); and the scope of public engagement in the exercise.

Geographically, the region of interest (ROI) defined in Manitoba Hydro's RCEA is said to capture "the main areas directly affected by Manitoba Hydro's northern developments associated with LWR [the Lake Winnipeg Regulation Project], CRD [Churchill River Diversion], associated transmission projects, and other associated infrastructure."[20] However, notably, the RCEA ROI does not include the southern portion of the Bipole I and II transmission line corridor, or the planned Bipole III transmission line corridor. The ROI also does not include portions of the Grand Rapids to Ponton 230 kV line, the Herblet Lake to Ralls Island 230 kV line, or the Herblet Lake to Cliff Lake 230 kV line. The explanation for this may be that the ROI is already larger than that recommended in the CEC's Bipole III report. However, the RCEA would be considered more complete if *all* of the hydroelectric infrastructure were captured. As well, the spatial scope of the ROI may exclude some potentially affected communities, such as the Shamattawa First Nation, "because current understandings suggest the community is not directly affected by the historic hydroelectric developments under consideration."[21] The RCEA does not say anything as to whether future hydroelectric development may alter this assumption.

Further, it is important to consider all linear developments—such as roads, pipelines, seismic lines, and river crossings—when assessing land-based cumulative effects. The RCEA's assessment does not fully account for the effects of road building on the environment over time. Road developments are captured in an intactness assessment, but the impacts of roads are very complex, far- and long-reaching, and multi-faceted. The indirect effects of road building are arguably far more insidious than the direct effects of their initial construction. Roads bring people in and resources out of a region, forever altering the environment, economy, and culture of a region. Wildlife (and humans) are killed on roads; air, noise, light, and heat pollution keep animals away from roads, fragmenting their natural habitats and altering the chemical environment. In the long term, carbon dioxide emissions from increased road traffic contribute to global warming.[22] To take a less obvious example, there have been significant effects on the commercial fishery for lake sturgeon on the Nelson River[23] and other nearby commercial fisheries. The presence of roads may have facilitated some of this pressure, as they provide commercial fisheries with easier access to local and other markets.

It is important to recognize that other factors, such as mining, highway developments, and the introduction of Western churches, schools, and government policies, have also affected the RCEA ROI.[24] However, there is no evidence in Phase II of the RCEA document indicating whether the effects of other projects were systematically examined and factored into the RCEA's conclusions. They may or may not have been.

The RCEA on Manitoba Hydro developments adjusts the spatial scope of analysis to suit each Regional Study Component, which is widely considered good practice in CEA (Cumulative Effects Assessment). Typically, RCEA uses a sub-regional (sometimes location-specific) approach to assessing effects, and there is ample evidence throughout the Manitoba Hydro RCEA that these regions are respected in its cumulative effects assessment. For example:

> The assessment of the aquatic environment divided the RCEA Region of Interest into four areas.... These areas were used for the Lake Sturgeon, mercury in fish, fish quality, seals, and beluga RSCs. For the water quality ... and fish community ... RSCs, each area was further subdivided ... to facilitate the discussions.[25]

> The effects of hydroelectric development on each RSC will be discussed first by area (or subdivision within the area where applicable) and then for the RCEA ROI as a whole.[26]

That being said, the temporal scope of the RCEA is retrospective only and focused on "the effects of previous hydroelectric development in the ROI,"[27] using mostly information and data up to 2013. It states: "The cumulative effects of any potential future hydroelectric developments (i.e. those not currently being constructed or part of any formal regulatory process) will be addressed outside of the RCEA, during the regulatory review process for those developments."[28] Thus, the temporal scale of the assessment does not include any aspect of future hydroelectric development in northern Manitoba. Past developments considered in the RCEA include generation and water regulation projects, converter stations and associated infrastructure projects, and transmission projects.[29] The RCEA did also include the Bipole III Transmission Project, Keewatinohk Converter Station and associated infrastructure projects, the Keeyask Generation Project, and the Keeyask Transmission Project.

With respect to RSCs, a limited number were scoped in to the RCEA. Some of the RSCs were chosen based on perceived importance/value to residents in the Churchill, Burntwood, and Nelson river systems.[30] However, Manitoba and Manitoba Hydro selected all of the RSCs without any public input. Certain potential RSCs were considered and dropped or not evaluated in certain areas of the ROI, with rationales provided. For example:

> It should be noted that the aquatic assessment of effects to the Nelson and Churchill River estuaries was limited to beluga and seals, which are the species of greatest concern. Due to the large tides that make it difficult to work in the estuary, there is an almost complete absence of historic, qualitative data for water quality and the fish community, which are subsequently not discussed for estuaries.[31]

> With further research, it has become apparent that there are few to no population data available for terrestrial furbearers in Manitoba, and limited information regarding their distribution within the RCEA ROI . . . the greatest impacts on furbearers have likely resulted within the riparian zones affected by flooding or dewatering. Therefore, the effects assessment for furbearers will focus on aquatic furbearers, using beaver as the focal species.[32]

Although the RCEA cannot include all affected species, as this defeats the purpose of scoping, the rationale for why certain Water and Land RSC were selected over others is at times questionable.

Regarding aquatic furbearers (e.g., beaver and muskrat, as we read about in Chapter 7 in this volume), flooding and dewatering have likely equally impacted other important species apart from the beaver, a keystone species. No terrestrial furbearers at all were selected as RSCs, which could have included mink, marten, fox, wolverine (listed as "Special Concern" by the Committee on the Status of Endangered Wildlife in Canada, [COSEWIC]),[33] otter (listed as "Threatened" by COSEWIC), wolves, lynx, or bobcat.[34] Of all possible bird species, the RSC list is limited to just waterfowl and colonial birds. According to the Nature Conservancy, more than 300 bird species rely on the boreal forest for nesting or migratory stopover habitat.[35]

Manitoba Hydro's RCEA identifies seals and beluga as RSCs (very little is known about the cumulative impacts upon them related to hydroelectric development) but does not make the connection among the abundance, quality, and availability of fish in the Nelson and Churchill estuaries (which are especially important and sensitive habitats) and those impacts to seals and beluga, even though it is noted that "evidence suggests that estuaries may be important feeding areas for seals,"[36] and beluga are listed as "Near Threatened."[37]

It is quite probable that certain important RSCs are missing from the RCEA list, given that impacts are likely to be noticeable sooner at other levels of ecosystem organization than they are at the species level.[38] For example, biodiversity underlies all ecosystem services and could constitute an RSC. Although the Phase II reports of the Province's and Manitoba Hydro's RCEA disclose a final selection of RSCs, unless that list is publicly and independently vetted, it is not possible to determine if it is complete or appropriate.

In terms of who was involved in preparing the RCEA, the Province and Manitoba Hydro did not directly engage regional stakeholders, though this is a core principle of good practice for any environmental assessment process. The RCEA's reliance on secondary sources and data (though extensive) misses the unprecedented opportunity for communities to contribute their knowledge of the full impact of hydroelectric development in the area over time. While it is certainly a challenge to "definitively or quantitatively separate the impacts of these other developments, events and policies from hydroelectric development," as the assessment states,[39] this challenge is outweighed by the potential benefits to affected Indigenous communities of disclosing, debating, and anticipating further impacts of hydro development, and by benefits of the socio-economic trends and patterns in the region that the RCEA would reveal.

Retrospective Analysis

Manitoba and Manitoba Hydro largely approached the RCEA as a descriptive exercise, with no new data collected; however, some new analysis of existing data was performed.[40] The RCEA addresses both environmental and socio-economic effects. Its information sources include findings of scientific and community-based studies, ongoing monitoring programs, regulatory processes, and settlements negotiations and claims processes.[41] Part III People provides a very detailed historical account of the socio-economic effects of hydroelectric development in the Churchill, Burntwood, and Nelson river systems area, while Part IV Physical Environment elaborately describes Manitoba Hydro's physical environmental impacts on the hydraulic zones identified. Both sections are used to support Part V Water and Part VI Land, which are the strongest parts of Phase II in terms of retrospective analysis.

The RCEA consistently attempts to summarize the cumulative impact to each RSC from the pre-development period through to the year 2013 and to assess that RSC's overall health, while clearly identifying information sources and acknowledging data limitations. Past assessments in the region typically did not attempt to integrate information collected under various programs in the same body of water,[42] whereas, notably, the RCEA does. This is a significant contribution, given that this effort contributes new information about the state of these river systems. Also, notably, the RCEA compares pre-development conditions with conditions during the development period where data are available for parts III to VI: People, Physical Environment, Land, and Water. The RCEA also compares on-site/on-system conditions with off-site/off-system conditions in many instances where data are available for Part V Water and Part VI Land. Both of these are good practices.

That being said, data were very limited in most cases for pre-development periods and there was often not enough data collected over the years to assess change over time.[43] Other data limitations included an almost total lack of data on furbearers (information on the single furbearer RSC—beaver—was available in just two terrestrial regions, yet impact assessment results were extrapolated to the whole ROI); there is essentially nothing known about impacts to seals and beluga, or to colonial seabirds (although, as Annette Luttermann describes in Chapter 7 in this volume, there has likely been a large impact), or why lake sturgeon populations remain stressed and depressed. These are significant data gaps for the relatively few RSCs chosen. Despite these gaps, the RCEA consistently strives to characterize the direct effects of past hydroelectric development within the ROI. The assessment clearly acknowledges that hydro development has directly impacted the natural variations in water flow in the Churchill, Burntwood and Nelson river systems, for example. Flooding, reversal of flow patterns, transmission lines, and linear developments such as access roads are all listed as key drivers of regional change.[44] Direct effects[45] in areas with significantly affected water levels include changes in ice cover/slush ice and timing of freezing, changes in water quality due to decomposing vegetation and leaching of materials from flooded soils, increased erosion and loss of habitat (both on land and in water), the blockage of upstream fish movements, and increased debris in the water and along the shorelines.

. However, as previously mentioned, the RCEA does not analyze indirect effects in detail. For example, the assessment states, with regard to the effects of hydroelectric development on fish quality: "it should be noted that hydroelectric development can cause changes to fish diet, water quality, water temperature, algae, and growth rates, all of which can, in turn, affect the taste and texture of fish. These potential indirect linkages have not been subject to scientific studies in the RCEA ROI."[46]

The RCEA consistently uses a range of indicators, metrics, and benchmarks to assess impacts to Part V Water and Part VI Land RSCs. These were aimed at describing and/or characterizing, in a measurable way, the state of that RSC to facilitate a clearer picture of its overall health. However, these metrics were chosen with no apparent public engagement or scrutiny.[47] The use of indicators or benchmarks is not evident in Part III People or Part IV Physical Environment.

Using driver and response indicators to assess RSCs is a useful, innovative practice. However, save for a few instances, the RCEA avoids using environmental thresholds (e.g., management targets, benchmarks, or ecological limits) that could help assess the significance of historical impacts on RSCs, although the use of thresholds is an accepted good practice in CEA. In Part V Water and Part VI Land, the RCEA's short timeline was often cited as the reason why thresholds could not be developed. The reason cited in Part III People is "lack of socio-economic and demographic-specific data pre-1980s,"[48] and in Part IV Physical Environment it is the "absence of high-quality, long-term records with good spatial coverage."[49]

Based on the retrospective analysis, Manitoba and Manitoba Hydro conclude that multiple hydroelectric developments have resulted in certain direct cumulative impacts to RSCs.[50] They acknowledge shoreline erosion, sedimentation, and the accumulation of debris that continue to the present, almost forty years after flooding in many areas of the region. For shorelines that have retreated through mineral erosion, banks and bluffs have not stabilized, and peatland continues to disintegrate or break down. Loss of high-quality habitat has directly affected wildlife, though it is repeatedly stressed that disturbances on species such as caribou, moose, beaver, waterfowl, and colonial water birds are relatively minor and constitute very low-level impacts.

Beyond the discussion of direct effects, a general lack of attention to the synergistic effects of hydroelectric development in the region is one of the biggest weaknesses of the RCEA, which by definition is supposed to capture important effects beyond those most obvious and immediate. Often missing is the assessment of impacts to important connections among people, the physical environment, water, and land. Arguably, a synergistic approach linking multiple stressors to each component in both quantitative and qualitative terms is more likely to yield a useful perspective for answering questions about the total impact of developments on the social and biophysical environment. For example, the assessment states: "While the changes in aquatic biota are strongly linked to changes in the physical environment, they are also linked to socio-economic conditions (e.g. changes in fish prices can result in the targeting of specific species by commercial fishers)."[51] Unfortunately, insightful statements like these—which explicitly recognize the potential for synergistic interactions in the region—are not explored in depth.

It is very important to identify where synergistic interactions affecting Land and Water RSCs might also affect People RSCs. For example, with respect to mercury concentrations in fish, the assessment states: "Based on the entire data set for the ROI, mean mercury concentrations of piscivorous fish species from on-system waterbodies have regularly and often substantially exceeded the 0.5ppm Health Canada standard for the commercial sale of fish. These exceedances have typically been observed for 5–25 years but in some cases for more than 35 years after flooding."[52] It is also noted that: "Hydroelectric development considerably changed Lower Churchill shoreline ecosystems as indicated by surface water area, shoreline length, waterbody morphology, water and ice regimes, bank and beach attributes, the distribution and abundance of shore zone, offshore and tall shrub vegetation and large woody debris accumulation."[53] The same "high" cumulative effects are noted for Nelson River shoreline ecosystems.[54]

From a cumulative effects perspective, it seems important to explore how high mercury concentrations in fish and the major alteration of shoreline ecosystems, combined with lower-quality fish (according to Indigenous people) and fewer fish available per cubic metre in the Nelson and Churchill river estuaries, together have synergistically impacted food security and cultural intactness for Indigenous communities in the region. The RCEA does make a couple of attempts to identify synergistic impacts, but the effort should be expanded. Without a deliberate effort to characterize the synergistic impacts of natural and human perturbations (including hydro) on each RSC, the cumulative effects cannot truly be understood.

It is apparent in the RCEA that the total stress on certain sub-regions of the ROI is much greater than others (the sub-region "Area 2"—the Nelson River and estuary—being the most stressed). Yet, the RCEA does not attempt to qualify the total, cumulative stress placed on any given sub-region, or on the ROI as a whole. In other words, despite the volume of information provided, Manitoba and Manitoba Hydro do not integrate their observations to arrive at a statement about the overall well-being and/or sustainability of the environment or communities of the region. In fact, the RCEA avoids the issue of the significance of the impacts it describes altogether. There is no attempt to evaluate significance either by using the classic criteria (magnitude, duration, likelihood, etc.) or by applying a "sustainability test." Further, the RCEA does not address the societal significance of the cumulative effects of hydro impact. Assigning significance to the impacts caused by hydropower development in northern Manitoba is not merely a scientific exercise. Determining significance is dynamic, contextual, political, and ultimately a judgment call: scientists evaluate significance differently from one another and from local communities.[55] If an assessment deems that a threshold has been crossed, any future impact on a Regional Study Component must be considered significant.

Prospective Analysis

Prospective analysis is an extension of the retrospective analysis—the next step in CEA—in which change trends are projected forward into the future to compare different future development scenarios. However, Manitoba and Manitoba Hydro's RCEA does not include prospective analysis: "environmental trends are discussed, where appropriate, to understand and provide context for environmental change over time, but predictions of future conditions due to climate change, introduction of non-native species, and other ongoing anthropogenic effects are limited, as they are new, evolving and currently not available in the literature."[56]

Prospective analysis is a core element of good-practice CEA and the lack of it must be considered a major shortcoming of the RCEA. It is unclear why the Terms of Reference precluded prospective analysis, given that a major question regarding the future welfare of northern Manitoba is whether to build more dams—particularly, whether or not to sanction development of the Conawapa Generating Station. Manitoba has significant undeveloped hydro potential remaining in the North and has already invested approximately $380 million on the Conawapa Project.[57] While the Province halted construction on the multi-billion-dollar project in 2014, after the Public Utilities Board (PUB) recommended its cancellation due to an increasingly weak business case, it is difficult to imagine it will stay "off the books" forever.

Management

One of the biggest opportunities in a regional scale assessment is to identify ways to coordinate region-wide mitigation efforts across multiple partnerships (the "management" phase of CEA). In this case, the RCEA does not address management beyond providing a list of past and current remediation programs in the region.[58]

Phase II, Part III People documents Manitoba Hydro's past/ongoing efforts at mitigating hydro-related effects in the region, some of which are collaborative in nature: for example, the Lake Sturgeon Stewardship and Enhancement Program,[59] and Coordinated Aquatic Monitoring Program.[60] Most of the effects (Resource Use, Navigation, Transportation, Public Safety, etc.) are mitigated via existing settlement agreements that stipulate compensation agreements for affected communities. Other location-specific initiatives (e.g., Kischi Sipi Namao, formally Lower Nelson River Sturgeon Stewardship Agreement) and programs (e.g., Waterways Management Program, including the Boat Patrol Program, Debris Management Program, and Water Level Forecast Notice Program) are documented as "mitigation measures" for Navigation, Transportation, and Public Safety. The RCEA largely presents these efforts in the context of hydro development, and not in the context of offsetting significant cumulative effects affecting the people in the Region of Interest.

Part IV Physical Environment is silent on the topic of impact mitigation and management measures, although it alludes to the value of collaborative monitoring without elaborating on what such collaborative efforts could look like for managing cumulative effects. For example, the section states: "Water Survey of Canada (WSC) and Manitoba Hydro are part of the National Hydrometric Program—a cooperative endeavour between the federal, provincial, and territorial governments to provide accurate, timely, and standardized data and information on the current and historic availability of surface water."[61] The reason advanced for this collaborative initiative is to support operational and cost efficiencies but not to offset significant cumulative environmental effects.

Thus, although the RCEA's list of past remediation and compensation programs is useful to identify strengths, weaknesses, gaps, and opportunities to strengthen regional impact management, this work has yet to be done: "Following completion of the Phase II report and the public outreach program, Manitoba and Manitoba Hydro will review all of the RCEA documents, the outcomes of the public outreach program, as well as current monitoring and planning/licensing initiatives and consider next appropriate steps. Efforts will be made to develop next steps in a comprehensive and coordinated fashion. Next steps will be outlined in a final RCEA Next Steps document, available in spring 2017."[62] To date, the Next Steps document has not been completed.

Conformity to RSEA Principles and Process

Tables 9.1 and 9.2 summarize the extent to which the northern Manitoba RCEA currently conforms to the core and methodological principles for Regional Strategic Environmental Assessment (RSEA), as set forth by the Canadian Council of Ministers of the Environment (CCME).

Table 9.1. Conformity to the CCME Regional Strategic Environmental Assessment Core Principles

Core Principles	
Strategic	Not yet. The exercise should be "objectives-led." At present the goals and objectives of the Regional Cumulative Effects Assessment (RCEA) are not explicitly stated and there is no clear, publicly endorsed vision for the future of the Region of Interest (ROI).
Futures-oriented	Not yet. The RCEA is currently retrospective in nature only, with no prospective analysis, strategic alternatives for development, or assessment of the likely cumulative effects of these alternatives.
Planned early commencement	The RCEA was completed approximately sixty years after hydroelectric development began in northern Manitoba. However, at least half of the capacity for hydroelectric power in the province has yet to be developed, with more generating stations being considered for future development. This is a very significant amount of further development to a region that has already been acknowledged as significantly altered. It is still "early" if one considers the development that still may come in northern Manitoba.
Cumulative effects focused	Yes. However, prospective analysis of strategic alternatives for the ROI is recommended.
Multi-tiered	Not yet. There is no deliberate connection with project-based environmental impact assessment identified, or any connection to "upstream" policy or planning decisions affecting the ROI.
Multi-scaled	Yes. The scale of analysis in the retrospective analysis is adjusted to suit each Regional Study Component.
Participatory	Not yet. The RCEA process should meaningfully engage affected northern communities and other stakeholders in all key phases of assessment.
Opportunistic	Not yet. The RCEA does not identify opportunities to enhance institutional policies or arrangements, for example.
Adaptive	Not yet. Although a comprehensive list of past and current remediation and compensation efforts by Manitoba Hydro is identified, no changes to existing management or monitoring plans in the region are suggested as yet.

The RCEA was not designed as a strategic exercise. Rather, it simply describes the past cumulative effects in the region. Manitoba Conservation and Water Stewardship and Manitoba Hydro agreed to Terms of Reference for the RCEA in May 2014, in which they agree that the best option to address the Clean Environment Commission's concerns is to develop an RCEA document that is "retrospective in nature"[63] and "describes environmental change over time as a result of previous hydro development, including impacts, mitigation measures, community issues, compensation and the current quality of the environment."[64] Although the Clean Environment Commission does not specifically ask for a strategic assessment in Bipole III Recommendation 13.2, it has registered previous calls for strategic assessment in the region in 2004 and 2012.[65]

Positioning the RCEA as a retrospective, descriptive exercise forestalls a significant opportunity to publicly debate alternative development scenarios and identify the best possible future development path for northern Manitoba. It also precludes stipulating the desired nature and pace of development in the future and/or establishing criteria to evaluate the acceptability of proposed future projects. The RCEA's terms of reference do not state its intended purpose, other than that it will serve "as a resource."[66] It does not specify whether it should be used as a resource to perhaps inform the Manitoba provincial Clean Energy strategy, a regional sustainable development plan (e.g., the Growing Outcomes in Watersheds initiative, which encourages the delivery of ecological goods and services), future project impact assessment approvals or conditions (e.g., Conawapa), or a future regional strategic assessment exercise. Without a clear statement of the tactical purpose of the RCEA, it is difficult to conceptualize the influence of this work, and its value as a resource and to whom.

Previous calls[67] for a collaborative approach to assessing the cumulative effects of past, present, and future development in northern Manitoba were overlooked. The RCEA's terms of reference greatly restrict meaningful, face-to-face participation from northern residents, which was established as the standard for consultation as early as the Berger Inquiry in 1974.[68] There appears to have been no consultation with the public or Indigenous communities in scoping Regional Study Components, creating and analyzing alternative development scenarios, determining significance, creating impact mitigation and monitoring strategies, or integrating adaptive feedback. As well, various important sections are currently missing from the RCEA.[69] However, the RCEA states, "Communities will have the opportunity to review and comment on their summaries [of cumulative effects of development on them] before they are made public. This review and comment will occur throughout the RCEA Public Outreach Program being undertaken by the CEC."[70] At the time of this book's publication, plans for public consultation had been greatly reduced, and the sections are still incomplete.

Not surprisingly, then, the retrospective analysis of cumulative effects on Water and Land RSCs is stronger than that for People. Considerable work remains to be done to adequately characterize cumulative impacts on affected Indigenous communities, and analysis of synergistic and indirect environmental effects on Water and Land RSCs is also rather weak. There are Western scientific and Indigenous traditional knowledge disparities of opinion regarding the cumulative effects on certain Water and Land RSCs and the total stress on sub-regions and the ROI as a whole that have not been characterized yet, and the RCEA has not yet evaluated the significance of the cumulative effects it describes.

Current strengths of the RCEA with respect to the methodological principles set forth by the Canadian Council of Ministers of the Environment (see Table 9.2) include that its current RSC list does include species of noted concern and importance in the ROI, and that it has adopted a structured, systematic approach to the retrospective analysis. To become a strategic assessment, the RCEA would need to be integrated with other regional policy and planning initiatives to ensure a mutually reinforcing relationship; it would need to assess the future cumulative effects of alternative development scenarios in preparation to select a desired path forward; and the interdisciplinary aspects of cumulative effects—in particular, to explore synergistic and total impacts to the region—would need to be improved. For example, the RCEA claims it cannot properly understand the cumulative effects of hydroelectric development on fish quality, because there is no direct scientific linkage. Thus, the RCEA must explore noted indirect linkages; and if an interdisciplinary team does this, the cumulative effects might become much more readily apparent.

Table 9.2. Conformity to CCME Regional Strategic Environmental Assessment Methodological Principles

Methodological Principles	
Integrated	Not yet.
Focused on alternatives	Not yet.
Regional VEC-based	Yes, the Regional Study Components (RCSs) selected appear to be sensitive to the regional context (e.g., water quality, fish community), though their numbers are small, and their appropriateness has not been publicly or independently vetted. Until they are, it will remain unclear as to whether these are the "only" or "best" RSCs to focus on.
Interdisciplinary	Not yet. Assessment is not interdisciplinary in that it does not evaluate the status of any RSC based on integrated scientific perspectives from various branches of knowledge. However, the Regional Cumulative Effects Assessment (RCEA) is cross-disciplinary in that there are various kinds of scientific analysis provided.
Structured and systematic	Yes, in the sense that the RCEA systematically examines existing information, evaluates new information, looks at changes in indicators over time, and summarizes change for RSCs over the period of development to the extent possible, given data limitations.

Table 9.3. Conformity to the Basic Stepwise Process for Regional Strategic Environmental Assessment

Pre-Assessment	
Develop a reference framework	Yes. The RCEA does provide and conform to a Terms of Reference, though current Terms of Reference are non-strategic and greatly limit opportunities for public engagement.
Scope the regional baseline	Yes. This is done reasonably well, with the caveat that there are many data gaps that need to be addressed through additional research in the Region of Interest (ROI). There is a strong basis for prospective analysis for many of the Regional Study Components (RSCs) that are used in the Regional Cumulative Effects Assessment (RCEA), although the RSC list should be publicly and independently vetted, and possibly expanded.

Identify regional stressors and trends	The RCEA does identify hydroelectric developments driving regional stressors or trends and does name other developments affecting the condition of RSCs in the ROI via network diagrams (however, this analysis should be performed in greater depth if and when possible).
Assessment	
Identify strategic alternatives for the region	Not yet. The RCEA does not currently identify strategic development alternatives for the region.
Assess cumulative effects of each alternative	Not yet. The RCEA does attempt to assess cumulative effects but not for strategic alternatives for the region, and not projected into the future.
Identify a preferred strategic alternative	Not yet. The RCEA does not identify a preferred strategic alternative that meets stated goals and objectives for development of the ROI.
*Post-Assessment**	
Identify mitigation needs and management actions	Not yet. The RCEA does provide a comprehensive overview of past and current mitigation and compensation initiatives in Part III People. However, the RCEA does not revisit those strategies based on the results of a prospective analysis or significance determination. Ideally these activities would inform a coordinated regional mitigation and monitoring plan going forward.
Develop a follow-up and monitoring program	Not yet.
Implement the strategy, monitor, and evaluate	Not yet.
Provide adaptive follow-up and review	Not yet. As the preferred scenario is implemented, lessons learned should be used to adapt development initiatives, programs, plans, and policies for the region to ensure desired outcomes are achieved.

* Manitoba and Manitoba Hydro have not yet issued the Next Steps document following public consultation on the RCEA. Therefore, information regarding follow-up and monitoring, including any intended mitigation and management actions, is unavailable at the time of writing of this volume.

With respect to the phases of a basic stepwise process established for Regional Strategic Environmental Assessment,[71] the RCEA is missing many key components. Table 9.3 summarizes which steps have been addressed and which are outstanding.

Looking at these methodological steps, the RCEA addresses only two pre-assessment phases reasonably well at present: scoping the regional baseline and identifying stressors or trends. If the RCEA were to be transformed into a strategic exercise, a new Terms of Reference would have to be issued to reflect the activities still to come in the assessment and post-assessment phases of the framework. The assessment phase would be centred on identifying and evaluating strategic alternatives to the "status quo" hydroelectric development path. The post-assessment phase would be focused on carefully adapting the current mitigation and monitoring regime in the ROI, based on how significant cumulative impacts in the region are determined to be. The approach would become proactive, with the sustainability of its RSCs—seals, beluga, sturgeon, water quality, habitat, biodiversity, and more—at its heart. That being said, compensation programs such as the Northern Flood Agreement (NFA) would naturally retain their importance and be maintained into the future.

Revisiting the RCEA: The Path Forward

Despite multiple earlier calls for strategic RCEA in northern Manitoba, the RCEA is not strategic in nature. While it would not be appropriate to criticize the lack of strategic elements in the RCEA, given the stated Terms of Reference, unless the RCEA is revisited as a strategic exercise that is objectives-led, includes alternative development scenarios, and selects a preferred scenario that details the desired nature and pace of future development in northern Manitoba, the citizens of Manitoba will lose out on much of the potential value-add of an RCEA. While the RCEA does offer a strong retrospective analysis of historical impacts to select land and water RSCs,[72] it could offer so much more: not in terms of pages added, but in terms of perspective added through increased attention to indirect and synergistic impacts, particularly on affected Indigenous communities and their ways of life.

On balance, the Manitoba and Manitoba Hydro RCEA falls short of good-practice CEA. While many elements of good practice were present—for example, in scoping, and in adapting the geographic scale of analysis to suit the nature of each Regional Study Component—the selection of RSCs itself remains unvetted, and the RCEA does not include the very futures-focused and innovative, alternatives-based analysis that makes it so valuable to decision makers. It was also disappointing that some of the same limitations of the Keeyask's CEA, examined in Chapter 4 in this volume, arose again in the RCEA a few years later. For example, both were missing major best-practice components of their assessments: in the project CEA, potentially helpful management and mitigation plans were absent, because of the finding of "no significant adverse effects"; for the RCEA, the future analysis was missing. Both had issues with selecting the valued components to study; both failed to adequately address the differing conclusions within their reports between the Western scientific knowledge and Indigenous knowledge presented. It was a missed opportunity not to make better use of lessons learned.

Based on these observations and given that the provincial environmental minister and the Clean Environment Commission have requested assistance in identifying next steps for the RCEA,[73] the RCEA should be revisited in the near future. A publicly endorsed strategic RCEA should be used to inform future hydroelectric development project approvals in northern Manitoba, including the Conawapa Generating Station and associated infrastructure, as well as related regional policy and planning processes. The current RCEA can be transformed into a forward-looking document, can still achieve the original intent of CEC's advice in the Wuskwatim hearing, and can better conform to the Canadian Council of Ministers of the Environment's established principles and process for Regional Strategic Environmental Assessment. Transforming the RCEA from non-strategic to strategic is essential in order to reach its fullest potential in strengthening Manitoba's environment, economy, and people, particularly the Indigenous communities of the North.

The author would like to acknowledge Dr. Ayodele Olagunju's contributions to parts of the technical report on which this chapter is based.

Notes

1   Government of Canada, *Reference Guide: Addressing Cumulative Environmental Effects (The Concept of Cumulative Environmental Effects)*, 2017, accessed 14 May 2021, https://www.canada.ca/en/impact-assessment-agency/services/policy-guidance/reference-guide-addressing-cumulative-environmental-effects.html.

2   United States Environmental Protection Agency (US EPA), *What Is Acid Rain?* accessed 26 September 2019, https://www.epa.gov/acidrain/what-acid-rain.

3   Wanda Leung, Bram Noble, Jochen Jaeger, and Jill Gunn, "Disparate Perceptions About Uncertainty Consideration and Disclosure Practices in Environmental Assessment and Opportunities for Improvement," *Environmental Impact Assessment Review* 57 (2016): 89–100.

4   J. Gélinas, D. Horswill, R. Northey, and R. Pelletier, *Building Common Ground: A New Vision for Impact Assessment in Canada: The Final Report of the Expert Panel for the Review of Environmental Assessment Processes* (Ottawa: Canadian Environmental Assessment Agency, 2017), accessed 14 May 2021, https://www.canada.ca/content/dam/themes/environment/conservation/environmental-reviews/building-common-ground/building-common-ground.pdf.

5   Jill Blakley and Ayodele Olagunju, *Critical Review of the Regional Cumulative Effects Assessment (RCEA) for Hydroelectric Developments on the Churchill, Burntwood and Nelson River Systems*, technical report prepared for the Public Interest Law Centre Manitoba under contract agreement, Manitoba, Canada, 2017.

6   See, for example, Great Sand Hills Scientific Advisory Committee (GSH RES), *Great Sand Hills Regional Environmental Study* (Regina: Canadian Plains Research Center, 2007); "Beaufort Sea Strategic Regional Plan of Action" (BSStRPA), accessed 26 September 2019, http://www.bsstrpa.ca/pdf/bsstrpa/BSStRPA%20RPA%20March2009.pdf; Jill Gunn and Bram Noble, "A Conceptual Basis and Methodological Framework for Regional Strategic Environmental Assessment (R-SEA)," *Impact Assessment and Project Appraisal* 27, no. 4 (2009): 258–70; Denis Kirchhoff, Dan McCarthy, Debbe Crandall, Laura McDowell, and Graham Whitelaw, "Strategic Environmental Assessment and Regional Infrastructure Planning: The Case of York Region, Ontario, Canada," *Impact Assessment and Project Appraisal* 29, no. 1 (2010): 11–26; Denis Kirchhoff, Dan McCarthy, Debbe Crandall, Laura McDowell, and Graham Whitelaw, "A Policy Window Opens: Strategic Environmental Assessment in York Region, Ontario, Canada," *Journal of Environmental Assessment Policy and Management* 12, no. 3 (2011): 333–54; Dallas Johnson, Kim Lalonde, Menzie McEachern, John Kenney, Gustavo Mendoza, Andrew Buffin, and Kate Rich, "Improving Cumulative Effects Assessment in Alberta: Regional Strategic Assessment," *Environmental Impact Assessment Review* 31, no. 5 (2011): 481–83, http://doi.org/10.1016/j.eiar.2011.01.010; Courtney Fidler and Bram Noble, "Advancing Regional Strategic Environmental Assessment in Canada's Western Arctic: Implementation Opportunities and Challenges," *Journal of Environmental Assessment Policy and Management* 15, no. 1 (2013): 1350007; Bram Noble and Jill Gunn, *Review of KHLP's Approach to the Keeyask Generation Project Cumulative Effects Assessment* (Winnipeg: Public Interest Law Centre, 2012), accessed 14 May 2021, https://www.researchgate.net/publication/272791007_Review_of_KHLP%27s_Approach_to_the_Keeyask_Generation_Project_Cumulative_Effects_Assessment; Cheryl Chetkiewicz and Anne Lintner, *Getting It Right in Ontario's Far North: The Need for a Regional Strategic Environmental*

Assessment in the Ring of Fire [Wawangajing] (N.p.: Wildlife Conservation Society Canada, 2014), accessed 14 May 2021, https://www.wcscanada.org/Portals/96/Documents/RSEA_Report_WCSCanada_Ecojustice_FINAL.pdf.

7   See Keeyask Hydropower Limited Partnership, *Keeyask Environmental Impact Statement,* Manitoba Hydro, 2012, ch. 6, 6–12, accessed 14 May 2021, https://keeyask.com/project-timeline/environment-assessment-process/environmental-licensing-process/.

8   Jim Waldram, "Hydro-Electric Development and the Process of Negotiation in Northern Manitoba, 1960–1977," *Canadian Journal of Native Studies* 4, no. 2 (1984): 205–39.

9   Ibid.

10 Information on the Northern Flood Agreement in this paragraph is drawn from: Know History, *Hydroelectric Development in Northern Manitoba: A History of the Development of the Churchill, Burntwood and Nelson Rivers, 1960–2015* (Winnipeg: Manitoba Clean Environment Commission, 2016), accessed 14 May 2021, http://www.cecmanitoba.ca/cecm/hearings/pubs/Regional_Cumulative_Effects_Assessment/BackgroundInformation/Hydroelectric_Development_in_Northern_Manitoba.pdf.

11 See Noble and Gunn, *Review of KHLP's Approach;* Jill Gunn and Bram Noble, *Review of the Cumulative Effects Assessment Undertaken by Manitoba Hydro for the Bipole III Project* (Winnipeg: Public Interest Law Centre, 2013), accessed 14 May 2021, https://sitecstatement.files.wordpress.com/2016/02/gunn-j-and-b-noble-november-2012-critical-review-of-the-cumulative-effects-assessment-undertaken-by-manitoba-hydro-for-the-bipole-iii-project-prepared-for-the-public-interest-law-c1.pdf.

12 The Legislative Assembly of Manitoba, Bill 18, The Path to Reconciliation Act, 2016, accessed 14 May 2021, https://web2.gov.mb.ca/bills/40-5/b018e.php.

13 Manitoba Hydro, *"Who We Are,"* accessed 26 September 2019, http://www.manitobahydropower.com/who-we-are.shtml.

14 Canadian Council of Ministers of the Environment, *Canada-Wide Definitions and Principles for Cumulative Effects* (Winnipeg: Canadian Council of Ministers of the Environment, 2014), accessed 14 May 2021, https://ccme.ca/en/res/cedefinitionsandprinciples1.0e.pdf.

15 James Careless, "Metropolitan-Hinterland Thesis" (N.p.: *The Canadian Encyclopedia,* 2018), accessed 14 May 2021, https://www.thecanadianencyclopedia.ca/en/article/metropolitan-hinterland-thesis.

16 See Jill Harriman and Bram Noble, "Characterizing Project and Strategic Approaches to Regional Cumulative Effects Assessment in Canada," *Journal of Environmental Assessment Policy and Management* 10, no. 1 (2008): 25–50.

17 Canadian Council of Ministers of the Environment, *Regional Strategic Environmental Assessment in Canada: Principles and Guidance* (Winnipeg: Canadian Council of Ministers of the Environment, 2009), accessed 14 May 2021, https://ccme.ca/en/res/rseaincanadaprinciplesandguidance1428-secure.pdf.

18 Ibid.

19 Blakley and Olagunju, *Critical Review.*

20 Government of Manitoba and Manitoba Hydro, *Regional Cumulative Effects Assessment,* 2015, Phase II, Part I, 1.3-2, https://www.hydro.mb.ca/regulatory_affairs/regional_cumulative_effects_assessment/.

21 Ibid., Phase II, Part I, 3.2-3.

22 S. Trombulak and C. Frisell, "Review of Ecological Effects of Roads on Terrestrial and Aquatic Communities," *Conservation Biology* 14 (2000): 18–30; Ayodele Olagunju, "Selecting Valued Ecosystem Components for Cumulative Effects in Federally Assessed Road Infrastructure Projects in Canada," Master's thesis, University of Saskatchewan.

23 Manitoba and Manitoba Hydro, *Regional Cumulative Effects Assessment*, Phase II, Part V, 5.4-5.

24 Ibid., Phase II, Part I, 2.6-1.

25 Ibid., Phase II, Part V, 5.1-1.

26 Ibid., Phase II, Part V, 5.1-1.

27 Ibid., Phase II, Part I, 1.2-1.

28 Ibid., Phase II, Part I, 1.3-8.

29 Ibid., Phase II, Part I, Table 1.3.2-1.

30 Ibid., Phase 1, Part II, 1.3-14.

31 Ibid., Phase II, Part V, 5.1-5.

32 Ibid., Phase II, Part VI, 6.1-6.

33 Brian Slough, "Status of the Wolverine *Gulo* in Canada," *Wildlife Biology* 13 (2007): 76–82.

34 See The Association for the Protection of Fur-Bearing Animals, "*What is a Fur-Bearer?*" 2013, accessed 26 September 2019, http://thefurbearers.com/about-us/who-are-the-fur-bearers.

35 C. Richards, "The Importance of Boreal Forests," *Land Lines: The Nature Conservancy of Canada* (blog), 2018, accessed 26 September 2019, http://www.natureconservancy.ca/en/blog/the-importance-of-boreal-forests.html#.XY2Oxy3MyuU.

36 Manitoba and Manitoba Hydro, *Regional Cumulative Effects Assessment*, Phase II, Part V, 5.7-2.

37 Ibid., Phase II, Part V, 5.8-2.

38 Jo Treweek, *Ecological Assessment* (Oxford: Blackwell Science, 1999).

39 Manitoba and Manitoba Hydro, *Regional Cumulative Effects Assessment*, Phase II, Part III, 3.2-6.

40 Ibid., Phase II, Part I, 1.1-2.

41 Ibid., Phase II, Part I, 1.1-2.

42 Ibid., Phase II, Part V, 5.2-13 and 5.3-9.

43 Ibid., Phase II, Part V, 5.3-9.

44 Ibid., Phase II, Part V, 5.1-2.

45 Ibid., see Figure 5.1.2-1 in Phase II, Part V.

46 Ibid., Phase II, Part V, 5.6-32.

47 Ibid., see sections 5.1.2.3. (Water) and 6.1.2.3 (Land).

48 Ibid., Phase II, Part III, 3.3-33.

49 Ibid., Phase II, Part IV, 4.2-5.

50 Government of Manitoba and Manitoba Hydro, *Regional Cumulative Effects Assessment*.

51 Ibid., Phase II, Part V, 5.1-2.

52 Ibid., Phase II, Part V. 5.5-98.

53 Ibid., Phase II, Part VI, 3-431.

54   Ibid., Phase II, Part VI, 6.3-442, 6.3-451, 6.3-452.

55   Bram Noble, *Introduction to Environmental Impact Assessment: Guide to Principles and Practice,* 3rd ed. (Toronto: Oxford University Press, 2015).

56   Manitoba and Manitoba Hydro, *Regional Cumulative Effects Assessment,* Phase II, Part I, 1.3-5.

57   Manitoba Hydro, "2017/18 and 2018/19 General Rate Application," accessed 26 September 2019, https://www.hydro.mb.ca/regulatory_affairs/pdf/electric/general_rate_application_2017/full_rate_application_2017.pdf, see: tab 3, 18.

58   Manitoba and Manitoba Hydro, *Regional Cumulative Effects Assessment,* Phase II, Part I, 1.2-6.

59   Ibid., Phase II, Part III, 3.4-26.

60   Ibid.

61   Manitoba and Manitoba Hydro, *Regional Cumulative Effects Assessment,* Phase II, Part IV, 4.3-5.

62   Ibid., Phase II, Part I, 1.1-2.

63   Ibid., Terms of Reference, 1.

64   Ibid., Terms of Reference, 3.

65   See the Clean Environment Commission's 2004 Wuskwatim recommendation; and Gunn and Noble's 2012 Bipole III recommendation in *Review of the Cumulative Effects.*

66   Manitoba and Manitoba Hydro, *Regional Cumulative Effects Assessment,* Terms of Reference, 5.

67   See the Clean Environment Commission's 2004 Wuskwatim recommendation; and Gunn and Noble's 2012 Bipole III recommendation in *Review of the Cumulative Effects.*

68   Peter Mulvihill and Doug Baker, "Ambitious and Restrictive Scoping: Case Studies from Northern Canada," *Environmental Impact Assessment Review* 21, no. 4 (2001): 363–84; Robert Gibson, "Why Sustainability Assessment?" in *Sustainability Assessment: Pluralism, Practice and Progress,* ed. A. Bond, A. Morrison-Saunders, and R. Howitt (London: Routledge, 2013), 3–17.

69   Manitoba and Manitoba Hydro, *Regional Cumulative Effects Assessment;* sections 3.5.4 through 3.5.19 of Phase II, Part III People are missing.

70   Manitoba and Manitoba Hydro, *Regional Cumulative Effects Assessment,* Phase II, Part III, 3.5-9.

71   Jill Gunn and Bram Noble, "A Conceptual Basis and Methodological Framework for Regional Strategic Environmental Assessment (R-SEA)," *Impact Assessment and Project Appraisal* 27, no. 4 (2009): 258–70.

72   Regional study components are defined in the report as "topics that have been selected to focus the assessment, represent the overall effects of hydroelectric developments within the Region of Interest and reflect key ecological and social concerns, or are of key importance to the people living in the area." See: Manitoba and Manitoba Hydro, *Regional Cumulative Effects Assessment,* Phase II, Part I, xxv.

73   C. Cox, Letter to Mr. Serge Scrafield, Chair, Clean Environment Commission, written by Ms Cathy Cox, Minister of Sustainable Development (Government of Manitoba, 2017), accessed 26 September 2019, http://www.gov.mb.ca/sd/eal/registries/5714hydro/revised_cec_t_of_r2017-03-02_v1.pdf.

"We Are the Family"

TRAPLINE 15 FAMILY, REPRESENTED BY JANET MCIVOR,
ILLA DISBROWE, MARY WAVEY, MARILYN MAZURAT,
NORMA MCIVOR, ROBERT SPENCE, GLORIA KITCHEKEESIK,
AND JONATHAN KITCHEKEESIK

*Excerpt from the transcript of the Keeyask CEC hearing in Winnipeg,
14 November 2013.*

We are the family whose ancestral land is on the Gull Lake Trapline 15 area . . . we are here to talk about traditional land use.

The Clean Environment Commission has already been told that the Gull Lake area will be the most devastated land and water . . . when the Keeyask Generating Station [(KGS) is built]. You have already been told time and time again that in our Cree [culture] Aboriginal and Treaty harvesting practices and rights are exercised by our family on the land we know, love and is our home.

We sit before you, CEC, to hear our voice for our rights as descendants of the keeper[s] of the land. Our ancestral land has already been disrupted by the worst kind. From what we have seen, when the KGS is built, our lives, our heritage, our ancestral lands will be altered and destroyed forever. . . .

All the money in the world is not going to replace the lost ways of our ancestral connection to the Gull Lake Trapline 15. That will forever change. Our relationship with the land runs deep. Our way of life on Gull Lake, as we have come to live, it will be wiped out when the Keeyask Generating Station is completed.

We want to talk to the CEC about two things; the way the Keeyask Generating Station project has . . . affected our family physically, mentally and socially and spiritually. And second, the kind of accommodations that Manitoba Hydro should provide to try and ease the damage and the mental stress and the personal turmoil done to each and every one of us. We implore [the] CEC to make a condition on the licence for Keeyask Generating Station that our family be provided this accommodation.

Keeyask has and will affect us. We are a traditional Cree family carrying on our Cree culture as our inherent right to do so. From all our commotion from the so-called progress, we are from the land and live with the land and . . . care for it.

We have had to deal with a lot of changes forced on us over the years, but by far the worst change imposed on us has been the building of the Keeyask Generating Station. Yes, we know there have been agreements between our First Nation and Manitoba Hydro. We feel the First Nation got boxed in by all the pressure. There was the pressure from all the damage that Hydro—that the existing Hydro projects have done to all of us, and the pressure that came from KGS itself. Many of us believe that KGS will get built regardless of what we want. The Manitoba Hydro has so much power that they will get what they want no matter what.

So there was a real pressure to agree to get something from this . . . project instead. But we think that the damage from KGS will be so great and that . . . what TCN [Tataskweyak Cree Nation] is getting in return is so little that TCN should have never agreed to KGS.

We think it goes against our Cree world view to allow such permanent and widespread damage and harm, especially when so little is being offered in return.

This is what the damage will be to our family and homeland alone, displacing our way of life, flooding us out, disconnecting the integrity of our connection [with] our past, ruining our relationship to our land. Destroying the way of the hunting and fishing, affecting [what] we harvest the land and waters to sustain life on this land, reducing mercury and affecting the fish, taking away our fishing, taking away our plants, waters and shorelines that severely affects the habits of different species that make it a beautiful sanctuary.

———

Keeyask dam will be built in the heart of Gull Lake. To us, the family that is—this is the last place we had seen our brother, Leon, alive. He couldn't speak but we understood him. To this day, we still search and scour the shorelines when the water level is low. After the Keeyask dam is built, this will be gone. It will be a reservoir, gone forever.

Our trust has been compromised. How can we trust Manitoba Hydro to do the right thing? When they were doing the supposed consultation process, the year they did the referendum, there were people that had questions and seeing things that needed change in the JKDA [Joint Keeyask Development Agreement], but were told they can't change it because it was a frozen draft. But in the presentation, it only said draft, not frozen draft. So how can we trust anything we are told when Manitoba Hydro lawyers, consultants can easily change the meaning of a word ["draft"] in a dictionary?

We were part of the protest and we were served [a] court injunction. We were told we were trespassing in our own traditional territory. This court injunction is still held over our heads.

RCMPs were like messengers. They told us Hydro would deal with outstanding issues. To this day, we haven't seen nothing.

There is no amount of money that would replace what we will lose. I had heard numerous times people say this, this is just a formality. In today's world, CEC will grant Manitoba Hydro this licence because Manitoba Hydro already spent millions. Money talks.

So I come back to trust. How can we trust Manitoba Hydro to do the right thing? But I believe there are still some good people out there, so I trust CEC to put in a condition. Before Manitoba Hydro builds Keeyask dam, to deal with all the outstanding issues and concerns.

PART 3

Partnership Builiding and Hydroelectric Development

" Is it the intention of this government and Manitoba Hydro to try and destroy the Treaties that were signed by our people, as long as the river flows, the grass grows and the sun shines? I would love to see you try and stop that sun from shining, and the grass [from growing], but you are doing your best with the rivers, aren't you?"

Tom Nepetaypo, Fox Lake Cree Nation, CFLGC Presentation at CEC hearings (9 December 2013), 5497–98

CHAPTER 10

The Honour of the Crown and Hydroelectric Development in Manitoba

AIMÉE CRAFT

This chapter probes a concept that is widely recognized in Canadian law relating to Indigenous peoples—the Honour of the Crown. This duty to act honourably governs all relations between the Crown and Indigenous peoples in Canada. When considering how this overarching duty applies to hydroelectric projects in Manitoba, and to the planning, approval, and construction of the Keeyask Dam, two major questions arise: Who is the Crown? and What is the extent of the duty to act honourably? These questions are significant in the context of continuing hydroelectric development over more than half a century, through a highly integrated system of generation and distribution that continues to grow. These questions are also particularly relevant when continued development directly affects the exercise of Treaty and Aboriginal rights that many First Nations and other Indigenous peoples in northern Manitoba hold, and where extensive cumulative impacts continue to put pressure on Indigenous territories and communities.

The Supreme Court of Canada (SCC) has confirmed that the Honour of the Crown is an overarching duty that governs all of the Crown's interactions with Indigenous peoples in Canada. This duty applies to Treaty making, interpretation, and implementation; to the Crown duty to consult and accommodate impacts on Indigenous rights, lands, and waters; and to the negotiation of claims. It grounds the interpretation and application of section 35 of the Constitution

Act 1982[1] ("the Constitution"), which recognizes and affirms Treaty and Aboriginal rights, ensuring that those rights cannot be infringed upon without justification.[2]

While many have celebrated the genesis and confirmation of the Honour of the Crown in multiple SCC cases, its application has been fraught with controversy. Its meaning and intent are somewhat ambiguous. Indigenous peoples, government, and third parties each see the normative obligations associated with the duty differently, particularly in relation to natural resource extraction.

Indigenous nations exercise constitutionally protected Treaty and Aboriginal rights in Manitoba. They also have harvesting rights guaranteed to "Indians"[3] by the Natural Resources Transfer Agreement and Act that are constitutionally protected. Where there may be an impact on those rights, the Crown has a duty to consult and accommodate, which flows from the broader duty of the Crown to act honourably.

The relationship between Manitoba Hydro—acting as an agent of the Crown—and the Province of Manitoba (including its various departments and agents) is oftentimes perplexing to Indigenous peoples, and has remained somewhat obscure in law and its practical application. However, the SCC has confirmed that the Honour of the Crown "is not a mere incantation, but rather a core precept that finds its application in concrete practices."[4] The Crown and all its delegates have a duty to act honourably in relation to Indigenous peoples.

In the context of continued hydroelectric development in Manitoba, all Crown conduct must be honourable and held to the highest standard, as required by law—in the Treaties, the Constitution, and the United Nations Declaration on the Rights of Indigenous Peoples (UNDRIP). This includes adhering to the standard of free, prior, and informed consent (FPIC, explored in more depth in Joseph Dipple's chapter in this volume) where critical Indigenous interests and constitutionally protected rights are potentially impacted. As argued in this chapter, agents of the Crown (including Manitoba Hydro) must be held to this highest standard in relation to potential impacts on Indigenous peoples, lands, resources, and rights—past, present, and future. The Keeyask context illustrates the need for such a high standard, where the Cree environmental assessments found in sum that the significance of the impacts outweighed the proposed mitigation (particularly in relation to sturgeon and caribou populations), and yet the Keeyask partnership's

Environmental Impact Statement found that there were no significant residual adverse effects. In another example, Jerry Buckland, Melanie O'Gorman, and Joseph Dipple in this volume point to the potentially coercive nature of securing First Nations' consent for the Keeyask Project if they did not genuinely believe they had a choice. In cases where such a discrepancy arises over the competing interests between Indigenous peoples and the Crown, the highest standard of honourable conduct should be required of all Crown agents and representatives.

The Honour of the Crown—An Overarching Constitutional Duty

The Honour of the Crown is a constitutional duty that "refers to the principle that servants of the Crown must conduct themselves with honour when acting on behalf of the sovereign."[5] It is an overarching duty that applies to all interactions between the Crown and Indigenous peoples, and particularly to the solemn promises it has made, including fulfilling Treaty obligations. As stated by the SCC in the MMF (Manitoba Metis Federation) decision, "In its most basic iteration, the law assumes that the Crown always intends to fulfill its solemn promises, including constitutional obligations."[6]

Reconciliation is the purpose underlying the Honour of the Crown.[7] The Honour of the Crown requires that the Crown (a) broadly and purposively interpret their promises made under section 35, and (b) act diligently to fulfil this purpose. This precludes the Crown from engaging in sharp dealing[8] or creating legislation contrary to reconciliation. As stated in *R v. Badger*: "the honour of the Crown is always at stake in its dealing with Indian people. Interpretations of treaties and statutory provisions which have an impact upon Treaty or Aboriginal rights must be approached in a manner which maintains the integrity of the Crown."[9]

The Honour of the Crown gives rise to a duty of purposeful fulfillment of the Crown's promises. This means that the Crown must interpret legislation affecting section 35 rights in an intentional and deliberate manner, and the Crown must diligently try to fulfill the underlying intent of its constitutional obligation.[10] *Haida Nation v. British Columbia* states, "From the assertion of sovereignty to the resolution of claims and the implementation of treaties, the Crown must act honourably."[11]

Furthermore, the Honour of the Crown applies to the Crown in all its forms, including the federal and provincial Crown, and to other agents who act as representatives of the Crown in various capacities, including boards, tribunals, and agencies. This supports the argument that the duty applies to Manitoba Hydro in its capacity as an agent of the Crown.

What constitutes honourable conduct varies with the context and circumstances.[12] Distinct duties flow from the Honour of the Crown, including the duty to consult and accommodate. The duty to consult, as stated in *Mikisew Cree First Nation v. Canada (Minister of Canadian Heritage)*, is "an essential corollary to the honourable process of reconciliation."[13] To fulfill this duty, Crown servants must seek to perform the obligation in a way that pursues the purpose behind the promise. As *R v. Marshall* states, the Aboriginal group must not be left "with an empty shell of a Treaty promise."[14] The SCC has found that the cumulative effects of an ongoing project and historical context may inform the scope of the duty to consult.[15]

The Crown can delegate the duty to consult to a regulatory body. Where the Crown intends to rely on the regulatory body's process, it must make that clear to the affected Indigenous group.[16] Regulatory bodies with final decision-making power (for example, the National Energy Board)[17] are subject to the duty to consult. A regulatory body can fulfill the Crown's duty to consult by demonstrating institutional expertise and by having the appropriate powers. For example, appropriate powers might be (1) the procedural powers necessary to implement consultation; and (2) the remedial powers to, where necessary, accommodate affected Aboriginal claims, or Aboriginal and Treaty rights.[18] If these terms are met, the Crown can rely on the regulatory body's process to completely or partially fulfill the Crown's duty to consult.[19] Regardless of the regulatory bodies' obligations with respect to consultation and accommodation, as an agent of the Crown they are necessarily vested with the underlying duty of the Honour of the Crown.

The Honour of the Crown and Manitoba Hydro

Manitoba Hydro has stated numerous times that it does not consider itself to be the "Crown" for the purposes of fulfilling the Crown's duty of consultation and accommodation.[20] However, it has indicated that it is an agent of the Crown, as stated in the Manitoba Hydro Act.[21] Manitoba Hydro's role as an agent of the Crown engages its duty to act honourably.

In its 2016 application to the National Energy Board for a certificate to build the Manitoba-Minnesota Transmission Project, Manitoba Hydro indicated that it views the First Nations and Métis Engagement Process (referring to the leadership meetings, open houses, field visits, letters, phone calls, and self-directed studies that took place between Manitoba Hydro and First Nations, Métis, and Indigenous organizations from August 2013 through to filing the transmission project's Environmental Impact Statement) "as distinct from Crown consultations conducted pursuant to section 35 of the Constitution Act, 1982.... Manitoba Hydro submits that the legal obligation to undertake section 35 consultations with respect to the Manitoba-Minnesota Transmission Project lies with Canada and the Province of Manitoba and has not been delegated to Manitoba Hydro."[22] Manitoba Hydro took a similar position in relation to the Keeyask Project and negotiations, stating clearly in the 2009 Joint Keeyask Development Agreement that Manitoba Hydro would provide information to Manitoba and Canada for the purpose of their consultations.[23]

In other circumstances, Crown corporations, like BC Hydro, have been delegated some or all of the Crown's duty to consult.[24] The SCC in *Rio Tinto* found that BC Hydro was an agent of the Crown, acting "in the place of the Crown"—in that case, for the purpose of making an agreement with Alcan to purchase energy.[25] It was, therefore, subject to the Crown's duties to consult and correspondingly to act honourably in all its dealings.

In 2015, the superior court of Manitoba was asked to prevent Manitoba Hydro from further cutting down boreal forests for the Bipole III transmission line until the duty to consult and accommodate had been discharged. The underlying question—Does Manitoba Hydro have a duty to consult and accommodate?—was answered negatively in the injunction application. In the *Sapotaweyak Cree Nation et al. v. Manitoba et al.* case, Justice Bryk of the Manitoba Court of Queen's Bench confirmed that "Hydro is a Manitoba Crown corporation established pursuant to *The Manitoba Hydro Act*, C.C.S.M., c. H190 ('Hydro Act'), and pursuant to s. 4(2) of that Act is an agent of Her Majesty."[26] However, he stopped short of finding a duty to consult and accommodate, and distinguished the *Sapotaweyak* case from the *Rio Tinto* case, finding that Manitoba Hydro did not have a duty to consult and accommodate the Sapotaweyak First Nation. In his decision, Justice Bryk found "that the duty on Crown corporations to consult only arises when that Crown corporation is specifically charged with a duty to act in accordance with the Honour of the Crown. [The Supreme Court of Canada] did not say that all Crown corporations, under any circumstances, are charged with the responsibility to consult."[27] He went on to say:

> [42] In *Rio Tinto Alcan,* the trial court decided that B.C. Hydro had been specifically charged with the responsibility and duty to consult and that under those circumstances, its proposal to enter into an agreement to purchase electricity from Alcan amounted to Crown conduct. It was because of those unique circumstances that the trial court concluded that B.C. Hydro acted in place of the Crown.
>
> [43] There was no similar delegation of authority between Manitoba and Hydro. Moreover, in these circumstances, the law of agency does not establish that the obligations of the principal Manitoba automatically apply to its agent Hydro.
>
> [44] I have not been directed to any jurisprudence which would indicate the requirement for two separate simultaneous consultations by two separate entities.[28]

The trial judge in the *Sapotaweyak* case appears to have conflated two concepts: the Honour of the Crown and the duty to consult. While they are connected, the Honour of the Crown is an underlying section 35 duty that engages the honourable fulfillment of constitutional obligations (with the purpose of promoting reconciliation). The Honour of the Crown is necessarily broad, applies to a variety of circumstances, and is an inherent aspect of all Crown-Indigenous relations. The duty to consult and accommodate flows from the Honour of the Crown but is a specific duty that arises where there is potential impact on Treaty and Aboriginal rights. Therefore, the duty to consult may apply only in certain circumstances and may be delegated to a Crown corporation, whereas the overarching duty to act honourably applies to all agents of the Crown in all dealings with Indigenous peoples.

In the *Sapotaweyak* case, Manitoba Hydro accepted that it is an agent of the Crown. Manitoba Hydro never claimed that it did not have a duty to act honourably. Its claim was, rather, that it did not have a constitutional duty separate and apart from the Province's to consult and accommodate the rights and interests of the impacted First Nations.[29]

The Honour of the Crown and the duty to consult and accommodate are two related yet separate constitutional obligations. The jurisprudence is clear: the duty of the Crown applies to all its interactions with Indigenous peoples. An agent of the Crown should also uphold the Honour of the Crown in all of its interactions. While the agent may not have been delegated the duty to consult, this would not absolve it from the duty to act honourably. Manitoba Hydro may not have all of the specific duties of Manitoba. However, as a Crown corporation and an agent of the Crown, Manitoba Hydro does have a duty to act honourably in all its dealings with Indigenous peoples.

The duty to act honourably is heightened in the context of hydroelectric development since, in the majority of approvals processes, Manitoba Hydro (an agent of the Crown) is the proponent and Manitoba (the Crown) is the administrative decision maker and the consultative body.

In sum, Manitoba Hydro is an agent of the Crown and therefore should be subject to the duty of the Honour of the Crown. Even if one accepts Manitoba Hydro's position that, despite being an agent of the Crown, it does not have an obligation to consult and accommodate, it is evident that, at the very least, the underlying duty to act honourably applies to Manitoba Hydro in all its dealings with Indigenous peoples. As such, Manitoba Hydro should be held to a high standard of conduct in relation to Indigenous communities affected by hydroelectric projects—ongoing, future, and past—in northern Manitoba.

The Honour of the Crown in the Context of Keeyask and Future Projects

While Manitoba Hydro has invoked the language of meaningful and respectful relationships in its "strong and fair partnership"[30] with the four First Nations partners in the Keeyask Project, and while it committed to honouring Treaty and Aboriginal rights, it did not engage in constitutional (or section 35) consultation and accommodation.[31]

As has been thoroughly explored in this volume so far, the history of hydroelectric projects and their impacts on Indigenous peoples in Manitoba has been devastating. Current and potential future impacts of Keeyask have been documented in the 2012 Environmental Impact Statement (EIS) submitted on behalf of the Keeyask partnership,[32] the separate environmental assessments prepared by the Cree Nations (see Chapter 13 in this volume),[33] and through the evidence at the Clean Environment Commission (CEC) hearings.[34]

What, then, becomes of the duty to act honourably for Manitoba Hydro? What are the promises that it must fulfill to ensure the Crown's honour is maintained, and, as stated in *Haida Nation v. British Columbia (Minister of Forests)*, that it "is not a mere incantation, but rather a core precept that finds its application in concrete practices"?[35]

Manitoba Hydro has acknowledged that "the numbered Treaties in Manitoba are the cornerstone of the relationship between the First Nation signatories and the Crown."[36] Furthermore, the Northern Flood Agreement[37] has been deemed a modern Treaty, containing mutual rights and obligations and a solemn promise not to repeat the past practices of hydroelectric development without the consent of Indigenous peoples.[38]

In the *Daniels v. Canada (Indian Affairs and Northern Development)* decision, Justice Abella notes that the Government of Canada's goal is reconciliation with Indigenous peoples. This would recognize Indigenous peoples as equal partners in Confederation, rather than subjects of it:[39] "The constitutional changes, the apologies for historic wrongs, a growing appreciation that Aboriginal and non-Aboriginal people are partners in Confederation, the Report of the Royal Commission on Aboriginal Peoples, and the Final Report of the Truth and Reconciliation Commission of Canada, all indicate that reconciliation with all of Canada's Aboriginal peoples is Parliament's goal."

Justice Abella wrote that the *Daniels* decision itself "represents another chapter in the pursuit of reconciliation and redress in that relationship."[40] She defined the relationship in the context of the "history of Canada's relationship with its Indigenous peoples," and recalls that "the 'grand purpose' of s. 35 is '[t]he reconciliation of Aboriginal and non-Aboriginal Canadians in a *mutually respectful long-term relationship*.'"[41]

Given the current imperative of reconciliation, the adoption of UNDRIP (endorsed by both Manitoba and Canada), Manitoba's Path to Reconciliation[42] legislation, and the Treaties, this duty to act honourably must be enforced to a high degree, and corresponding acts must be significant and meaningful. For example, the Honour of the Crown requires that decision-making processes relating to lands and territories that may be impacted by development take into account Indigenous perspectives of the Treaty (an agreement to share in the land and resources) and Indigenous laws. This moves Canada closer to its goal of recognizing Indigenous peoples as equal partners in key decision making that greatly impacts shared land.

The government of Manitoba has affirmed its commitment to reconciliation as set out by the Truth and Reconciliation Commission of Canada (TRC) and UNDRIP,[43] guided by the following principles:

Respect: Reconciliation is founded on respect for Indigenous nations and Indigenous peoples. Respect is based on awareness and acknowledgement of the history of Indigenous peoples and appreciation of their languages, cultures, practices and legal traditions.

Engagement: Reconciliation is founded on engagement with Indigenous nations and Indigenous peoples.

Understanding: Reconciliation is fostered by striving for a deeper understanding of the historical and current relationships between Indigenous and non-Indigenous peoples and the hopes and aspirations of Indigenous nations and Indigenous peoples.

Action: Reconciliation is furthered by concrete and constructive action that improves the present and future relationships between Indigenous and non-Indigenous peoples.[44]

As an agent of the Crown, Manitoba Hydro, as part of its duty to uphold the Honour of the Crown, is subject to this same standard of commitment to reconciliation, the Calls to Action and UNDRIP. Scott Thomson, President and CEO of Manitoba Hydro, has clearly stated the Crown corporation's commitment to reconciliation with Indigenous people who are impacted by hydroelectric development in

Manitoba: "We continue to be committed to working with Aboriginal communities affected by our development and operations in a spirit of reconciliation."[45]

A Framework for Reconciliation

The framework for reconciliation, as put forward by the TRC and endorsed by the federal government, applies to the current and ongoing relationship between Manitoba Hydro, as an agent of the Crown, and Indigenous peoples in Manitoba.

According to the TRC, reconciliation is rooted in "the establishment and maintenance of mutually respectful relationships."[46] Manitoba has adopted this same definition of reconciliation.[47] This requires, amongst other things, the recognition of Indigenous self-determination and Indigenous legal orders. It necessitates the implementation of UNDRIP, which the TRC names as the framework for reconciliation,[48] and calls for real societal change.[49]

During its mandate, the TRC detailed ten principles of reconciliation that it viewed as essential for Canada to "flourish in the twenty-first century."[50] These principles informed the TRC's work and shaped the TRC's Calls to Action.

TRC PRINCIPLES OF RECONCILIATION[51]

1. The *United Nations Declaration on the Rights of Indigenous Peoples* is the framework for reconciliation at all levels and across all sectors of Canadian society.

2. First Nations, Inuit, and Métis peoples, as the original peoples of this country and as self-determining peoples, have Treaty, constitutional, and human rights that must be recognized and respected.

3. Reconciliation is a process of healing of relationships that requires public truth sharing, apology, and commemoration that acknowledge and redress past harms.

4. Reconciliation requires constructive action on addressing the ongoing legacies of colonialism that have had destructive impacts on Aboriginal peoples' education, cultures and languages, health, child welfare, the administration of justice, and economic opportunities and prosperity.

5. Reconciliation must create a more equitable and inclusive society by closing the gaps in social, health, and economic outcomes that exist between Aboriginal and non-Aboriginal Canadians.

6. All Canadians, as Treaty peoples, share responsibility for establishing and maintaining mutually respectful relationships.

7. The perspectives and understandings of Aboriginal Elders and Traditional Knowledge Keepers of the ethics, concepts, and practices of reconciliation are vital to long-term reconciliation.

8. Supporting Aboriginal peoples' cultural revitalization and integrating Indigenous knowledge systems, oral histories, laws, protocols, and connections to the land into the reconciliation process are essential.

9. Reconciliation requires political will, joint leadership, trust building, accountability, and transparency, as well as a substantial investment of resources.

10. Reconciliation requires sustained public education and dialogue, including youth engagement, about the history and legacy of residential schools, Treaties, and Aboriginal rights, as well as the historical and contemporary contributions of Aboriginal peoples to Canadian society.

The government of Canada, following the TRC, has confirmed its statement of principles regarding its relationship with Indigenous peoples in Canada.

PRINCIPLES RESPECTING THE GOVERNMENT OF CANADA'S RELATIONSHIP WITH INDIGENOUS PEOPLES[52]

The Government of Canada recognizes that:

1. All relations with Indigenous peoples need to be based on the recognition and implementation of their right to self-determination, including the inherent right of self-government.

2. Reconciliation is a fundamental purpose of section 35 of the *Constitution Act*, 1982.

3. The Honour of the Crown guides the conduct of the Crown in all of its dealings with Indigenous peoples.

4. Indigenous self-government is part of Canada's evolving system of cooperative federalism and distinct orders of government.

5. Treaties, agreements, and other constructive arrangements between Indigenous peoples and the Crown have been and are intended to be acts of reconciliation based on mutual recognition and respect.

6. Meaningful engagement with Indigenous peoples aims to secure their free, prior, and informed consent when Canada proposes to take actions which impact them and their rights on their lands, territories, and resources.

7. Respecting and implementing rights is essential and any infringement of section 35 rights must by law meet a high threshold of justification which includes Indigenous perspectives and satisfies the Crown's fiduciary obligations.

8. Reconciliation and self-government require a renewed fiscal relationship, developed in collaboration with Indigenous nations, that promotes a mutually supportive climate for economic partnership and resource development.

9. Reconciliation is an ongoing process that occurs in the context of evolving Indigenous-Crown relationships.

10. A distinctions-based approach is needed to ensure that the unique rights, interests and circumstances of the First Nations, the Métis Nation and Inuit are acknowledged, affirmed, and implemented.

Reconciliation itself, while an urgent and important project aimed at repairing and rebuilding relationships, has been fraught. There have been, and continue to be, conflicting views between Crown perspectives and Indigenous understandings of reconciliation. As stated by the TRC, "What is clear to this [Truth and Reconciliation] Commission is that Aboriginal peoples and the Crown have very different and conflicting views on what reconciliation is and how it is best achieved. The Government of Canada appears to believe that reconciliation entails Aboriginal peoples' accepting the reality and validity of Crown sovereignty and parliamentary supremacy in order to allow the government to get on with business. Aboriginal people, on the other hand, see reconciliation as an opportunity to affirm their own sovereignty and return to the 'partnership' ambitions they held after Confederation."[53]

In the *Mikisew Cree Nation* case, Justice Binnie (for the court) pointed out that the relationship between the Crown and Indigenous nations has been poisoned over time. Justice Binnie observed that "the multitude of smaller grievances created by the indifference of some government officials to Aboriginal peoples' concerns, and the lack of respect inherent in that indifference has been as destructive of the process of reconciliation as some of the larger and more explosive controversies."[54]

The TRC found that, particularly with respect to land use and development, or "economic reconciliation": "sustainable reconciliation on the land involves realizing the economic potential of Indigenous communities in a fair, just, and equitable manner that respects their right to self-determination. Economic reconciliation involves working in partnership with Indigenous peoples to ensure that lands and resources within their traditional territories are developed in culturally respectful ways that fully recognize Treaty and Aboriginal rights and title."[55]

The TRC also found that "Aboriginal peoples' right to self-determination must be integrated into Canada's constitutional and legal framework and into its civic institutions in a manner consistent with the principles, norms, and standards of [UNDRIP]."[56] The TRC rejected Canada's unilateral Crown-based approach to sovereignty and called for a shared sovereignty based on the recognition of Indigenous sovereignty to give effect to reconciliation: "The most significant damage is to the trust that has been broken between the Crown and Aboriginal peoples. This broken trust must be repaired. The vision that led to this breach in trust must be replaced with a new vision for Canada—one that fully embraces Aboriginal peoples' right to self-determination within, and in partnership with, a viable Canadian sovereignty."[57]

Canadian courts and the TRC have clearly identified the importance of Indigenous sovereignty and laws in the process of reconciliation. Leading Indigenous legal scholar John Borrows explains that "Canada cannot presently, historically, legally, or morally claim to be built upon European-derived law alone."[58] The TRC understands and applies this insight, concluding that "establishing respectful relationships also requires the revitalization of Indigenous law and legal traditions."[59] In its final report, the TRC observed: "Unfortunately, Canadian law has discriminatorily constrained the healthy growth of Indigenous law contrary to its highest principles. Nevertheless, many Indigenous people continue to shape their lives by reference to their customs and legal principles. These legal traditions are important in their own right. They can also be applied towards reconciliation for Canada, particularly when considering apologies, restitution, and reconciliation."[60]

There is a Canadian imperative for reconciliation that works towards the self-determination of Indigenous peoples, the implementation of UNDRIP, and the recognition of Indigenous legal orders. This requires implementing Treaty agreements—including modern-day Treaties, such as the Northern Flood Agreement—in ways that reflect Indigenous perspectives and laws, which were and still are vital to the making of those Treaties. Further, reconciliation requires a robust application of the Honour of the Crown, which extends to all agents of the Crown, including Crown corporations in the business of natural resource extraction.

Applying UNDRIP to the Keeyask Context

In May 2016, Carolyn Bennett, Minister of Indigenous and Northern Affairs, officially endorsed UNDRIP at the United Nations Permanent Forum on Indigenous Issues.[61] This distinguished the Liberal government of the day from the previous Conservative government's position, which held that UNDRIP was aspirational and not legally binding. On 21 June 2021 legislation came into force that advances a framework for the implementation of UNDRIP in Canadian law, as part of the renewed relationship between the government and Indigenous peoples.[62] The United Nations Declaration on the Rights of Indigenous Peoples Act requires the government to ensure laws are consistent with UNDRIP, co-create an action plan for implementation, and report on progress.[63] While the full impact of UNDRIP is somewhat uncertain in domestic law and policy,[64] it is likely to influence the interpretation and implementation of section 35 of the Constitution, Treaties, and Indigenous laws.[65]

As stated earlier in this chapter, the TRC recommended UNDRIP as the framework for reconciliation. In its preamble, UNDRIP considers that "treaties, agreements and other constructive arrangements, and the relationship they represent, are the basis for a strengthened partnership between Indigenous peoples and States." Article 37 provides for the right of Indigenous peoples to "recognition, observance and enforcement of treaties, agreements and other constructive arrangements concluded with States or their successors and to have States honour and respect such treaties, agreements and other constructive arrangements."[66]

The Keeyask development, and essentially all of the interconnected hydroelectric system in northern Manitoba, is in Treaty 5 territory.[67] Courts have attempted to interpret and define Treaties many times over. Through a series of cases that span a few decades, the SCC has developed principles for Treaty interpretation. The SCC views Treaties as unique agreements made by the Crown and Indigenous peoples. Treaties do not fit into international law boxes or regular contractual-type arrangements. As defined in *R v. Badger*, Treaties are "sacred promises and the Crown's honour requires the Court to assume that the Crown intended to fulfill its promises."[68] In order to honour those sacred promises, ambiguities are to be resolved in favour of Indigenous peoples,[69] and "Aboriginal understandings of words and corresponding legal concepts in Indian treaties are to be preferred over more legalistic and technical constructions."[70] Legal duties, such as the Honour of the Crown, serve to protect the solemn promises that were made as part of the Treaties.

In Manitoba (as well as Saskatchewan and Alberta), the federal government transferred jurisdiction over natural resources to the province in 1930.[71] In all three provinces, a clause was included in the Natural Resources Transfer Act (NRTA) to protect the right of "Indians"[72] to harvest food throughout the year.

Harvesting rights under the NRTA permit hunting, trapping, fishing, and gathering throughout the year on Crown lands and lands to which Indians have a right of access.[73] The NRTA has shaped the relationship between the Crown (Manitoba) and Indigenous peoples. In particular, the Honour of the Crown is heightened in the following ways by the obligations created in the harvesting clause. First, it allows for harvesting throughout the year, unrestricted by seasonal hunting regulations. Second, harvesting is not restricted to unoccupied Crown lands or reserves but rather includes other lands to which Indians may have a right of access. The right to harvest is met with corresponding obligations for the Crown to act honourably when allocating lands for purposes that may be incompatible with harvesting.

In Manitoba, NRTA harvesting rights are exercised similarly to Treaty rights to harvest. In the *Grassy Narrows* case, the SCC clearly expressed that if the taking up of land (which is permitted in the written text of the Treaty) were to result in so little land that it left the Ojibway with no meaningful right to hunt, fish, or trap, there could be an action for infringement against the Crown.[74] More recently, in the *Yahey* case, Justice Burke of the BC Supreme Court commented that a "meaningful diminishment" of the right would constitute an infringement, in accordance with the Sparrow framework of analysis.[75]

Indigenous understandings of impacts on their lands must be defined in their own terms. In addition to explicitly recognizing Treaties and constructive agreements as foundational to relationships between Indigenous peoples and the Crown, Article 26 of UNDRIP affirms the land rights of Indigenous peoples and state obligations to recognize and protect those lands in accordance with Indigenous systems of land tenure.

Article 26:

1. Indigenous peoples have the right to the lands, territories and resources which they have traditionally owned, occupied or otherwise used or acquired.

2. Indigenous peoples have the right to own, use, develop and control the lands, territories and resources that they possess by reason of traditional ownership or other traditional occupation or use, as well as those which they have otherwise acquired.

3. States shall give legal recognition and protection to these lands, territories and resources. Such recognition shall be conducted with due respect to the customs, traditions and land tenure systems of the Indigenous peoples concerned.[76]

UNDRIP also calls for the *free, prior, and informed consent* of Indigenous peoples (FPIC) prior to the approval of projects affecting their lands, and redress where this consent has not been obtained.[77] UNDRIP acknowledges the right of Indigenous peoples to create land policies, priorities, and strategies relating to the use and development of their lands, territories, and resources.[78] UNDRIP also requires consultation and cooperation through Indigenous governance mechanisms prior to project approvals relating to Indigenous lands and resources.[79]

Read together, the rights contained in UNDRIP demonstrate a clear intention to ensure states honour the agreements that have forged relationships between Indigenous peoples and the state, and to recognize Indigenous peoples' ability to determine and consent to the use of their lands, territories, and resources. Applied to a Keeyask context and to hydroelectric development more broadly, the Honour of the Crown is meant to uphold the substantive promise of UNDRIP, which, in turn, requires that Manitoba Hydro acknowledge and respect Treaty 5, and uphold the standard of FPIC and the rights of Indigenous peoples.

Having reviewed the Cree environmental assessments (EAs) in the Keeyask CEC hearings, it was clear that the Cree First Nations all found that there was significant harm and that, in sum, the significance of the impacts outweighed the mitigation Manitoba Hydro proposed. They were each concerned with the erosion of their Treaty rights, including the right to continue to hunt for food, as reflected in the Adverse Effects Agreements concluded with Manitoba Hydro. As is explored in more detail in Chapter 13 in this volume, the Keeyask EIS's finding that there would be "no significant adverse effects" contradicted the Cree EAs.[80] The fact that the EIS finding trumped the Cree assessments reflects an industry- and state-centred view of what is a significant and acceptable infringement of Indigenous rights. This does not align with honourable conduct aimed at reconciliation.

In addition, without oversimplifying the issue, there is ample evidence within the chapters of this book to conclude that the Honour of the Crown was not respected in the Keeyask process. Upholding the Honour of the Crown requires a high level of engagement by Manitoba Hydro in ensuring the meaningful and ongoing consent of Indigenous peoples, with adequate compensation for past and continuing harms, in accordance with Indigenous processes of decision making. This standard has not been met to date.

Conclusion

The Province of Manitoba's Path to Reconciliation Act, enacted in 2016, affirms that "the Government of Manitoba is committed to reconciliation and will be guided by the calls to action of the Truth and Reconciliation Commission and the principles set out in the United Nations Declaration on the Rights of Indigenous Peoples."[81]

Manitoba Hydro, as a Crown corporation and agent of the Crown, has an obligation to fulfill the intent of the Path to Reconciliation Act, and to act honourably in all of its dealings with Indigenous peoples. In a context of overlapping duties and interests, such as with hydroelectric development that may impact on Indigenous rights and interests, the duty to act honourably must be exercised to its fullest. By virtue of the Honour of the Crown, both Manitoba and Manitoba Hydro are subject to the underlying purpose of section 35, which is reconciliation between the Crown and Indigenous peoples. The Honour of the Crown requires a robust understanding of the Treaty and corresponding obligations and relationships within this decision-making context.

Historically and today, the law of Canada has been employed as a tool of dispossession in relation to Indigenous peoples, lands, and resources. Treaties are legal instruments that confirm obligations between nations, are constitutional documents, and are living, breathing affirmations of relationships between nations of people. The law, however, as applied by Canadian courts and governments, has erroneously been used to allow for the infringement and erosion of Treaties. This undermining of Treaty promises and disregard for Indigenous understandings of the Treaty relationship persisted in Canadian law to the point where, in some cases, there is no more meaningful ability to exercise the rights that the Treaty aims to protect.

The SCC has ruled that the cumulative effects of an ongoing project and historical context may inform the scope of the duty to consult.[82] Correspondingly, the cumulative effects and historical context of hydroelectric development in Manitoba should inform the duty to act honourably, presumably enhancing its application in this social, cultural, economic, and geographical landscape.

In order to give effect to the Honour of the Crown in the context of hydroelectric development, the Province of Manitoba and Manitoba Hydro, as the Crown, should:

- affirm that Manitoba Hydro is subject to the Honour of the Crown and must demonstrate a high standard of conduct in relation to Indigenous peoples who are potentially affected by hydroelectric development;

- consider the appropriateness of concurrent processes relating to Hydro projects to ensure that the duty to consult and accommodate and the highest standards of the Honour of the Crown are met;

- adopt a framework of reconciliation (modelled on the TRC principles for reconciliation and the Government of Canada's relationship principles) for the conduct of negotiations and decision making, including for cumulative, ongoing, and past projects and impacts;

- adopt the United Nations Declaration on the Rights of Indigenous Peoples as a framework for the conduct of negotiations and decision making, including adherence to the principles of free, prior, and informed consent;

- seek advice from Indigenous nations as to how Indigenous legal principles apply from both a procedural and substantive standpoint, from the evaluation of the project to the negotiations and the implementation of any agreements; and

- engage all Indigenous nations and peoples who are potentially affected (and who perceive themselves to be impacted) by the project to determine a process to engage Indigenous perspectives and laws in relation to the disposition of land and to the impact on kinship relationships (human and non–human).

The World Commission on Dams affirmed that "[d]ams are a means to an end, not an end in themselves."[83] Therefore, the approval of the Keeyask Dam, or any other dam, should not displace the constitutionally affirmed duties that arise in the relationship between the Crown and Indigenous peoples. As illustrated above, these duties flow from the Constitution, Treaties, Canadian law, international commitments, and overarching duties. Manitoba Hydro, as an agent of the Crown, must adhere to the most fundamental duty that guides all dealings with Indigenous peoples—that of the Honour of the Crown, rooted in the presumptions of fair dealing and honourable conduct. Read through the lens of constitutional and international obligations, and framed in the current imperative of reconciliation, this requires free, prior, and informed consent; direct involvement in decision making; and adequate compensation for past and future harms.

Notes

1   Constitution Act, 1982, Schedule B to the Canada Act 1982 (UK), 1982, c 11, s 35-35.1 [Constitution Act, 1982].
2   Ibid.
3   "Indian" is the technical legal term used in Canadian law (including the NRTA and the Indian Act); however, "First Nations" is a more commonly used term.
4   *Haida Nation v. British Columbia* (Minister of Forests), 2004 SCC 73 at para 16, [2004] 3 SCR 511 at para 16 [*Haida Nation*].
5   *Manitoba Metis Federation Inc. v. Canada (Attorney General)*, 2013 SCC 14, at para 65 [2013] 1 SCR 623 [*Manitoba Metis Federation*].
6   Ibid., para 77.
7   *Taku River Tlingit First Nation v. British Columbia (Project Assessment Director)*, 2004 3 SCR 550 at para 24 [*Taku River*].
8   *Manitoba Metis Federation*, para 79.
9   *R v. Badger*, [1996] 1 SCR 771 at para 41 [*Badger*].
10 Ibid.
11 *Haida Nation*, para 16.
12 Ibid., para 18; *Manitoba Metis Federation*, para 74.
13 *Mikisew Cree First Nation v. Canada (Minister of Canadian Heritage)*, [2005] 3 SCR 388, 2005 SCC 69 at para 38 [*Mikisew Cree*].
14 *R v. Marshall*, [1999] 3 SCR 456 at para. 52.
15 *Chippewas of the Thames First Nation v. Enbridge Pipelines Inc*, 2007 SCC 41 at para. 42, [2017] 1 SCR 1099 [*Chippewas*].
16 Ibid., para 44; *Clyde River (Hamlet) v. Petroleum Geo-Services Inc*, 2017 SCC 40 at para 23, [2017] 1 SCR 1069 [*Clyde River*].
17 *Chippewas*, para 42.
18 Ibid., para 32; *Clyde River*, para 30.
19 *Clyde River*, para 34.
20 As illustrated in the *Sapotaweyak* case discussed below.
21 *Sapotaweyak Cree Nation et al v. Manitoba*, 2015 MBQB 35 at para 9 [*Sapotaweyak*].
22 "A81054 Manitoba Hydro Application for Authorizations Related to the Manitoba-Minnesota Transmission Project," Canada Energy Regulator, Government of Canada, accessed 28 April 2021, https://apps.cer-rec.gc.ca/REGDOCS/Item/Filing/A81054.
23 *Joint Keeyask Development Agreement*, PDF file, 29 May 2009, https://www.hydro.mb.ca/projects/keeyask/pdf/JKDA_090529.pdf. The JKDA reads at page 48: "3.1.7 The Parties agree to provide such information with respect to the Keeyask Project to

Canada and Manitoba as reasonably may be required to enable Canada and Manitoba to consult Aboriginal people pursuant to section 35 of the *Constitution Act, 1982* (Canada)."

24 *Rio Tinto Alcan Inc. v. Carrier Sekani Tribal Council,* 2010 SCC 43, [2010] 2 S.C.R. 650 [*Rio Tinto*].

25 Ibid.

26 *Sapotaweyak,* para 13.

27 Ibid., para 41.

28 Ibid., paras 42–44.

29 Ibid., para 9.

30 Manitoba Clean Environment Commission, *Keeyask Generation Project*, 3493, accessed 28 April 2021, http://cecmanitoba.ca/cecm/hearings/keeyask.html.

31 Ibid., 3533.

32 Keeyask Hydropower Limited Partnership, *Environmental Impact Statement*, accessed 28 April 2021, https://keeyask.com/project-timeline/environment-assessment-process/environmental-licensing-process/>.

33 Fox Lake Cree Nation, *FLNC Environment Evaluation Report*, September 2012, https://www.ceaa-acee.gc.ca/050/documents_staticpost/64144/83657/Cree_-_02_Fox_Lake_Environment_Evaluation_Report_Sept_2012.pdf; Cree Nations Partners, *Keeyask Environmental Evaluation: A Report on the Environmental Effects of the Proposed Keeyask Project on Tataskweyak Cree Nation and War Lake First Nation*, PDF File, January 2012, https://www.ceaa-acee.gc.ca/050/documents_staticpost/64144/83657/Cree_-_01_Cree_Nations_Partners_Keeyask_Environmental_Evaluation_Report_Jan_2012.pdf; York Factory First Nation, *KIPEKISKWAYWINAN: Our Voices,* June 2012, https://www.ceaa-acee.gc.ca/050/documents_staticpost/64144/83657/Cree_-_03_Kipekiskwaywinan_Our%20 Voices_June_2012.pdf.

34 Manitoba Clean Environment Commission, *Keeyask Generation Project.*

35 *Haida Nation,* para 16.

36 National Energy Board—Manitoba Hydro Application for Authorizations Related to the Manitoba-Minnesota Transmission Project MH Response to Intervenor IR: NEB_WNST-IR-001.3 (lines 1–2).

37 Manitoba Hydro, *Indigenous Agreements*, accessed 29 April 2021, https://www.hydro.mb.ca/community/indigenous_relations/indigenous_agreements/.

38 CBC News, "Manitoba Apologizes to First Nation for Environmental Damage," CBC/Radio Canada, 20 January 2015, https://www.cbc.ca/news/canada/manitoba/manitoba-apologizes-to-first-nation-for-environmental-damage-1.2919768.

39 *Daniels v. Canada (Indian Affairs and Northern Development),* 2016 SCC 12, [2016] 1 S.C.R. 99 at para 37 [*Daniels*].

40 Ibid., para 1.

41 Ibid., para 34; emphasis added.

42 C.C.S.M., The Path to Reconciliation Act, c R30.5 [The Path to Reconciliation Act].

43 Ibid.

44 Ibid., s. 2.

45 Province of Manitoba, "Manitoba Government Issues Apology Over Past Hydro Development," news release, 20 January 2015, http://news.gov.mb.ca/news/index.html?item=33753.

46 Canada, Truth and Reconciliation Commission, *Canada's Residential Schools: Reconciliation*, vol. 6, *The Final Report* (Montreal: McGill-Queen's University Press, 2015), 11–12.

47 C.C.S.M., Path to Reconciliation Act, s. 1(1).

48 Ibid., s. 28.

49 Ibid., s. 1(1).

50 Ibid., s. 28.

51 Canada, Truth and Reconciliation Commission, *Canada's Residential Schools: Reconciliation*, 3–4.

52 Government of Canada, Department of Justice, "Principles Respecting the Government of Canada's Relationship with Indigenous Peoples," last modified 14 February 2018, https://www.justice.gc.ca/eng/csj-sjc/principles-principes.html.

53 Canada, Truth and Reconciliation Commission, *Canada's Residential Schools: Reconciliation*, 9.

54 *Mikisew Cree*, para 1.

55 Canada, Truth and Reconciliation Commission, *Canada's Residential Schools: Reconciliation*, 207.

56 Ibid., 28.

57 Ibid., 20.

58 John Borrows, *Canada's Indigenous Constitution* (Toronto: University of Toronto Press, 2010), 15.

59 Canada, Truth and Reconciliation Commission, *Canada's Residential Schools: Reconciliation*, 11–12.

60 Ibid., 78.

61 Minister of Indigenous and Northern Affairs Carolyn Bennett, Northern Public Affairs, "Announcement of Canada's Support for the United Nations Declaration on the Rights of Indigenous Peoples," statement delivered at the 15th session of the United Nations Permanent Forum on Indigenous Issues, 10 May 2016, www.northernpublicaffairs.ca/index/fully- adopting-undrip-minister-bennetts-speech/.

62 See Bill C-15, https://www.parl.ca/LegisInfo/en/bill/43-2/c-15.

63 See Statutes of Canada, Chapter 14, https://parl.ca/DocumentViewer/en/43-2/bill/C-15/royal-assent.

64 See, for example, Sheryl R. Lightfoot, "Adopting and Implementing the United Nations Declaration on the Rights of Indigenous Peoples: Canada's Existential Crisis," in *Surviving Canada: Indigenous Peoples Celebrate 150 Years of Betrayal*, ed. Kiera L. Ladner and Myra Tait (Winnipeg, MB: ARP, 2017), 440–59.

65 For an extensive review of perspectives on UNDRIP implementation, see the edited volume by the Centre for International Governance and Innovation: *Braiding Legal Orders: Implementing the United Nations Declaration on the Rights of Indigenous Peoples*, ed. John Borrows, Larry Chartran, Oonagh E. Fitzgerald, and Risa Schwartz (Waterloo: Centre for International Governance and Innovation, 2019).

66 United Nations Declaration on the Rights of Indigenous Peoples (UNDRIP), 13 September 2007, 61/295 at art. 37 [UNDRIP].

67 Treaty 5 was made in 1875 and adhesions were made for First Nations starting in 1908. *Treaty 5*, Her Majesty the Queen and Saulteaux and Swampy Cree Tribes of Indians, 20 September 1875, Cat No R33-0557 (transcribed from The Queen's Printer, Ottawa).

68   *Badger*, para 47.

69   *Nowegijick v. The Queen*, [1984] 1 SCR 29 at para 36 [*Nowegijick*].

70   *Mitchell v. Peguis Indian Band*, [1990] 2 S.C.R. 85 Dickson J.

71   The Manitoba Natural Resources Transfer Act Amendment Act, RSM 1987, c N60 [NRTA].

72   "Indians," as defined by law, are persons registered as Indians under the terms of the Indian Act, RSC 1985, c I-5, s 2(1). Note that the SCC has ruled that the NRTA does not apply to Métis Harvesters. *R v. Blais*, 2003 SCC 44, [2003] 2 SCR 236. The Métis have a Harvesting Agreement with the Province of Manitoba. See: "Province Partners with Manitoba Metis Federation to Uphold Métis Harvesting Rights, Natural Resource Conservation," Province of Manitoba, news release, 29 September 2012, http://news.gov.mb.ca/news/?item=15364&posted=2012-09-29.

73   NRTA, s. 13.

74   *Grassy Narrows First Nation v Ontario (Natural Resources)* 2014 SCC 48 at para 52, [2014] 2 SCR 447 [*Grassy Narrows*], as cited in *Mikisew Cree*, para 48.

75   *Yahey v British Columbia*, 2021 BCSC 1287 at para 158 [*Yahey*].

76   UNDRIP, art. 26.

77   UNDRIP, arts. 32, 38; emphasis added.

78   UNDRIP, art. 32 (1), "Indigenous peoples have the right to determine and develop priorities and strategies for the development or use of their lands or territories and other resources."

79   UNDRIP, art. 32 (2), "States shall consult and cooperate in good faith with the Indigenous peoples concerned through their own representative institutions in order to obtain their free and informed consent prior to the approval of any project affecting their lands or territories and other resources, particularly in connection with the development, utilization or exploitation of mineral, water or other resources."

80   For more on this, see Chapter 13 in this volume by Craft on the two-track approach.

81   C.C.S.M., Path to Reconciliation Act.

82   *Chippewas*, para 42.

83   World Commission on Dams, *Dams and Development: A New Framework for Decision-Making, The Report of the World Commission on Dams* (London, VA: Earthscan Publications Ltd, 2000), 2, https://archive.internationalrivers.org/sites/default/files/attached-files/world_commission_on_dams_final_report.pdf.

"Act of God"

ROBERT SPENCE, LAND AND RESOURCE USER, TATASKWEYAK CREE NATION

Excerpt from the transcript of the Keeyask CEC hearing in Winnipeg, 14 November 2013.

Note: Robert Spence testified in both English and Cree. CEC hearing transcripts note when he switches languages with "(Cree spoken)."

Thank you Lord for giving me the chance to come and speak here today in front of the CEC. (Cree spoken) And I never thought I was going to be able to come up here to talk in front of all you people. But I asked the Creator for help. And thank God he gave me the courage to come up here and talk on behalf of the people of Split Lake. And [on] behalf of the people that have gone. On behalf of the people that Manitoba Hydro ignored. And passed on. (Cree spoken) A lot of elders are gone, our elders, who taught us to respect the land, to carry on the teachings and the traditions of the First Nations people. I carry those with pride. Every day. (Cree spoken). . . . I came here to voice the concerns that my people have, our people as a First Nations people. A lot of people who wanted to come up here today can't come up here. They never had this opportunity. (Cree spoken) A lot of them left us already. A lot of good people (Cree spoken). But I hope through me that they can speak.

Hydro, since day one, has done nothing but harm to the environment. (Cree spoken) I'll tell you a story . . . (Cree spoken) My late grandfather John George Garson, I was out with him on the lake when he was commercial fishing in a chestnut canoe. I was just a young guy. Boy I was proud to be out there out in the lake with my grandfather. I thought I was doing something worthwhile and meaningful. (Cree spoken) That means a lot to a lot of us people who work hard. We are hardworking people. But to us, it's not work. That's a white man word. To us, it's just living. We are out on the lake and I went with [him] to check his net. We drove up to his net. Well, I looked down into the water (Cree spoken) and I saw the bellies of the fish under the water.

About a foot and a half to two feet down I saw them (Cree spoken). Boy we've got a lot of fish in the net. Honestly, that's how far I was able to see down into the water. (Cree spoken)

You won't see nothing. This is the water today, this is a fish today you try to look at a fish underwater. It's like you can't see it. But back in the day, you could see it that far. (Cree spoken).... A lot of the weeds, the vegetation are gone that I grew up with seeing. I said to my grandpa, boy (Cree spoken). One of these days, my grandpa, I said, I'm going to do that too when I become a fisherman I said. I'm going to be able to see all those fish in my net when [I] get old enough to fish.

Now, (Cree spoken) not even this close, can't see anything under the water. (Cree spoken) They invited aquatic environmental specialist. I thought I was doing really good going to work with these people, I thought I was making friends. But you know what I learned over the years, you can't make friends with people who are in it for money. You can't do that.

Now I realize I'm going to say what I have to say regardless of who I thought I made friends with. Sure we tag sturgeon. I didn't feel right about it, I felt really bad for the sturgeon. How would you feel if I stuck prongs in your ass and put wires through it? You wouldn't like it. (Cree spoken) He's got a life. He suffers too. We see it. We have seen it in the tags, aquatic and acoustic tags we put in the sturgeon.

And recently, I have seen the damages. (Cree spoken) I said to my grandfather, (Cree spoken) I'm going to get lots in my net. What he said next dumbfounded me because I never thought in my wildest dreams that anybody can be so capable of so much destruction. And he said to me (Cree spoken) when you get older, you're not going to have the same shorelines, they are going to be gone, the trees will be gone, they will be floating by. (Cree spoken)

I see it today. I thought (Cree spoken) that's what I said to him. (Cree spoken) And he said to me (Cree spoken) my grandson, they act like God. They have the power to destroy the land. And I say you are crazy in Cree. (Cree spoken) And he chuckled at me. Now I see it! "Act of God" that we hear all the time when floods occur. The over-manipulations of the water systems in Manitoba, Churchill River, Nelson River.

CHAPTER 11

Social Licence, Consent, and the Keeyask Project

JOSEPH DIPPLE

In recent history, the expanded need for energy and minerals has come in direct conflict with communities living in areas capable of producing these resources. This conflict has tarnished the social image of natural resource industries and has created major difficulties for mining, forestry, and energy corporations. These confrontations are strikingly prevalent in Manitoba, particularly surrounding past, present, and future hydro power projects. Hydro power production has been a contentious issue across the globe; however, Manitoba Hydro has promoted a "new" approach to relationships with affected Indigenous communities in recent years.

As a means of addressing these difficult relationships, corporations in the natural resource extraction and exploitation industries have promoted the idea of "social licence to operate" (explored earlier in Chapter 2 in this volume). This concept is based on the idea that affected communities can provide an informal licence, similar in nature to formal licensing from the state, but without any legal means of guaranteeing full consideration or compliance.[1] Some argue that Manitoba Hydro's recent actions provide social licence for its megaprojects in Manitoba's North; however, those who make this statement do not qualify their claim with a definition of "social licence," or present a thorough analysis of how communities provided said social licence. It is difficult to come to a conclusive statement about the nature of social licence in northern Manitoba, as there are wide divides between and within communities in their perception of hydro power production and community impacts.[2] However, it is possible to gauge the degree to which social licence might exist, as it is currently defined by Manitoba Hydro. In order to consider the possibility of social licence, this chapter will use a free, prior, and informed consent (FPIC) model to question whether the Province of Manitoba and Manitoba Hydro's claims to have secured a social licence for the Keeyask Project are valid. As Aimée Craft's previous chapter on Crown–Indigenous relations lays out, free, prior, and informed consent is laid out in the Truth and Reconciliation Commission's Call to Action #92, stating corporations must "commit to meaningful consultation, building respectful relationships, and obtaining the free, prior, and informed consent of Indigenous peoples before proceeding with economic development projects."[3] The United Nations Declaration on the Rights of Indigenous Peoples consistently uses the concept of free, prior, and informed consent, including it in considering compensation for lands that have been "confiscated, taken, occupied, used, or damaged without free, prior, and informed consent."[4] Given that, as Toyah Rodhouse and Frank Vanclay have discussed, "the concept of free, prior, and informed consent arose in the Indigenous rights discourse as a mechanism to ensure respect for Indigenous peoples,"[5] the use of this concept in relation to claims of social licence can help provide a nuanced understanding of the discussion. This chapter will use the FPIC model to consider both past and present hydroelectric generating stations in northern Manitoba and the use of concepts of "consultation" and "consent" to establish social licence.

History of Hydro Power Production in Manitoba

Byron Williams, in Chapter 1 of this volume, laid out much of the history of hydroelectric projects in Manitoba, as well as the political climates they were built in. These projects affected many Indigenous communities in both southern and northern Manitoba, with some communities being forced to relocate in order to accommodate flooding. In general, projects dating back to the early twentieth century were planned, initiated, and completed without any consultation or consent from communities that would be directly affected by their negative impacts. In northern Manitoba, the two foundational projects for Manitoba Hydro were the Churchill River Diversion and Lake Winnipeg Regulation Project, both started in the early 1970s. However, these projects—which brought about great destruction to the land and immense change to the river systems—were not constructed with the knowledge or consent of local Indigenous communities, who have relied upon these waterways since time immemorial. Many Indigenous communities along these river systems began a struggle to defend their ecosystem. In particular, five Cree communities formed the Northern Flood Committee to address the issue and pressured the federal and provincial governments as well as Manitoba Hydro into a modern-day Treaty known as the Northern Flood Agreement.[6] As time passed without effective implementation of the promises made in the Northern Flood Agreement, signed in 1977, Comprehensive Implementation Agreements were proposed and signed in the 1990s.[7] These were effectively one-time buyouts of the promises made in the modern-day Treaty.[8]

As discussed early on in this volume, Manitoba Hydro and the provincial government have taken a "new approach" to relationships with Indigenous communities affected by the construction of hydroelectric generating stations as of the early 2000s. Manitoba Hydro has used "partnership agreements" that allow First Nations to purchase shares in Hydro projects built in their homelands with Nisichawayasihk Cree Nation, in regards to the Wuskwatim Generating Station, and with Tataskweyak Cree Nation, Fox Lake Cree Nation, York Factory First Nation, and War Lake First Nation, in conjunction with the Keeyask Generating Station.[9] Former Manitoba premier Greg Selinger stated that these partnerships established "phenomenal social licence" from the related communities.[10] However, as we have heard from Dr. Ramona Neckoway (Nisichawayasihk Cree Nation), harvester Robert Spence (Tataskweyak Cree Nation), councillor Conway Arthurson, Elder and trapper Noah Massan (Fox Lake Cree Nation), Cheryl Flett (York Factory First Nation), Chief Betsy Kennedy (War Lake First Nation), and other community voices, there is far from consensus. Do these partnerships actually establish a social licence provided by the communities to move ahead with future generating stations? And if not, why and how does this claim of a "phenomenal" social licence fall short?

Social Licence

"Social licence to operate" is a concept that was initially developed in the mining sector.[11] Recently, it has been used in multiple industries including wind and geothermal in Australia.[12] However, the relatively recent use of the term in multiple industries has brought about the question of consistency between different industries. In their article about the concept, Nina Hall, Justine Lacey, Simone Carr-Cornish, and Anne Maree-Dowd found that different industries address social licence in varying ways.[13] There is no one definition of "social licence" within industry, and neither is there a predetermined means of establishing and maintaining the community support once it has been provided.

Given the variety of definitions and means of implementing the idea of social licence, scholars have begun to critically review the concept as a whole. In many cases, these scholars find that the discourse surrounding "social licence to operate" is directed towards a business or managerial view of costs and benefits. Business and managerial views generally perceive a situation in a cost-benefit analysis, and consider any costs as replaceable costs, allowing for a financial replacement of any detriment consequent from a corporate action. In other words, any negative outcome can be offset with enough money as compensation. As an outcome of this defining world view, much of the discussion of social licence is grounded in how industry forces the idea of "payment for costs" upon communities as the minimum amount of money necessary to curtail any potentially disruptive behaviours from the affected communities.[14] This approach fails to consider the community's perception of the costs they will bear, any intangible losses that will result from natural resource exploitation, how impacted ecosystems may cease to function, or the possibility that some losses may be irreplaceable. Indigenous perspectives and relationships with the land are likely not fully considered under this corporate world view of social licence. Replacing the loss of land with financial compensation would be perceived as a strong approach to relationship building from a corporate standpoint. However, this perspective does not take the irreplaceable nature of relationships with the land into account.[15]

Despite the immensely problematic use of social licence as natural resource extraction and exploitation industries have defined it, there are ways in which social licence can be used to support communities. One argument suggests that "free, prior, and informed consent" can be part of a formalized process of gaining and maintaining social licence.[16] Generally, industry prefers to avoid the term "consent" in favour of "consultation," as "consent" may provide some legal right to reject a project.[17] If corporations are required to gain consent that falls into all three categories (free, prior, informed), and if the corporations undergo this process with the goal of gaining and maintaining communities' long-term approval (ongoing consent), any affected community would have the opportunity to make a decision based on a full understanding of what they are being asked. In the future, social licence conversations should move in a new direction towards a more community-oriented understanding of costs, benefits, and acceptance or approval of projects. However, for the purposes of this chapter, the "free, prior, and informed consent" definition of social licence should constitute the "minimum standard" achieved prior to any corporate suggestion that affected communities have provided their social licence.

Social Licence and the Keeyask Project

Wuskwatim Generating Station (2012), along the Burntwood River and near the community of Nisichawayasihk Cree Nation (NCN), constituted Manitoba Hydro's first "new" approach to partnerships with First Nations along the Nelson River (hereafter Kichi Sipi). Manitoba Hydro's partnership originally provided NCN with the possibility of purchasing 33 percent of Wuskwatim, effectively allowing them the opportunity of gaining 33 percent of the profit.[18] However, current prospects for the Wuskwatim partnership are looking grim. For a number of years, the Wuskwatim Project was losing money and the agreement between Manitoba Hydro and NCN have been adjusted to prevent NCN from owing Manitoba Hydro millions of dollars for their portions of the losses.[19] Following in the style of the Wuskwatim partnership, the Keeyask partnership "allows" the four Keeyask First Nations to purchase a total of 25 percent of shares in the Keeyask Project.[20] Another option exists, if communities do not wish to purchase such a large share, that guarantees payment regardless of generating station profit but for only 2.17 percent of the project.[21]

In addition to financial requirements, these partnerships also require the community to provide political support for the generating stations. If the generating stations are seen as having no positive impacts on the communities, energy sales to the United States, who may purchase hydro power over fossil fuels because it is seen as "socially responsible," may suffer, reducing community profits. Additionally, Indigenous leaders in negotiations with Manitoba Hydro regarding the project are required to sign confidentiality agreements, forbidding them from discussing certain aspects of negotiations with the community members they are expected to represent.[22] When former premier Greg Selinger stated that these partnership agreements provided "phenomenal social licence," it seems he was arguing that the communities' agreement to join in on the construction of generating stations for the small possibility of profit was a sign of community support and approval. However, this falls into the managerial and corporate world view that many scholars question regarding what having a "social licence to operate" really means.

Free Consent

First in the definition of social licence is the concept of "free" consent. Free consent is consent provided with the perception that the decision will not cause harm to the community, and that there is "no coercion, intimidation or manipulation."[23] A consistent theme throughout the narratives provided in Gillam and Split Lake (the community of Tataskweyak Cree Nation) was the perception that Keeyask would bring immense and long-lasting destruction to the communities. Throughout the personal interviews conducted for this chapter, people cited a multitude of aspects of community life that would be forever impacted by building Keeyask. Many community members discussed the damage to land that would result from flooding produced by the construction and operation of Keeyask, as well as all past and future projects.[24] Robert Spence, who lends his voice to other sections of this book as well, stated, "I was born under the shadow of the Kelsey dam ... I'll die underneath the shadow of another."[25] Additionally, community members discussed the destruction of culturally important locations as well as habitat for wildlife, impacts that also weigh heavily on the community's ability to pursue economic and cultural pursuits such as gathering, hunting, fishing, and trapping.[26] Robert Spence encapsulates this sentiment through the statement, "How is it development when it pushes him and I off the lake and into the welfare line?"[27] People raised concerns about having a large work camp nearby, with major concerns about the increased introduction of hard drugs to the community as well as the possibility of assault.[28] These immensely negative impacts are just some of the many impacts community members know will arrive with the construction of Keeyask, based on their experience with the other four generating stations along Kichi Sipi. There are those who support the Keeyask Project because they see the possibility of greater benefits for the communities rather than the costs. Many who adopt this stance cite jobs, potential infrastructure "development," contracts for community businesses, and other financial benefits from both the construction and future profits of the generating station.[29] In many regards, this is what Premier Selinger was basing his argument on when he stated that the partnership agreement provides social licence.

Despite these possible Western-capitalist benefits, many community members who are cited in this chapter, and who spoke in opposition at the Clean Environment Commission and Public Utilities Board hearings on Keeyask, stated that they viewed the project as guaranteed no matter the outcome of the local community referendum on the Joint Keeyask Development Agreement.[30] It is indeed very possible that the Crown corporation would have proceeded with the project regardless of whether communities provided their social licence through part-nership agreements. Manitoba Hydro has a history of moving forward with generating station projects regardless of community consultation or consent, providing precedence for the communities' perception that there was no real ability to veto the project.[31] If Manitoba Hydro did move forward despite a community's refusal of partnership, that community would then suffer all the aforementioned negative impacts without any of the benefits. This essentially forces communities into partnership as the lesser of two bad options. Yet again, this shows Manitoba Hydro's managerial view of social licence, as these four Cree communities have no real power to decide the fate of the project. They are instead offered rather terrible business deals and financial compen-sation in return for not revolting against the project. With this in mind, and with multiple community members stating that this was present in their minds when they ratified the partnership agreement, there was no free consent. This already removes one of the three required forms of consent necessary for the FPIC definition of social licence.

Prior Consent

For the purposes of this chapter, "prior consent" is defined as community consent for a project before the proponents initiate the project, as well as before the final decision to complete the project is made.[32] Regarding the Keeyask Project, it is quite clear that Manitoba Hydro did not adhere to this definition. Manitoba Hydro very obviously planned the project far in advance of their conversations with affected communities, with the regulatory licence perceived as a "rubber stamp" that would be granted regardless of the Clean Enviroment Commission (CEC) hearing outcome.[33] Approximately $140 million, or 2 percent of the then project cost, went towards legal and technical advice for the communities, which on the surface is a very beneficial use of money.[34] However, as Byron Williams argued in Chapter 1 of this volume, the immense expenditure of money on the project prior to approval provides a justification for continuing with the project despite requests to cancel it, as the money has already been spent. During the CEC hearings for the Keeyask Project, Elder Noah Massan (see Chapter 6 of this volume) questioned the size of the sewage lagoon at the then Keewatinoow camp site. The size of this lagoon, he argued, was much larger than those on the construction sites of past generating stations. He was concerned that this infrastructure was instead being built for the yet-to-be-licensed Conawapa Generating Station.[35] It seems that money continued to be spent and construction camps built before any partnerships had been established or formal licensing processes had begun.[36]

Another aspect of "prior consent" is whether consent was given to prior projects of a similar nature or with the same corporation. Did communities consent to the many interrelated Hydro projects that are foundational to the perceived benefits of Keeyask? In order to examine this aspect of prior consent, we will look at Tataskweyak's history of consent, or lack thereof, as a test case.[37] As the Manitoba government and Manitoba Hydro moved towards the construction of the Churchill River Diversion and Lake Winnipeg Regulation projects, they made little to no attempts to consult with local First Nations. The Indigenous community at South Indian Lake was informed of initial plans for the Churchill River Diversion only when the Province publicly informed the rest of Manitoba.[38] Ultimately, this lack of prior knowledge as well as the failure to consult communities brought about the Northern Flood Committee, a coalition of five First Nations communities affected by the projects. This included Split Lake Cree Nation, now Tataskweyak Cree Nation.[39] The Northern Flood Committee worked to gain some form of compensation for the immense damages caused, resulting in the Northern Flood Agreement. As Manitoba Hydro continued to build new generating stations, the Crown corporation and the Manitoba government were forced to address questions of Aboriginal rights established in both the Canadian Constitution and the Northern Flood Agreement. Following the age-old "divide and conquer" tactics prominent in the historic Treaty days, the government and Crown corporation succeeded in buying out the rights of the Northern Flood Agreement from four of the five committee communities by 1997.[40] Compensation agreements in no way show consent for the projects. Rather, they demonstrate the desire to gain some compensation from the Northern Flood Agreement they fought for, which remained relatively unfulfilled for fifteen to twenty years following its ratification.

Considering the lack of consultation and the immense efforts communities were forced to expend to gain some form of compensation for Hydro impacts in northern Manitoba—not just for Tataskweyak, but throughout the history of hydro development in northern Manitoba—it is fair to say there was no consent for the projects before they first began along Kichi Sipi. The only situations in which consent can be considered possible is the recent "partnership" agreements, which is questionable, as this chapter explains.

Informed Consent

The last aspect of the FPIC definition of social licence is "informed consent." In many ways, this is the most difficult form of consent to gain, as well as to argue that it has not been provided. When considering informed consent, the community must be given full disclosure on the project in a way that is understandable and with enough information to make a decision with full knowledge of what they face in the future.[41] Complicating this question is the fact that communities granting consent may have very different perceptions from industry proponents on how well this was accomplished.

Manitoba Hydro has taken a number of steps to provide information to communities, while also including Indigenous community members in the process of obtaining and generating information on the impacts of the project. During its assessment of which species to include in its Environmental Impact Statement as Valued Ecological Components, Manitoba Hydro and its scientific consultants spoke with Indigenous community members from "partner" communities to review wildlife and plants that are of interest to both non-Indigenous (endangered species) and Indigenous community members (culturally important).[42] Including Indigenous knowledge in the consideration of project impacts is an important step toward a more sustainable form of energy production. Additionally, Manitoba Hydro held multiple community consultation sessions regarding the Keeyask Project, attempting to provide community members with some knowledge of what the project would include and the partnership itself.[43] Manitoba Hydro and the leadership of the four partner communities describe the planning of the Keeyask Generating Station as a collaborative effort.[44] Hearings regarding the Keeyask Project, particularly the 2013–2014 Clean Environment Commission hearings, took place in both northern Manitoba and Winnipeg. These hearings provided community members with an opportunity to see documents created by Manitoba Hydro and hear expert consultants addressing different aspects of the project, and allowed for direct community intervention from Pimicikamak Okimawin, the Concerned Fox Lake Grassroots Citizens discussed in Chapter 6 of this volume, and others.[45] Community members were also able to provide their perceptions at the Manitoba Public Utilities Board's Needs For and Alternatives To hearings in 2014 through presentations from interveners, such as the Consumers' Association of Canada. Although these hearings are expensive and difficult to organize, they provide some opportunities for community voices to be heard on issues important to their way of life and relationship to their lands. They also generate a large quantity of information through the public transcripts such hearings establish.

Despite Manitoba Hydro's aforementioned actions, it is quite obvious through conversations with community members that they did not do enough, and that the relatively little they did was not up to community standards.[46] One of the most easily addressed concerns is that regarding the approach taken to identifying Valued Ecological Components, mentioned earlier. Community members participating in the Clean Environment Commission hearings took issue with Manitoba Hydro's approach, as Elders who were involved feel their knowledge was rarely, if ever, used and that many of the plants and animals they identified as important were not actually addressed in the environmental reports.[47] Failure to include and address what the Indigenous communities consider important both reduces their ability to participate in gaining the information they need to provide informed consent and restricts the information Manitoba Hydro and consultants obtain through studies on the implications of the project. Community members also took issue with the consultation process, stating that many of the consultation sessions with Manitoba Hydro were held in Winnipeg and include only certain members of the chief and council government.[48] Additionally, as Aimée Craft explores more thoroughly in Chapter 13 of this volume, community members were concerned about the actual inclusion of Indigenous voices and Indigenous knowledges in the "two-track" environmental assessments and other consultative processes.[49] Some community members questioned the extremely tight timelines set out for consultation processes and the affirmation of agreements.[50] In some instances, Manitoba Hydro actually pushed forward the timelines that had been set out in their partnership agreements. In particular, Elder Noah Massan and then councillor Conway Arthurson expressed concern over the timeline for the South Access Road. Based on the Joint Keeyask Development Agreement (JKDA), ratified in 2009, the South Access Road would be constructed after Keeyask had been completed. However, Manitoba Hydro required an additional construction site and thus required the South Access Road for 2015, only approximately one year after the CEC hearings.[51] These last-minute changes to large and important aspects of the project can seriously damage any trust created in the partnership process and can call into question all of the supposed inclusion of Indigenous perspectives in the consultation process.

In addition to the problems associated with having consultation sessions away from communities and only with select community members, many people questioned the relatively recent introduction of confidentiality agreements regarding the consultation process.[52] Reducing or eliminating community leaders' ability to discuss the consultation process with their respective communities significantly reduces the rest of the community's ability to obtain information. As a result, they cannot provide informed consent. These confidentiality agreements not only reduce the ability of community members to keep up to date with negotiations as they happen, they also create divisions among the community, their leaders, and Manitoba Hydro as well, as it increases distrust. During the CEC hearings in Split Lake, then councillor Conway Arthurson spoke openly about his concerns over the confidentiality surrounding the project. During his presentation, he discussed his legal advisors warning him against speaking to the CEC during their hearings in his own community of Fox Lake. He consistently returned to the challenge of having a true partnership and trust when he was being warned not to speak publicly about his concerns.[53] Although he continued to support the project, he was critical about the fact that lawyers had scripted the presentations of his fellow leaders, effectively preventing them from sharing their knowledge with their community and the commission.[54] He punctuated the end of his presentation by speaking directly to Manitoba Hydro when he stated, "We don't trust you. It is as simple as that."[55] Arguably, one of the most foundational aspects of a partnership and the provision of a social licence is creating and maintaining a trust relationship. Lack of trust can also create a dilemma in the process of ongoing consent and long-lasting social licence for a project.

Conclusion

Although there has been some form of concerted effort by Manitoba Hydro and the provincial government to change their relations with affected First Nations in the North, these attempts to redefine a long history of adversarial relations have somewhat failed. Manitoba Hydro has attempted to address these problems by establishing partnership agreements with affected communities in order to provide the perception that communities support these projects. "Social licence to operate" is an industry-defined means of conveying this argument and provides an opportunity for Manitoba Hydro and the provincial government to convince both other Manitobans as well as consumers in the United States that they have secured community support and will address any social problems in a community-oriented manner. However, their approach has failed to address a fuller, more socially just, meaning of social licence. Rather, it continues to represent an industrial, managerial, and Western capitalist world view on how to address costs that fails to consider the irreplaceable nature of costs to Indigenous relationships with the land, cultural activities, and human lives.

This chapter used the concept of "free, prior and informed consent," endorsed by the Truth and Reconciliation Commission of Canada and embedded within the United Nations Declaration on the Rights of Indigenous Peoples, to assess whether Manitoba Hydro and the Province obtained a true social licence to operate even within this managerial, cost-benefit analysis framework. After reviewing the historical and current perceptions of hydro power production in the Keeyask partner communities, it is quite obvious that Manitoba Hydro has not received the social licence they believe the partnership agreements establish. Ivan Keeper and Robert Spence effectively summed this sentiment up in their discussion of the Bipole III powerline when they wrote, "Manitoba Hydro recently informed Tataskweyak Cree Nation it has 'all necessary permits and authorizations' for construction, but Manitoba Hydro is wrong."[56] Although this statement is directed towards the Bipole III Project, this sentiment is held by many in the community regarding the Keeyask Project.

That said, it is still possible to express social licence as a more holistic definition. If Manitoba Hydro wants to follow a community-oriented framework of free, prior, and informed consent, communities must be provided with as much information as is available to the Crown corporation itself, and the forced use of confidentiality agreements and narrowly defined "valued ecological components" must end. Prior consent is a difficult form of consent to receive but must be fulfilled in a meaningful way to allow the community to make a decision in a comprehensive manner. Communities must be given time to review the process of construction and partnership formation and must be allowed to do so in such a manner that their decision can direct future decisions prior to finalized Manitoba Hydro plans. Free consent cannot be provided by communities who are unable to effect change as they find necessary. If a community is expected to provide free consent, power must be afforded to the communities such that they are able to defeat plans for a project if they perceive the costs as too high.

Additionally, social licence to operate cannot be viewed merely as a one-time licence with no consideration for ongoing consent through future review or maintenance. The four First Nations involved with Keeyask ratified the Joint Keeyask Development Agreement in 2009; by the time this volume is published in 2022, the projected cost of the project has increased significantly.[57] For social licence to be meaningful in the lives of affected community members, it must be reviewed and evaluated constantly throughout the process of construction and operation of any natural resource extraction or exploitation project. In northern Manitoba, this means any decision made that allows Manitoba Hydro social licence must be evaluated constantly to allow communities the greatest ability to participate in the project and truly provide social licence.

There is an argument to be made for the creation of jobs and economic opportunities for communities through Manitoba Hydro partnerships, with the possibility of a bright and prosperous future for all involved. However, for every statement in support of more generating stations and partnership agreements, there is a tsunami of voices in opposition, citing a long and trying history of destruction and corporate failure to mitigate damages or consult. The controversial and dividing nature of the partnership agreements set out for the Keeyask Project makes it immensely difficult to definitively determine whether social licence has been provided. However, based on a free, prior, and informed consent model of social licence, there are clearly serious flaws in Manitoba Hydro's claims to social licence. Manitoba would do well to reconsider the problematic term of "social licence to operate" to allow for a more progressive and less industrially focused means of addressing the social costs of resource extraction and exploitation.

If Manitoba Hydro honestly wishes to establish a positive and mutually beneficial relationship with affected communities in northern Manitoba, the relentless attempts to purchase social licence through partnership agreements and compensation agreements must stop. Instead, they must thoroughly review their approaches in the past and Indigenous communities' views of what must happen in the future to truly construct and support a strong relationship. There is a consistent lack of trust for Manitoba Hydro in northern Manitoba, and social licence cannot be established without a new legacy and a positive relationship.

This research would not have been possible without the generous financial support of the Social Sciences and Humanities Research Council of Canada through the Manitoba Research Alliance Partnering for Change— Community-Based Solution for Aboriginal and Inner-City Poverty grant, as well as the University of Manitoba's Graduate Enhancement of Tri-Council Stipends Program and the Duff Roblin Fellowship.

Notes

1   John R. Owen and Deanna Kemp, "Social Licence and Mining: A Critical Perspective," *Resources Policy* 38 (2013): 31.

2   Joseph Dipple, "Implications of Hydroelectric Partnerships in Northern Manitoba: Do Partnership Agreements Provide Social Licence?" Master's thesis, University of Manitoba, 2015, 66–67.

3   Truth and Reconciliation Canada, *Truth and Reconciliation Commission of Canada: Calls to Action* (Winnipeg: Truth and Reconciliation Commission of Canada, 2015), 10.

4   United Nations, *United Nations Declaration on the Rights of Indigenous Peoples* (New York: United Nations General Assembly, 2008), 10.

5   Toyah Rodhouse and Frank Vanclay, "Is Free, Prior, and Informed Consent a Form of Corporate Social Responsibility?" *Journal of Cleaner Production* 131 (2016): 786.

6   James Waldram, *As Long as the Rivers Run: Hydroelectric Development and Native Communities in Western Canada* (Winnipeg: University of Manitoba Press, 1988), 147.

7   David Newman, "History of NFA Implementation by the Government of Manitoba," in *First Nations and Hydroelectric Development in Northern Manitoba: The Northern Flood Agreement: Issues and Implications*, ed. Jean-Luc Chodkiewicz and Jennifer Brown (Winnipeg: The Centre for Rupert's Land Studies at the University of Winnipeg, 1999), 47–49.

8   Peter Kulchyski, *Aboriginal Rights Are Not Human Rights* (Winnipeg: Arbeiter Ring Press, 2013), 141.

9   Will Braun, "What About Aboriginal Partners?," *Interchurch Council on Hydropower*, 20 March 2017, https://hydrojustice.org/2017/03/20/cree-fortunes-hitched-to-hydro-wagon/.

10 Will Braun, "Dam Deal Loses Shine: First Nations Gambled on Bold Talk of Prosperity," *Winnipeg Free Press*, 24 April 2014, http://www.winnipegfreepress.com/opinion/analysis/dam-deal-loses-shine-256479261.html.

11 Nina Hall, Justine Lacey, Simone Carr-Cornish, and Anne Maree-Dowd, "Social Licence to Operate: Understanding How a Concept Has Been Translated into Practice in Energy Industries," *Journal of Cleaner Production* 86 (2015): 301–07.

12 Ibid.

13 Ibid.

14 Richard Parsons and Kieren Moffat, "Constructing the Meaning of Social Licence," *Social Epistemology* 28 (2014): 347–51; Owen and Kemp, "Social Licence and Mining," 31–32.

15 Manitoba, Ministry of Conservation, *Keeyask Generation Project Public Hearings,* Hearing 8 January 2014 (Winnipeg: Manitoba Clean Environment Commission), 6811.

16 Rodhouse and Vanclay, "Is Free, Prior, and Informed Consent," 789.

17 Parsons and Moffat, "Constructing the Meaning," 345.

18 Braun, "Dam Deal Loses Shine."

19 Braun, "What About Aboriginal Partners?"

20 Manitoba Hydro, *Keeyask Project,* accessed 29 April 2015, https://www.hydro.mb.ca/projects/keeyask/index.shtml?WT.mc_id=2613.

21 Braun, "What About Aboriginal Partners?"

22 Manitoba Hydro, *Confidentiality Agreement,* accessed 29 April 2015, https://www.hydro.mb.ca/projects/keeyask/pdf/Schedule_24_1_090529.pdf.

23 Rodhouse and Vanclay, "Is Free, Prior, and Informed Consent," 788.

24 Robert Spence, personal communications; Noah Massan, personal communications; Dipple, "Implications of Hydroelectric Partnerships in Northern Manitoba," 49.

25 Manitoba, Public Utilities Board, *Manitoba Hydro Needs For and Alternatives To Review of Manitoba Hydro's Preferred Development Plan,* Hearing 25 April 2014 (Winnipeg: Public Utilities Board, 2014), 8271–72.

26 Noah Massan, personal communications; Robert Spence, personal communications.

27 Dipple, "Implications of Hydroelectric Partnerships in Northern Manitoba," 83.

28 Ibid., 70–71.

29 See John Loxely, *Aboriginal, Northern, and Community Economic Development: Papers and Retrospectives* (Winnipeg: Arbeiter Ring Press, 2010); Marcel Moody, "This Hydro Partnership Is Working," *Winnipeg Free Press,* 3 May 2014, http://www.winnipegfreepress.com/opinion/analysis/this-hydro-partnership-is-working-257773111.html.

30 Noah Massan, personal communications; Robert Spence, personal communications; Ivan Moose, personal communications.

31 Kulchyski, *Aboriginal Rights,* 131; Manitoba, Ministry of Conservation, *Keeyask Generation Project Public Hearings,* Hearing 8 January 2014 (Winnipeg: Manitoba Clean Environment Commission, 2014), 6785.

32 Rodhouse and Vanclay, "Is Free, Prior, and Informed Consent," 788.

33 Robert Spence, personal communications; Ivan Moose, personal communications; Noah Massan, personal communications.

34 Manitoba, Ministry of Conservation, *Keeyask Generation Project Public Hearings,* Hearing 24 September 2013 (Winnipeg: Manitoba Clean Environment Commission, 2013), 26.

35 Manitoba, Ministry of Conservation, *Keeyask Generation Project Public Hearings,* Hearing 31 October 2013 (Winnipeg: Manitoba Clean Environment Commission, 2013), 1698–1700.

36 Noah Massan, personal communications.

37 Manitoba Hydro, *History and Timeline,* accessed 29 April 2015, https://www.hydro.mb.ca/corporate/history/history_timeline.html.

38 Hugh McCullum and Karmel McCullum, *This Land Is Not for Sale* (Toronto:

Anglican Book Centre, 1975), 106.

39   Waldram, *As Long as the Rivers Run*, 147.

40   Kulchyski, *Aboriginal Rights*, 141.

41   Rodhouse and Vanclay, "Is Free, Prior, and Informed Consent," 788.

42   Manitoba, Ministry of Conservation, *Keeyask Generation Project Public Hearings*, Hearing 23 October 2013, vol. 3 (Winnipeg: Manitoba Clean Environment Commission, 2013), 645–46.

43   Manitoba Hydro, "Round One the Public Involvement Program for the Keeyask Generation Project," accessed 29 April 2015, https://www.hydro.mb.ca/projects/keeyask/pdf/summary_round_one.pdf.

44   Keeyask Hydro Power Limited Partnership, *The Partnership*, accessed 29 April 2015, http://keeyask.com/wp/the-partnership.

45   Clean Environment Commission, *Keeyask Generation Project*, accessed 29 April 2015, http://www.cecmanitoba.ca/hearings/index.cfm?hearingid=39#2.

46   Robert Spence, personal communications.

47   Noah Massan, personal communications.

48   Noah Massan, personal communications; Robert Spence, personal communications; Ivan Moose, personal communications.

49   Manitoba, Ministry of Conservation, *Keeyask Generation Project Public Hearings*, Hearing 8 October 2013 (Winnipeg: Manitoba Clean Environment Commission, 2013), 52.

50   Ibid., 86–87, 93.

51   Ibid., 86–87; Manitoba, Ministry of Conservation, *Keeyask Generation Project*, Hearing 31, 1715–16.

52   Ivan Moose, personal communications; Manitoba Hydro, *Confidentiality Agreement*.

53   Manitoba, Ministry of Conservation, *Keeyask Generation Project*, Hearing 8, 90–99.

54   Ibid.

55   Manitoba, Ministry of Conservation, *Keeyask Generation Project*, Hearing 8, 93.

56   Ivan Keeper and Robert Spence, "Hydro Lacks Authority to Build Bipole," *Winnipeg Free Press*, 20 January 2015, http://www.winnipegfreepress.com/opinion/analysis/hydro-lacks-authority-to-build-bipole-289114941.html.

57   Keeyask Hydro Power Limited Partnership, *The Partnership*; CBC News, "1st Female Manitoba Hydro President and CEO Appointed," *CBC News*, 1 November 2018, https://www.cbc.ca/news/canada/manitoba/jay-grewal-manitoba-hydro-1.4887410.

" It is important that we work together as partners to continuously reconcile a role in a partnership to heal past wounds related to the Hydro development, to build trustworthy relationships with our partners. We especially want our children and future generations to know that we entered into this partnership with these feelings and deep misgivings, but insisted on a long-term, ongoing commitment to healing, reconciliation, mutual respect and self-determination."

Ted Bland, York Factory First Nation, Partnership Panel at CEC hearings (21 October 2013), 163

CHAPTER 12

The Keeyask Model from a Community Economic Development Perspective

JERRY BUCKLAND AND MELANIE O'GORMAN

All across Canada, natural resource development is occurring at a rapid pace. From forestry in British Columbia and the oil sands in Alberta to mining in Ontario, resource development is generating huge sums of money and driving local economic development. We are in a new era, however, when the sharing of opportunities stemming from natural resource development among Indigenous peoples, companies, and governments is becoming commonplace. Across Canada there is now a patchwork of resource agreements, all recognizing that Indigenous peoples have a right to share in the wealth generated and that Indigenous peoples must participate in natural resource development if such development is to be sustainable.[1]

Hydroelectric development is no different. Whereas large-scale dam projects were once viewed as socially and environmentally destructive, they have come back into favour on the presumption that hydroelectric generation is a relatively clean energy source in terms of greenhouse gas emissions.[2] As previous chapters of this volume have discussed, Manitoba Hydro is now attempting to recognize past harms and respond to calls for redistributive justice through partnership agreements with local First Nations—first with Wuskwatim and now with Keeyask. Politicians, Manitoba Hydro representatives, and leaders from Indigenous communities have argued that these agreements will bring much-needed community economic development to Keeyask partner communities. While this is an important goal, how do the Keeyask agreements measure up against recognized standards for economic development?

Community Economic Development Framework

According to the literature, hydro dams and local community development do not often sit well with each other. For instance, the World Commission on Dams' high-level review of dam projects concluded that while dams can contribute to economic growth, they often place heavy and involuntary burdens on local, and often Indigenous, peoples: "Large dams have had serious impacts on lives, livelihoods, cultures and spiritual existence of indigenous and tribal peoples. Due to neglect and lack of capacity to secure justice because of structural inequities, cultural dissonance, discrimination and economic and political marginalization, indigenous and tribal people have suffered disproportionately from negative impacts of large dams, while often being excluded from sharing in the benefits."[3]

The disturbance of the landscape and changes in water quality and biodiversity resulting from hydroelectric dams disrupt the harmony of human–ecological relations so crucial to Indigenous well-being. In contrast to an anthropocentric view of land and water as resources to be exploited, Indigenous peoples view themselves as "relatives of the land," so that dam development may be viewed as especially harmful.[4]

In a report by the Manitoba Research Alliance, community economic development (CED) is defined as "placing the community at the centre of economic development—such that the community is both the beneficiary and the prime mover. By matching local resources with local needs, community members are able to realize their higher-order non-economic needs, as well as their basic material needs."[5] Based on a survey of the CED literature, below we identify five common principles cited in the CED literature for projects to engender sustainable CED.[6] We use these principles as a framework to evaluate the Keeyask Project.

CED Principles

1. *Project impacts/benefits should align with community values.* A project must bring large benefits for the affected community relative to other available projects. Such benefits should fulfill the goals of the

community, whether economic, social, cultural, ecological, and so forth.

2. *"Small is beautiful"; once established, scaling up a project or business may be appropriate.* For communities to maintain control over their lives, it is important to start small. Once communities have established an effective model, scaling up may be possible and consistent with community ideals.

3. *Protection of the environment and community interests: project benefits should be holistic.* A healthy economy cannot continue if it is achieved at the expense of community vitality and environmental health. A range of community interests—not just economic—should be served by the project.

4. *All stakeholders should participate in project decision making.* Decision making must take into account all stakeholders, including less vocal community residents and future generations. These stakeholders are critically important to the success of projects, yet often marginalized.

5. *There should be continuous building of local capacity.* A central issue in the CED literature is that development leads to the growth of individual and community capacity to work toward goals.

While these principles dominate the CED literature, we acknowledge that there are a multitude of views on what constitutes CED. As views on CED involve social norms, world views, and ideologies, as well as one's socio-economic circumstances, even within a small community there will be divergent opinions of what an appropriate CED path is. A set of five criteria cannot possibly represent this diversity. However, the literature from which they are drawn is vast and established, so these are long-standing themes. For example, it includes the landmark publication *Wahbung: Our Tomorrows.* This powerful vision laid out by the Manitoba Indian Brotherhood emphasized the crucial role of hunting, fishing, trapping, and gathering for Indigenous economies, the need for consistent economic development efforts, and the importance of training/education. More recently, *Indigenomics* by Carol Anne Hilton discusses similar principles as those above, including an emphasis on economic self-determination and holistic development for future generations—"the seventh generation economy."[7]

The Keeyask Generation Project as a Community Economic Development Model

The Keeyask Generation Project is a joint effort of Manitoba Hydro and Tataskweyak Cree Nation (TCN), War Lake First Nation (WLFN), York Factory First Nation (YFFN), and Fox Lake Cree Nation (FLCN).[8] This joint effort is referred to as the "Keeyask Hydropower Limited Partnership" (KHLP).[9] Keeyask itself will be located in the Split Lake Resource Management Area of northern Manitoba, 725 kilometres northeast of Winnipeg on the lower Nelson River. The Generating Station will be the fourth largest generating station in Manitoba.[10]

Manitoba Hydro began discussing the Keeyask Generation Project with TCN in 1998. War Lake, Fox Lake, and York Factory eventually joined the discussion, and all five parties signed the Joint Keeyask Development Agreement (JKDA) in 2009.[11] This agreement governs all activities related to the project, including training, employment, financing, business opportunities, and so forth. Manitoba Hydro will provide administrative and management services for the KHLP and will own at least 75 percent of the equity of the partnership. The four First Nations, which Manitoba Hydro refers to as the "Keeyask Cree Nations" (KCNs), collectively have the right to own up to 25 percent of the partnership—although that would cost millions of dollars up front. Construction on Keeyask began in 2014, after the KHLP secured the final regulatory approvals from the Province following the Clean Environment Commission's recommendation to approve the project. The first of seven units officially went into operation on 16 February 2021.

The Pre-construction Phase (1998–2014)

Key to the Keeyask model as a CED model is the extent to which Manitoba Hydro consulted the community, and the community's subsequent ratification of the decision to participate in the Keeyask Project. Starting in 1998, the Crown corporation held information meetings in each KCN and in Winnipeg, Thompson, Gillam, and Churchill. All adult KCN community members were invited to participate in referenda to gauge support for the JKDA as well as to ratify the Adverse Effects Agreement (AEAs) meant to address unavoidable harms from the construction project for each community.[12] The referenda results were interpreted as supportive of the Keeyask Project in each community, given that greater than one-third of eligible voters came to vote, and a majority of votes were cast in favour of the JKDA and AEAs.

Also relating to the CED principles above—in particular, capacity building—is the training conducted to prepare local workers for work on the Keeyask Project. Between 2001 and 2010, multiple levels of government carried out a large training initiative, called the "Hydro Northern Training and Employment Initiative," to ensure skilled local labour would be available for Wuskwatim, Keeyask, and other major Manitoba construction projects.[13] This $60.3 million multi-year initiative aimed to train over 1,000 First Nations workers for approximately 800 jobs with the Wuskwatim and Keeyask projects. By 2010, 1,876 individuals had successfully completed at least one course within the initiative[14] for designated trades such as iron-working and plumbing; non-designated trades such as heavy equipment operation; construction support; professional and administrative positions; and non-occupational training such as life skills.[15] As of August 2020, individuals from the KCNs accounted for 35 percent of all on-the-job training and 9 percent of all other training that has occurred.[16]

The Construction Phase (2014–2021)

The construction phase of the Keeyask Project began in July 2014 and will continue until 2021, with cleanup occurring until 2022. The KHLP notes that contracts worth over $730 million have been awarded for work on the Keeyask infrastructure and generation projects, and that over $33 million has been spent in the KCNs.[17] Originally roughly $200 million of contracts were reserved for KCN businesses or joint-venture partnerships; however, we could not find information on what proportion of direct negotiated contracts have been secured by KCN businesses.

In total, the construction of the Keeyask Generating Station is estimated to have required a total of 4,225 person-years of employment from 2014 to 2021, with peak employment in 2017. The JKDA identified a target of at least 630 (15 percent) of these person-years of employment for KCN communities. The Burntwood/Nelson Agreement gave "Qualified Northern Aboriginals" preference for hiring for the Keeyask Project. As of December 2020, a total of 10,615 individuals had been hired to work on the Keeyask Project. Of those, 19 percent were KCN members and 39 percent were Indigenous.[18]

The Post-construction Phase[19]

The JKDA Benefits Summary notes that "Manitoba Hydro and the KCNs have agreed to a 20-year target for the employment of 182 Members of the KCNs in Manitoba Hydro's ongoing operations."[20] If this target is met, and assuming that each operational position pays $60,000 per person per year, this will bring $10.8 million in total ($540,000 per year) into the KCNs.

While the KCNs have the option to invest in up to 25 percent equity of the $8.7 billion project, their current capacity to purchase equity is likely lower, perhaps between 1.9 percent and 2.5 percent (costing approximately $29.45 million to $38.75 million). The KCNs can purchase shares according to two options, but they are predicted to invest via the Preferred Unit option, which guarantees a return on their investment. In particular, this return will be the higher of the Preferred Minimum Distribution (PMD) or the Preferred Participating Distribution (PPD). If the Keeyask Project has low revenues, then the PMD will prevail, and we estimate that the PMD will provide the KCNs with a stable stream of investment income.[21] Assuming that the KCNs invest a 1.9 percent equity stake, the PMD would bring revenue of $1.25 million per year. If, however, annual revenue of the Keeyask Project were high (say $260 million), then the PPD would be the higher distribution, and it would bring $5.9 million per year if the KCNs invested 1.9 percent equity, or $7.8 million per year if the KCNs invested 2.5 percent equity.

In addition to investment revenue, the Keeyask Project includes Adverse Effects Agreements with all four KCNs, which provide "replacements, substitutions or opportunities to offset unavoidable Keeyask Adverse Effects."[22] Each KCN is responsible for managing, implementing, and operating each offsetting program. Examples of AEAs include hunting/fishing programs, infrastructure projects, museums, and language and cultural programming. Each AEA includes annual supporting funds from the KHLP and residual compensation, and will compensate licensed trappers for loss of revenue and for infrastructure damage due to the Keeyask Project. These AEA obligations were estimated to total $169 million as of March 2015.[23]

Analysis of the Keeyask Model according to CED Principles

Achievements of the Keeyask Model

The Keeyask Project embeds certain community economic development features within its partnership between Manitoba Hydro and the KCNs. In this regard, it is an improvement from a CED perspective over past hydroelectric projects. Other positive features include improved financial arrangements and training/employment initiatives.

The Partnership

Drawing on the precedent set by Wuskwatim, the Manitoba Hydro–KCN partnership gives the KCNs a substantial stake in the ownership of the Keeyask Project. This point relates to the CED principle number four, participatory decision-making.

Our literature review has identified mutual interests between the hydroelectric industry and communities living near dam sites. Pierre Fortin argues that northern rivers and landscapes are an important common interest between the hydroelectric industry and Indigenous people.[24] He asserts that what is needed is an effective process that allows these groups to engage in equitable agreements, plans, implementation, and monitoring/evaluation for revised implementation. Speaking from the perspective of the hydroelectric industry, Fortin concludes that these building blocks are in place with the Keeyask partnership.

Unlike previous hydroelectric projects before Wuskwatim, the Keeysak model has involved community members from local First Nations in a number of processes ranging from joint management of environmental assessment to negotiation over the AEAs and representation on the project board of directors. Manitoba Hydro consulted communities regarding project design. For example, they modified their design to minimize flooding and limit water level fluctuations to one metre, based on community consultations.[25]

More Equitable Sharing of Benefits

By providing greater community economic development opportunities to the KCNs from the start, the Keeyask Project improves on many CED aspects of early hydroelectric dam projects in northern Manitoba. This relates to CED principle number one, project alignment with community interests.

Proponents view the Keeyask Generation Project as an opportunity to improve economic conditions in relatively economically depressed northern communities.[26] The investment income the project generates for the KCNs offers an income stream that can be used to fund housing or other community economic development initiatives. In the news release announcing the signing of the JKDA, Tataskweyak Chief Duke Beardy said, "Keeyask provides an opportunity for us to join the mainstream Manitoba economy to build a future of hope that will sustain and provide for all citizens of Tataskweyak Cree Nation."[27]

In the case of Wuskwatim, Nisichawayasihk Cree Nation (NCN) shares both gains and losses with Manitoba Hydro. Hence NCN faces financial risk, and will be left with a large debt load if Manitoba Hydro revenues do not materialize.[28] As Dr. Ramona Neckoway shares in this volume, low revenues to date mean that NCN members are currently "born into debt." The Keeyask agreement improves on this aspect of the Wuskwatim agreement in that it allows the KCNs to purchase preferred shares that offer a guaranteed financial return for investing in the project.

Ciaran O'Faircheallaigh notes that revenue from natural resource development also gives communities access to a steady (non-governmental) income stream, which they can use as they see fit, independent of government priorities.[29] War Lake Chief Betsy Kennedy noted this when she said, "We are very optimistic that the JKDA will provide significant benefits now and for future generations of War Lake Members. It paves the way for economic development through business, employment and income opportunities—leading, we trust, to self-sufficiency."[30]

Training and Employment Creation

The Hydro Northern Training and Employment Initiative was the first large-scale training initiative designed and managed by, for, and in northern Manitoba First Nations. This is a significant achievement not only to the Keeyask partnership's credit, but also to that of the provincial and federal government agencies and the First Nations that supported it. As noted earlier, the initiative surpassed its goal of training 1,000 First Nations workers for positions with the Keeyask Project and other northern Manitoba employment opportunities. This may bring significant wage increases to KCN members after Keeyask construction has ceased.[31]

Having employment targets at all is also a significant improvement over the Wuskwatim Project, which included no explicit employment targets. The JKDA specified short- and medium-term employment targets, and entails that the Keeyask partnership may be held accountable if they do not meet such targets.

Challenges Embedded within the Keeyask Model

Despite the improvements of the Keeyask model over past models, the Keeyask model is not associated with a number of CED principles. Significant risks stem from the project's large size, the sizable power imbalance between Manitoba Hydro and the KCNs, and the fact that economic compensation may not offset ecological, social, or spiritual costs.

Local Harm and Inadequate Compensation

A large number of studies, internationally and in Canada, have documented the negative social, economic, and environmental impacts from dam projects on Indigenous peoples, and that these impacts tend to persist for generations. James Waldram undertook an early and comprehensive study on dams in northern Manitoba and concluded that Indigenous peoples generally have not adequately benefited from these projects.[32] This relates to a number of CED principles, but most specifically to CED principle number three, the need for holistic community benefits from a project.

J.E. Windsor and J.A. McVey examined the impact of the Kenney Dam, a private dam on the Nechako River in northwestern British Columbia, built in 1952 to power Alcan's aluminum smelter on the Cheslatta T'En community in the interior of British Columbia.[33] The Cheslatta were relocated to make space for the new reservoir, and this led to a drastic loss of a "sense of place." Before their community was flooded, the Cheslatta were self-sufficient. In their new territory, many felt uncomfortable that they were in the ancestral territory of the Wet'suwet'en. Alcan destroyed their entire former community before it was flooded—buildings, including the community church, homes and ranches were burned. The graveyard was washed away. In 1984, the Carrier Sekani Tribal Council described the impact of the Cheslatta relocation as follows: "They were forced to build a new life in a farming community with which they had little in common. Many were forced to abandon their traditional occupations of hunting, trapping and fishing. A once proud people had for a time lost all dignity and succumbed to despair and alcohol. Whereas no Indians living at Cheslatta had been reliant on social assistance, now Band members have very few other sources of income."[34]

Suicide and violence—once rare occurrences—became common. Relocation led to a loss of identity and community collapse. Windsor and McVey conclude, "We do not consider it unfair to conclude that the benefits of most large dams—especially hydroelectric dams—have been achieved at the expense of the displacement and impoverishment of others, generally low-income, rural peoples and, all too frequently, native peoples."[35]

Martin Loney, examining the impact of dam projects in northern Manitoba, describes Manitoba Hydro's approach to dealing with Indigenous communities as "forced modernization."[36] Loney documented the negative outcomes of dam projects on local people, including declining incomes, rising rates of substance abuse, and declining food security. While the construction phase did create some short-term, low-waged employment, medium- to long-term employment did not arise. Loney notes, "In some cases it may be possible to argue that a new development has had an almost immediate traumatic effect, sending a community into a spiral of decline from which there seems no prospect of recovery."[37]

Disruptions to Traditional Livelihoods

A major concern raised in the literature has to do with disruption of traditional livelihoods. This point relates most closely to CED principle number one, the protection of environmental and community interests, and to CED principle number three, the need for holistic benefits from projects.

As Elder and harvester Noah Massan argues in Chapter 6 of this volume, Indigenous peoples' traditional livelihoods in northern Manitoba provide holistic, physically and intellectually demanding work; income (in-kind, for trade, and for sale); and cultural and spiritual identity. Since there is less demarcation between "nine-to-five" job activities and recreational, spiritual, and cultural activities outside of that time, flooding lands traditionally used for hunting, gathering, trapping, and fishing will have interconnected economic, socio-cultural, and spiritual effects. While the Keeyask Project AEAs propose moving individuals to new hunting or fishing grounds for short time periods, this is an untested idea with little uptake to date.

Ronald Niezen examined the social impacts of hydroelectric development on the Indigenous people of James Bay, Québec,[38] and found that communities more directly affected by hydroelectric development experienced negative social outcomes such as suicide, violence, substance abuse, and child neglect. Less-affected communities that were able to continue hunting, trapping, and fishing saw fewer social problems. Niezen's results support the view that traditional livelihoods are more than a "job" and that their loss has wide-ranging consequences.

Steven Hoffman examined the Northern Flood Agreement (NFA) and found that it does not support traditional livelihoods but rather leads to the erosion of these livelihoods.[39] He explains that the NFA and associated implementation agreements represent "once-and-for-all" payments that are meant to extinguish liabilities for past harm caused by hydroelectric development. The NFA does not even purport to rectify the near collapse of the South Indian Lake fishery or any of the other negative impacts resulting from the flooding of South Indian Lake. He argues it is misguided to assume that the provision of funds under the NFA (similar to the Keeyask provision of funds for substitution of traditional livelihoods under the AEAs) can replace traditional livelihood activities, which are interwoven with socio-cultural and spiritual well-being.

Loney reports on a range of studies that find that hydroelectric development has been impoverishing and creates dependency for Indigenous communities in northern Manitoba.[40] He notes that in all of these communities, before the dam, the local community was active in a number of traditional livelihoods that provided "highly nutritional food supplies and afforded a lifestyle which provided significant physical, as well as spiritual rewards."[41] After flooding, for example in Chemawawin (Easterville) due to the Grand Rapids Dam, moose habitat declined and fishing and trapping activities became less viable. This affected the self-esteem and identity of both individuals and their families, and led to mental health problems and consequent increases in alcoholism and crime. Loney notes that while many northern First Nations might have been, relative to urban standards, materially poor, they had a strong and resilient economy.[42]

In 1995, Loney again studied Grand Rapids, finding that the dam caused long-term trauma to the community. Once again, he found that the compensation being offered in the form of piecemeal services and modern-sector jobs cannot substitute for a more holistic traditional livelihood system.

Even in the more recent Wuskwatim agreement, Peter Kulchyski notes that Manitoba Hydro continues to be critical of traditional livelihoods.[43] For example he says, "While our society at least pretends to pay respect to preserving the family farm as a foundation for rural communities in southern areas, no parallel (even pretence of) respect is paid to hunting families as the foundation of community life in northern regions. . . . Hunters are often classed as 'unemployed' and are not seen as contributors to the gross domestic product. Their economy and rights are off the map of planners and economic advisors. Yet they have sustained their families, communities and nations in northern regions for millennia."[44]

He notes that the Wuskwatim Project—with its promises of destroying the land in exchange for modern-sector jobs—indicates a modern bias. He notes that because of the holistic set of benefits traditional livelihoods provide, "hunters are among the wealthiest of peoples."[45] Based on this body of evidence, the Keeyask Generation Project almost certainly runs the risk of harming local communities due to a lack of respect for traditional livelihoods.

These studies demonstrate that even in the best-case scenario, where First Nations communities receive strong social services and modern employment, the consequences could be harmful because the separateness of these components is fundamentally different from the traditional livelihoods of First Nations. Hence, if benefits promised to First Nations members through the JKDA do not materialize, these individuals will be doubly harmed.

KCN Participation

CED principle number four draws attention to the importance of local participation in decision making on development projects. The literature identifies power asymmetry as an important challenge regarding Indigenous people's participation in hydro projects when these hydroelectric projects are driven by large state or corporate bureaucracies.[46] This power imbalance makes it difficult for Indigenous stakeholders to participate freely and fairly in decision making on projects "in their backyard." A power asymmetry indeed exists between the four First Nations involved in this project and Manitoba Hydro.

Referenda were held in each Keeyask community to decide on whether to proceed with the Keeyask Project. The high proportion of members in each KCN who voted in favour of the project may be viewed as representing widespread support for the project. It should be noted, however, that only 37 percent of eligible voters in York Factory and 47 percent of eligible voters in Fox Lake voted in the referenda.[47] Another concern regarding these referenda relates to whether their style—a majority rule vote of all adults in the community—is compatible with Cree culture and values. For example, perhaps consensus-based decision making and a transparent vote could have been used instead.[48]

Further, as Joseph Dipple discusses in Chapter 11 in this volume, members may not have felt that they had a genuine choice in the matter—Manitoba Hydro would proceed with the project with or without their support.[49] At the Clean Environment Commission (CEC) hearings in 2013–14, the Concerned Fox Lake Grassroots Citizens noted that the smaller KCNs (York Factory, Fox Lake, and War Lake) may have felt that Tataskweyak's vote was decisive, given its larger size, and if they had not consented, the dam would still be built but with fewer benefits and more harmful consequences for them. They suggested that very few community members actually attended information sessions on Keeyask. This raises some doubt about how engaged and informed community members ultimately were in the decision making.[50]

There are also concerns with how Manitoba Hydro framed the Keeyask Project to the Indigenous communities. For instance, Dr. Ramona Neckoway argues that, in the case of the Wuskwatim hydro-electric project, members of Nisichawayasihk Cree Nation First Nation were attracted to the project by the perceived short-term benefits.[51] Hydro representatives prominently highlighted the project's short-term benefits, such as cash payouts, while the long-term costs (i.e., loss of land and traditional livelihoods) were comparatively understated. Michael Foth highlights what he describes as the coercive nature of the Wuskwatim consultative process and argues that dissent against Wuskwatim was highly controlled.[52] For example, Foth quotes Carol Kobliski of the Justice Seekers of Nelson House:

Many in our community want to speak out, but keep silent in fear of personal reprisals from our Chief and Council. For example, our Chief and Council are taking vindictive action against Reverend Nelson Hart for participating in these hearings. They have taken formal action to try and have him removed as a Reverend in our community. Where is our freedom of speech? This is an example of what will happen leading up to the Wuskwatim project development agreement vote. The misinformation had already started as our Chief and Council tried to intimidate Nelson House band members to support Wuskwatim.[53]

This relatively recent evidence of proponents deliberately manipulating how a hydro project's costs and benefits are framed to gain local support casts doubt on the legitimacy of First Nations' participation in decision making for Keeyask as well.[54]

Dynamic Capacity Building

CED principle five relates to individual and collective capacity building. Establishing the Keeyask partnership is an achievement in this regard. However, in order for the partnership to "bear fruit," community members must not only have job and business opportunities during the dam construction period but experience those benefits long-term. Much of this will come through training and education in a diverse range of fields.

In order for the partnership to be truly participatory, it is important that Keeyask Cree Nation members are equipped with the capacity to address the challenges that are posed by a large project like the Keeyask Generation Project. Whereas Manitoba Hydro is in the business of building and operating hydroelectric dams, the Keeyask communities are not. While the Keeyask project trains local residents for employment in construction and trades, there is little evidence of training and education in fields other than those that directly benefit hydroelectric development. Given that construction jobs will taper off once the project is complete, the Keeyask partnership should support long-term economic development opportunities that do not derive from hydroelectric power generation. For example, Manitoba Hydro could provide funds to launch training programs in health care or early childhood development, or build high schools in Fox Lake, York Factory, and War Lake First Nations so that students do not have to leave their communities to complete their education. This would ensure there are diverse skills in the community for long-term CED.

Evidence of the Keeyask partnership taking ownership of this broad approach to human capital development is not particularly apparent in the Keeyask partnership agreement or in the Clean Environment Commission hearings process. Instead, Manitoba Hydro seems to view the capacity-building issue as outside of its purview. See, for example, this response from the hearings: "Funding capital projects or upgrades in KCNs communities is beyond the scope and responsibility of the Keeyask Hydropower Limited Partnership. On-reserve education is the responsibility of the federal government. As stated in SE SV Section 3.4.2.3, each of the Keeyask Partners has the opportunity to invest in the Project and, after the Project is operational, receive income based on Project revenues. As such, the distribution of annual Project dividends is expected to increase the amount of discretionary income the KCNs have to address economic, infrastructure and social needs."[55]

While it is true that First Nations must take the lead in deciding the nature of socio-cultural capacity-building initiatives, it is disingenuous for the Keeyask partnership to say that it has no role here.

"Small Is Beautiful," and Meeting Local Needs Is Essential
At a cost of $8.7 billion, the Keeyask Project will take about seven years to complete. It will have a net capacity of 695 megawatts and will flood approximately forty-five square kilometres. Compared with dams around the world—such as Three Gorges in China and Itaipu in South America—the Keeyask Dam is not large. But within the context of the First Nations communities affected in the region, its size and significance are immense. Moreover, the dam is designed primarily to provide electricity to southern Manitoba and northern U.S. consumers. These two features of the Keeyask Project make it particularly risky from a CED perspective. This point relates to CED principle number two, the idea that, at least in the beginning, "small is beautiful," and number three, holistic benefits and protecting environment and community interests.

The main benefit of starting projects small is that it allows the community to engage in planning and testing the project, to ensure it aligns with their interests before scale-up occurs. But Keeyask is very large compared with other economic activities in the KCNs. While the CED literature is quite consistent about the need to "start small," there is more debate about whether local production must remain small or, out of necessity, grow larger.[56]

From a CED perspective, it would have been preferable if Manitoba Hydro had worked with local communities on developing smaller-scale projects first to develop a trusting relationship and build capacity.[57] Once they established an effective partnership model, then better conditions would exist to scale up the hydroelectric project to the order of the Keeyask Dam. As it stands, the four Cree Nations involved must "take a leap of faith" in agreeing to partner with Manitoba Hydro on a large project from which there is no turning back. This directly contravenes the "small is beautiful" principle.

Economic Development and Compensation

A final challenge of the Keeyask Project, relating to CED principle number three, is the protection of the environment and community interests. Given the scarcity of modern economic opportunities in many of the communities surrounding the proposed Keeyask Generating Station, some see hydroelectric development as a rare economic opportunity that these communities should take advantage of. However, a number of risks relating to modern economic development and compensation exist.

First, most employment resulting from the Keeyask Project will be short-term. As discussed, higher paid and more stable jobs will not accrue to the First Nations communities to the same extent as these relatively lower-waged construction jobs. The boom-bust nature of this employment is known to be damaging: people abandon (or are forced out of) traditional livelihoods to take up short-term jobs requiring specific skills, only to find that those skills are not rewarded in other areas of the local economy. Waldram refers to the "severe social disintegration" resulting from the Grand Rapids hydroelectric development, noting that "this disintegration was caused by the declining economic potential of the region, the subsequent unemployment, and a general community-wide depression, all of which were the result of the hydroelectric project and relocation."[58]

Even the short-term employment benefits of Keeyask should be viewed with caution. The Burntwood/Nelson Agreement governs labour relations, as noted above. This agreement prevents collective action of any kind,[59] taking away a key form of recourse against poor labour practices, should they arise.

First Nations band councils are to administer all funds received for offsetting programs and from profit sharing with Manitoba Hydro. Strong local governance is therefore essential for First Nations members to benefit. First Nations councils are required to provide their members with an annual report on revenue versus spending, and any concerns may be referred to an arbiter—although it is costly, both in terms of time and money, to do so.[60] The Hydropower Sustainability Assessment Protocol, a global framework for assessing hydro projects, emphasizes public disclosure of all project benefits.[61]

Spending arising from the Keeyask Project requires funding to flow from the KHLP to the individual KCN (for example, spending on the AEAs). If KCN members are to hold their leaders accountable for this spending, they must have information on resource flows to those leaders; however, there is no requirement that KCN members receive information on this. Representatives of the Concerned Fox Lake Grassroots Citizens noted that they have not personally observed the impact from money that has already flowed from Manitoba Hydro to Fox Lake Cree Nation, which amounted to just under $8 million.[62] The cause of this disconnect—between Manitoba Hydro's spending and the (ideally positive) impact on the community—is unclear. For the Keeyask Project to be a success, it is important that the KHLP report all financial flows of the Keeyask Project to KCN members.

Representatives from the grassroots citizens group note that in addition to the concerns with transparency noted above, confidentiality agreements signed by Fox Lake Cree Nation leadership restricts information about the Keeyask Project as well (see Joseph Dipple, Chapter 11 in this volume).[63] These agreements restrict a community's ability to place political pressure on a government or company if a deal is harmful, as they cannot publicize harmful aspects of the agreement in the media. O'Faircheallaigh calls this the loss of a "crucial lever," the capacity of a community to threaten a corporation or government's reputation.[64]

Overall, the Keeyask Project does not meet many of the CED criteria laid out at the beginning of this chapter. These include the significant harm that the KCNs will likely incur in terms of social, ecological, and spiritual well-being; that it is a large-scale dam with irreversible

effects; that the KCNs' participation in decision making for the dam
was inadequate; that the economic benefits promised to them may be
less than expected; and that the project does not take a long-term view
on training and education for Keeyask Cree Nations members beyond
the direct construction-related skills needed to build Keeyask.

Conclusion

Shortly after he was elected, Assembly of First Nations National Chief
Perry Bellegarde said, "To the people across this great land, I say to you,
that the values of fairness and tolerance which Canada exports to the
world, are a lie when it comes to our people. . . . Canada will no longer
develop pipelines, no longer develop transmission lines, or any infrastructure, on our lands as business as usual. That is not on."[65]

The Keeyask hydroelectric project as a model of CED aims to respond
to this call. As noted by KCN leadership in documents submitted to the
Clean Environment Commission hearings, the Keeyask model reflects
economic sovereignty as embodied in Article 3 of the United Nations
Declaration on the Rights of Indigenous Peoples. The Keeyask Project's
Joint Keeyask Development Agreement represents a turning point in
the relationship between First Nations and Manitoba Hydro—the
culmination of over a decade of negotiation between Manitoba Hydro
and the KCNs. It is clear that time and money were explicitly set aside
for building partnerships. It is also clear that the Keeyask Project could
bring revenue that could stimulate KCN businesses and create jobs.

We argue in this chapter, however, that the Keeyask agreement is
not a model of community economic development with a consensus
of support from the KCNs. Large projects such as Keeyask will have a
dramatic effect on these communities. A flooded landscape has a ripple
effect into livelihoods, society, and the individual psyche. Further, as
Loney says, "what has happened to many communities must be understood as more than simply the sum of a series of discrete impacts. The
cumulative effects of hydroelectric regulation strike at the very core of
a community's sense of self-confidence and well-being."[66] The AEAs
attempt to make up for these losses, but whether they will succeed is
yet to be seen. As Eric Saunders notes in York Factory First Nation:

> The proposed development of Keeyask and Conawapa,
> and any other future developments will continue to erode

our traditional way of life into the future. Our ancestors have always been conservationists and keepers of the land. Destruction of land and its resources is not a part of our tradition and this is what concerns me most. We have to respect and uphold what our Elders taught us in terms of how we use the land and how to take care of it. It is important for our younger generations to be taught and learn the traditional ways of life, so that these teachings can be passed on to future generations.[67]

Additionally, the project may affect communities other than the KCNs (e.g., Shamattawa First Nation, Norway House Cree Nation, and Cross Lake (Pimicikamak Okimawin), but these communities will receive no benefits or compensation agreements from the project. This chapter has presented risks associated with characteristics of the Keeyask CED model, including how implementation will compare with or deviate from the plans on paper. Manitoba Hydro's track record in fostering sustainable development in the North is not strong. Hoping that Keeyask will be different will therefore involve a major "leap of faith" in trusting Manitoba Hydro's new intentions toward affected First Nations and the effectiveness of an untested partnership model.

We are very grateful for research assistance provided to us by Jazmin Alfaro, Alain Beaudry, and Heidi Cook.

Notes

1   Some examples include the Gwich'in and Sahtu final agreements, which concern oil and gas development; the Cameco/Areva collaboration with English River First Nation regarding uranium mining in northern Saskatchewan; La Paix des Braves between the Government of Quebec and the Grand Council of the Crees on forestry, mining, and hydroelectric development; and the Voisey's Bay mining partnership with the Innu in Labrador. It should be noted that the details of some of these partnerships are often confidential, making it more difficult for First Nations, Métis or Inuit communities in similar sectors/geographic areas to bargain for a fair share of resources.

2   Howard Schneider, "World Bank Rethinks Stance on Large-Scale Hydropower Projects," *The Guardian*, 14 May 2013.

3   World Commission on Dams, "Dams and Development: A New Framework for Decision-Making: The Report of the World Commission on Dams," Earthscan

Publications Ltd., December 2001, 110, https://pubs.iied.org/sites/default/files/pdfs/migrate/9126IIED.pdf.

4   Gail Whiteman, "All My Relations: Understanding Perceptions of Justice and Conflict between Companies and Indigenous Peoples," *Organization Studies* 30, no. 1 (2009): 114.

5   Manitoba Research Alliance, *Potential of CED as a Response to the New Economy* (Winnipeg: Canadian Centre for Policy Alternatives, 2003), 8.

6   Gerald Taiaiake Alfred, "Colonialism and State Dependency," *Journal de la santé autochtone* (2007): 42–60; Carol Anne Hilton, *Indigenomics* (Gabriola Island, BC: New Society Publishers, 2021); John Loxley, *Transforming or Reforming Capitalism: Towards a Theory of Community Economic Development* (Winnipeg: Fernwood, 2007); Manitoba Indian Brotherhood, *Wahbung: Our Tomorrows*, October 1971, https://manitobachiefs.com/wp-content/uploads/2017/12/Wahbung-Our-Tomorrows-Searchable.pdf; Eric Shragge, *Community Economic Development: In Search of Empowerment* (Montréal: Black Rose Books, 1997).

7   Hilton, *Indigenomics*, 7.

8   Data for this section are compiled from a number of sources including general information from the Keeyask Hydropower Limited Partnership website, the Environmental Impact Statement responses (found on the KHLP website), and the Joint Keeyask Development Agreement (available on the Manitoba Hydro website).

9   Keeyask Hydropower Limited Partnership (KHLP), "Press Release: Manitoba Hydro and Four Cree Nations Sign Historic Joint Keeyask Development Agreement," 29 May 2009, https://keeyask.com/2009/05/manitoba-hydro-and-four-cree-nations-sign-historic-joint-keeyask-development-agreement/.

10   Keeyask Hydropower Limited Partnershiop, https://keeyask.com/the-project/.

11   Keeyask Hydropower Limited Partnership, *Joint Keeyask Development Agreement*, 2009, accessed 13 July 2013, https://www.hydro.mb.ca/docs/regulatory_affairs/projects/keeyask/JKDA_090529.pdf.

12   For instance, the Cree Nations Partners Tataskweyak (TCN) and War Lake First Nations (WLFN) voters were asked the following: "Do you support the Chief and Council of [either TCN or WLFN] signing the proposed Joint Keeyask Development Agreement?" and "Do you support the Chief and Council of [either TCN or WLFN] signing the Keeyask Adverse Effects Agreement?" See Keeyask Hydropower Limited Partnership (KHLP), *Keeyask Generation Project—Environmental Impact Statement*, Responses to Information Requests, Clean Environment Commission, Rounds 1, 2013b, https://keeyask.com/project-timeline/environment-assessment-process/regulatory-process/responses-to-information-requests-cec-new/Response to EIS, 2-23, 2-24.

13   Water Power and Dam Construction, "Employment Initiative," 15 May 2007, https://www.waterpowermagazine.com/features/featureemployment-initiative/.

14   Wuskwatim and Keeyask Training Consortium Inc. (WKTC), "Annual Report for the Year Ending March 31, 2010," 8, https://www.hydro.mb.ca/docs/regulatory_affairs/pdf/gra_2012_2013/Appendix_42.pdf.

15   Funding for the initiative was provided by Manitoba Hydro, the Province of Manitoba, Indian and Northern Affairs Canada (INAC), Western Economic Diversification, and Human Resources Skills Development Canada, and in-kind support was provided by Nisichawayasihk Cree Nation, TCN, War Lake First

Nation, Fox Lake First Nation, York Factory First Nation, Manitoba Keewatinowi Okimakanak Inc. (MKO), and the Manitoba Metis Federation (MMF).

16   Keeyask Hydropower Limited Partnership (KHLP), "Training," August 2020, https://keeyask.com/the-project/employment/training/.

17   Keeyask Hydropower Limited Partnership (KHLP), "Business Opportunity Statistics," accessed 7 May 2021, https://keeyask.com/the-project/contracts/business-opportunity-statistics/.

18   Keeyask Hydropower Limited Partnership (KHLP), "Total Project Hires," December 2020, https://keeyask.com/the-project/employment/employment-statistics/total-hires-by-trade/.

19   Justification of these figures can be found in Jerry Buckland and Melanie O'Gorman, *Re-envisioning the North? A Critical Socio-economic Assessment of Manitoba Hydro's 2012/13 to 2047/48 Preferred Development Plan*, report written for the Consumers Association of Canada—Manitoba Branch (Winnipeg) for submission to the Public Utilities Board Hearing on Manitoba Hydro's Need For and Alternatives To its Preferred Development Plan, 18 March 2014, http://www.pub.gov.mb.ca/nfat/pdf/socio-economic_buckland_ogorman.pdf.

20   Manitoba Hydro, "Appendix 2.2, Joint Keeyask Development Agreement—Benefits Summary," *Needs For and Alternatives To (NFAT)*, 3, accessed 27 October 2013, http://www.pub.gov.mb.ca/nfat/pdf/hydro_application/appendix_02_2_jkda_benefits_summary.pdf.

21   This is because this return is the thirty-year bond rate minus 1.5 percent, and we estimate this thirty-year bond rate to be approximately 5.7 percent. Hence, as long as this rate is above 1.5 percent, there would be a positive return. To maintain a positive real rate of return, the thirty-year bond rate would have to remain higher than roughly 3.5 percent to account for 2 percent inflation, which is likely, given historical long-term bond rates.

22   Tataskweyak Cree Nation, "Adverse Effects Agreement with Manitoba Hydro," 2009, accessed 23 October 2013, 13, https://www.hydro.mb.ca/docs/regulatory_affairs/projects/keeyask/JKDA_090529.pdf.

23   Office of the Auditor General (Manitoba), *Manitoba Hydro: Keeyask Process Costs and Adverse Effects Agreements with First Nations*, September 2016, https://www.oag.mb.ca/audit-reports/report/manitoba-hydro-keeyask-process-costs-and-adverse-effects-agreements-with-first-nations/. The Wuskwatim Project also included an AEA similar to that of the Keeyask Project. However, it was more focused on compensating trappers whose trapline was disrupted by the Wuskwatim Project. It also contains funds for "ceremonies, language programs and other initiatives designed to protect, restore and enhance their Cree culture and language." Wuskwatim Power Limited Partnership (WPLP), "Schedule 11-1—NCN Adverse Effects Agreement," 29 June 2006, 35, https://www.hydro.mb.ca/docs/community/indigenous_relations/wuskwatim_pda/Schedule_11-1_NCN-Adverse-Effects-Agreement.pdf.

24   Pierre Fortin, "The Hydro Industry and the Aboriginal People of Canada," *International Journal on Hydropower and Dams* 8 (2001): 47–50.

25   Bernt Rydgren, Aida Khalil, Doug Smith, and Joerg Hartmann, *Hydropower Sustainability Assessment Protocol—Official Assessment: Keeyask Hydropower Limited Partnership*, 18 July 2013, https://keeyask.com/wp-content/uploads/Keeyask-Official-Assessment-FINAL-18July2013.pdf.

26 Keeyask Cree Nations, "Final Argument of the Keeyask First Nations Partners: Needs For and Alternatives To (NFAT) Hearing," 26 May 2014, http://www.pub. gov.mb.ca/nfat_hearing/NFAT%20Exhibits/MH-207.pdf; Leandro Freylejer, *Under-Development of Northern Manitoba Communities Over the Past Two and a Half Decades* (Winnipeg: Canadian Centre for Policy Alternatives, 2012).

27 Keeyask Hydropower Limited Partnership, News Release, "Manitoba Hydro and Four Cree Nations Sign Historic Joint Keeyask Development Agreement," https:// keeyask.com/2009/05/manitoba-hydro-and-four-cree-nations-sign-historic-joint-keeyask-development-agreement/; Keeyask Hydropower Limited Partnership, *Joint Keeyask Development Agreement*, 2009b, accessed 13 July 2013, https://www.hydro. mb.ca/docs/regulatory_affairs/projects/keeyask/JKDA_090529.pdf.

28 Peter Kulchyski, "A Step Back: The Nisichawayasihk Cree Nation and the Wuskwatim Project," in *Power Struggles: Hydro Development and First Nations in Manitoba and Quebec*, ed. T. Martin and S.M. Hoffman (Winnipeg: University of Manitoba Press, 2008), 136.

29 Ciaran O'Faircheallaigh, "Aboriginal Mining Company Contractual Agreements in Australia and Canada: Implications for Political Autonomy and Community Development," *Canadian Journal of Development Studies* 30, no. 1–2 (2010): 69–86.

30 Manitoba Hydro, http://www.hydro.mb.ca/projects/keeyask/news_release_090529. pdf.

31 Reviews of the literature on the impact of training programs indicate that there are large wage returns to training, especially to apprenticeships; see, for example, Robert J. Lalonde, "The Promise of Public Sector-Sponsored Training Programs," *The Journal of Economic Perspectives* 9, no. 2 (1995): 149–68; and Elchanan Cohn and John T. Addison, "The Economic Returns to Lifelong Learning in OECD Countries," *Education Economics* 6, no. 3 (1998): 253–307.

32 James B. Waldram, *As Long as the Rivers Run: Hydroelectric Development and Native Communities in Western Canada* (Winnipeg: University of Manitoba Press, 1988).

33 J.E. Windsor and J. A. McVey, "Annihilation of Both Place and Sense of Place: The Experience of the Cheslatta T'En Canadian First Nation within the Context of Large-Scale Environmental Projects," *The Geographical Journal* 171, no. 2 (2005): 146–65.

34 Ibid., 156.

35 Ibid., 159.

36 Martin Loney, "Social Problems, Community Trauma and Hydro Project Impacts," *Canadian Journal of Native Studies* 15, no. 2 (1995): 231–54.

37 Ibid., 235.

38 Ronald Niezen, "Power and Dignity: The Social Consequences of Hydro-Electric Development for the James Bay Cree," *Canadian Review of Sociology and Anthropology* 30, no. 4 (1993): 510–29.

39 Steven M. Hoffman, "Engineering Poverty: Colonialism and Hydroelectric Development in Northern Manitoba," in *Power Struggles: Hydro Development and First Nations in Manitoba and Quebec*, ed. Thibault Martin and S.M. Hoffman (Winnipeg: University of Manitoba Press, 2008): 103–28.

40 Martin Loney, "The Construction of Dependency: The Case of the Grand Rapids Hydro Project," *Canadian Journal of Native Studies* 7, no. 1 (1987): 57–78.

41 Ibid., 61.

42 Ibid., 62.

43 Kulchyski, "A Step Back."

44 Ibid., 142.

45 Ibid.

46 William F. Fisher, "Going Under: Indigenous Peoples and the Struggle against Large Dams," *Cultural Survival* 23 (1999): 29–32.

47 These statistics were found at the following links, respectively: http://www.yffd. ca/YFFD%20update_Newsletter_letter_size.pdf, and http://www.cecmanitoba. ca/resource/hearings/39/KHLP-032%20Appendix%20C%20-%20FLCN%20 KJDA%20and%20AEA%20Referendum%20Results1.pdf.

48 Leanne Simpson, Sandra Storm, and Don Sullivan, "Closing the Economic Gap in Northern Manitoba: Sustained Economic Development for Manitoba's First Nations Communities," *Canadian Journal of Native Studies* 27, no. 1 (2007): 75.

49 Jerry Buckland and Melanie O'Gorman, "The Keeyask Hydro Dam Plan in Northern Canada: A Model for Inclusive Indigenous Development?" *Canadian Journal of Development Studies* 38, no. 1 (2017): 72–90.

50 Keeyask Hydropower Limited Partnership (KHLP), "Gillam Public Hearing— September 24, 2013," *Keeyask Environmental Impact Statement, Supporting Volume: Public Involvement*, 53, https://keeyask.com/project-timeline/public-involvement/. Others may not have participated in discussions about the Keeyask Project as a form of resistance to the project. This was noted in the Gillam Public Hearing for the Keeyask EIS: a participant said, "A lot of people are not here, they are hurt, they are boycotting this."

51 Ramona Neckoway, "Electric Beads and Our Dam Future: Hydroelectric Development on Cree Territory," *E-misférica* 2.1, accessed 25 August 2013, http:// hemi.nyu.edu/journal/2_1/necaway.html.

52 Michael Foth, "Barriers to Aboriginal Participation in Environmental Assessment: A Case Study of the Wuskwatim Generating Station," PhD diss., University of Manitoba, 2011.

53 Ibid., 133.

54 Neckoway, "Electric Beads"; Foth, "Barriers to Aboriginal Participation."

55 Keeyask Hydropower Limited Partnership (KHLP), *Keeyask Generation Project—Environmental Impact Statement, Responses to Information Requests, Clean Environment Commission, Round 1*, 2013b, Response to CEC Rd 1 CAC-0091a, https://keeyask.com/project-timeline/environment-assessment-process/regulatory-process/responses-to-information-requests-cec-new/.

56 Maryam Razaei and Hadi Dowlatabadi, "Off-Grid: Community Energy and the Pursuit of Self-Sufficiency in British Columbia's Remote and First Nations Communities," *Local Environment* 21, no. 7 (2016): 789–807; Fred Schwartz and Mohammad Shahidehpour, "Small Hydro as Green Power," IEEE Power Engineering Society General Meeting, 2006, 1–6.

57 For instance, Manitoba Hydro might have developed partnerships with the KCNs to undertake a local needs assessment. If the needs assessment found that the communities wanted locally generated electricity, a plan might have been developed to build micro dams. With a smaller project, there would be less risk of local environmental and social harm, and this small project could form the foundation for a scaled-up hydroelectric project.

58 Waldram, *As Long as the Rivers Run*, 109.

59 Burntwood/Nelson Agreement (BNA), 17, accessed 12 July 2013, http://www.hydro. mb.ca/projects/bna_agreement.pdf.BNA.

60 KHLP, *Keeyask Generation Project—Environmental Impact Statement*, Round 1 information request 79c.

61 International Hydropower Association, *Hydropower Sustainability Assessment Protocol*, 70, 193, accessed 25 September 2013, https://www.hydrosustainability.org/ assessment-protocol.

62 Fox Lake Concerned Citizens Group (FLCCG), interview by Melanie O'Gorman, 27 September 2013.

63 The representatives noted that many residents are concerned about the negative social effects of the Keeyask Project, especially about the abuse of women by construction workers, entry of drugs into the community, and increased racism. According to the representatives, in a previous Hydro project, a woman who was raped by a project worker was discouraged from telling her story to prevent a negative impression of the construction project. At the same time, members feel there is nothing they can do about these things—the Keeyask Project will be approved, they think, regardless of their views on it.

64 O'Faircheallaigh, "Aboriginal Mining Company."

65 Mark Elyas, "Perry Bellegarde Elected National Chief of the Assembly of First Nations," *First Nations Drum*, 13 January 2015.

66 Loney, "Construction of Dependency," 248.

67 York Factory First Nation, *KIPEKISKWAYWINAN: Our Voices*, June 2012, 3, https://keeyask.com/wp-content/uploads/2012/07/Kipekiskwaywinan_Our-Voices_June_2012_Part-1.pdf.

" Pimicikamak's survival is at stake. Its own critical infrastructure that has sustained it for thousands of years is being washed away. Its traditional economies have been washed away. Its history is being washed away."

David Muswaggon, Pimicikamak,
CEC hearings (4 December 2013), 5039

PART 4

What Is Good Development?
Legacy Building in the North

Hiding from Hydro
by Ovide Mercredi

The water flows secretly
Hiding from Hydro
Lest it be seen
As wealth and power.

It lies motionless
Breathing selectively
Lest it be discovered, and
Captured for electricity
For those in the south.

Here in the far north
Where First People live
It hides with them,
Kindred spirits
Of unjust exploitation,
Glancing around
In four directions,
Hoping for reprieve
Looking skyward
For divine intervention
And sacred intention
Lying close to the heart
Of Mother Earth
For their safety.

The water speaks in silence
To nature's forgotten children:
The four-leggeds, the crawlers,
The swimmers and the winged ones.
Each time Nature's children come
Crying for their loss of habitat
The water takes their suffering
And speaks of healing.

Nature's children,
Like First Peoples hide from Hydro
Lest they be discovered, and
Exploited unjustly for electricity

The water flows slowly
Quietly and secretly
To save them.

29 May 2005

The Two-Track Approach: Foundations for Indigenous and Western Frameworks in Environmental Evaluation

AIMÉE CRAFT

Environmental evaluation and assessment is premised on the idea that it is possible to estimate potential impacts and mitigate potentially harmful short- and long-term project outcomes (see Chapter 4 by Jill Blakely and Bram Noble and Chapter 9 by Blakely in this volume). Environmental evaluation has historically relied heavily on Western scientific methods to evaluate impacts on species within designated project areas, including within Indigenous lands, territories, and waters.[1]

Narrowly defined evaluation approaches (which affects the list of components designated as "worthy of evaluation") and limited geographical scoping of projects have often led to the exclusion of identification of cumulative and regional impacts, as well as socially and culturally significant long-term effects. For example, in their evaluation of the Keeyask Project, the Cree Nation Partners (representing the Tataskweyak Cree Nation and War Lake First Nation) explained: "TCN members do not view the potential environmental effects of Keeyask as being primarily related to resources or to particular physical elements of our homeland ecosystem. Rather, our members see them as effects on our customs, practices, traditions, and relationships that comprise our distinctive cultural identity."[2]

While the field of environmental evaluation and assessment has evolved to more carefully consider past impacts on people within broader geographies and demographies, there are still some important limitations as to how Western frameworks approach environmental evaluation from the point of view of justifying the project itself. Furthermore, proponents such as Manitoba Hydro have fragmented project licensing and evaluation as a strategy to have less destructive project phases approved first, while further phases then use the existing infrastructure to justify approval of subsequent megaproject phases.[3]

In addition to these inherent limitations, the struggle to evaluate based on Indigenous forms of knowledge within a Western evaluative context persists. As stated by Marie Battiste and James Youngblood Henderson in their seminal work on Indigenous knowledges, Indigenous ways of knowing are "the expression of the vibrant relationships between the people, their ecosystems, and the other living beings and spirits that share their lands."[4] As James Robson explores in Chapter 5 of this volume, resource managers and bureaucrats may see Indigenous knowledge as compatible with Western scientific knowledge to a degree—but there is much room for misinterpretation and poor application. And when it comes to the ultimate decision making regarding project approval, as Sarah Morales says, "there is still a long way to go before Indigenous perspectives are appropriately integrated into decision making."[5]

While policy-makers have often used Indigenous knowledges[6] (IK) as a supporting source of data to validate Western science,[7] there is often tension between IK and non-Indigenous knowledges when it comes to the level of influence each has on decision-making processes and outcomes. Indigenous knowledge has been placed in the position of being either a source of data for Western scientific research or a means to validate Western science's conclusions. Very rarely has IK been the point of departure in an environmental assessment, from which Western science acts in a supportive role. Even more rarely has IK formed the environmental decision making itself.

Compounding this narrow view of environmental evaluation, which relies almost exclusively on Western science, is the improper characterization of Indigenous knowledge as "world view." Indigenous knowledges are based on a study of the environment that arises out of an Indigenous ontological and epistemological context. While Western scientific methods and areas of study derive from Western scientific traditions, IK draws its methods and study from Indigenous paradigms and frameworks. Therefore, the often alluded-to distinction between Western science and Indigenous world view is a false dilemma, resulting from comparing the study (Western science) to the framework (world view).

For example, the Clean Environment Commission (CEC) spoke to the challenge of bringing the Cree world view and technical science together, as though they were of the same fundamental nature. They suggested that "it may be necessary to establish a mechanism for reconciling differences of opinion between practitioners of the two approaches."[8] As illustrated through a case study of the Keeyask Dam, a more appropriate approach is to treat Western science and Indigenous knowledges as methods of study, applied in their corresponding frameworks and world views (Western and Indigenous). For example, during the CEC hearing, there was discussion about the scientific reports on sturgeon moving to new spawning areas, to which the Elder responded: "Who is the scientist that spoke to a sturgeon?"[9]

As methods of study, IK and Western scientific knowledge can be assessed through the world view or lens of either Indigenous or Western epistemological frameworks.[10] For example, where IK and Western scientific data provide different metrics or results, one could assess either or both sets of data and aggregated knowledge, or their respective conclusions, through environmental evaluation frameworks that derive from either world view, to decide which conclusion to follow. Arguably, Indigenous frameworks of evaluation, rooted in Indigenous world views that consider interconnections between environment and people in less capitalistic and reductive terms, could provide a more appropriate set of decision-making principles grounded in concepts of sustainability and relationality.

Manitoba Hydro and the First Nations partners made an attempt to resolve some of these imbalances through the *two-track assessment approach* they adopted when preparing the environmental assessment for Keeyask. In that process, IK would purportedly both inform the Keeyask partnership's Western scientific approach as well as exist independently through the environmental evaluations prepared by each of the Keeyask Cree Nations (KCNs). Both the Cree environmental evaluation reports and the Western science were meant to influence the final outcome of the assessment. According to the Keeyask Hydro Limited Partnership (KHLP), the two-track approach aimed to ensure that "information and concerns arising from the two tracks would be considered throughout the assessment process and throughout the final Environmental Impact Statement (EIS). The collaborative nature of the two tracks was intended to ensure that concerns and predictions arising from the First Nations' assessments were employed in the regulatory assessment and in Project planning, mitigation, management and monitoring."[11]

This chapter probes the Keeyask partnership's attempt to equally value IK and "technical" science, as described in the EIS. Using a few examples that arose during the CEC hearings and from the EIS, I consider how significantly Indigenous knowledge factored into the CEC's decision to approve the project. The chapter closes with some recommendations to ensure IK is incorporated into important decision-making processes regarding project development and in defining the evaluation and assessment process throughout. Otherwise, IK will continue to sit uncomfortably alongside, but never fully integrated into, the decisions affecting Indigenous interests and communities, and the web of relationships they have with the natural environment and non-human relatives.

The Two-Track Approach

Figure 13.1 shows the Keeyask Hydropower Limited Partnership's approach in the Keeyask process. Although this figure refers to the monitoring process, the KHLP referred to the two-track approach throughout the CEC hearing and the EIS as being the "regulatory assessment" track and in contrast to the Keeyask Cree Nations' three independent environmental evaluations.

When the Keeyask hydroelectric generating project was originally proposed, Manitoba Hydro first partnered with the Tataskweyak Cree Nation (TCN) with an agreement that, as partners, TCN would bring its collective knowledge to the table. As we know, the KHLP was ultimately composed of Manitoba Hydro and the four Keeyask Cree Nations.[12] Figure 13.2. is a map of the area surrounding the Keeyask Dam, along with the First Nations' locations and the existing dams in the area.

Two core sets of agreements between the project partners, the KCNs and Manitoba Hydro, were negotiated as part of the public consultations between 1998 and 2009: the Joint Keeyask Development

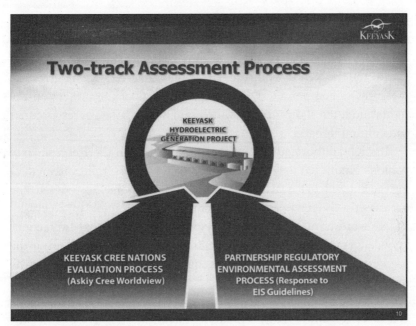

Figure 13.1. The Two-Track Process. Source: Manitoba Hydro EIS.

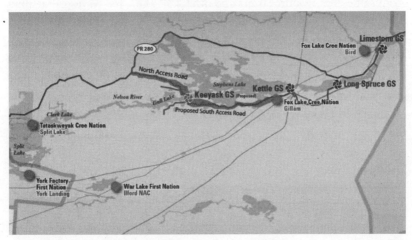

Figure 13.2. Keeyask Area, First Nations, and Existing Dams. Source: CEC Final Report.

Agreement (JKDA) and the Adverse Effects Agreements (AEAs) for each of the Keeyask Cree Nations. The JKDA describes the legal, governance, and financial structures of the partnership between Manitoba Hydro and the KCNs, while the AEAs include agreed-upon mitigation measures to compensate for potential impacts of the project on the rights and interests of members, including such matters as resource use and cultural impacts.

The KHLP boasted that the consultations with the Keeyask Cree Nations[13] impacted the project early in its design by significantly reducing the flooding to a quarter of the area that was originally proposed. The partnership also renamed the project from "Gull Rapids" to "Keeyask," a Cree word translating to "Gull Rapids." All agreed that Indigenous knowledges (IK) (or Aboriginal Traditional Knowledge [ATK], as the partners described it) should have equal weight in the project's environmental assessment.

As the CEC's final report describes, "each of the Keeyask Cree Nations (KCNs) therefore led its own environmental assessment process, consulting with its own community and forming its own expert groups of elders, resource users and others."[14] The Cree Nations Partners' *Keeyask Environmental Evaluation* considered environmental effects of the proposed project based on Cree world view, consultation with community members, and their Ancestral Homeland Ecosystem Model to assess major changes to the determinants of harmony and balance in past, present, and future.[15] Fox Lake Cree Nation's *Environment Evaluation Report* centred on mino pimatisiwin, the overall health of the people and the corresponding values relating to language, culture, values and beliefs; the transmission of knowledge and heritage; human health and wellness; and their land and animal relationships.[16] York Factory First Nation (YFFN) prepared the *KIPEKISKWAYWINAN: Our Voices* report that centred YFFN voices to tell their story; illustrate their history and values; reflect on change and damage to the land, water, and people; and consider ways forward and their hopes and expectations for the future.[17]

This resulted in three Cree Nations environmental evaluation reports: a joint report from the Cree Nation Partners (Tataskweyak and War Lake First Nations), one from York Factory First Nation, and one from Fox Lake Cree Nation. The KCNs' environmental evaluations, based on their Cree world views and their experience with hydroelectric development,[18] formed one track. In the other track, the KHLP conducted a regulatory assessment. "The regulatory assessment track included preparation of that portion of the final EIS that employed a standard valued environmental component (VEC) approach, and used both technical science and Aboriginal traditional knowledge (ATK) in a manner intended to meet federal and provincial regulatory requirements."[19]

In preparation for the EIS, Manitoba Hydro and the four Keeyask Cree Nations agreed to the following principles: "Giving equal weight to the two approaches to knowledge, ensuring visibility of ATK in the EIS, maintaining Aboriginal people's authority over their knowledge and treating the knowledge confidentially, employing documentation and rigorous methods to gather ATK, acknowledging the distinct worldviews of technical science and the Cree partners, building and sustaining respectful relationships, acknowledging the past, reflecting cultural and spiritual values, and addressing uncertainty and employing a precautionary approach."[20]

Information and concerns arising from the two tracks would be considered throughout the assessment process and throughout the final EIS. The original intention was that the two tracks would be collaborative and that the Cree evaluations would inform the outcomes of the regulatory assessment. The collaborative nature of the two tracks was intended to ensure that concerns and predictions arising from the First Nations' assessments were employed in the regulatory assessment and in project planning, mitigation, management, and monitoring.[21]

While the two-track approach aimed to equally weigh and integrate ATK into the environmental evaluation, the ultimate result was somewhat unsatisfactory. According to the CEC final report: "concerns were expressed that the technical science track ultimately dominated the decision making."[22] In addition to the caribou and sturgeon issues discussed in this chapter, there were incompatible conclusions between the Cree environmental evaluations and the EIS about the fluctuation of water levels on Split Lake.[23] The report noted: "Within the EIS, there are a number of issues in which the KCNs' assessments and technical science assessments reach different conclusions,"[24] and that "within the KCNs' assessments, it was acknowledged that there was at times a philosophical disagreement between the two approaches."[25] The evaluative framework employed for the Cree environmental assessments/

evaluations (EAs) was grounded in Cree world view, epistemologies, and ontologies, whereas the EIS was grounded in Western environmental traditions that defined the Keeyask decision-making process. The Cree environmental evaluations stood apart (both physically and conceptually) from the EIS. In the end, their differing conclusions were not advanced in the EIS, in the project proposal, or at the CEC hearing as the partnership's ultimate environmental finding.

The Regulatory Assessment and Cree Environmental Evaluations

Each of the three Cree environmental evaluations centred on relationships, including those with the land, animals, families, communities, and nations. These included special relationships with other than human beings, like the caribou and sturgeon, whom the Cree referred to in their evaluations as "their kin."[26]

In contrast to the relational paradigm advanced in each of the Cree environmental evaluations, the regulatory assessment evaluated thirty-eight aquatic, terrestrial, and socio-economic valued environmental components (VECs).[27] As discussed in Chapters 5 and 6 of this volume, examining the significance of potential impacts on individual components contradicts a Cree framework focused on the interconnectedness of human and non-human relationships.

Table 13.1. Valued Environmental Components (VECs) Included in the Keeyask Environmental Impact Statement

Aquatic VECs (5)	Water quality, walleye, pike, lake whitefish, lake sturgeon
Terrestrial VECs (13)	Ecosystem diversity, intactness, wetland function, priority plants, Canada goose, mallard, bald eagle, olive-sided flycatcher, common nighthawk, rusty blackbird, beaver, caribou, moose
Socio-economic VECs (20)	Employment opportunities, business opportunities, income, cost of living, resource economy, housing, infrastructure and services, transportation infrastructure, land, governance goals and plans, community health, mercury and human health, public safety and worker interaction, travel access and safety, culture and spirituality, aesthetics, domestic fishing, domestic hunting and gathering, commercial trapping, heritage resources

There was also a contrast in the way the environment was evaluated. The regulatory assessment included nine steps in its analytical framework of impact assessment, rather than a holistic approach:

1. Project Description
2. Scope of Assessment
3. Environmental Setting
4. Identification of Potential Effects
5. Mitigation of Adverse Effects
6. Assessment of Residual Effects
7. Regulatory Significance of Residual Effects
8. Cumulative Effects
9. Monitoring and Follow-up

Where the Cree EAs and the regulatory assessment (or EIS) differ most drastically is in steps 5, 6, and 7. The regulatory assessment presumes that measures can be used to prevent or reduce adverse effects and that, where effects remain, their significance is not great enough to warrant revising or deciding not to proceed with the project. This approach considered federal and provincial benchmarks for acceptable risk and effects in relation to the VECs. However, what is deemed acceptable risk and effect from a regulatory perspective did not always align with the Cree perspective. For example, where the regulatory assessment found that there were no significant adverse effects on caribou and sturgeon populations, some of the KCNs were of the view that the residual effects on caribou and sturgeon were significant, and not adequately mitigated.[28]

Each of the Cree environmental evaluations had problems with the VEC approach because of its misalignment with the interrelated and interconnected approach featured in the Cree reports. The Cree EAs, taken as a whole, suggested that the selected VECs were problematic in the face of their preferred holistic approach, and that, from their perspective, some different VECs would have been chosen, or perhaps VECs would have been entirely discounted as a method of evaluating. As the Fox Lake Cree Nation evaluation states: "By its very nature, the VEC approach tends to ignore interrelatedness of people, animals, water, landscape and plants. . . . Our people do not place greater importance on certain species and all are valued equally. The entire Kischi Sipi [Nelson River] including the Inninuwak [the Cree people], fish, birds, plants and wildlife, all of whom use, inhabit and benefit from the river would constitute a VEC."[29]

In its final report the CEC recommended that the province develop criteria for selecting VECs. What would ultimately benefit assessment would be to have evaluative criteria that are integrated and holistic, and that consider relationships between the "components" that Western approaches are designed to sever.

The relationship with the land and concern for the land were core features of each of the Cree environmental reports in a very different way from in the EIS. The York Factory First Nation report said, "Askiy is the whole of the land, water, people, plants, animals and all things. We are part of Askiy and we have relied on Askiy since we have existed. We respect Askiy and we are affected by even the smallest changes to Askiy. Askiy is beyond value."[30] It also stated, "To live a good life we respect and care for Askiy, other people, and all things in this world for our ancestors and for future generations. We call this minopimatisiwin."[31]

The following are two glaring examples of how, if Indigenous knowledges had been weighted equally in the environmental evaluation, the Keeyask Project would not have met the Western standard of environmental evaluation that was applied: that of no significant adverse effects.

STURGEON/NAMEO

In the Cree evaluations and throughout the CEC hearing, Indigenous community members and other advocates expressed concern about the project's potential impact on sturgeon.[32] A senior vice-president at Manitoba Hydro and chair of the Keeyask Hydropower Limited Partnership, Ken Adams, indicated that he could "categorically state that sturgeon in the Keeyask region will be better off with the project than without it."[33] However, the Cree environmental evaluations and the Cree Nations' evidence supported a different finding. In their view, the sturgeon were likely to be significantly and negatively impacted by the project.

Sturgeon is considered to be an endangered species, largely because of hydroelectric generating stations[34] and commercial overharvesting (1940s to 1970s).[35] Building the Keeyask Dam means losing the Gull Rapids spawning ground, which would have further effects (see Chapter 7 in this volume). Although the proponents have proposed constructing artificial spawning reefs, modifying shorelines, and building new habitat, these mitigation measures remain experimental and uncertain in terms of ensuring continued sturgeon stock.

Many participants and experts at the CEC hearing expressed concern that Manitoba Hydro was being overly optimistic in assessing the success of proposed mitigation measures. The Keeyask partnership's proposed methods for mitigating sturgeon loss were predicated on restocking and relocating fish, based on summary surveys of the existing population. However, Indigenous knowledge contested the potential success of both. Tataskweyak harvester Robert Spence provided IK evidence that sturgeon at Keeyask were spawning, despite Hydro's claiming they don't spawn in that location.[36] Elders from the Kaweechiwasihk Kay-Tay-A-Ti-Suk testified that sturgeon are especially sensitive to changes in the environment and this is long-standing knowledge. Elder Flora Beardy stated, "Na May O is a Cree word for sturgeon. This is a very clean fish. When their present habitat is polluted or changed, the fish will leave the area. Even when ashes fall on the river from a forest fire, the fish leave the area."[37] The Elders called for a study, including both Western scientific knowledge and Aboriginal traditional knowledge, to review fish passages and innovative approaches to mitigating impacts on lake sturgeon.[38] The CEC panel agreed that the KHLP's certainty was not warranted,[39] and that determining if the population is sustainable would take approximately fifty years. The panel recommended that: a) sturgeon be stocked for fifty years, b) sturgeon be tagged to evaluate the success of the recovery program, and c) the KHLP consult widely on successful techniques for rearing and release.

CARIBOU/ATIK

As James Schaefer brought up in Chapter 8 in this volume, another issue that arose in the hearing was whether the "summer-resident" caribou that occupied the area and calved on islands in the Gull Rapids area were boreal woodland caribou, which are listed as threatened under the federal Species at Risk Act and the Manitoba Endangered Species Act. At the time of the EIS, Manitoba Conservation and Water Stewardship did not recognize a boreal woodland caribou range as far north as Gull Rapids. The Keeyask partnership also stated that summer-resident caribou may have spent only one summer in the area and were possibly not boreal woodland caribou. Subsequent studies have shown that there are caribou that have likely inhabited Gull Rapids throughout the summer.[40]

The KCNs were of the view that there is a herd of boreal woodland caribou that resides and calves in the area. The difference of opinion on caribou became central to the CEC hearing. The CEC's final report stated that "representatives of the Partnership characterized this difference of opinion regarding caribou as an instance in which the regulatory assessment makes use of the findings of the KCNs' assessments."[41] However, the EIS's ultimate conclusion that there would be no significant adverse effects on caribou directly contradicted the findings of two of the Keeyask Cree Nations and their land users.[42]

The CEC was of the view that "several factors support the conclusion that the 'summer resident' caribou in the Project area are more likely to be boreal woodland caribou."[43] The report indicated that among the list of factors was traditional knowledge presented by Elders and resource harvesters: "Elders who gave testimony at the hearing have provided personal observations and history on the distribution and abundance of these animals."[44] The CEC did not share the Keeyask Partnership's "moderate to high degree of certainty" that impacts on caribou would be small. The CEC recommended genetic testing and an assumption that the summer-resident caribou are boreal woodland caribou,[45] as well as a long-term coordinated monitoring study and a regional caribou management strategy.[46] They also recommended that the KHLP and Manitoba government "further investigate and incorporate ATK and local knowledge of historical 'summer resident caribou' distributions and populations to inform current status and their management."[47] The CEC suggested that a First Nations harvester's "personal observations of caribou in the Keeyask region, and those of his friends and fellow resource users, could have helped to clarify the issue regarding summer resident/boreal woodland caribou.... The Province and the Proponent should take more notice of these observations and the Cree worldview and incorporate them to a greater degree."[48]

Regardless of their classification, the summer-resident caribou would be impacted by the loss of islands in the Gull Rapids area and the reduction in size of Caribou Island, which reduces calving habitat.[49] Caribou are known to be sensitive creatures, and the Elders, Knowledge Keepers, and land users of the area were particularly concerned that not only would available habitat be reduced but the caribou would stay away altogether.

Benchmarks used to assess caribou included four factors: total physical habitat loss, intactness, linear feature density, and grey wolf density. The EIS indicated that disturbance levels were already so high around Keeyask that it could not support a self-sustaining population of woodland caribou.[50] However, the Keeyask Partnership did not propose any positive habitat-enhancement measures, only mitigation measures to ensure less disruption, such as avoiding caribou calving areas, taking steps to avoid vehicle collisions with caribou, and prohibiting firearms in work camps in order to minimize additional hunting.[51]

Indigenous Evaluation and Decision Making

To understand the potential contained in Indigenous knowledge and its application to environmental assessment both in Canada and around the world, it is important to look to international conventions on Indigenous rights and the advancement of Indigenous law and self-governance within Canada. As established in Chapter 10 of this volume, the United Nations Declaration on the Rights of Indigenous Peoples (UNDRIP) recognizes that Indigenous peoples have the "right to determine and develop priorities and strategies for the development and use of their lands or territories and other resources."[52] Furthermore, UNDRIP recognizes the "right to participate in decision-making in matters which would affect their rights, through representatives chosen by themselves in accordance with their own procedures, as well as to maintain and develop their own Indigenous decision-making institutions."[53] The United Nations Special Rapporteur James Anaya reflected that the right to participate in decision making relating to industry and extractive development extends to situations where Indigenous peoples own, use, develop, and control land, territories, and resources under their own Indigenous laws near to where, or on which, extractive activities take place or are proposed to take place.[54]

In its final report, the Truth and Reconciliation Commission of Canada observed that Indigenous laws, policies, and decision-making frameworks have a critical role to play in setting out a framework for reconciliation.[55] Additionally, the Supreme Court of Canada has acknowledged that customary laws of Indigenous peoples have survived the assertion of sovereignty by the Crown and continue to apply today.[56]

Indigenous laws and legal traditions are relevant to hydroelectric environmental impact assessments in four distinct ways. First,

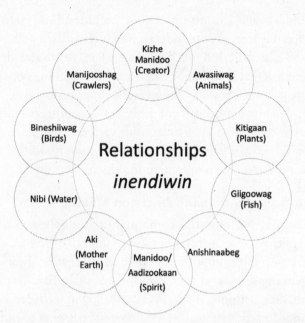

Figure 13.3. Anishinaabe Legal Relationships. Illustration: Aimée Craft.

Indigenous laws are an important interpretive tool for understanding Treaty perspectives, including how Indigenous peoples entered into the Treaty relationship with the Crown.[57] Some of these ramifications are explored in Chapter 10 of this volume.

Second, Indigenous laws are based in complex systems of kinship that include both human and non-human kinship. Human kinship relationships extend far beyond the boundaries of the Treaty territories, traditional territories, reserves, or state boundaries (such as provincial or nation-state borders). Historically, mobility along the rivers, pre-dating and including the fur trade period, have supported relations among communities in extended territories.[58] Non-human kinship relationships are similarly far-reaching. Figure 13.3[59] illustrates the interconnected web of responsibilities and obligations that derive from Indigenous epistemologies and philosophical frameworks.

Third, Indigenous laws depict very different relationships to lands and resources from what Euro-Canadian common law perspectives offer. For example, state jurisdictions and geopolitical boundaries depart from Indigenous perspectives relating to lands and resources.[60] In addition, Indigenous perspectives view the significance of impacts differently and more holistically, as the Clean Environment Commission explained: "Given that a WSK [Western Scientific Knowledge] environmental assessment seeks to find no residual effects after mitigation on individual VECs, when viewed from a global ecosystem perspective, this can be seen as a flawed process. ATK, on the other hand, places paramount importance on protecting the whole of the ecosystem. Incorporating the two approaches could well provide great benefits to our environment."[61]

Fourth, Indigenous principles of sustainability are an integral part of Indigenous perspectives. In particular, intergenerational principled decision making is referred to in Anishinaabe world view in the context of seven generations. They place the individual in a web of responsibilities to all of creation.[62] According to the World Commission on Environment and Development, sustainable development is that which meets the needs of the present without compromising the ability of future generations to meet their own needs.[63] While similarly future-focused, this Western definition of sustainability is human-centric and does not consider the well-being of all beings in creation. Furthermore, Elders continue to teach us that reconciliation has to take place with the Earth, our mother, before it can happen between people.[64] We find guidance for this approach within many Indigenous legal systems.

Evaluative Principles in the Cree Environmental Evaluations

Core values were listed and explained in the Cree EAs. For example, the York Factory First Nation listed the following principles as important to their evaluation of the project:

- Kiskinohamakaywina (Teachings) have been handed down through the generations and offer daily guidance. These teachings are relevant and applicable to the assessment, planning, construction, and operation of Keeyask.

- Kistaynitamowin (Respect) is very important when speaking and acting towards Askiy. One must understand that everything of Askiy has a place and purpose.

- Kistaynitakosewin (Honour)—It is important to honour life and Askiy through ceremonies.

- Tapwaywin (Truth)—It is important that we speak truth-fully based on our knowledge and experience.

- Aspehnimowin (Trust) is important to our relationships and is developed over time.

- Ohcinewin—This difficult-to-translate term means that because of the interconnectedness of Askiy, if you harm anything, including land, water, people, plants, or animals, you will experience harmful repercussions, which may affect your children or grandchildren.

- Ayakohmisewin (Caution) is essential so that individuals and the community can avoid disrespectful and harmful actions towards others or towards Askiy.

The Fox Lake Cree Nation spoke to three important evalu-ative principles:

- Oochinewin ("the belief that a negative action against an animal, a person or the land could negatively impact the fate of a person, or family members of the next genera-tion"),[65]

- Pastamowin (making "inappropriate, hateful, untrue comments about someone else"),[66] and

- Mitewewin ("the traditional and spiritual ways of life").[67]

The York Factory report proposed that for the partnership to suc-ceed, "We need to make the Partnership work—to reconcile and build trust among the partners. We need to follow our cultural values—to come to terms with the damage that will be caused by the project and to fulfill our obligations as stewards of the land. We need to prepare our young people—to build the identity and values that will guide them in managing the project."[68]

Fox Lake framed their environmental analysis around the concept of mino pimatisiwin: "Mino pimatisiwin includes the protection of Aski, our health and social wellbeing, socio-economic prosperity, integrity of culture and language, integrity of governance and autonomy, and healthy local ecosystems."[69]

While some might consider these statements of values to be part of the holistic or "world view" preamble to the project's evaluation of impacts, when seen through a lens of Indigenous law and governance they become the core evaluative principles for environmental decision making. However, the Keeyask partnership did not take up these evaluative principles in the conclusions of the EIS or the CEC hearing; neither, ultimately, did the decision maker and licensing authority: Manitoba Conservation. The Province, Manitoba Hydro, and the Clean Environment Commission made all decisions and formed their analyses from a Western legal and regulatory framework, informed primarily (if not wholly) by Western evaluative criteria.

CEC Commissioner Reg Nepinak explained that the Cree were not given credit for sustaining the environment prior to hydroelectric development. He indicated that the values of managing a sustainable environment and environmental decision making should be considered through Indigenous lenses.

> In these hearings, it has been maintained that the Cree worldview is equal to Western science. However, the Cree are still not given credit for maintaining the environment for 5,000 years. We are aware that Manitoba Hydro is not the only contributor to the condition of the water; still, it has contributed a major portion to its condition and continues to do so.
>
> The Indigenous people did have a governance structure that was unlike the western model and if the Europeans recognized it, it was dismissed, much the same way the Indigenous worldview is dismissed today.
>
> In order for our two societies to come together, the whole of immigrant societies need to recognize that the Indigenous people understood and managed the concept of a sustainable environment. Learn who we are, why our ceremonies are so important, learn about our languages. [70]

Therefore, Indigenous nations should be engaged in the decision-making process relating to hydroelectric development according to their world view, including their Indigenous decision-making processes and on the basis of Indigenous law. This would include engagement with Indigenous procedural and substantive laws.[71]

Commissioner Nepinak put forward the idea of a circle of grandmothers as a decision-making mechanism: "Final decisions in

governing our Indigenous societies were made by our grandmothers—
Ke nocominanak. The minister should support these long-standing and
successful methods of the Cree/Indigenous worldview by incorporating
a circle of Ke nocominanak with a mission to oversee safeguarding the
environment."[72]

Options do exist to engage people in environmental decision making using non-Western principles. However, it requires a fundamental
shift in thinking to seize opportunities to engage with Indigenous
knowledges, laws, and legal orders, on Indigenous peoples' own terms.

The CEC's Findings:
"No Significant Residual Adverse Effects"

The attempt at bringing together Western science and ATK as equal
sources of knowledge in the Keeyask two-track approach was an important effort. However, the results were decidedly mixed. The CEC
report states, "While the Commission commends the Proponent for
an innovative approach in bringing the Cree worldview and technical
science together, the approach to regulatory environmental assessment
was at times plagued by inconsistency and confusion."[73] The Keeyask
partnership's efforts to truly equally value both forms of knowledge were
plagued by biases towards Western science, a misunderstanding of what
Indigenous knowledge can offer, and a structural system of decision
making that continues to privilege Western values and methods of evaluating, grounded in Western philosophical and theoretical paradigms.

The entire decision-making framework for the environmental
evaluation of the Keeyask proposal rested on the finding of *no residual
significant adverse effects*. Deconstructed, this means that there may be:

a) significant effects that can be mitigated; or that

b) there are residual effects that are not significant.

This decision-making framework supposes that an impact can be
mitigated and lessened by other corresponding/correlating/unrelated/
compensatory actions.

The Adverse Effect Agreements concluded between Manitoba
Hydro and each of the Keeyask Cree Nations played an important part
in concluding that there were no significant residual adverse effects on
each of the VECs. The CEC final report states, "Each AEA includes
certain one-time payments, typically for capital costs of mitigation

programs, and a guaranteed annual payment for costs of the programs described in the agreement. All the AEAs set out that the priorities for addressing adverse effects from the Keeyask Project are, in order, to prevent or avoid causing adverse effects, to lessen or reduce unavoidable adverse effects, to provide replacements, substitutions or opportunities to offset adverse effects, and to pay fair compensation for loss or damage caused by adverse effects."[74]

This contrasts deeply with the holistic approach to evaluation that was put forward in each of the Cree environmental evaluations, with impacts being felt across sectors. None of the Cree assessments endorsed or recommended the Keeyask Project. If the Keeyask partnership's approach had incorporated Cree normative values into the ultimate evaluative framework, the results would have made for more equal engagement with Indigenous knowledges (which include criteria and process for decision making). Although the Environmental Impact Statement alluded to these decision-making criteria in its world view and values descriptions, they are not explicitly built into the EIS's decision-making criteria. This would have made it fit better with the objectives of the two-track approach: giving equal weight to Indigenous knowledge and Western scientific knowledge in the environmental assessment, where Indigenous knowledge would inform the Western scientific approach while also existing independently.

Conclusion

The principled, long-term view of the Keeyask Cree Nations demonstrates intimate knowledge of the lands, waters, and other beings that have inhabited the whole region for an extended period of time. As the CEC final report notes: "The viewpoint of the three reports, which takes a long view of the region and does not distinguish impacts on a project-by-project basis, is especially worthwhile in understanding the cumulative effects of hydroelectric development in northern Manitoba."[75]

These observations, based on Cree land users' long-term baselines and study of the environment, as well as their direct relationships with land, water, and other non-human beings, were guided by Indigenous methods and framed in Indigenous world views, including the evaluative principles described in each of the Cree EAs. The environmental evaluations also considered the region as a whole, without dissociating the proposed Keeyask Project from the other hydroelectric development and industrial pressures within the territory. These are the forms of knowledge and evaluative frameworks that are essential to principled decision making within Indigenous territories. Cultivating Indigenous knowledge and practices has the potential to radically transform scientific research.[76] While Western science and technologies are powerful tools for understanding natural phenomena, they do not tell the entire story.[77]

In its report on Keeyask, the CEC concluded that there is a great deal of work left to do between Manitoba Hydro and Indigenous nations in Manitoba. "The Commission is of the view that there is a need for a more formal process of reconciliation ... [and] recommends a process to rebuild trust and respect, for what was lost, what remains and what may be in the future."[78] The continued impact of development in the North and the corresponding displacement of Indigenous people from their homelands, either directly or through loss of way of life, can be seen as a forced migration resulting in "ecosystem people" becoming "ecological refugees."[79]

There is a Canadian imperative for reconciliation that works towards the self-determination of Indigenous peoples, the implementation of UNDRIP, and the recognition of Indigenous legal orders. This reconciliation must be built on the basis of nation-to-nation relationships grounded in the implementation of Treaty agreements in ways that reflect Indigenous perspectives and laws. Deborah McGregor reminds us that when researching and assessing, we "should draw upon Indigenous research paradigms, which privilege Indigenous worldviews, epistemologies and knowledges as a productive way forward."[80] A reconciliation paradigm also requires the free, prior, and informed consent of Indigenous peoples in their land and territories, and their full participation in decision making relating to the use of "resources."

In light of past loss and damage to the land and people, and in order to give effect to the constitutionally and internationally protected rights of Indigenous peoples, any future decision making—for example, if and when Manitoba Hydro revisits the question of building Conawapa, or when it delivers on the promised programs and mitigation efforts that are part of the AEAs—this decision making must take into account Indigenous decision-making matrices and substantive legal norms. As the CEC final report states, "A narrow approach to doing this will not succeed. The work must be collaborative with Aboriginal communities, with academics and with groups across the country who are also pursuing respect for and incorporation of ATK and Aboriginal worldviews into environmental decision-making."[81]

Manitoba Hydro, the Province of Manitoba, the Clean Environment Commission, and the National Energy Board should continue to seek submissions as to how Indigenous legal principles apply in a decision-making matrix that reflects Indigenous perspectives from both a procedural and substantive viewpoint. Environmental evaluation must be done on the basis of principled decision making relying on Indigenous evaluative frameworks if we are to move forward with development in Indigenous territories.

Notes

1   When I refer to "decision making" and "environmental evaluation," I am not speaking to the constitutional duty (section 35) of consultation and accommodation that relates to potential infringement of Aboriginal and Treaty rights. This chapter focuses solely on the context of decision making relating to environmental decisions in an administrative context.

2   Cree Nation Partners, *Keeyask Environmental Evaluation: A Report on the Environmental Effects of the Proposed Keeyask Project on Tataskweyak Cree Nation and War Lake First Nation* (Manitoba: Cree Nation Partners, January 2012), 40, keeyask. com/wp-content/uploads/2012/07/CNP-Keeyask-Environmental-Evaluation-Web-Jan2012.pdf.

3   See Byron Williams's piece in Chapter 1 of this volume.

4   Marie Battiste and James Youngblood Henderson, *Protecting Indigenous Knowledge and Heritage: A Global Challenge* (Saskatoon: Purich, 2000), 42.

5   Sarah Morales, "Canary in a Coal Mine," in *Braiding Legal Order: Implementing the United Nations Declaration on the Rights of Indigenous Peoples*, ed. John Borrows et al. (Waterloo: CIGI Press, 2019), 119.

6   Also referred to as "traditional knowledge" (TK) and "Aboriginal traditional knowledge" (ATK).

7   Also referred to as "scientific knowledge" (SK), "Western science" (WS), and "Western scientific knowledge" (WSK).

8   Manitoba Clean Environment Commission, *Report on Public Hearing: Keeyask Generation Project*, Manitoba, April 2014, 45, http://www.cecmanitoba.ca/cecm/archive/pubs/commission%20reports/keeyask%20web%20final2.pdf [CEC Final Report].

9   Manitoba Clean Environment Commission, *Keeyask Generation Project*, 9 October 2013, 72, http://www.cecmanitoba.ca/resource/hearings/39/Public%20Hearing%20Oct%209,2013%20Cross%20Lake.pdf.

10 Leroy Little Bear, "Jagged Worldviews Colliding," in *Reclaiming Indigenous Voice and Vision*, ed. Marie Battiste (Vancouver: University of British Columbia Press, 2000), 77–85.

11 CEC Final Report, 39.

12 Ibid., 2.

13 A term used to refer to all four Cree Nations that became partners in the project.

14 CEC Final Report, 47.

15 Cree Nation Partners, *Keeyask Environmental Evaluation*, 63–73.

16 Fox Lake Cree Nation, FLCN Environment Evaluation Report (Winnipeg: Fox Lake Cree Nation, Sept. 2012), https://www.ceaa-acee.gc.ca/050/documents_staticpost/64144/83657/Cree_-_02_Fox_Lake_Environment_Evaluation_Report_Sept_2012.pdf.

17 York Factory First Nation, *KIPEKISKWAYWINAN: Our Voices* (York Landing, MB, June 2012), https://www.ceaa-acee.gc.ca/050/documents_staticpost/64144/83657/Cree_-_03_Kipekiskwaywinan_Our%20Voices_June_2012.pdf.

18 There were three EAs; each was different in approach, style, and format: Cree Nation Partners, representing Tataskweyak Cree Nation (TCN) and War Lake First Nation (WLFN), prepared the report *Keeyask Environmental Evaluation*. Fox Lake Cree Nation (FLCN) prepared the *Fox Lake Cree Nation Environment Evaluation Report*. York Factory First Nation (YFFN) prepared *KIPEKISKWAYWINAN: Our Voices*.

19 CEC Final Report, 39.

20 Ibid., 41–42 (EIS 2A-1-2A-2).

21 Ibid., 39.

22 Ibid., 42. For a description of these perspectives, including suggestions for a three-track approach, see CEC Final Report, 42–43.

23 CEC Final Report, 42.

24 Ibid.

25 Ibid., 44.

26 Cree Nation Partners, *Keeyask Environmental Evaluation*, 48.

27 CEC Final Report, 41.

28 Manitoba Clean Environment Commission, *Keeyask Generation Project*, 26 September 2013, 33–34, http://www.cecmanitoba.ca/resource/hearings/39/Public%20Hearing%20Sept%2026,%202013%20York%20Factory.pdf; Manitoba Clean Environment Commission, *Keeyask Generation Project*, 31 October 2013, 1704–5 and 1745–47, http://www.cecmanitoba.ca/resource/hearings/39/Transcripts%20-%20Keeyask%20Winnipeg%20Hearing%20Oct%2031,2013.pdf; Manitoba Clean Environment Commission, *Keeyask Generation Project*, 9 January 2014, 6808–9, http://www.cecmanitoba.ca/resource/hearings/39/Transcripts%20-%20Keeyask%20Winnipeg%20Hearing%20v.31%20Jan%209,%202014.pdf.

29 Fox Lake Cree Nation, *FLCN Environment Evaluation Report*; Cree Nation Partners, *Keeyask Environmental Evaluation*, iv–v.

30 York Factory First Nation, *KIPEKISKWAYWINAN: Our Voices*, 15.

31 Ibid., 20.

32 Cree Nation Partners, *Keeyask Environmental Evaluation*, 38; York Factory First Nation, *KIPEKISKWAYWINAN: Our Voices*, 80; Fox Lake Cree Nation, *FLCN Environment Evaluation Report*, vii.

33 Manitoba Clean Environment Commission, *Keeyask Generation Project*, 21 October 2013, 92, http://www.cecmanitoba.ca/resource/hearings/39/Transcripts%20-%20Keeyask%20Winnipeg%20Hearing%20Oct%2021,2013.pdf.

34 See CEC Final Report, 72. Note that Kelsey and Kettle dams were built on known sturgeon spawning sites.

35 CEC Final Report, 76.

36 Manitoba Clean Environment Commission, *Keeyask Generation Project*, 14 November 2013, 3364, http://www.cecmanitoba.ca/resource/hearings/39/Transcripts%20-%20Keeyask%20Winnipeg%20Hearing%20Nov%2014,2013.pdf.

37 Manitoba Clean Environment Commission, *Keeyask Generation Project*, 12 December 2013, 6226, http://www.cecmanitoba.ca/resource/hearings/39/Transcripts%20-%20Keeyask%20Winnipeg%20Hearing%20Dec%2012,2013.pdf.

38 Manitoba Clean Environment Commission, *Keeyask Generation Project*, 9 January 2014, 6915–16, http://www.cecmanitoba.ca/resource/hearings/39/Transcripts%20-%20Keeyask%20Winnipeg%20Hearing%20v.31%20Jan%209,%202014.pdf.

39 CEC Final Report, 76.

40 Wildlife Resource Consulting Services MB Inc., *Caribou Winter Abundance Estimates Report. Keeyask Generation Project Terrestrial Effects Monitoring Plan Report #TEMP-2016-06*, June 2016, https://keeyask.com/wp-content/uploads/2014/08/KGP-TEMP-2016-06-Caribou-Winter-Abundance.pdf; Wildlife Resource Consulting Services MB Inc., *Summer Resident Caribou Range Monitoring Report. Keeyask Generation Projects Terrestrial Effects Monitoring Plan Report #TEMP-2016-07*, June 2016, https://keeyask.com/wp-content/uploads/2014/08/KGP-TEMP-2016-07-Summer-Resident-Caribou-Range.pdf; Wildlife Resource Consulting Services MB Inc., *Summer Resident Caribou Range, Keeyask Generation Project Terrestrial Effects Monitoring Plan Report #TEMP-2018-16*, June 2018, https://keeyask.com/wp-content/uploads/2018/06/TEMP-2018-16-Caribou-Summer-Resident-Range-Monitoring.pdf; Wildlife Resource Consulting Services MB Inc., *Caribou Sensory Disturbance Monitoring, Keeyask Generation Project Terrestrial Effects Monitoring Plan Report #TEMP-2019-15*, June 2019, https://keeyask.com/wp-content/uploads/2019/07/TEMP-2019-15-Caribou-Sensory-Disturbance-Monitoring.pdf.

41 CEC Final Report, 42.

42 York Factory First Nation, *KIPEKISKWAYWINAN: Our Voices*, 92–94; Fox Lake Cree Nation, *FLCN Environment Evaluation Report*, 78–79, 87.

43 CEC Final Report, 94.

44 Ibid., 94–95.

45 Ibid., 165, recommendation 10.14.

46 Ibid., recommendation 10.15.

47 Ibid., recommendation 10.13.

48 CEC Final Report, 94–95.

49 Ibid., 90.

50 Cree Nation Partners, *Keeyask Environmental Evaluation*, 38.

51 CEC Final Report, 91.

52 United Nations Declaration on the Rights of Indigenous Peoples (UNDRIP), 13 September 2007, 61/295 at art 18 [UNDRIP], https://www.un.org/development/desa/indigenouspeoples/wp-content/uploads/sites/19/2018/11/UNDRIP_E_web.pdf.

53   UNDRIP, 18.

54   United Nations General Assembly, James Anaya, Report of the Special Rapporteur on the Rights of Indigenous Peoples, A/HRC/18/35, 11 July 2011, 10, https://www. ohchr.org/Documents/Issues/IPeoples/SR/A-HRC-18-35_en.pdf.

55   Canada, Truth and Reconciliation Commission, *Honoring the Truth, Reconciling for the Future: Summary of the Final report of the Truth and Reconciliation Commission of Canada* (Montreal: McGill-Queen's University Press, 2015), 199.

56   *Mitchell v Minister of National Revenue*, 2001 SCC 33, [2001] 1 SCR 911.

57   See, for example, Aimée Craft, *Breathing Life into the Stone Fort Treaty* (Saskatoon: Purich Publishing, 2013); Heidi Kiiwetinepinesiik Stark, "Respect, Responsibility and Renewal: The Foundations of Anishinaabe Treaty Making with the United States and Canada," *American Indian Culture and Research Journal* 34, no. 2 (2010): 156; Harold Johnson, *Two Families: Treaties and Government* (Saskatoon: Purich, 2007). See also Office of the Treaty Commissioner, *Treaty Implementation: Fulfilling the Covenant* (Saskatoon: Office of the Treaty Commissioner, 2007); John Borrows, "Wampum at Niagara: The Royal Proclamation, Canadian Legal History, and Self-Government," in *Aboriginal and Treaty Rights in Canada: Essays on Law, Equality, and Respect for Difference*, ed. Michael Asch (Vancouver: University of British Columbia Press, 1997), 155; Sharon Venne, "Understanding Treaty 6: An Indigenous Perspective," in *Aboriginal and Treaty Rights in Canada: Essays on Law, Equality, and Respect for Difference*, ed. Michael Asch (Vancouver: University of British Columbia Press, 1997), 173; Robert A. Williams Jr, *Linking Arms Together: American Indian Treaty Visions of Law and Peace, 1600–1800* (New York: Routledge, 1999), 12.

58   *Canadian Geographic*, "Fur Trade," 2019, https://indigenouspeoplesatlasofcanada.ca/ article/fur-trade/.

59   Figure reproduced from Aimée Craft, "Neither Infringement nor Justification—The SCC's Mistaken Approach to Reconciliation," in *Renewing Relationships: Indigenous Peoples and Canada*, ed. Brenda Gunn and Karen Drake (Saskatoon: Native Law Centre, University of Saskatchewan, 2019), 56.

60   See, for example, Sarah Hunt, "Ontologies of Indigeneity: The Politics of Embodying a Concept," *Cultural Geographies in Practice* 21, no. 1 (2013): 27; Michelle Daigle, "Awawanenitakik: The Spatial Politics of Recognition and Relational Geographies of Indigenous Self-determination," *The Canadian Geographer* 60, no. 2 (2006): 1–11; Lindsay Naylor et al., "Interventions: Bringing the Decolonial to Political Geography," *Political Geography* 66 (2017): 199–209.

61   CEC Final Report, 160.

62   See, for example, Aimée Craft, "Giving and Receiving Life from Anishinaabe Nibi Inaakonigewin (Our Water Law) Research," in *Methodological Challenges in Nature-Culture and Environmental History Research*, ed. Jocelyn Thorpe, Stephanie Rutherford, and L. Anders Sandberg (New York: Routledge, 2016), 105–119; Deborah McGregor, "Anishinaabe Environmental Knowledge," in *Contemporary Studies in Environmental and Indigenous Pedagogies*, ed. A. Kulnieks, D.R. Longboat, and K. Young (Rotterdam: SensePublishers, 2013); Basil Johnston, *Honour Earth Mother* (Cape Croker Reserve, Wiarton, ON: Kegedonce Press, 2003), 77–88; Kyle Whyte, Joseph Brewer II, Jay Johnson, "Weaving Indigenous Science, Protocols and Sustainability Science," *Sustainability Science* 11, no. 25 (2016): 25.

63 World Commission on Environment and Development, *Our Common Future*, 1987, https://sustainabledevelopment.un.org/content/documents/5987our-common-future.pdf.

64 Treaty Relations Commission of Manitoba and Assembly of Manitoba Chiefs, *Untuwe Pi Kin He—Who We Are: Treaty Elders' Teachings,* vol. I, by Doris Pratt, in Joe Hyslop, Harry Bone, and the Treaty and Dakota Elders of Manitoba, with contributions by the AMC Council of Elders (Winnipeg: TRCM & AMC, 2014) [TRCM vol. 1]; see also D'Arcy Linklater in TRCM, vol 1.

65 Fox Lake Cree Nation, *FLCN Environment Evaluation Report,* 13.

66 Ibid., 15.

67 Ibid., 15.

68 York Factory First Nation, *KIPEKISKWAYWINAN: Our Voices,* 107.

69 Fox Lake Cree Nation, *FLCN Environment Evaluation Report,* ii.

70 CEC Final Report, 161.

71 Craft, *Breathing Life,* 83.

72 CEC Final Report, 161.

73 Ibid., 45.

74 Ibid., 31.

75 Ibid., 59.

76 Deborah McGregor, Jean-Paul Restoule, and Rochelle Johnston, eds., *Indigenous Research: Theories, Practices, and Relationships* (Toronto: Canadian Scholars' Press, 2018).

77 Manulani Aluli-Meyer, "Changing the Culture of Research: An Introduction to the Triangulation of Meaning," in *Hulili: Multidisciplinary Research on Hawaiian Well-Being,* ed. Shawn Kanaiaupuni (Saline: Kamehameha Schools, 2006), 269.

78 CEC Final Report, 163.

79 Anaya, "Report of the Special Rapporteur," 10.

80 Deborah McGregor, "Truth Be Told: Redefining Relationships through Indigenous Research," in *Renewing Relationships: Indigenous Peoples and Canada,* ed. Karen Drake and Brenda L. Gunn (Saskatoon: Wiyasiwewin Mikiwahp Native Law Centre, 2019), 1.

81 CEC Final Report, 160.

"The Relation to Our Land"

TRAPLINE 15 FAMILY, REPRESENTED BY JANET MCIVOR,
ILLA DISBROWE, MARY WAVEY, MARILYN MAZURAT,
NORMA MCIVOR, ROBERT SPENCE, GLORIA KITCHEKEESIK,
AND JONATHAN KITCHEKEESIK

*Excerpt from the transcript of the Keeyask CEC hearing in Winnipeg,
14 November 2013.*

When I was out and about on the land trying to feed my kids their food from where I come from, I used to see these little damages a long time ago that seem so tiny today. I used to see all these things from way back in 1979 when my dad and I used to go out on the land there. We used to pull our skidoos through about a foot of ice water with about an inch of ice on top. I used to think oh, this is part of life. And then as I got older, I had some kids, and everything started to change....

But meanwhile hydro never sleeps....

And in 1992, I had a dream of my grandfather and a little child. There was three of us standing there, holding hands. My grandfather spoke to me in that dream and he said look at the little child. There was no place for him to play. That's the way it looks now in Split Lake with all the sharp rocks along the shoreline.

We live in a prison of Manitoba Hydro dyke....

I seen Manitoba Hydro's commercials, clean environment. But if you walked a day in my shoes, I don't think he would think it was clean.

I think I got so used to the way that Hydro treated the land that my system got really strong. Like I drink water that was brown, just that's how I used to see it. And in the springtime, when Hydro would let go of some water and then they'd choke up the river and then more water would come and then the ice dam would break and then it came to our camp. There was no way we could get some more water except for where we used to get it. And all the little minute particles in the ice melted on top of that. It settled on top of the ice that when spring came around, it melted the snow because [the] particles absorbed the sand.

It took my brother away that way.

Every little change that we had experienced before now became something that we must adapt to.

————

We have been forced to negotiate for some sort of accommodations under Article 10 of Adverse Effects Agreement. That says Hydro will remain liable to compensate any member who is a licensed trapper, not traditional land user, for any loss of revenue from commercial trapping and any direct loss or damage to any buildings, structure or other infrastructure located on the registered trapline used by a member which resulted from a construction and operation of the KGS project. . . .

Our Cree Nation partner Keeyask environmental evaluation registered trapline system [and] traditional family territories. We had family, traditional territories before licence, trapline licence. Traditional land uses [have] been passed on from generation to generation in our culture. Each family has their own territory. And to impose this on them will create conflict between families. That's what Hydro is trying to do to us, is to find another trapline for us. But every family member in our community has their own traditional land use. We can't go and impose on them. Because every time we have a meeting with Hydro, that's what they put on the table.

Manitoba Hydro has suggested to us that all they have to do is to pay us a very small amount of money and perhaps find us another trapline area. But this is not a trapline issue, we have been given very few choices and all very poor.

First of all, we find another—if we find another suitable trapline area, it will never substitute for our homeland, where we have always been. It will be like [a forced relocation]. Anyone who understands Cree culture would never say to a Cree person, just pack up and move on. That would degrade who we are because we are about the relation to our land. The land . . . the creator gave to us to live on and take care of it.

Second, we are about to lose everything, including use of our land, trees, rocks, shoreline. These are structures and infrastructures to us, yet Hydro refuses to accept this and say we only get bare bones compensation for our homes on the land.

What if I go to your territory and said I want to move my family here? What if I go next door to your place? This is our homeland.

Everybody has—every culture has [a] system. And I know that everybody in our Cree culture knows this.

We asked CEC to consider recommending conditions to put on the licence [for] Hydro to make best efforts in good faith and on a good urgent basis to negotiate [a] compensation package for our family that includes infrastructure....

Leon's Island is our Memorial site. This is where we lost our brother. And what they wanted to compensate for us is a Memorial and a picnic table. I already got a picnic table, I can make my [own] picnic table.

And Lillian's Island. How much do you think that is? ... Whenever we take our children out, that's where they go swim and that's where we go have our picnics as a family. We have our gathering here as a family. It will be under water. This is named after our oldest sister, Lillian.

Our dad's main camp. It had a tepee in it and that's where we had our kids, we had our traditional gathering in there. What is Hydro willing to put on the table for that land?

Looking Back Lake ...

They are displacing us with all this Keeyask dam. [These are] very important and spiritual and cultural places to our family. Cabins, travel access safety to our family, ceremonies and memorial sites, and heritage sites. We want to be left alone, undisturbed and protected.

CHAPTER 14

Good Development Should Not End with Environmental Assessment: Adaptive Management in Northern Development

PATRICIA FITZPATRICK, ALAN P. DIDUCK,
AND JAMES P. ROBSON

There is no such thing as a perfect decision. People must make choices about the best course of action based on the information available to them at the time. Large-scale hydroelectric projects in northern Manitoba are situated in, and thus become part of, complex social-ecological systems. Project impacts are therefore often highly uncertain, project planning and decision making are usually imperfect, and choices about the best course of action are regularly made with incomplete or changing information. Despite these challenges, project planning, decision making, and development must and often do proceed.

Given these realities, assessing the environmental impacts of hydroelectric projects is of paramount importance. Environmental assessment (EA) helps proponents, regulators, rights holders, and stakeholders address uncertainty by helping them first predict a project's impacts, then eliminate or mitigate negative effects and optimize positive ones. Moreover, integrating adaptive management into EA and using it during the construction and operation of a project (if approved) can actually make it easier to deal with uncertainty. J. Brian Nyberg and J. Taylor define adaptive management as a "formal process for continually improving management strategies and practices by ensuring learning from the outcomes of operational programs."[1] In doing so, adaptive management systematically allows natural resource development to proceed using the best available knowledge, while ensuring that project design and implementation are modified as new information becomes available. Adaptive management is thus often considered an important component of robust approaches to EA.[2]

The Keeyask Generating Station represented an important opportunity to embed adaptive management practices into hydroelectric development as a best practice for all future projects. However, the difficult legacy of hydro development in Manitoba's North necessarily raised key questions. For example, how can local communities and stakeholders have confidence that monitoring programs for Keeyask would be fully implemented when the record for other projects, such as the devastatingly destructive Churchill River Diversion, built in the 1960s, is not transparent? Can a proponent realistically predict and mitigate negative impacts of a new development in the absence of a robust understanding of the cumulative impacts of past hydroelectric development in the region? This lack of certainty provides critical context for understanding how important adaptive management can be for guiding monitoring and follow-up programs in more recent and new developments.

The purpose of this chapter is to assess how adaptive management was treated in the EA of the Keeyask Project and in its licence approval. We have a particular focus on monitoring, because it is a critical aspect of both EA and adaptive management, and it received considerable attention during the Keeyask proceedings.

From Managing Adaptively to Adaptive Management

As noted, adaptive management is a systematic process for improving strategies and practices by learning from and acting on the outcomes of management experiences.[3] The literature on adaptive management is rich and provides considerable guidance for the design and implementation of adaptive management strategies.[4] In this chapter, we adopt an Australian model that links results from management experiences to policy objectives through a cyclical, iterative process of planning, doing, evaluating, learning, and adjusting (Figure 14.1).[5] Each stage and activity in the adaptive management cycle is necessary, but monitoring

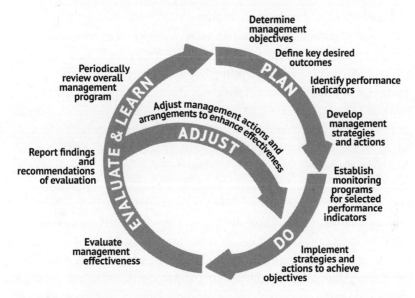

Figure 14.1. Adaptive Management Cycle for the Tasmanian Wilderness World Heritage Area. Image credit: W. Hiebert.

is the most important element because it provides the information for rational, evidence-based decision making in later stages of the cycle.

Similarly, monitoring plays a vital role in EA. The introduction of the provincial Environment Act in 1988 and similar legislative changes at the federal level now require that new developments undergo an EA before they are approved. Such processes may require follow-up and monitoring programs. Policy makers now recognize monitoring and follow-up as an EA best practice that can achieve various objectives.[6] For example, governments can use monitoring to ensure compliance with resource development requirements set out in laws, permits, and authorizations. Researchers can use monitoring to assess the accuracy of assessment predictions, thereby adding to broader knowledge of the system. More recently, and in the context of hydroelectric development in northern Manitoba, Lydia Dobrovolny proposed that a well-designed monitoring program could be used to meet requirements for environmental and social accountability, required in some U.S. jurisdictions that purchase power from Manitoba (e.g., Minnesota).[7] Monitoring can be particularly effective when it is designed for adaptive management.

Resource management practitioners widely acknowledge that determinations about environmental impacts of proposed developments are made in the context of uncertainty. Uncertainty arises from a variety of issues, including incomplete or imperfect understanding of the system being affected, natural variability in the system, multi-scale human impacts on the environment (including climate change), different societal and political agendas, and questionable research approaches and techniques being used to study potential impacts and mitigation measures.[8] Additionally, biophysical and human systems are often unpredictable, and society's management goals and priorities can and do change over time. Studies of uncertainty provide a framework for analyzing different gaps in understanding: those we can currently identify, those we are aware of but cannot describe, and those we cannot foresee.[9]

While such uncertainties can sometimes paralyze decision making, identifying them can actually help in making decisions about developments and their impacts. EA processes should ideally make sure projects are legally required to include adaptive management.[10] Adaptive management is designed to minimize the risks of development by creating a robust system of monitoring, evaluation, learning, and adapting in order to deal with uncertainties as they emerge. Adaptive management, then, as J.B. Ruhl states in an article in the *University of Kansas Law Review*, is adopted at the "back end" in "monitoring-adjustment frameworks that allow incremental policy and decision adjustments."[11] In this way, follow-up and monitoring programs become central to ensuring that a development continues to reflect new and emerging information throughout its life cycle.

While people will often informally learn and adapt as part of their experiences, or "manage adaptively,"[12] what distinguishes adaptive management from such reactive learning is purposeful planning. Beyond the "manage adaptively" approach, there are two main categories of adaptive management—passive and active—distinguished by the degree to which management actions are treated as experiments.[13] "Passive adaptive management" (a form of sequential learning) is where historical data are used to frame a single best approach, along a path that is assumed to be correct. Faced with uncertainty, managers implement the alternative they think is "best" (with respect to meeting management objectives), and then monitor to see if they were right, adjusting as needed.

"Active adaptive management" is explicitly designed to provide data and feedback on the relative effectiveness of multiple management or policy options. Faced with uncertainty, managers implement more than one strategy as simultaneous experiments to see which is best. While both passive and active adaptive management are characterized by iterative (step by step) decision making, feedback between monitoring and decisions made (learning), and embracing risk and uncertainty as a way to better understand your project, only active adaptive management deliberately probes the system to test competing hypotheses. When a policy succeeds under active adaptive management, your hypothesis is validated. When the policy fails, you learn, adjust, and base future initiatives on your new understanding. Part of the power of adaptive management is that it is meant to be both scientific and pluralistic; with forethought, design should include all good sources of information, including Western science, Indigenous knowledge, and local expertise. This form of civic "learning by doing"[14] is the essence of adaptive management, and the means by which we winnow down uncertainty.[15]

Importantly, not all aspects of a monitoring program can or should be subject to experimentation (either active or passive). However, as Alana Moore and co-authors indicate, "there is no simple rule for when learning is worthwhile."[16] According to them, a proponent needs to optimize "its investment in learning,"[17] taking into account the costs of the exercise, the opportunity cost of implementing each experiment, and the potential benefit from learning from the experiment.

We founded our analysis of how the Keeyask EA treated adaptive management on the model depicted in Figure 14.1 and on five best practices derived from the literature:[18]

1. *Adopt a comprehensive definition of adaptive management (including uncertainty and complexity)*: To what degree did the monitoring program recognize adaptive management and incorporate uncertainty and socio-ecological complexities in program design? Monitoring programs should clearly articulate that they are a departure from historic practice and are guided by adaptive management.

2. *Be deliberate in design and implementation*: To what extent did program planning begin with good questions to frame research monitoring and evaluation? Whenever practicable, monitoring programs should be purposefully designed to address uncertainty,

and interventions should rely on the scientific method, i.e., be active management "experimental probes."

3. *Promote learning that influences action*: How much did the program design include systematic and continual review of monitoring results? Monitoring programs should be based on an iterative approach that emphasizes feedback and learning, meaning that not only should monitoring results be incorporated into future activities but so too should new and emerging information and technologies.

4. *Ensure transparent decision making*: To what degree was the program design broad-based, inclusive, and participatory? Monitoring programs should include careful documentation and monitoring results, and decision making about future modifications should be publicly accessible.

5. *Have (and/or develop) requisite capacity*: To what extent did the program include adequate financial and human resources? Monitoring programs must have flexibility to allow for increased expenditure, when warranted, and staff of these programs must have appropriate qualifications and decision-making authority within the organization.

Our integrative review of academic literature on adaptive management subsequently guided our analysis of the EA documentation (which included the Keeyask Environmental Impact Statement and supporting documents, the Adverse Effects Agreements, preliminary Environmental Protection Program documents, and hearing documentation) in preparing for our involvement as witnesses in the Keeyask Clean Environment Commission (CEC) public hearings. During the hearings, we advocated for a robust, transparent follow-up and monitoring program, designed and implemented in the spirit of adaptive management. We also argued that the results of the monitoring program should be publicly available, and that the project be subject to an external audit once construction of Keeyask was complete.

In addition to our literature review and analysis of EA documentation, we also based this chapter's findings on documentation that the project regulators created after the CEC public hearings. This material was important because it contained specific recommendations and licensing conditions related directly to adaptive management.

Adaptive Management in Monitoring Design

Keeyask was the first hydroelectric project EA in Manitoba that required the proponents to consider adaptive management in designing its monitoring programs. Adaptive management was first raised during the hearings for the Wuskwatim projects,[19] and served as a governing principle for the draft environmental protection program submitted during the Bipole III assessment.[20] However, guidelines issued for the Keeyask impact statement specified the EA should address "monitoring activities that will be undertaken to evaluate the effectiveness of mitigation and the need for management responses (adaptive management)."[21] Recognizing that in Manitoba, the Keeyask partnership itself drafted these guidelines, and that it narrowly defined adaptive management in this instance, the inclusion was nonetheless important. This is a subtle but potentially significant change that could set a precedent that would enhance EA requirements for hydroelectric development.

Adaptive management, and its associated best practices, became an important design feature of the Keeyask Project's proposed monitoring regime.[22] The definition of "adaptive management" used in later EA documentation is consistent with best practices in the literature, and reflects the definition we used earlier in this chapter. The EA documents also highlighted how uncertainty is a condition resulting (in part) from inadequate scientific information, and that some "effects are predictable with a high level of certainty while other effects may be unknown until they occur."[23] Overall, our assessment of the Keeyask partnership's approach to adaptive management as articulated in the EA documentation (Practice 1), including addressing uncertainty and complexity, was favourable.

Our analysis of the Keeyask partnership's specific management plans and monitoring programs was more variable. With respect to design (Practice 2), a positive feature was the submission of draft environment protection and monitoring plans as part of the EA. However, five important programs, including the vegetation rehabilitation plan and the Aboriginal[24] traditional knowledge monitoring plans, were not available during our review. Furthermore, what emerged during the EA was that, given the high uncertainty associated with some impact areas (e.g., sturgeon, cumulative effects), specifying additional, targeted monitoring programs would have strengthened the project application (see Chapter 4 in this volume by Jill Blakely and Bram Noble).

In the Keeyask partnership's plans submitted to the CEC, we found only a limited number of examples of predetermined experimentation, important for active adaptive management. When prompted, the proponents identified examples where it would need to experiment, and it outlined potential modifications that could be tested during the monitoring phase; that is, it offered two potential adjustments should monitoring reveal that lake sturgeon do not gather where expected or if cycling at the dam impacts survivability. This illustrated that, at least for some components, the proponent was thinking about active adaptive management opportunities. If more information like this had been included in the proponent's original draft plans, that would have strengthened its application, and given us, as external reviewers, more confidence in the proposed monitoring program. Overall, then, we found that there were multiple opportunities to strengthen the design of the monitoring program.

Similarly, we found that the monitoring program demonstrated some aspects that promoted learning (Practice 3), but there was room for improvement. Identifying when and how results would be used across different monitoring programs and plans, also known as "integration," is a critical design element for fostering learning. Our analysis of the EA documentation found only limited evidence of such integration. For example, the terrestrial and aquatic effects assessments used an ecosystem-based approach, which is in itself integrative,[25] and the monitoring plans discussed the need for the plans themselves to be integrated. A basic example is integrating mercury monitoring results from the aquatic effects program with the human health risk assessment proposed for the socio-economic monitoring plan. However, there was a lack of specificity about when and how results from lateral programs would inform related monitoring plans. Moving beyond an overarching commitment, tangible examples would have strengthened opportunities for learning.

Likewise, the Keeyask partnership referenced integrating Western science and Aboriginal traditional knowledge in the adaptive management strategy, but this integration was not considered in any full sense of the word. This lack of integration of results from different knowledge sources in the adaptive management strategy was not surprising, given that a choice was made not to integrate the technical and Indigenous EAs[26] (see Aimée Craft, Chapter 13 of this volume), but in our view it should have been a critical component of design.

In regard to transparency (Practice 4), we found mixed results. A troubling feature was the lack of information about the Keeyask partnership's proposed process for evaluation and adjustments after the project was approved.[27] Although the monitoring plans established different time frames for obtaining results, the Keeyask partnership did not identify how or when adjustments would be made.[28] As well, there were no opportunities to engage the public in changes to monitoring programs, putting this important component of adaptive management at risk of being abandoned post-approval. On a more positive note, project documentation indicated that the Keeyask partnership would communicate any changes to its monitoring programs to the public. This includes a commitment to post to a project website annual reports to the province. Additionally, EA documentation indicated that a Monitoring Advisory Committee would regularly review monitoring results and discuss whether monitoring plans needed to be revised, which showed a degree of transparency and openness beyond the project proponent's formal corporate bounds.[29]

Our review also raised significant concerns with respect to whether the Keeyask partnership had devoted adequate resources to monitoring (Practice 5). As adaptive management is built on monitoring and refining that monitoring over time, program design should clearly detail financial resources committed to this process. However, there was little information as to how the Keeyask partnership would support key personnel throughout the life cycle of the project. The proponents relied on past experience—specifically the range of personnel used to develop impact statements and the associated monitoring programs and plans—as evidence that monitoring would continue after project approval. Likewise, although the monitoring plan included a contingency fund, we were unable to ascertain the size and duration of the fund, and how it would be made available during the life of the project. A more robust monitoring plan would have explained the process for adding capacity and for funding changes to monitoring programs, either as a whole or for each key component. In addition, we were concerned about the Monitoring Advisory Committee's general lack of resources, capacity, and authority. The committee was charged with reviewing monitoring reports, providing advice and guidance, and acting as a liaison with the partner First Nation communities. However, it did not have an externally funded budget and the proponents did not anticipate that it would engage outside expertise to review monitoring plans or results. Further, it would not conduct independent studies, and it had no access to dispute resolution, should the Keeyask partnership not follow its advice.

Adaptive Management at the Post-review Stage

Monitoring programs and plans submitted as part of an EA are considered incomplete drafts. Proponents are meant to adjust or modify programs based on the information collected through the public review. For the Keeyask Project, two regulatory agencies reviewed the proponent's impact statement for approval (the provincial CEC and the federal Canadian Environmental Assessment Agency).

Recommendations in the CEC's report strengthened elements of transparency lacking in the proponent's draft documentation. Echoing similar provisions identified for Bipole III, the CEC advised that the licence include conditions for: a third-party audit evaluating how accurate the proponent's assessment of impacts was once construction is completed, and then again ten years later (recommendation 13.1); more systematic and ongoing information tools, specifically maintaining the Keeyask website for the project's entire lifecycle (recommendation 13.2); and, more effort to build learning into monitoring by preparing annual reports to government (posted on the project website) with "sufficient detail that assessment can be made as to the accuracy of predictions, success of mitigation actions and commitment to future actions (recommendation 13.3)."[30]

Each of these conditions was included in the environmental licence issued by the Province of Manitoba (conditions 67, 68, and 20, respectively). In doing so, the province strengthened the transparency aspect of program design; if the conditions are met, the public will have online access to that information on a regular basis. As well, the licence bolstered transparency, and the potential for broad-based learning, by including condition 18q for timely provision of monitoring information regarding offsetting programs to the partner First Nations' resource management boards.[31] Conditions requiring the proponents to incorporate both Western science and Aboriginal traditional knowledge in environmental protection, management, and monitoring plans enhanced the project's potential for cross-cultural learning (16a, 17a, 18a).

The licence also included recommendations for monitoring specific components. In some instances (17e and 21b, related to sturgeon), the licence specified that adaptive management should guide the monitoring. In other instances, including a condition related to the general approach to the monitoring program (18f), the licence sought information about how negative impacts would be "adaptively managed." This terminology raises the question of how the province understood the phrase "adaptively managed." Did it mean the reactive learning associated with "managing adaptively," or did it mean the more purposeful "adaptive management" (in either of its passive or active variations)? Nonetheless, including these recommendations addresses, in part, some of the design flaws identified in the previous section.

The Canadian Environmental Assessment Agency's report prepared as part of the federal EA process also referenced adaptive management.[32] In addition to sporadic references to adaptive management for monitoring specific components (e.g., mercury, sturgeon, and revegetation), the report specified that once the proponents completed the design of their monitoring programs, subsequent revisions should be addressed through adaptive management. This can be seen as reinforcing the proponent's commitment to adaptive management, particularly as the federal approach is consistent with the more robust approaches presented earlier.

Discussion and Conclusion

Our analysis found that the adaptive management strategy and monitoring programs for the Keeyask Project, as designed, showed a marked improvement over earlier projects.[33] Recognizing and including adaptive management in EA reviews has been slow to come, and its inclusion in this case is an important step in modernizing the EA process in Manitoba and, more broadly, Canada. We have hope that future assessments will require proponents to consider adaptive management in the design and implementation of monitoring programs. With respect to the Keeyask Project, we note that the partnership clearly indicated throughout the EA documentation their intention to adopt adaptive management in monitoring and follow-up programs. It also clearly recognized uncertainties associated with the project and espoused a best-practice definition of adaptive management.

However, there were significant issues related to how monitoring was planned, reviewed, and conducted. First, more consistent treatment of each element of the adaptive management cycle would have strengthened monitoring program design. This would have included having clear indicators of how results would inform subsequent monitoring activities, including proposed timelines for integrating results across different monitoring programs. While project documentation included some examples, the proponents needed to do more to communicate their interest in and capacity for adaptive management. In addition, there should have been significantly more information available about the decision-making processes and resources available for future changes to the different monitoring programs. Relying on a track record limited to three very recent projects simply cannot allay concerns, particularly given the outstanding issues associated with the Churchill River Diversion and Manitoba Hydro's troubled legacy in the North.

Proponents, in crafting EA documents, often make broad commitments as to how they will construct and operate their planned development. A long-standing challenge of EA processes is how regulatory authorities can hold companies accountable for those things that fall outside a government department's mandate. In other words, what are the consequences should a company fail to implement its plan? Conditional licences and other permits and interdepartmental coordination are the main means of enforcing compliance, and of course both were used in the Keeyask case. And although the licence for Keeyask helped address shortcomings in the proponent's adaptive management strategy and related monitoring programs, we believe the government could do more to strengthen the role of adaptive management in EA. For adaptive management to become an effective practice for good development in the North, we need to strengthen regulations to ensure that systematic learning remains a priority, even once project approval is granted—for example, with clear legislative requirements for adaptive management.

Furthermore, the licence should have included more direct requirements to follow adaptive management, with more clarity in the technical language employed: Does the province see "adaptively managed" as the same as "adaptive management"?

The biggest elephant in the room was, and continues to be, the lack of a meaningful and public review of the impacts and mitigation measures in the Churchill River Diversion. While the Northern Flood Agreement was developed, it has been largely toothless (see Joseph Dipple, Chapter 11 in this volume). For example, can proponents realistically predict and mitigate negative impacts of development in the absence of a robust, detailed, and well-implemented regional cumulative effects assessment of past development? Furthermore, how can there be confidence that monitoring programs for new dams will be fully implemented when the record for the Churchill River Diversion and associated hydroelectric development is not transparent? This lack of certitude provides critical context for understanding the importance of adaptive management in guiding monitoring and follow-up programs in more recent developments such as Keeyask.

Such a review also needs to consider how to develop meaningful relationships with northern First Nations—not only in future developments but also for existing dams. For example, is there a way to share decision making? As Aimée Craft argues in Chapter 10, what concrete steps do the Province and Manitoba Hydro need to take to move from incorporating Aboriginal traditional knowledge in EA to following Indigenous legal traditions throughout the review? Are there other models of economic partnership—for past and future development—that should be implemented? If done well, this type of review could provide a strategic roadmap for future projects, strengthen public confidence in Manitoba Hydro, and minimize uncertainty for those who live in the North. In the absence of such a review, systematically analyzing uncertainty for new projects in the same social-ecological system as the Churchill River Diversion remains elusive. Good adaptive management and the lessons it provides cannot rest on a weak foundation.

In February 2021 the Keeyask Generating Station went into service. With growing access to annual monitoring data, we have an opportunity to get a better understanding of post-assessment activities. Such analysis might consider a range of questions, including:

> Were the design and implementation of plans appropriate? For example, did the methodologies meet best practices in Indigenous and Western sciences? Did the design and implementation include experts representing all of the partners? Does the program, as currently implemented, meet the commitments made by the proponents (including those related to human and financial resources)?

Were the predictions accurate? For example, did the Keeyask proponent monitor the "correct" ecosystem components? Was the determination of effects presented in the EA borne out?

How did the Keeyask proponent employ adaptive management? For example, are there instances when monitoring programs or protocols were changed to reflect more current understanding of project impacts? Did the proponent add new ecosystem components to its monitoring regimes?

How do follow-up and monitoring document and demonstrate learning by the Keeyask partnership?

Only once we have access to findings from the monitoring programs can we determine how to further enhance adaptive management in northern development.

Although there is now greater involvement by affected First Nations, and a regulatory system that may include adaptive management, we cannot evaluate the significance of each until we can see how lessons learned from this development are implemented during operation and influence newer developments. In our view, best-practice adaptive management that relies on Western science, Indigenous legal traditions and practices, and local expertise, which is also inclusive and participatory for all rights holders and stakeholders, will help usher in a new era of hydroelectric development in Manitoba.

We would like to acknowledge that the Keeyask Project is built in Treaty 5 territory. This manuscript was drafted in Treaty 1. Winnipeg is in the territory of the Anishinaabeg, Cree, Oji-Cree, Dakota and Dene peoples, and the homeland of the Métis Peoples. The water we drink comes from Treaty 3, and the power we use comes from Treaty 5 and beyond. Acknowledging this truth is important, yet only a small part of building a relationship with those in whose territories we live. We would like to thank the Public Interest Law Centre, and the Consumers Association of Manitoba, who first raised our interest in adaptive management in Manitoba energy projects and then supported our efforts to provide an independent analysis of this project. We also wish to acknowledge Aimée Craft and Jill Blakley for their work to bring this important case study forward. Portions of this paper are adapted from Diduck and Fitzpatrick, Assessing Adaptive Management,[34] *and Diduck et al.,* Guidance from Adaptive Environmental Management.[35]

Notes

1   J. B. Nyberg and B. Taylor, "Applying Adaptive Management in British Columbia's Forests" (paper presented at the Proceedings of the FAO/ECE/ILO International Forestry Seminar, Prince George, BC, 1995), at para. 2.

2   For example, Bram Noble, "Adaptive Environmental Management," in *Resource and Environmental Management in Canada*, ed. Bruce Mitchell (Don Mills, ON: Oxford University Press, 2015), 87–111.

3   Carl J. Walters and Crawford Stanley Holling, "Large-scale Management Experiments and Learning by Doing," *Ecology* 71, no. 6 (1990): 2060–68.

4   For example, Catherine Allan and George H. Stankey, "Synthesis of Lessons," in *Adaptive Environmental Management: A Practitioner's Guide*, ed. C. Allan and George H. Stankey (New York: Springer Verlag, 2009), 341–46.

5   Modified from G. Jones, "The Adaptive Management System for the Tasmanian Wilderness World Heritage Area: Linking Management Planning with Effective Evaluation," in *Adaptive Environmental Management: A Practitioner's Guide*, ed. C. Allan and George H. Stankey (New York: Springer Verlag, 2009), 237.

6   For example, Joanne Moyer, Patricia Fitzpatrick, Alan P. Diduck, and Beverly Froese, "Towards Community-based Monitoring in the Hog Industry in Manitoba: A Paper Submitted to the Manitoba Clean Environment Commission," *Canadian Public Administration Journal* 51, no. 4 (2008): 637–58; Bram Noble, *Introduction to Environmental Impact Assessment: A Guide to Principles and Practice*, 3rd ed. (Don Mills, ON: Oxford University Press, 2015).

7   Lydia Dobrovolny, "Monitoring for Success: Designing and Implementing a Monitoring Regime for Northern Manitoba," in *Power Struggles: Hydro Development and First Nations in Manitoba and Quebec*, ed. Thibault Martin and Steven M. Hoffman (Winnipeg: University of Manitoba Press, 2008), 169–202.

8   Allan and Stankey, "Synthesis of Lessons"; Ray Hilborn, "Living with Uncertainty in Resource Management," *North American Journal of Fisheries Management* 7, no. 1 (1987): 1–5; Kai N. Lee, *Compass and Gyroscope: Integrating Science and Politics for the Environment* (Washington, DC: Island Press, 1993).

9   Karen S. Christenson, "Coping with Uncertainty in Planning," *Journal of the American Planning Association* 51, no. 1 (1985): 63–73; Brian Wynne, "Uncertainty and Environmental Learning: Reconceiving Science and Policy in the Preventive Paradigm," *Global Environmental Change* 2, no. 2 (1992): 111–27.

10   Robert Gibson, "In Full Retreat: The Canadian Government's New Environmental Assessment Law Undoes Decades of Progress," *Impact Assessment and Project Appraisal* 30, no. 3 (2012): 179–88.

11   J.B. Ruhl, "Taking Adaptive Management Seriously: A Case Study of the Endangered Species Act," *University of Kansas Law Review* 52 (2003), para. 3; see also Noble, "Adaptive Environmental Management."

12   Noble, "Adaptive Environmental Management."

13 Walters and Holling, "Large-Scale Management Experiments."

14 Ibid.

15 Lance H. Gunderson, "Adaptive Dancing: Interactions between Social Resilience and Ecological Crises," in *Navigating Social-Ecological Systems*, ed. Fikret Berkes, Johan Colding, and Carle Folke (New York: Cambridge University Press, 2003), 33–52.

16 Alana L. Moore, Leila Walker, Michael C. Runge, Eve McDonald-Madden, and Michael A. McCarthy, "Two-Step Adaptive Management for Choosing between Two Management Actions," *Ecological Applications* (2017): 1214.

17 Ibid., 1211.

18 Developed from Catherine Allan and George H. Stankey, eds., *Adaptive Environmental Management: A Practitioner's Guide* (New York: Springer Netherlands, 2009); modified from Alan P. Diduck, Patricia Fitzpatrick, and James P. Robson, *Guidance from Adaptive Environmental Management, Monitoring and Independent Oversight for Manitoba Hydro's Upcoming Development Proposals: A Report Prepared for the Consumers Association of Canada (Manitoba) and the Public Interest Law Centre of Legal Aid Manitoba*, Public Interest Law Centre (Winnipeg, MB, November 2012).

19 Clean Environment Commission, *Wuskwatim Generation and Transmission Project Hearing Transcript*, Clean Environment Commission, 77 (2004), http://www.cecmanitoba.ca/cecm/archive/pubs/commission%20reports/commissioned-reports-2004-2005-wuskwatim_generation_transmission_projects_full_report.pdf.

20 Alan P. Diduck, Patricia Fitzpatrick, and James P. Robson, *Guidance from Adaptive Environmental Management, Monitoring and Independent Oversight for Manitoba Hydro's Upcoming Development Proposals: A Report Prepared for the Consumers Association of Canada (Manitoba) and the Public Interest Law Centre of Legal Aid Manitoba*, Public Interest Law Centre (Winnipeg, MB, November 2012).

21 Keeyask Hydropower Limited Partnership, *Executive Summary* (Winnipeg, MB: Manitoba Hydro, 2012), xxxii.

22 Alan P. Diduck and Patricia Fitzpatrick, *Assessing Adaptive Management in the Keeyask EIS: A report prepared for the Consumers Association of Canada (Manitoba) and the Public Interest Law Centre of Legal Aid Manitoba*, Public Interest Law Centre (Winnipeg, MB, November 2013).

23 Keeyask Hydropower Limited Partnership, *Response to the EIS Guidelines*, Manitoba Hydro (Winnipeg, MB, 2012), 5–14.

24 We use the term "Aboriginal" to reflect its usage in documentation prepared by the Keeyask partnership for the EA process.

25 Bruce Mitchell and Dan Shrubsole, "An Overview of Integration in Resource and Environmental Management," in *Integrated Resource and Environmental Management: Concepts and Practice*, ed. Kevin Hanna and D. Scott Slocombe (Toronto: Oxford University Press, 2007), 21–35.

26 The partnership chose to undertake two tracks of analysis and to present both in the filing (CEC Rd1 CAC-0013), and made no attempts to integrate them. The analysis and conclusions of the two assessments were never meant to be reconciled. This approach may pose problems over time.

27 Diduck and Fitzpatrick, *Assessing Adaptive Management*.

28 As would be expected, and appropriate, different time periods were proposed for integrating results, depending upon the specific objective. For example, the socio-

economic monitoring program indicated that a food-consumption survey would be done every five years, whereas the aquatics effects program employed a minimum ten-year post-impoundment time horizon for addressing things like water quality and aquatic habitat.

29 The Monitoring Advisory Committee is comprised of representatives of each of the project proponent's partners, and advisors from the First Nation partners may attend meetings under specific circumstances.

30 Clean Environment Commission, *Keeyask Generating Project: Report on Public Hearing*, Winnipeg, MB, April 2014, 148, http://www.cecmanitoba.ca/resource/ hearings/36/FINAL%20WEB%20Bipole%20III%20Transmission%20Project_ WEB3.pdf.

31 Offsetting programs "provide appropriate replacements, substitutions or opportunities to offset unavoidable adverse Project effects on the practices, customs and traditions integral to the First Nations' distinctive cultural identity," and include access to alternative resource use locations and Cree language and cultural programming; see Keeyask Hydropower Limited Partnership, *Response to the EIS Guidelines*, 14.

32 Canadian Environmental Assessment Agency, *Keeyask Generation Project: Comprehensive Study*, Canadian Environmental Assessment Agency (Ottawa, April 2014).

33 Diduck and Fitzpatrick, *Assessing Adaptive Management*.

34 Ibid.

35 Diduck, Fitzpatrick, and Robson, *Guidance from Adaptive Environmental Management*.

" No longer will I remain quiet. No longer will I regret being silent. No longer will I allow Hydro's timeline to go ahead without us being ready. Starting today. Manitoba Hydro, you need to consider our timeline. Which means slow down."

Conway Arthurson, Fox Lake Cree Nation, CEC hearings (8 October 2013), 93

CHAPTER 15

Will There Be Lasting Gains?
Sustainability Assessment, Keeyask, and the
Manitoba Power System Plan

KYRKE GAUDREAU AND ROBERT B. GIBSON

Few proposed resource extraction projects are subjected to serious analysis of whether they are the best option for delivering lasting contributions to well-being. That statement is true for many jurisdictions in the world, including Manitoba. It is also regrettable everywhere. This chapter reports on what would have been involved in doing a reasonably comprehensive sustainability-based analysis of the Keeyask Generating Station project and Manitoba Hydro's Preferred Development Plan to determine how best to meet Manitoba's energy needs.[1]

Our goal is not to evaluate the dam or to make a pronouncement on particular issues. Rather, we propose a framework for clarifying and choosing among the energy choices that would best serve the long-term and immediate public interest, including the interests of the Indigenous communities most directly affected, and to explain why using such a framework is appropriate.

A framework of some sort was clearly needed to conceive and evaluate the two linked undertakings. As proposed, the Keeyask Dam and Manitoba Hydro's preferred power system plan were big, expensive undertakings that would have major effects for many generations, on top of existing impacts. Moreover, the two undertakings raised a wide range of highly complex issues and options.

Using a sustainability-based criteria framework makes sense for four key reasons. First, the concept of sustainability covers the full suite of social, economic, and ecological concerns that affect our long-term and immediate prospects. Second, we now know enough to identify the core requirements for moving towards sustainability that apply everywhere,[2] with considerable experience in specifying those requirements for particular cases.[3] Third, while the term "sustainability" is frequently confused and abused, its key components were widely embraced, including by the Province of Manitoba, Manitoba Hydro, and the Indigenous communities of the Nelson watershed.[4] And last, sustainability-based criteria set an appropriately high standard. They test whether a proposed undertaking is the best option for delivering lasting gains and avoiding significant negative effects. That is a reasonable expectation, including for hydro dams and provincial electric power systems.

Applying a comprehensive framework of sustainability-based criteria to any new hydroelectric project or system plan would deliver the most positive contributions to lasting well-being if used to determine what purposes to pursue, what options to consider, and what to approve. This work has important implications for establishing a new, positive legacy for development in northern Manitoba. This chapter aims to provide a broad structure for considering the issues raised in other chapters of this book, and for future undertakings in the region.

Sustainability-Based Assessments

The Basic Concept

Sustainability assessment is an updated version of very old wisdom about the merits of looking ahead—anticipating the future effects of possible innovations and figuring out how to minimize the risks of trial and error, how to protect what is most valuable, and how to extend the benefits. The updating recognizes the global as well as local character of the issues before us. It also incorporates new knowledge, especially about the interconnections, feedbacks, and uncertainties of social and ecological systems.

The global roots of sustainability assessment lie in the challenge that the United Nation's Brundtland Commission identified back in the mid-1980s. The commission saw increasingly unsustainable pressures on the biosphere and billions of people without basic material security as one problem. In response it proposed a "sustainable development" transition that would apply precautionary care, participatory engagement, and continuous learning to deliver both environmental stewardship and better livelihoods for all.

Local and regional pressures have pointed in the same direction. Global concerns about unsustainability are mostly the cumulative results of concerns within nations and communities. Economic uncertainties, stressed ecosystems, and struggling communities have undermined people's faith that current approaches to the future will automatically deliver increasing well-being and security while fixing any adverse side effects. Consequently, we have seen more active local engagement to protect valued qualities (traditions, resources, etc.) and to seek improvements even when this means challenging proponents of conventional undertakings. As Chapters 3, 6, and 13 in this volume attest, northern Manitoba is one place where this has been happening.

Unlike many established evaluation and approval processes, sustainability assessment is not focused only on mitigating adverse effects. It aims higher, seeking to identify the best options for progress towards desirable and durable futures, while also avoiding the negatives. In this role, sustainability assessment compares options and judges' proposals not only on individual effects but also on combinations, interactions, and interdependencies between humans and the biophysical foundations for life.

To identify best options for the long haul, sustainability assessment relies heavily on applying explicit sustainability-based criteria for each case it reviews. These criteria combine the global and local. The basic idea is that, for every new undertaking, we should combine attention to the core requirements for progress towards sustainability that apply everywhere and the specifics of the particular context—its interacting systems of socio-ecological relations, capacities, limitations, trajectories of change, and aspirations for the future—to see more clearly what is prudent, possible, and desirable.

Sustainability-Based Assessment Practice So Far

Because sustainability-based approaches to decision making are meant to encourage change, they threaten "business as usual." At the same time, they fit well with rising demands for corporate responsibility and offer important advantages for jurisdictions seeking to enhance the effectiveness, efficiency, fairness, and credibility of their decision making. Consequently, sustainability-based assessments have been initiated, and in some places required by law, for a host of applications around the world.[5] Sustainability-based approaches can apply to new or renewing projects, policies, and programs; reviews of past experience; reconsideration of ongoing activities; and comparison of future scenarios. In Canada, the most visible applications of "contribution to sustainability" tests have been in a series of joint environmental assessment panel reviews on major projects across the country.[6] But others have used similar approaches in urban growth management planning, regional resource management, and reviews of institutional practice, among others,[7] and the Canadian federal government has recently legislated sustainability-based assessment.[8]

While Manitoba has not yet embraced sustainability assessment as a legal requirement in provincial decision making, the province has legislated core sustainability principles[9] and the Manitoba Law Reform Commission has recommended that the Province develop "a strategy and timeline for transitioning Manitoba to a system of sustainability assessment."[10] As we discuss below, the Keeyask and Manitoba Hydro system plan reviews, presented at the Clean Environment Commission (CEC) and Public Utilities Board (PUB) public hearings, made tentative steps towards a sustainability-based approach. However, they represented at best a bare beginning.

Sustainability Assessment for Keeyask and the Manitoba Power System

For practical application, the broad objective of progress towards sustainability needs to be translated into a set of criteria to guide deliberative processes and decision making. As noted above, the criteria must recognize both general requirements for sustainability and the particularities of the local context. Also, they must be applied explicitly in deliberations that not only engage the key authorities and stakeholders but also build as much public capacity as possible.

In simple cases, the essential steps are quite straightforward. Assessment begins with thinking about the needs and opportunities you want to address, what purposes they will serve, and the potentially feasible options (or alternatives) for serving those purposes. You must then describe the options in enough detail to identify and compare their potential impacts or effects. You then choose the best option, paying careful attention to minimizing trade-offs, mitigating the risks, and enhancing the benefits. Last comes monitoring and adjusting through the life of the undertaking. Throughout the process, applying explicit sustainability-based criteria is an important way to stay focused on all the interrelated objectives, imposing rigour and building credibility for the decisions you make.

The Keeyask Dam and the Manitoba power system plan were not and are not simple. The dam was being considered for a watershed already heavily disturbed by hydropower projects. The proposal was submitted as a collaboration between Manitoba Hydro and the four Keeyask First Nations who were negatively affected by the earlier developments. Also, the project was intended to serve multiple regional purposes in addition to generating electricity for the provincial power system and anticipated electricity exports.

Even the initial purposes and alternatives involved a complex mix. For power system purposes, alternatives to the dam were mostly outside the region (including conserving energy to reduce demand, building more dispersed and smaller-scale renewable electricity projects, reducing the province's ambitions towards exports, etc.). For the purposes of restitution and well-being in northern Manitoba, especially for the Nelson watershed communities, Manitoba Hydro did not bring any regional development alternatives to the table, either in the planning work or at the hearings.

Moreover, Manitoba's regulatory process for public deliberation and decision making separated assessing the Keeyask Dam and reviewing Manitoba Hydro's entire power system plan, something several other chapters in this volume have noted as problematic. Neither process considered other regional development options for the communities and region to be affected by the Keeyask Project.

As part of a sustainability assessment process, it is important to consider alternatives to the Keeyask Dam in particular and to Manitoba's power system plans as a whole. All proper sustainability assessments should undertake a comparative evaluation of options and select the best. This chapter therefore sets out to develop a reasonably comprehensive framework of criteria that covers the key factors involved in evaluating the Keeyask Dam proposal in light of other, little-explored alternatives.

Sustainability Assessment Criteria for the Case

The Province of Manitoba should have carefully developed a sustainability-based criteria framework much earlier as a broadly participative process, with key roles for Manitoba Hydro, the Indigenous communities of the Nelson watershed, and other relevant authorities and stakeholders. The process should have linked long-term provincial objectives with those for the electric power system, regional well-being in the North, especially for Indigenous communities, and more focused attention to the potential role of an additional dam or dams.

The sustainability assessment framework that we developed for this chapter, and to present to the CEC hearings on Keeyask and the PUB's Needs For and Alternatives To assessment of Manitoba Hydro's Preferred Development Plan, occurred only after the Keeyask proposal had entered the licensing process. This creates major limitations. We are outsiders, with no opportunity to formally consult with anyone. Instead, we have relied on the literature on electric power planning and dam projects (including the work of the World Commission on Dams),[11] documents from the project proponents and other commentators, records on the context for the project in Manitoba and the Nelson watershed, and our own previous experience elsewhere.

From this material we attempted to identify what were likely the key issues specific to the Keeyask case, and to integrate them with the core requirements for progress towards sustainability. We have summarized the resulting framework in Table 15.1, below.

Table 15.1. Primary Sustainability Criteria for Evaluation and Decision Making in the Keeyask Case

---

Improving the ecological basis of our livelihoods and wealth

Goal/criterion: Build human–ecological relations to establish and maintain the long-term integrity of socio-biophysical systems and protect the irreplaceable life-support functions upon which human as well as ecological well-being depends.

Themes: Maintaining ecological functions and services and the ecological basis of traditional livelihoods; improving habitats and habitat intactness; mitigating climate change; ensuring immediate and long-term adaptive planning; and avoiding and mitigating adverse effects.

Fostering desirable and durable livelihoods

Goal/criterion: Expand the range and availability of desirable and durable livelihood opportunities while helping to ensure sufficiency for all.

Themes: Ensuring livelihood foundations; protecting the most vulnerable; fostering local economic development and self-determination; preventing "boom and bust" economies; and establishing shared responsibility for livelihood maintenance.

Enhancing well-being and self-determination for Indigenous communities

Goal/criterion: Enhance Indigenous community well-being and respect traditional livelihoods while allowing those communities to benefit from development projects as appropriate.

Themes: Strengthening Indigenous ways of living and self-determination; enhancing determinants of health; supporting Indigenous infrastructure; furthering Askiy (the traditional Cree recognition of ties to and responsibility for the land); and fostering community well-being and empowerment.

Ensuring fairness in process and outcomes

Goal/criterion: Ensure that sufficiency and effective choices for all are pursued in ways that reduce dangerous gaps in sufficiency and opportunity (and health, security, social recognition, political influence, etc.) between the rich and the poor.

Themes: Distributing benefits and risks fairly; providing fair access to resources and opportunities; mitigating unavoidable losses; accounting for the past; and establishing shared responsibility for promoting equity.

Leaving a positive legacy

Goal/criterion: Favour options and actions that are most likely to preserve or enhance the opportunities and capabilities of future generations to live sustainably.

Themes: Securing long-term availability of energy and resources; securing future opportunities; saving for the future; ensuring lasting benefit; establishing shared responsibility for a positive legacy; and developing energy bridges.

Promoting resource maintenance, conservation, and efficiency

Goal/criterion: Provide a larger base for ensuring sustainable livelihoods for all, while reducing threats to the long-term integrity of socio-ecological systems by reducing extractive damage, avoiding waste, and cutting overall material and energy use per unit of benefit.

Themes: Reducing overall energy and resource consumption; fostering responsible use of energy; developing resilient energy supplies; avoiding resource conflicts; and mitigating adverse effects.

Prioritizing precautionary and adaptive management

Goal/criterion: Favour undertakings that respect uncertainty and avoid risks of serious or irreversible damage to the foundations of sustainability, and act on incomplete but suggestive information where there may be risks to social and/or ecological systems that are crucial for sustainability.

Themes: Ensuring responsive monitoring and adaptive management; developing baseline data; respecting uncertainty; anticipating climate change; and avoiding lock-in.

Ensuring due process and an informed citizenry

Goal/criterion: Build individuals', communities', and other collective decision-making bodies' capacity to apply sustainability requirements through more open and better-informed deliberations, greater attention to fostering reciprocal awareness and collective responsibility, and more integrated use of various decision-making practices.

Themes: Maintaining traditional ways of knowing and deciding; promoting good governance; fostering informed and responsible citizenry; accounting for all costs; promoting open and informed decision making; and ensuring proper problem formulation.

Integrating immediate and long-term planning objectives

Goal/criterion: Apply all principles of sustainability at once, seeking mutually supportive benefits and multiple gains so as to ensure the overall cumulative effects of the chosen alternative will make the strongest feasible contribution to sustainability while avoiding trade-offs.

Themes: Promoting integrated assessment to seek the best alternative; seeking mutually reinforcing positive gains; and avoiding trade-offs.

The framework of criteria developed in Table 15.1 above was originally intended as a core structure for the Clean Environment Commission and the Manitoba Public Utilities Board to use in their assessments. Initiating a participative process before hydroelectric projects, including Keeyask, were selected would have delivered a better set of criteria, and more specific matters raised in both sets of hearings could then have been incorporated. Nevertheless, the basic framework illustrates the nature and potential utility of explicit sustainability-based grounds for evaluations and decisions about the Keeyask Dam.

The following discussion addresses four key questions for the Keeyask assessment in which applying the basic framework criteria could have helped the proponents, the CEC, the PUB, and others work towards an enlightened decision.

Four Big Questions Raised When Applying Sustainability Criteria to Keeyask

Applying sustainability-based criteria to projects and plans involves three basic steps: defining the project's purpose, comparing alternatives, and picking options most likely to deliver multiple, mutually reinforcing benefits while avoiding potential damage. For the Keeyask case, including both the hydropower project and associated electricity system plans, these basic steps must also involve special attention to major energy issues and Indigenous rights.

Overall, the standard questions facing a sustainability assessment can be represented as the following:

1. What is the public interest need for and purpose of the undertaking?

2. What are the major alternatives for meeting the need?

3. Would the alternatives help to meet sustainability objectives (with emphasis on the objectives most salient to the local context)?

4. How do the alternatives compare when considered in light of an explicit set of context-specific sustainability criteria?

Most of the time, governments and regulators neglect these key questions for major energy undertakings or consider them only after the proponents have submitted their projects for approval. However, applying a sustainability criteria framework from the outset of planning ensures more illuminating and helpful answers to all four questions. As the criteria summary in Table 15.1 indicates, many interconnected factors are involved that interact in complex ways. The following discussion provides an overview of what happens when we ask the four big questions of the Keeyask case, using the criteria listed in Table 15.1.

Question 1. What Is the Public Interest Need for and Purpose of the Undertaking?

Manitoba Hydro and the Province evidently conceived the Keeyask Dam chiefly to meet anticipated domestic demand and facilitate electricity exports for provincial economic gain. However, it was proposed by a partnership—the Keeyask Hydropower Limited Partnership (KHLP), comprising Manitoba Hydro and four First Nations in the lower Nelson watershed—in part to secure benefits for the communities. Thus, the project's purposes combined province-wide energy needs and regional community needs, both of which properly involve the full range of sustainability considerations.

Other chapters in this book have already revealed the importance and complexity of the regional communities' needs, and how they may be addressed and/or compromised by the Keeyask Project. Many of these needs are immediate and pressing. However, they all rest in commitments to land and culture that stretch back beyond memory and ahead without end. This is inherently a sustainability perspective, which has evidently mixed implications for the Keeyask Project. For a proper sustainability-based assessment in the Keeyask case, the general criteria outlined in Table 15.1 would have to be adjusted and specified by the Indigenous communities and authorities whose rights and interests may be affected and whose free, prior, and informed consent is needed.

The issues surrounding Manitoba's perceived energy needs underlying the Keeyask proposal are also complex. For sustainability purposes, it's useful to focus on energy "need" considerations before launching into options for generating more. This begins with understanding that energy is only a means to social ends. People generally do not want energy per se, but rather the services it provides—comfortable homes, mobility, convenience, entertainment, light, and so on.[12] Consequently, assessing electrical energy needs raises three initial questions centred on the services:[13]

(i) What energy services are desirable now and in the roughly foreseeable future?

(ii) Is electricity the most appropriate form of energy for the desired services?

(iii) What is the most efficient way to provide the desirable services for which electricity is the best option?

The question about desirable services is tricky, because social norms—including technological possibilities, expectations, fashions, and moral judgments—can and do change. Choices about future options matter. For example, we might encourage a transition to electric cars, or reduce car dependence through better public transit, teleconferencing, and Internet shopping, or some of each. What we choose affects how much electricity we need to generate.

The second question involves matching the quality of electricity as an energy source to the quality of energy needed for the end use. Electricity is a high-quality energy source, best for applications that are very delicate (advanced computing) or very demanding (laser cutting metals). It is not well matched for low-quality tasks, such as space heating, which can be better supplied through heat pumps, solar heating, or biomass.[14] End-use matching can be a far more efficient and effective means of achieving our goals than building more generating stations. Beginning with the end use and working backwards to the ideal energy source also opens up a wider range of possibilities to meet needs, and tends to encourage adopting a diversity of energy-related technologies.

The third question, about using electricity responsibly when it is the best option for the services we need, is more familiar. The *Manitoba Clean Energy Strategy* highlights several opportunities for efficiency, conservation, and demand-side management, including raising energy efficiency standards for high-energy consuming products, financing programs to lower upfront retrofit costs, and updating building codes to reflect new designs.[15] British Columbia has already achieved considerable savings by supporting technological upgrades (e.g., installing LED lights and continuously variable drive motors), continually optimizing building operations, and raising awareness of the need to conserve energy.[16]

In advanced electric power system planning, where these three need questions have been asked, "conservation and demand management" efficiency initiatives have been overtaking new electricity generation projects as the most attractive option.[17] Reducing demand is typically cheaper, more flexible, more likely to reduce ecological stress, and more likely to distribute jobs and other social benefits throughout the province than building new dams or other power plants and their attendant transmission lines. Energy conservation and efficiency efforts are easily linked with widespread and long-standing respect for thrift, simplicity, diversity, neighbourliness, humility, and craftsmanship. Moreover, they help people see that requiring large amounts of energy to accomplish social goals is a better indicator of failure than of success.[18]

Failure to examine energy needs carefully can lead to oversupply and wasteful use.[19] A useful approach is to start with the desired future state and then work backwards to the present to determine the required changes. "Backcasting," as this approach is called, promotes reflection on what is unattractive about present arrangements and trends, such as modern societies' currently inequitable use of resources.[20] This allows us to pursue the futures we want, rather than accepting projections based on what we have now.

Question 2. What Are the Alternatives?

In the Keeyask case, there were two potential alternatives: alternatives for meeting the regional communities' socio-economic needs, and alternatives for meeting provincial energy needs (or the services underlying these energy needs). Only the latter received careful attention. In the Clean Environment Commission's public hearings concerning the Keeyask Dam proposal, the only seriously explored alternative to approving the project was the null option—continuing with existing conditions and any future regional opportunities that might arise in the absence of the Keeyask Dam. In contrast, the Public Utilities Board review compared Manitoba Hydro's preferred system plan (including Keeyask) with multiple alternative portfolios.

The main issue for the Clean Environment Commission's proceedings was whether or not to issue an Environment Act licence for the Keeyask Project—to determine whether the proposed project was "acceptable," not whether it was the most desirable option. Unfortunately, there is rarely a credibly delineated line to distinguish an acceptable undertaking from an unacceptable one. Moreover, as Chapter 4 in this volume demonstrates, project-centred assessments typically lack adequate information on cumulative adverse effects[21] as well as the anticipated positive effects and the implications of resulting trade-offs. The proponents did not present any alternative ways of spurring regional development or otherwise addressing communities' needs because such matters were beyond the core mandate of Manitoba Hydro (except as aspects of electrical energy project delivery), and the project-centred process was not designed to seek or attract proponents of other options.

The Public Utilities Board's electric power system plan review was very different. Energy system alternatives were central and debates focused on the adequacy of Manitoba Hydro's work in identifying and comparing the many available options. Wrestling with the many options is now a major challenge for power system planning. Apparent electricity "needs" can be addressed by different sources of energy, more efficient electricity use, and various combinations of conservation and demand-side management initiatives.[22] Regulators can also compare the merits of these combinations with other options for generating new electricity supply, which are also varied—large and small, centralized and dispersed, renewable and non-renewable, and so forth.

Moreover, in the dynamic field of electrical energy planning, the options and their relative merits are changing constantly. They are affected, for example, by advances in technology (e.g., solar generation), price and supply shifts (e.g., natural gas), disasters (e.g., the Fukushima nuclear plant disaster), experience (e.g., with energy efficiency incentives), influence of affected stakeholders and authorities (e.g., Aboriginal rights rulings), and policy shifts (e.g., carbon pricing). These uncertainties mean that governments and corporations need to revisit conventional assumptions often, and they should favour flexibly diverse options over single inflexible ones. In this shifting landscape, it is especially important to have specified sustainability criteria that favour precaution (Table 15.1, criterion 7) to guide the evaluation of options, and to subject the criteria themselves to regular review.

Like other electric power system authorities, Manitoba Hydro assembled several different portfolios with varying sets of generation, transmission, and conservation components and compared them before identifying the preferred plan presented to the Public Utilities Board. The portfolio approach to alternatives can help build a system with complementary components—for example, by ensuring that hydro dams' long lead times do not divert resources away from smaller renewable or efficiency options,[23] or by using hydro dams to support other technologies, such as wind power, to overcome the issue of intermittent supply.[24] Portfolio use does not, however, avoid problems arising from commonly entrenched utility biases favouring more generation over ambitious conservation and demand-side management, or a few large centralized projects over many diverse small ones. Such traditions tend to prevail, especially if approval processes do not insist on comparatively evaluating broad alternatives in light of the full suite of comprehensive, sustainability-based criteria. Additionally, comparatively assessing energy alternatives is best done at the power system level, rather than individual undertakings. It is difficult, if not impossible, to determine the relative value of a particular project, or even a particular electricity generation technology, without considering what position it may occupy in the larger system.

Unfortunately, the Clean Environment Commission was left in the unenviable position of evaluating a major project proposal without the overall power system alternatives, without regional development alternatives, and without a potentially adequate basis for considering the project's possible contributions to regional cumulative effects. Power system alternatives were only later examined in the Public Utilities Board process.

Question 3. Would the Alternatives Help to Meet Sustainability Objectives?

Sustainability-based decision making is designed to encourage significant changes in how our societies function. Those changes move us closer towards transitioning to a sustainable future. But sustainability assessments for energy systems include particular emphasis on two main shifts—transitioning from ever-rising consumption of energy (and associated stresses) to sustainable levels of reliance on renewable, climate-friendly resources,[25] and adopting technologies and systems that are flexible enough to accommodate the unexpected challenges and opportunities of an uncertain future.

The two shifts are closely linked and have mixed implications for big dams. Hydropower is a renewable energy source, but dams are ecologically and socially disruptive. Dams can be a reliable source of electricity for a century or more, and a stable base for an electrical power system, assuming water flows are consistent over time (perhaps a large "if," given climate change). At the same time, however, dams are very large and costly fixed components in the system. Building a hydropower dam involves making a big initial investment of capital to obtain a large chunk of generating capacity to meet a large chunk of demand that is expected to persist for many decades. The funds used for dam building will then not be available for other electrical energy options (such as wind and solar), and the substantial available supply may reduce motivations for conservation and efficiency efforts.

In contrast, a system constructed of multiple, modular, and scalable renewable generation sources (and efficiency programs) can be deployed more gradually and be adjusted more quickly to changes in demand, and can facilitate adopting more advanced technologies as they become available and affordable. Smaller and more innovative options also have their problems, including challenges in forecasting power output and conservation results, and in managing a grid with a high percentage of intermittent sources. Also, from a biophysical standpoint, the energy and other resources needed to produce renewable energy systems (e.g., solar photovoltaic) and their associated technologies (e.g., batteries) are still quite high.[26] That indicates a lower than desirable energy return on investment and requires careful attention to the systems' life-cycle effects.

In Manitoba and many other jurisdictions today, even medium-term future demand, technologies, and climatic conditions are minimally predictable, and system flexibility is a key consideration in energy system planning (Table 15.1, criterion 7).[27] While additional big dams may have a place in future electrical energy system portfolios,[28] they are not automatically the best option. What about the objectives most salient to the local context—in the Keeyask case, the Indigenous population and their traditional lands (Table 15.1, criterion 3)? Would the alternatives contribute to recovery and reconciliation for the Indigenous peoples of the region?

In the Keeyask case, local communities and ecosystems have already suffered significant adverse effects from previous hydropower projects built in an era of disempowerment, expropriation, and imposed assimilation (which many would argue is ongoing). Whether the Keeyask Project will contribute to recovery, reconciliation, and lasting well-being in the region is uncertain. Any additional hydropower projects will add further ecological and socio-cultural disturbance. To what extent the damage (e.g., to sturgeon populations) can be mitigated successfully was and remains an open question. The extent to which the employment opportunities, revenues, and broader empowerment associated with the project will be important contributors to lasting livelihoods and community well-being is similarly debatable.

The First Nations that voted to be equity partners in the Keeyask Project did so with reluctance, faced with the limited choice between Keeyask and no Keeyask. Fox Lake Cree Nation, for example, reported: "The decision to become a partner in the Keeyask Project was a difficult decision and for many members it will be difficult to reconcile being a partner in a process that will forever alter Askiy. The challenge for the Partnership is to ensure that it realizes on the opportunities presented while simultaneously making every effort to ensure that Askiy is protected."[29]

For the York Factory First Nation, the constraints were tighter because the project seemed certain to go ahead in any event: "We felt it was important to become a partner and have a voice in the Keeyask Project, rather than let it move forward without us."[30] For the purposes of deciding whether or not to support the project, to give or withhold "free, prior and informed consent" as required under the UN Declaration on the Rights of Indigenous Peoples[31] (see Chapter 10 in this volume), a choice constrained by the absence of other positive opportunities is not ideal.

Question 4. What Are the Relative Merits of the Alternatives?

Choosing among the alternatives properly involves applying specified sustainability-based criteria in comparative evaluations (Table 15.1).[32] Doing so identifies the strengths and limitations of each option, reveals the trade-offs involved, and facilitates a reasonably justified choice of the best option for delivering lasting positive contributions and avoiding negative effects and risks.

In the Keeyask case, neither the Clean Environment Commission nor the Public Utilities Board had a comprehensive set of case-specific sustainability criteria for their evaluations. However, both bodies could have chosen to prepare and apply sustainability-based criteria. As demonstrated by Table 15.1, and detailed in our submissions,[33] developing a reasonably complete set of sustainability-based criteria is not particularly difficult.

Of the submitted Environmental Impact Statement materials, serious commitment to the fundamental principles of sustainability was evident only in the environmental evaluation reports prepared by the Keeyask Cree Nations. These reports consistently emphasized the inseparability of caring for the land (Askiy) and maintaining livelihoods.[34] However, the reports were limited to considering the Keeyask Dam and the null alternative. No other options were available.

The Keeyask Environmental Impact Statement (EIS)[35] offered a version of sustainability assessment in a special chapter that considered the proposed undertaking in light of individual objectives drawn from an assortment of federal, provincial, and utility (Manitoba Hydro) principles, policies, and guidelines.[36] The EIS did not address interactions among social-ecological and economic considerations or any options beyond the project as proposed. As previous chapters have explored, the EIS tended to emphasize prospects for positive effects and skate over adverse effects and uncertainties.

In its preferred plan submission to the Public Utilities Board, Manitoba Hydro took a similar approach to sustainability assessment. They left the work to a concise appendix and did not apply a comprehensive and integrated set of criteria of the kind presented in Table 15.1. The appendix did compare four alternative plans using multiple accounts benefit-cost analysis, but focused primarily on hydropower and gas-thermal generation, with no integration of wind, solar, or conservation and demand-side management components. Both the sustainability chapter in the Keeyask EIS and the system plan appendix appeared to be post-planning justifications of the proposals on sustainability grounds, rather than evidence of sustainability-based planning and assessment.

Sustainability did not figure prominently in the final decisions on the Keeyask Project or Manitoba Hydro's preferred development plan. In its report recommending that Keeyask be licensed, the Clean Environment Commission noted several more and less comprehensive approaches to sustainability-based assessment[37] but chose not to apply any of them, declaring sustainability assessment to be "beyond the scope of our review" but "worthy of future consideration."[38] The Public Utilities Board recommended that Manitoba Hydro's preferred development plan be rejected, but approved the Keeyask component. Like the CEC, the PUB chose not to apply a sustainability-based test.[39]

A Sustainability-Based Assessment of Keeyask Decision Making

The Clean Environment Commission and Public Utilities Board reviews, and the public discussions surrounding them, clarified many of the key issues surrounding the Keeyask Project and the associated Manitoba power system plan. The province deserves credit for ensuring that the plan as well as the project were subjected to open examination in public hearings. Other Canadian jurisdictions, notably Ontario and British Columbia, could learn from Manitoba's example. Nevertheless, neither process delivered a clear picture of whether the Keeyask Project was likely to make a positive overall contribution to sustainability, in northern Manitoba or in Manitoba generally.

Our work did not attempt to assess the Keeyask proposal or Manitoba Hydro's preferred development plan and alternatives using the criteria framework summarized in Table 15.1. Such an assessment would have required expertise in every interrelated area covered by the criteria, plus a deep understanding of the proposals and the alternatives—well beyond our capacities. However, we did consider some of the strengths and limitations the proponents' efforts and the structure of the province's decision-making process in comparison with what would have characterized an approach that applied context-specific sustainability assessment criteria. The conclusions were mixed but include grounds for optimism and directions for future effort.

With the constrained exception of the Cree partners, Keeyask proponents did not apply a comprehensive sustainability framework in their planning and neither the Clean Environment Commission nor the Public Utilities Board carried out an integrated sustainability-based review. While all of these players recognized important sustainability-related objectives, and Manitoba, with its existing sustainable development principles, was well positioned to regularly adopt a serious sustainability-based approach to project assessment and decision making, this has not yet happened.

The main deficiencies in the Keeyask case, aside from the failure to construct and apply comprehensive sustainability-based criteria, involved the relationship between the Keeyask Project and Manitoba Hydro's plan level assessments. The Clean Environment Commission's review of the Keeyask Project was hobbled by inadequate cumulative effects information and the absence of a basis for comparing the proposed project with regional development and electricity system alternatives. The Public Utilities Board did compare system alternatives (though without comprehensive criteria and with consequently debatable results) and benefited from access to the CEC's review findings. But even for the Keeyask option, important uncertainties about sustainability effects remained.

These difficulties point to the need to more broadly integrate sustainability-based approaches and public engagement throughout Manitoba Hydro's planning process. In electrical power systems, individual project proposals and the evolution of overall plans influence each other over time. The dynamics are difficult to capture in public review processes that focus on informing decision making for approvals.[40]

If the Keeyask case is to leave a positive legacy, its lessons should inspire ongoing engagement and application of explicit sustainability-based criteria throughout the development and implementation of Manitoba Hydro's future plans. The Keeyask experience should inspire new efforts to identify options for enhancing prospects for lasting well-being where such prospects are currently lacking. In the Keeyask case, people in the Nelson watershed communities had two highly imperfect options. They could support the Keeyask Project with its mix of opportunities and risks, or rely on the existing status quo. Not surprisingly, many found both options unattractive. While finding better alternatives will not be easy, for communities in the Nelson watershed and elsewhere, developing innovative means of fostering sustainability-enhancing regional development alternatives remains a worthy priority for public authorities, especially in light of commitments to Treaty rights, reconciliation, and the implementation of the United Nations Declaration on the Rights of Indigenous Peoples.

There is an evident need for a longer-term sustainability agenda in Manitoba and beyond. Back in Chapter 8 of this volume, James Schaefer invited Manitobans to use prospects for the long-lived, far-ranging caribou as a call to something bigger—a plan for sustainability on a broader and forward-looking scale. Now is the time to accept that call. Most Manitobans now consume resources, produce waste, and contribute to global overconsumption of natural capital at a rate far beyond what is sustainable and equitable in this world. Many of Manitoba's and Canada's excesses are facilitated by access to high-quality energy sources, including electricity. While it is not impossible to justify new dams or expanded power systems, such proposals should be conceived, designed, and presented as initial parts of a larger and longer strategy that helps us transition to conditions that create lasting well-being. On that we have some distance to go.

Notes

1   The research and consulting that underlie this chapter were undertaken in partnership with the Manitoba Public Interest Law Centre, and on behalf of the Consumers' Association of Canada, Manitoba Branch. As part of this work, we prepared a sustainability-based framework of criteria for considering all major issues and options relating to Manitoba Hydro's preferred development plan (which includes Keeyask) as presented to the Public Utilities Board in June 2014.

2   Robert B. Gibson, Selma Hassan, Susan Holtz, James Tansey, and Graham Whitelaw, *Sustainability Assessment: Criteria and Processes* (London: Earthscan, 2005).

3   Robert Gibson, *Sustainability Assessment: Applications and Opportunities* (London: Taylor and Francis, 2017).

4   The province's core sustainability principles were set out in the Sustainable Development Act in 1998 (Manitoba Hydro, *Needs For and Alternatives To [NFAT]) Business Case Submission* [Winnipeg, 2013]). Manitoba Hydro's sustainable development policy and thirteen sustainability principles were adopted in 1993 (Manitoba Hydro, *Sustainable Development Policy*, Winnipeg, n.d., accessed 25 October 2021, https://www.hydro.mb.ca/environment/env_management/sdp/. The largely Indigenous communities in the Nelson watershed have a much longer record of commitment to sustainable understandings and practices, as represented, for example, by the concept of omâmawi-okâwîmâw askiy and its connections throughout Cree culture; see Marilyn Shirt, Kevin Lewis, and Wayne Jackson, "Cree Ontology, Epistemology and Axiology Research," in *Proceedings of the International Indigenous Development Research Conference* (Auckland: New Zealand Indigenous Centre of Research Excellence, 2012), 205–11.

5   Barry Dalal-Clayton and Barry Sadler, *Sustainability Appraisal: A Sourcebook and Reference Guide to International Experience* (London: Routledge, 2014).

6   Voisey's Bay Environmental Assessment Panel, *Report on the Proposed Voisey's Bay Mine and Mill Project* (Ottawa: Canadian Environmental Assessment Agency, 1999); Canadian Environmental Assessment Agency, *Kemess North Copper-Gold Mine Project: Joint Review Panel Report* (Ottawa: Canadian Environmental Assessment Agency, 2007); Canadian Environmental Assessment Agency, *Environmental Assessment of the Whites Point Quarry and Marine Terminal Project: Joint Review Panel Report* (Ottawa: Canadian Environmental Assessment Agency, 2007); Ministry of the Environment, *Foundation for a Sustainable Northern Future: Report of the Joint Review Panel for the Mackenzie Gas Project* (Ottawa: Ministry of the Environment, 2010); Canadian Environmental Assessment Agency, *Report of the Joint Review Panel—Lower Churchill Hydroelectric Generation Project, Nalcor Energy, Newfoundland and Labrador* (Ottawa: Canadian Environmental Assessment Agency, 2011).

7   Robert Gibson, "Sustainability Assessment in Canada," in *Sustainability Assessment: Pluralism, Practice and Progress*, ed. A. Bond, A. Morrison-Saunders, and R. Howitt (London: Taylor and Francis, 2012), 167–83; Gibson, *Sustainability Assessment*.

8   Meinhard Doelle and John Sinclair, eds., *The Next Generation of Impact Assessment: A Critical Review of the Canadian Impact Assessment Act* (Toronto: Irwin Law, 2021).

9   Manitoba, Sustainable Development Act, C.C.S.M. C. S270, 1998.

10 Manitoba Law Reform Commission, Final Report, *Manitoba's Environmental Assessment and Licensing Regime under the Environment Act* (Winnipeg: Manitoba Law Reform Commission, May 2015), 38.

11 World Commission on Dams, *Dams and Development: A New Framework for Decision-Making* (London: Earthscan, 2000).

12 Amory B. Lovins, "Energy Strategy: The Road Not Taken?" *Foreign Affairs* 55, no. 1 (1976): 12; Science Council of Canada, *Canada as a Conserver Society: Resource Uncertainties and the Need for New Technologies* (Ottawa: The Council, 1977).

13 Amory B. Lovins, "Soft Energy Technologies," *Annual Review of Energy* 3, no. 1 (1978): 477–517.

14 Manitoba, *Manitoba Clean Energy Strategy,* Winnipeg, 2012, 30, https://www.gov.
mb.ca/sd/environment_and_biodiversity/energy/pubs/energy_strategy_2012.pdf.

15 Ibid., 3.

16 BC Hydro, "Energy Manager Program," Vancouver, 2015, accessed 1 July 2015,
http://www.bchydro.com/powersmart/business/programs/energy-manager.
html?WT.mc_id=rd_energymanager.

17 World Commission on Dams, *Dams and Development,* 224.

18 Amory B. Lovins, *Soft Energy Paths: Towards a Durable Peace,* Friends of the Earth
Energy Papers (San Francisco: Friends of the Earth, 1977), chs. 1 and 2; Lovins,
"Soft Energy Technologies"; Ursula M. Franklin, *The Real World of Technology,* CBC
Massey Lectures, 1989 (Toronto: House of Anansi, 1999), ch. 6.

19 World Commission on Dams, *Dams and Development,* 179.

20 Ibid., 149; John Robinson, "Future Subjunctive: Backcasting as Social Learning,"
Futures 35, no. 8 (2003): 839–56, doi: 10.1016/S0016-3287(03)00039-9.

21 In the Keeyask case, assessment of regional cumulative effects in the Nelson
watershed and beyond was recognized as an issue but left to the future. See
Manitoba Clean Environment Commission, *Report on Public Hearing: Keeyask
Generation Project* (Winnipeg: Manitoba Clean Environment Commission, 2014),
ch. 12; Peter Duinker and Lorne Greig, "The Impotence of Cumulative Effects
Assessment in Canada: Ailments and Ideas for Redeployment," *Environmental
Management* 37, no. 2 (2006): 153–61, https://doi.org/10.1007/s00267-004-0240-5.

22 Philippe Dunsky, Martin Poirier, Brent Langille, Marina Malkova, and Bruno
Gobeil, "The Role and Value of Demand-Side Management in Manitoba Hydro's
Resource Planning Process," report submitted to the Manitoba Public Utilities
Board for Consumers' Association of Canada (Manitoba) and Green Action Centre
(February 2014).

23 World Commission on Dams, *Dams and Development,* 221.

24 Manitoba, *Manitoba Clean Energy Strategy.*

25 David B. Brooks and Sean Casey, "A Guide to Soft Energy Studies," *Alternatives*
8, no. 3/4 (1979): 10–26; Denton E. Morrison and Dora G. Lodwick, "The Social
Impacts of Soft and Hard Energy Systems: The Lovins' Claims as a Social Science
Challenge," *Annual Review of Energy* 6, no. 1 (1981): 357–78.

26 Mark Z. Jacobson, Mark A. Delucchi, Zack A.F. Bauer, Savannah C. Goodman,
William E. Chapman, Mary A. Cameron, Cedric Bozonnat et al., "100% Clean
and Renewable Wind, Water, and Sunlight All-Sector Energy Roadmaps for 139
Countries of the World," *Joule* 1, no. 1 (6 September 2017): 108–21.

27 Frans Berkhout, "Innovation Theory and Socio-Technical Transitions," in *Managing
the Transition to Renewable Energy: Theory and Practice from Local, Regional and
Macro Perspectives,* ed. Jeroen C.J.M. van den Bergh and Frank R. Bruinsma
(Cheltenham, UK: Edward Elgar Publishing, 2008), 129–47.

28 Some recent initiatives seeking to delineate pathways to meeting climate change
mitigation commitments have identified major expansion hydropower as a key
means of replacing fossil-based energy. See, for example, Trottier Energy Futures
Project, *Canada's Challenge and Opportunity: Transformations for Major Reductions
in GHG Emissions* (Vancouver: David Suzuki Foundation and Canadian Academy
of Engineering, 2016), https://davidsuzuki.org/wp-content/uploads/2017/09/
REPORT-canada-challenge-opportunity-transformations-major-reductions-
GHG-emissions.pdf.

29 Fox Lake Cree Nation, *Environment Evaluation Report,* September 2012, https://keeyask.com/wp-content/uploads/2012/07/FLCN-Environment-Evaluation-Report_Sept_2012.pdf.

30 York Factory First Nation, *KIPEKISKWAYWINAN: Our Voices,* June 2012, 24, https://keeyask.com/wp-content/uploads/2012/07/Kipekiskwaywinan_Our-Voices_June_2012_Part-2.pdf.

31 United Nations Declaration on the Rights of Indigenous Peoples, General Assembly Resolution 295, 61st Sess, A/RES/61/295, 2007, https://www.un.org/development/desa/indigenouspeoples/declaration-on-the-rights-of-indigenous-peoples.html.

32 Kyrke Gaudreau and Robert B. Gibson, *Framework for Sustainability-Based Assessment for the Keeyask Hydro Project* (Winnipeg: Consumers Association of Canada—Manitoba Branch, 2013); Kyrke Gaudreau and Robert B. Gibson, *Framework for Sustainability-Based Assessment for the Public Utilities Board's Needs For and Alternatives To (NFAT) Assessment of Manitoba Hydro's Preferred Development Plan and Alternatives* (Winnipeg: Consumers Association of Canada [Manitoba], 2014).

33 Ibid.

34 The Keeyask Cree Nations "environmental evaluation reports," which cover a broader agenda than the title suggests, are available online at https://keeyask.com/project-timeline/environment-assessment-process/activites/keeyask-cree-nations-enviro-evaluation-reports/.

35 Keeyask Hydropower Limited Partnership, *Keeyask Generation Project Environmental Impact Statement: Executive Summary Part 1.* (Winnipeg: Keeyask Hydropower Limited Partnership, 2012), ch. 9.

36 The individual objectives were drawn from the province's "Principles of and Guidelines for Sustainable Development" (Manitoba, Sustainable Development Act); the federal government's "Sustainable Development Strategy Goals" (Environment Canada, *Planning for a Sustainable Future: A Federal Sustainable Development Strategy for Canada,* 2010, https://publications.gc.ca/site/eng/450571/publication.html; and Manitoba Hydro's own Policies/Principles of Sustainable Development (Manitoba Hydro, *Sustainable Development Policy/Principles*).

37 CEC, *Report on Public Hearing,* 149–55.

38 Ibid., 159.

39 Manitoba Public Utilities Board, *Needs For and Alternatives To (NFAT): Review of Manitoba Hydro's Preferred Development Plan,* Winnipeg, June 2014, www.pubmanitoba.ca/v1/nfat/pdf/finalreport_pdp.pdf.

40 The Clean Environment Commission and the Public Utilities Board make recommendations to the Manitoba government, which makes the final decisions on reviewed cases.

> " We were raised to respect, love, protect the land. We used the land, animals and water as a gift from our Creator."

Janet McIvor and Mary Wavey, Split Lake/TCN,
CEC hearings (8 October 2013), 19

CONCLUSION

Pathways to a Better Legacy
of Development in Northern Manitoba

JILL BLAKLEY AND AIMÉE CRAFT

Hydroelectricity has been a driving economic force in Manitoba since the turn of the century and more intensively in the North in the last sixty years. It is the subject of environmental, economic, and social concern for all Manitobans, and particularly for Indigenous people affected by the complex web of development projects that have emerged one after another. Nations, communities, families, and individuals have seen their landscapes and waterways change dramatically over time and been affected by these changes—sometimes four generations within the same family.[1]

Through the lens of the Keeyask hydroelectric development project on the Nelson River, beyond the conclusion of the Clean Environment Commission's (CEC) environmental assessment hearings, we have sought to bring back into focus a question of provincial importance: Should the Keeyask Dam have been built? As community members, Knowledge Keepers, technicians, expert witnesses, and lawyers, we have asked: What is our personal and shared understanding and ex-perience of hydroelectric and other forms of development in northern Manitoba—past, present, and future? How have these projects benefited economies and who have they benefited? What are some of the lasting legacies of development, both positive and negative? What is the cumu-lative impact on the environment in the Nelson River sub-watershed? Can Indigenous partnership building serve as a model for collaborative resource development? What are the sustainability concerns unique to northern environments and people that policy makers must keep in mind? And, what would constitute "good hydroelectric development" in northern Manitoba and areas like it around the world?

Our authors have provided many useful observations and specific directives that are pertinent to future project hearings and development decisions in northern Manitoba. To begin, Byron Williams urges the government to find ways to democratize environmental oversight to better protect vulnerable communities and reminds us that Manitoba's highly politicized regulatory review process ultimately gave a green light of approval to a series of high-risk projects, particularly Keeyask. Will Braun agrees, believing the entire "commit-first-review-later" process must be reversed for any future projects.

James Robson contends that "fixing" impact assessment in cross-cultural settings will need to involve acknowledging that the regulatory test for significance, and the use of valued environmental components (VECs), sits awkwardly with a relational Indigenous world view, as does using offsetting programs that undermine the importance of place to local people. He suggests it will also have much to do with restructuring the very institutions, practices, and assumptions that underlie impact assessment itself.

In conversation with Noah Massan, Agnieszka Pawlowska-Mainville conveys that the time has come to deconstruct and maybe even reconstruct Hydro's metanarrative of progress. Braun similarly feels the government must do more to act as facilitator of mature, nuanced public discussion rather than pushing a narrow, oversimplified narrative. In this vein, Annette Luttermann aptly points out that hydroelectricity has long been marketed to the general public as "green" power since it is generated by harnessing the flow of water to spin turbines. The global cycle recirculates water, constantly returning it to rivers, and thus hydroelectricity is described as "renewable" compared with burning fossil fuels. However, she believes it is also essential to acknowledge the direct, widespread, and long-term negative environmental and social justice consequences that are related to river regulation, and to acknowledge the considerable uncertainties in attempting to mitigate adverse effects in complex ecological systems. Joseph Dipple challenges the dominant narrative of the partnership approach, arguing it has failed to address a fuller, more socially just meaning of "social licence" and rather is representative of an industrial and managerial viewpoint on how to address costs faced by communities. It also failed to consider the prospect of irreplaceable costs, such as relationships with the land, cultural activities, and human lives. He concludes that for social licence to be meaningful in the lives of affected community members, it must at minimum use a model of free, prior, and informed consent, and be reviewed throughout the process of construction and operation of any natural resource extraction or exploitation project.

A new narrative must also acknowledge the complexities that exist regarding the loss of knowledge and feelings of guilt that individuals and communities endure, some of which are party to the partnership model. Pawlowska-Mainville, in conversation with Massan, captures this well, saying that once the environment of the area is lost, the knowledge of the area is lost and few may have the opportunity to learn what was there. Massan reasons that no one will ever be able to access the knowledge of the area in the same way it took generations of individuals to learn about it through an interdependent relationship. Due to the immense loss of knowledge, then, the project is not about progressing forward but about being set back; a lot of new history must be relearned and recreated in a Manitoba Hydro–controlled space. Massan states: "I worked for Hydro, me. I helped destroy my community."

Several authors urge taking the long view of environmental protection and consequences of development. Braun, and Patricia Fitzpatrick, Alan P. Diduck, and James P. Robson identify the continued need to address upstream impacts related to the Churchill River Diversion as well as Lake Winnipeg regulation, and particularly to understand, and make public, the true environmental and social costs that northerners continue to pay for inexpensive electricity. James Schaefer explains that to conserve caribou, we must consider more than the short-term and the immediate; we must embrace whole landscapes and multiple decades. He casts caribou as a call to something even bigger: the opportunity to adopt a broader view of how we gauge success and an invitation to a world view that is expansive, forward-looking, and hopeful. He believes caribou can serve as a mark of our real accomplishments, if only we choose to scale up our thinking to match their biology. Kyrke Gaudreau and Robert Gibson, Luttermann, and Fitzpatrick et al. all suggest that far more data/information are needed, now and over time, with effective monitoring, to gain a clearer picture of whether the Keeyask Project is likely to make a positive overall contribution to sustainability.

Several broader observations have also come to light through our collective examination of the Keeyask experience, and we offer these below. These insights might be considered as principles upon which to base future development activity in northern Manitoba and in similar situations elsewhere.

A better legacy of development in areas rich in natural resources and therefore subject to development pressures should involve a sustained effort to establish truth about the harms of past development and to work towards reconciliation with the people and communities affected. According to the Truth and Reconciliation Commission of Canada (TRC), this is about doing whatever is needed to establish (in many regions for the first time) and maintain a mutually respectful relationship between Indigenous and non-Indigenous peoples, including the Crown (federal, provincial, territorial, and other agents of the Crown such as Manitoba Hydro).[2] At a minimum this involves being aware of the past, acknowledging the harm inflicted, and seeking atonement, followed by actions that result in real societal change.[3] In the context of environmental impact assessment, that could mean requiring, in the terms of reference for future projects' Environmental Impact Statements, that the proponent describe any planned or existing truth and reconciliation measures that coincide with the project or past projects, or delaying further construction of the project until they have instituted a truth and reconciliation process. This reflects the earlier recommendation of the Manitoba Clean Environment Commission, following the Bipole III project hearing, to implement a reconciliation process.

More generally, the Province of Manitoba, Manitoba Hydro, and all other stakeholders must address the impacts of the past in order to move forward with the ethical development, distribution, and sale of hydroelectric energy in Manitoba and beyond its borders. Apologies and meaningful reparation for past damages must be discussed between all parties. The Northern Flood Agreement must be given full effect for signatory communities, and further agreements must be negotiated with other impacted and not-yet-compensated communities.

Foundational to truth, reconciliation, and meaningful relationships is institutional honesty. Manitoba Hydro is not a homogenous organization in that there are many voices within it, and many perspectives on what might constitute good development and how best to achieve it alongside the goals of a corporation and its board of directors. Hierarchical organizations, by nature, tend to edit and filter information as it moves up and down the chain of communication, even suppressing certain knowledge as it passes from one organizational level to the next.[4] There is a known bias toward screening out certain types of information from upward transmission; as well, low trust in the message's receiver results in senders suppressing significantly more information, particularly when the information might reflect unfavourably upon the sender.[5] As Gerald Feltham and Christian Hofmann report, "Restricting the dissemination of information within organizations or releasing aggregated rather than specific information are two efficient [and common] avenues to suppress information."[6] What mechanisms does the Crown corporation have in place, and who is responsible to ensure that the truth, or truths, are wholly stated without reservation, and also made externally accessible to the public?

Corporate honesty in environmental decision making is critical because it factors into corporate credibility. Researchers have established that accepting blame for poor firm performance is in fact highly valued by investors.[7] What Manitobans need is an increased level of forthcomingness that meets or exceeds the expectations of those affected by the corporation's actions, informed by principles of institutional design for greater accountability.[8] A simple example might be that Manitoba Hydro host opportunities for their scientists and the scientists representing intervenor groups from its public hearings to communicate openly with one another, as well as with Indigenous and local Knowledge Keepers about predicted impacts and cumulative effects—*well ahead of the formal project hearing process*—to foster relationships and mutual learning, and to build more informed, balanced perspectives among all parties. It is also heightened in cases where the corporation acts as an agent of the Crown in the context of Indigenous–Crown relations.

A general shift in perspective is needed to ensure a better legacy of development in northern Manitoba. It is still a challenge in Canada for government and corporations to view northern and hinterland areas as homelands and multi-dimensional ecosystems, rather than as simple storehouses or repositories of natural resources. In his seminal work

Northern Frontier, Northern Homelands, Justice Thomas Berger in the late 1970s brought the concept of the Canadian North as "homeland" to southerners' attention and succeeded in alerting the public and governments to the deleterious effects of megaprojects and the need for balanced development.[9] Manitoba government leaders and decision makers need to shift their perspective to ensure they view the Nelson River, Lake Winnipeg, and all waters connected and affected by the northern hydroelectric complex within the context of responsible water management provincially and globally. This means implementing integrated watershed management and planning in the province in concrete ways, with bold strides to bridge the sharp land/water policy divide that has been entrenched since the advent of the grid road system in Manitoba in the late nineteenth century.[10]

In the future, achieving well-balanced, well-paced, integrated development will depend on decision makers' willingness to engage in collaborative, strategic visioning exercises about cumulative impacts and the future of a homeland region, in light of both Indigenous rights and needs and provincial, territorial, and national development agendas. Regional-scale, strategic environmental assessment provides a potential framework to undertake such work. To date, Manitoba has no formal development policy or vision for the North, or a northern or provincial energy strategy. Part of visioning means giving communities a voice in championing energy alternatives (demand-side management, supply efficiency, new supply options, novel supply mixes, and so on).

It is also necessary (and challenging) to shift the view of hydroelectric development in northern Manitoba away from the perception that it is a series of discrete projects, when in fact it has been and will continue to be a tightly integrated program of development. We must work toward communicating about new projects more honestly, acknowledging them as part of an ongoing, hundred-year energy and economic development program (if both past and potential future projects are taken into account); an interconnected system of megaprojects. The tendency has been to assess one project at a time and speak of each as though it were discrete: considering the Keeyask Dam separate from the Bipole III transmission line, even though the new transmission line will carry Keeyask's power south and eventually to the United States. The tendency has also been to distinguish and hive off the Lake Winnipeg regulation project from the Nelson River hydro complex to the north, even though they are connected by a diversion channel established to optimize power along the Nelson River. The same is true about hiving off the Nelson River dams from the Churchill River Diversion and the augmented flow program. Taking a holistic view of the total impacts of a development program is ultimately the only way to give a true account of the truth of past harms. It is the cumulative effects of all development that ultimately matters when estimating both the general viability and specific health status of northern people, communities, and ecosystems.

One of the most important lessons emerging from the Keeyask experience is how early some pieces of the project were approved, thus tipping the balance toward project approval without sufficient public input or "exit ramps" in place. There was little flexibility and few opportunities to backtrack in response to changing fiscal and political project conditions, which tend to plague megaprojects in the current global economy. As Bent Flyvbjerg states in his article about megaprojects, "Frequently, there is over-commitment to a certain [mega] project concept at an early stage, resulting in 'lock-in' or 'capture,' leaving analyses of alternatives weak or absent, and leading to escalated commitment in later stages. 'Fail fast' does not apply; 'fail slow' does."[11] Overcommitment in the early stages of megaproject development is often the result of a common mistake: overestimating the benefits of the project while underestimating costs. This results in a falsely high benefit-cost ratio for the project.[12] This may mean that a project is started despite the fact it will ultimately prove not to be financially and economically viable, or that one project may be started instead of another that could have yielded higher returns, had the real costs and benefits of both projects been known.[13] Many projects also become increasingly socially and environmentally unviable, as the true magnitude of their impacts become clearer. Approximately one in ten megaprojects is on budget, one in ten is on schedule, and one in ten delivers the promised benefits, and, according to Flyvbjerg, "approximately one in one thousand projects is a success, defined as 'on target' for all three."[14]

This becomes all the more relevant where, in the context of past development without Indigenous consent, resource development is now predicated on a partnership model that should benefit impacted communities and people. The Keeyask model proposed a unique model for collaborative resource development and decision making, which is essential for those with a stake in the future sustainability of the region in question. However, we must question the facts of decision-making power in the context of partnership development and probe the economic power of the respective parties in general and in relation to each other. This includes the economic partners and ultimately their constituents (in the case of First Nations, their citizens, and, in the case of Manitoba Hydro, all Manitobans). We must also consider and account for the many Indigenous parties and other affected northerners either not privy to or in support of the Keeyask partnership model. While Tataskweyak Cree Nation and War Lake First Nation (also known as the Cree Nation Partners) indicated in their environmental evaluation that they expected their relationship with their ancestral homeland to improve after the project,[15] these are not uniformly held views in these communities. Further, the depth of social, relational, and spiritual impacts could not be fully measured in the Keeyask Environmental Impact Statement or the Cree partners' environmental evaluations, and these perspectives were not fully considered in the decision making about the Keeyask Project.

We must also reconsider how development projects are assessed in an evolving context of Indigenous rights internationally and domestically, including the application of the doctrine of free, prior, and informed consent of Indigenous people in relation to development within their lands, territories, and waters. David Rossiter and Patricia Wood stress that Indigenous experiences in Canada must be "understood as a series of situated and grounded experiences of colonialism and capitalist production."[16] This requires engagement with concepts like the Honour of the Crown that permeate the whole of the relationship between Indigenous people and the Crown (including Crown corporations such as Manitoba Hydro) and require a standard of conduct that upholds the constitutional recognition and affirmation of Treaty and Aboriginal rights. It also requires careful consideration of Indigenous norms and legal principles that are to be equally weighted with common law property law concepts when considering Indigenous interests.[17]

Turning to the assessment process, what is the "sweet spot" in terms of how much information we need to make better development decisions, and how can we improve the mechanisms, power imbalance, and transparency in joint decision making? How do we reconcile the financial reality of running a Crown corporation, and the need to ensure an uninterrupted power supply, with the equally important reality that there are many other social and environmental dimensions to good development, including gender- and health-based impacts, and the need for climate responsibility? The challenge of sustainable development in the twenty-first century is to simultaneously solve a business dilemma and an environmental management dilemma. This also begs us to think about the deeper underlying question of the ultimate benefit of these hydroelectric megaprojects. Whose interests are they serving? Are they necessary? Who have they benefited in the past? Who do they benefit now and later? Who have they harmed? And who will they impact in the future? Manitoba Hydro as a Crown corporation has both corporate duties and duties to all consumers and citizens of Manitoba. How are these duties defined and how are benefits considered? How are relationships measured over time? What are the desired outcomes for the residents and environment of northern Manitoba in the future, and are these fundamentally different from what they were at the onset of hydro development, given the now significant impact to the region, and how do we connect these values with a given project assessment?

While the answers to such questions are clearly complex, the Keeyask experience suggests that the current "court-like" quasi-judicial administrative public hearing process model that typifies environmental assessment in Canada is perhaps not the most effective way to facilitate the constructive exchange of information or unity between otherwise different cultures and world views. Given that it is almost impossible to know if the "right" information has been procured to make "sound" predictions, the hearing process could shift to include activities that emphasize the relationship building and mutual learning aspects of environmental assessment and facilitate networked dialogue. Others have called for a more interactive format of consultation/engagement/consent that is still highly structured (has a clear agenda), yet far less formal or adversarial ("walks in the woods").[18] The director of the Public Interest Law Centre of Manitoba notes that the Fox Lake, Tataskweyak, War Lake (Cree Nation Partners), and York Factory Cree world view processes and the deliberations of the Public Utilities Board were quite effective relative to the formal CEC Keeyask hearing, although very different in format.[19] Both recognized the value of distinct voices, the need to provide proper resources to enable these distinct voices to be heard, and that Manitoba Hydro and the government of Manitoba did not have a monopoly on the truth.[20]

The Keeyask experience underscores the continuing need to adopt a more holistic, regional-scale view of the environment when assessing the impacts of any piece of a megaproject development program. In the earliest days of environmental assessment, the process was heavily criticized for being unfocused, unscientific, lacking in standardization, and, perhaps worst of all, politically motivated.[21] Many engaged in project hearings were dissuaded from participating fully by the voluminous Environmental Impact Statements, which often numbered in the thousands of pages, particularly those people lacking the scientific and technical parlance to understand and effectively respond to them. The EIS introduced the concept of a valued ecosystem component (VEC) as a way to focus the assessment not on "everything" but rather on the most important aspects of the environment perturbed by a project. However, it was seen as equally important to consider impacts on functional ecological relationships whenever possible[22] and to focus the assessment at biological levels higher than the population level—as Gordon Beanlands and Peter Duinker describe in their framework for ecological assessment, "the level at which our ability to predict or measure changes due to human activity is often weakest."[23] This advice was never more relevant than it is for the Nelson River sub-watershed, where hydro projects have direct impacts not only on VECs such as sturgeon but also through ecological relationships that unfold over space and time on the land, in the air, in the forests, and in communities. Knowing that the regional project environment has been significantly altered, *what is assessed and by whom* becomes ever more important. Our ability to make the connections among multiple projects, assess and protect ecosystem services, establish and adhere to environmental thresholds and limits when available, consider past and future impacts on Indigenous communities and people within their socio-legal frameworks, and handle the uncertainties created by disparate sets of data and historical data gaps will in no small part define the success of environmental assessment in the future.

Looking ahead, a better legacy of hydroelectric development in northern Manitoba and regions like it is possible. As pointed out by the World Commission on Dams, although dam building has made an undeniably significant contribution to human development, in too many cases an unacceptable and often unnecessary price has been paid by downstream communities, taxpayers, and the natural environment.[24]

Changing this legacy involves acknowledging the past litany of damages that have affected so many areas around the world, including community displacement, lost livelihoods, damaged ecosystems and drowned wildlife, massive debt burdens and unrealized benefits, and, in some cases, serious human rights violations.[25]

The ultimate questions related to any public hearing process remain, however: What is the appropriate process for gathering and considering different forms of knowledge relating to the potential impacts and benefits of a project, relating to a range of factors; and what are the values, policies, and principles that inform the decision making? And whose process, whose values, and whose decision making is at play? As argued in this book, Indigenous systems of evaluation and decision making must be central to any analysis of the merits of future and ongoing hydroelectric development in Manitoba.

The World Commission on Dams has emphasized that such legacies can be changed by achieving the following benchmark: "Outstanding social issues associated with existing large dams are identified and assessed; processes and mechanisms are developed with affected communities to remedy them."[26] Manitoba and Manitoba Hydro have taken important first steps in this regard through public apology and a commitment to regional cumulative effects assessment in the Nelson River sub-watershed. After many decades of dam building and development in the North, the conversation and the work ahead have only just begun. When further development is proposed within the region, as it most certainly will be, it should be held to a higher standard that engages with some of the ideas expressed in this volume, and others that will be brought forward by those people and communities most directly impacted.

Notes

1 Ramona Neckoway, personal communication, 2019.
2 John Ralston Saul, "Truth and Reconciliation Is Canada's Last Chance to Get it Right," *Globe and Mail*, 15 May 2018.
3 Truth and Reconciliation Commission of Canada, *Honouring the Truth, Reconciling for the Future: Summary of the Final Report of the Truth and Reconciliation Commission of Canada* (Ottawa: Government of Canada, 2015), accessed 18 June 2019, http://www.trc.ca/assets/pdf/Honouring_the_Truth_Reconciling_for_the_Future_July_23_2015.pdf.
4 Charles O'Reilly III, "The Intentional Distortion of Information in Organizational Communication: A Laboratory and Field Investigation," *Human Relations* 31, no. 2 (1978): 173–93.

5   Ibid.

6   Gerald Feltham and Christian Hofmann, "Information Suppression in Multi-Agent Contracting," *Review of Accounting Studies* 17 (2012): 254.

7   Don Chance, James Cicon, and Stephen P. Ferris, "Poor Performance and the Value of Corporate Honesty," *Journal of Corporate Finance* 33 (2015): 1–18.

8   Bent Flyvbjerg, "What You Should Know about Megaprojects and Why: An Overview," *Project Management Journal* 45, no. 2 (2014): 6–19.

9   Shelagh D. Grant, "Myths of the North in the Canadian Ethos," *Northern Review* 3, no. 4 (1989): n.p.

10 Henry Venema, Bryan Oborne, and Cynthia Neudoerffer, *The Manitoba Challenge: Linking Water and Land Management for Climate Adaptation* (Winnipeg: International Institute for Sustainable Development, 2010).

11 Flyvbjerg, "What You Should Know," 9.

12 Flyvbjerg, "What You Should Know."

13 Ibid.

14 Ibid., 11.

15 See sec. 11.3.4 of the Keeyask Environmental Evaluation completed by the Tataskweyak Cree Nation and War Lake First Nation, 2012, https://keeyask.com/wp-content/uploads/2012/07/CNP-Keeyask-Environmental-Evaluation-Web-Jan2012.pdf.

16 David Rossiter and Patricia Wood, "Fantastic Topographies: Neo-Liberal Responses to Aboriginal Land Claims in British Columbia," *Canadian Geographer/Le Géographe canadien* 49, no. 4 (2005): 352.

17 Reference to the Tsilhqot'in decision, *Tsilhqot'in Nation v. Bristish Columbia*, 2014 SCC 44.

18 Jennifer M. Stewart and A. John Sinclair, "Meaningful Public Participation in Environmental Assessment: Perspectives from Canadian Participants, Proponents, and Government," *Journal of Environmental Assessment Policy and Management* 9, no. 2 (2007): 161–83.

19 Byron Williams, personal communication, 2019.

20 Ibid.

21 Gordon E. Beanlands and Peter N. Duinker, *An Ecological Framework for Environmental Impact Assessment in Canada* (Halifax: Institute for Resource and Environmental Studies, Dalhousie University, and Federal Environmental Assessment Review Office, 1983).

22 Ibid.

23 Ibid., 5.

24 American University International Law Review, "The Report of the World Commission on Dams—Executive Summary," *American University International Law Review* 16, no. 6 (2001): 1435–52.

25 International Rivers Network, *The World Bank's Big Dam Legacy*, 2007, accessed 28 February 2019, https://www.internationalrivers.org/sites/default/files/attached-files/the_world_banks_big_dam_legacy.pdf.

26 Aviva Imhof, Susanne Wong, and Peter Bosshard, *Citizens' Guide to the World Commission on Dams* (Berkeley: International Rivers Network, 2002), accessed 11 May 2021, https://www.irn.org/files/wcd/wcdguide.pdf.

The Government of Manitoba's Apology

GREG SELINGER, FORMER PREMIER OF MANITOBA AND MLA FOR ST. BONIFACE
Pimicikamak Okimawin, 20 January 2015

Hydroelectricity is a reliable, sustainable, and secure source of energy for Manitoba. But as with all sources of energy, there are environmental effects of hydroelectric development. These effects include changes in water levels and flows on water bodies, particularly in Manitoba's north and in areas where Aboriginal people have lived for generations before European settlement and industrial development.

The reliable supply of renewable hydroelectric power with a low carbon footprint from Manitoba Hydro projects on the Winnipeg River, the Grand Rapids Project, and the Lake Winnipeg Regulation and Churchill River Diversion projects have been a great benefit to Manitobans. But we have discovered that the environmental effects of such projects were not considered fully, and the nature and extent of the effects were uncertain and unknown at the time the projects were developed.

We now have a growing appreciation of how important lands and waters are to the economies and cultures of Manitoba's Aboriginal peoples. Hydroelectricity development has changed the water regimes on some lakes and rivers and we now understand how significantly this affects many Aboriginal communities. The effects of hydro projects include effects on transportation in summer and winter, effects on hunting and trapping, effects on fishing, effects on water quality, and in some cases, includes significant flooding of First Nation reserve land and other lands traditionally used by Aboriginal people.

The effects are more than just those on land and water and on plants and animals. We recognize that hydro development can affect the cultural identities of Aboriginal peoples because of the close relationship of Aboriginal peoples to the land and resources.

Although some studies were conducted before these hydroelectric projects were developed, and measures were taken, these projects were developed at a time where the effects on Aboriginal peoples were not fully understood.

The studies commissioned by the Canada/Manitoba Lake Winnipeg, Churchill and Nelson Rivers Study Board (1971–75) considered the potential effects of the Lake Winnipeg Regulation and Churchill River Diversion projects then being developed. These studies and the summary report of the board were considered by many at the time to be state of the art in assessing the impacts of a project of the broad scope of the Lake Winnipeg Regulation and Churchill River Diversion projects.

However, looking back now it is clear that the interests of the Aboriginal peoples, particularly in the north, were not fully considered.

Further, these projects were developed before the recognition of the Crown's duty of consultation with Aboriginal peoples and before principles of environmental assessment and licensing were established in law. As a result, First Nations, Métis communities, and other Aboriginal communities were not fully consulted about these projects before they were developed. Canada, Manitoba, and Manitoba Hydro did not have the benefit of a comprehensive understanding of the issues and concerns of Aboriginal peoples and of potential ways to address those concerns from the people themselves.

Looking back on what has happened, and on the effects on Aboriginal communities in Manitoba, I wish now on behalf of the government of Manitoba to express my sincere apology to Aboriginal peoples affected by hydro development.

The Canadian Charter of Rights and Freedoms recognizes basic rights of liberty, democracy, and equality. Our constitution also recognizes the Aboriginal rights and the treaty rights of our Aboriginal peoples.

In December 2000, in a statement in the Manitoba Legislative Assembly, the Honourable Eric Robinson, Minister of Aboriginal and Northern Affairs, recognized the Northern Flood Agreement as a modern-day treaty. Minister Robinson also committed to an open, fair, and honest relationship with the five Northern Flood Agreement First Nations on a government-to-government basis. This was reaffirmed in the Manitoba Legislature in December 2014. On behalf of the government, I restate this commitment and hope that this statement will help us to continue to develop this relationship in a spirit of reconciliation.

We can also continue to learn from the Royal Commission on Aboriginal Peoples, the Manitoba Aboriginal Justice Inquiry, and the Aboriginal Justice Implementation Commission, and from our experience.

The Governments of Canada and Manitoba, and Manitoba Hydro, have negotiated comprehensive agreements with the NFA First Nations: Tataskweyak Cree Nation, York Factory First Nation, Nisichawayasihk Cree Nation, and Norway House Cree Nation. Manitoba and Manitoba Hydro also have entered into Comprehensive Forebay Agreements with the Mosakahiken and Chemawawin First Nations and the Moose Lake and Easterville communities. An agreement was reached in 1992 addressing the adverse effects of hydro development at the South Indian Lake community (now O-Pipon-Na-Piwin Cree Nation). An agreement addressing adverse effects of hydro development on Fox Lake Cree Nation was reached in 2004 and one with War Lake First Nation in 2005.

Many other agreements also have been reached with First Nations, communities, and resource users, and programs have been developed to address the effects of hydro development. Amongst others, Manitoba Hydro has entered into agreements intended to foster improved relationships with Chemawawin Cree Nation, Misipawistik Cree Nation, Mosakahiken Cree Nation, and Opaskwayak Cree Nation.

In November 2014, Manitoba, Manitoba Hydro, and the Manitoba Metis Federation entered into the Kwaysh-kin-na-mihk la paazh "Turning the Page" Agreement that will provide for an improved relationship with the Metis relating to hydro projects as it addressed the MMF concerns related to Hydro's past developments.

In December 2014, Manitoba and Manitoba Hydro entered into a Process Agreement with Pimicikamak (on its own behalf and on behalf of Cross Lake First Nation). The Process Agreement provides for those parties to work together on identified NFA relationship and policy issues. Importantly, the Process Agreement recognizes that the parties will work in a government-to-government relationship and in a spirit of reconciliation, mutual respect, good faith, openness, and accountability.

Manitoba Hydro is a Crown corporation of the Government of Manitoba. Manitoba Hydro is responsible for providing the continuous supply of energy to meet the needs of the province and to promote economy and efficiency in the development, generation, transmission, distribution, supply, and end-use of energy. Manitoba Hydro strives to operate in a socially and environmentally responsible way as befits its status as a Crown corporation. An important part of Manitoba Hydro's responsibility is to work with Aboriginal peoples to mitigate and address adverse effects on communities as part of this spirit of reconciliation.

The Government of Manitoba and Manitoba Hydro are also committed to providing opportunities for Aboriginal people and Aboriginal-owned business to participate in employment and business opportunities arising from Manitoba Hydro projects. Manitoba Hydro's partnership arrangements with First Nations on the Wuskwatim and Keeyask projects demonstrate a new way of doing business.

Although many initiatives have been undertaken to address adverse effects of hydro development, we recognize that reconciliation is an ongoing process and are committed to work with communities toward building respectful relationships.

I again express my apology on behalf of the Manitoba government.

Source: https://hydrojustice.org/2015/06/25/test-2/.

Comments on the Official Apology for Harms Caused by the Hydropower System

CHIEF CATHY MERRICK, PIMICIKAMAK OKIMAWIN
Pimicikamak Okimawin, 20 January 2015

On behalf of the Pimicikamak nation, I welcome the apology just spoken by Greg Selinger, Premier of Manitoba.

I thank you, Mr. Premier, for coming here to our traditional land to offer these words.

This is an important day for Pimicikamak and for Manitoba. This is an important step in reconciling our relationship.

This is a day our people will remember.

Today's apology is consistent with our national policy of healing Pimicikamak traditional territory, healing Pimicikamak people and healing Pimicikamak as a nation.

According to our ways, we stand here today before the Creator—the Creator who put a wild and free-flowing river in this land, the Creator who gave our people the sacred responsibility to care for these lands and waters, the Creator who can put love and respect in all of our hearts.

We are here today because many years ago Manitoba Hydro, with the permission of the governments of Manitoba and Canada, dammed the veins of our mother Earth. The changes began more than 50 years ago when the Kelsey dam was built in the Nelson River—Kichi Sipi—which flows through the heart of our nation. That dam affects a long stretch of the river as well as what is known today Sipiwesk Lake, one of our most important lakes.

Some of our people were forcibly displaced when Sipiwesk was flooded. Graves along the lakeshore have been exposed, disturbed and in some cases washed away.

In the '70s, another dam was put in Kichi Sipi—Jenpeg. This dam has caused both flooding and low water. It has disturbed the natural balance of seasonal fluctuations and has turned part of our territory into a floodway at times.

Pimicikamak citizens have died as a result of dangerous ice and floating debris caused by Jenpeg.

The hydro project has also contributed to mass unemployment and mass poverty for our people. It has piled on top of the other difficulties we have faced.

It is not possible to capture in words the damage done. Much of the harm is irreparable. It has forever changed our ways of life and our health. For us, hydropower is not clean.

Many elders have passed away without ever hearing what we heard today. We cannot do anything about that now. We can only honour their memory by working to make things better.

Nothing will truly replace what we have lost. That is a bitter reality we must live with. All we can do is stand here today to let out the grief and to heal our nation. Mr. Premier, you have contributed to that healing today.

We are here today because on 16 October 2014 several hundred of our citizens went to Jenpeg. They were upset. They were fed up. They were determined. And they sent a clear message: This is our home; we demand to be treated with respect; and things must change.

October 16 is another day our people will remember.

In the weeks that followed, many of our people spent a lot of time at Jenpeg. They organized events, they tended the fires, they spent nights there in the cold. I thank and honour everyone who contributed to that stand, including the people who were there in spirit.

I also want to acknowledge that our actions at Jenpeg created hardships for individual workers at the facility and their families. I humbly ask for your understanding.

Jenpeg is a prominent part of our history and our homeland. The dam will always be a symbol of loss for us, but now it is also a reminder of the strength and determination we demonstrated there.

Today's apology is an important symbol of that sort of shift from hurt to healing. It symbolizes new relationship. The apology does not fix the past. It does not even fix the present. Our lands, waters and resources are still a mess. Our people still lack a fair share of the opportunity generated by the river. Our people still have to face debilitating hydro bills.

But what this apology does, is create the foundation for a better future. It does not create that future, but it creates a foundation. Now we have to build that future together. The process ahead can be a turning point for our nation. It can have a direct impact on the well-being of a great many of our people, as well as our lands.

Not all of our people are ready to accept an apology. Some people will need to see what follows this apology before they are ready to accept it. I understand that. That is the nature of apologies.

Mr. Premier, I want you to leave here today knowing that this is our home and we love it. We love it and we will protect it. We *must* protect it because it is our Mother. She is sick, but she is still our Mother.

I want you to leave here today feeling beyond any shadow of a doubt that the Pimicikamak people are proud; the Pimicikamak people are strong; the Pimicikamak people will stand tall.

Mr. Premier, I thank you again for travelling here to deliver this apology. I hope this is part of a healing journey for all of us.

I assure you again that this is a day our people will remember.

Ekosani. Thank you.

Source: https://hydrojustice.org/2015/06/25/test-2/.

APPENDIX 3

Excerpts from *Economic Review of Bipole III and Keeyask*

BRAD WALL, COMMISSIONER
November 2020

Since the approval of the Keeyask generating station, there has been one major commissioned review of the project by Brad Wall, former premier of Saskatchewan. This appendix includes selected passages and quotations from Mr. Wall's report that examine both the efficacy and the motivations behind the decision taken by the province of Manitoba and Manitoba Hydro to pursue Keeyask, and whether Keeyask was, indeed, a good idea.

What has become clear through this review is that all too often the otherwise thorough and insightful analysis, presentation, and decision-making functions for major capital projects proposed by Manitoba Hydro were constrained. These constraints influenced the path to a decision to the point where decisions became questions of "how can it continue?" rather than questions of "does this still make sense?" The constraints were put into place much earlier than one would expect and were supported throughout the past decade by action and sometimes inaction. (8)

What were the motivating goals that led to decisions that resulted in a $9.4 billion combined generation and transmission project becoming a $13.4 (8.7 + 4.7) billion project even as the reservoir at Keeyask was still uncharged as of the beginning of this review? (9)

The concept of "Manitoba's Oil" is an analogy that must be limited in its application to the sale of power to external parties. In that respect, Manitoba's citizens, and not a private sector interest, bear the risk not only as involuntary venture capitalists for generation capacity for the export market, but also as customers (and payors) of last resort of the monopoly, Manitoba Hydro. (9)

Politicians wanted this export story, the "hydro is our oil" story, to be true to provide continued justification for new hydroelectric projects and related developments even as costs grew rapidly. It was a signature economic development plan for Manitoba. (10)

The $1.2 billion spent prior to approval to proceed with Keeyask suggests that pre-planned off-ramps or even rigorous evaluation of pre-approval spending of public dollars were not substantially in place. . . . Cabinet documents point clearly to Keeyask as effectively a merchant dam for export, not as a project needed to meet domestic power demand. As domestic demand forecasts have waned in recent years, the domestic need for Keeyask is even less certain. (11)

Domestic demand will likely grow to require the generation capacity eventually, but until that time these projects will be at the mercy of the international market. The implications of these significant capital investments and long-term risks now rest on the bottom line of the Crown corporation, its customers and its shareholder, the Government of Manitoba. (11)

The most dramatic influence, however, came from the "locked in" nature and co-dependence of the two projects that are the subject of this review. Bipole III, as presented in its mega-project form beyond the simple backup transmission project became "locked in" in 2007 with the Government's decision to preclude an east side routing. Once this decision was made, Keeyask became not just possible, but fundamental to help justify the economics of the Bipole III project. In the same manner, Keeyask became "locked in" when the prospect of increased export demand became apparent and with government-approved export contracts in 2011 acknowledged that new hydroelectric power generation would be necessary to fulfill Manitoba Hydro's commitments under the contracts. (13)

... It has become clear from the efforts of this review that the forces in play that led to the development of Bipole III and Keeyask are much more systemic and are a reflection of the magnitude of the projects and the potential positive impact of their completion. This led decision makers to commit to an outcome far too early in the process without due consideration to the complexities and risk inherent in projects of this scope and size. When the inevitable realities began to appear as the projects progressed, the decision makers could see no way out and were forced to defend escalating costs, slipping timetables, and eroding financial benefits. This can lead, and in this case certainly led, to narrow, incremental decisions rather than a step back to look at the project holistically and with a firm resolve to ensuring that proceeding remained in the public's interest. (14)

The Commissioner does not believe that Bipole III was built solely for reliability. If that were the primary motivation it would have been built years earlier. Rather, Bipole III was built to facilitate the construction of new electrical generation which logically makes the timing of Bipole III almost completely dependent on the timing of Keeyask. By focusing attention on the reliability element, this project was separated from the approval process normally associated with projects of this size and its need and cost were disaggregated from the analysis of Keeyask during the NFAT [Needs For and Alternatives To]. Bipole III did improve the reliability of the Province's electrical grid, but its construction and in-service date were driven by the desire to build new generation. (16)

It is the Commissioner's finding that Keeyask was not necessary at the time of the NFAT to meet the Province's then-anticipated electrical needs in a timely and cost-effective manner. ...

The decision to proceed with Keeyask was driven by momentum from previous decisions including reputational risk from export agreements that *required* new generation when that generation had not been approved, "sunk costs" of $1.2 billion in infrastructure spending to support the project, and partnership agreements that had already been executed with First Nations after significant effort and good faith on their part. These prior decisions effectively pre-determined that Keeyask would proceed even though that was not the lowest cost option to meet domestic need at the time of the NFAT. (17)

The division of the two projects and the designation of Bipole III as a reliability project masked the co-dependent nature of the two projects and allowed a $4.7 billion project to proceed with just environmental review. [It is] noted that while the Bipole III and Keeyask projects were disaggregated for public and regulatory consumption, they were inextricably linked and could not exist without each other. This precluded a review of the projects as a whole with the entire proposed investment on the table. (28)

Recommendation #1.3: The Government should pursue Indigenous partnerships including equity, means of mitigating project impacts (e.g., modified routing within a preferred corridor), and other means of addressing concerns when a particular project is the most economical way of providing for the supply of power adequate for the needs of the Province, as opposed to rejecting the most economical option out of hand in favour of a more expensive option. (45)

Recommendation #2.3: The Government should be open to equity options or other opportunities with Indigenous partners for all activities, including transmission projects like Bipole III. In addition to helping to fulfill the goal of reconciliation, such partnerships with Indigenous peoples may help to ensure that projects can be completed on schedule and on budget by allowing Manitoba Hydro to proceed with its preferred development option without delays caused by Indigenous opposition. (61)

The lack of oversight by government allowed the projects to become firmly established and entrenched long before they were subjected to an independent review at which point—given the sunk costs and executed agreements—they were effectively a *fait accompli*. (68)

Source: Manitoba, Ministry of Crown Services, *Economic Review of Bipole III and Keeyask*, Brad Wall, Commissioner, vol. 1 (Winnipeg: Economic Review Commission, November 2020). https://manitoba.ca/asset_library/en/proactive/2020_2021/ERBK-Report-Volume1.PDF.

ABBREVIATIONS

AEA – Adverse Effects Agreement

ATK – Aboriginal Traditional Knowledge

CCME – Canadian Council of Ministers for the Environment

CEAA – Canadian Environmental Assessment Agency

CEA – Cumulative Effects Assessment

CEC – Clean Environment Commission

CED – Community Economic Development

CNP – Cree Nation Partners [Tataskweyak Cree Nation and War Lake First Nation]

COSEWIC – Committee on the Status of Endangered Wildlife in Canada

CRD – Churchill River Diversion

EA – Environmental Assessment

EE – Environmental Evaluation

EIS – Environmental Impact Statement

FLCN – Fox Lake Cree Nation

FPIC – Free, Prior, and Informed Consent

IK – Indigenous Knowledge

KCN – Keeyask Cree Nation

KGS – Keeyask Generating Station

LWR – Lake Winnipeg Regulation project

NFA – Northern Flood Agreement

NFAT – Needs For and Alternatives To

NRTA – Natural Resources Transfer Act

RCEA – Regional Cumulative Effects Assessment

ROI – Region of Interest

RSC – Regional Study Component

SARA – Species at Risk Act

SCC – Supreme Court of Canada

SIL – South Indian Lake

TCN – Tataskweyak Cree Nation

TEK – Traditional Ecological Knowledge

UNDRIP – United Nations Declaration on the Rights of
         Indigenous Peoples

VEC – Valued Ecological Component

WLFN – War Lake First Nation

WSK – Western Scientific Knowledge

YFFN – York Factory First Nation

" And the water, why are you selling it?
Our way of life is our land and my home."

Cheryl Flett, York Factory First Nation,
CEC hearings (26 September 2013), 22

CONTRIBUTORS

Jill Blakley is an associate professor in the Department of Geography and Planning and Interim Vice-Dean, Faculty Relations, in the College of Arts and Science at the University of Saskatchewan.

Will Braun is with the Interchurch Council on Hydropower and performs research and advocacy on energy and Indigenous issues.

Jerry Buckland is a professor of international development studies at Menno Simons College.

Aimée Craft is an associate professor of law in the Faculty of Common Law at the University of Ottawa and holds a University Research Chair in Nibi miinawaa aki inaakonigewin: Indigenous governance in relationship with land and water.

Alan P. Diduck is a professor in the Department of Environmental Studies and Sciences at the University of Winnipeg.

Joseph Dipple is a PhD candidate in the Department of Native Studies at the University of Manitoba.

Steve Ducharme is the president of the South Indian Lake Fishermen's Association.

Leslie Dysart is the CEO of the Community Association of South Indian Lake.

Patricia Fitzpatrick is a professor in the Department of Geography and an instructor in the Master's of Development Practice—Indigenous Development Program at the University of Winnipeg.

Kyrke Gaudreau is an adjunct professor of natural resources and environmental studies at the University of Northern British Columbia.

Robert B. Gibson is a professor in the School of Environment, Resources and Sustainability at the University of Waterloo.

Asfia Gulrukh Kamal is an assistant professor of Aboriginal and northern studies at the University College of the North.

Annette Luttermann is principal consultant with A.L. Ecologic based in Golden, British Columbia, specializing in river and wetland ecology.

Noah Massan is an Elder, trapper, and harvester from Fox Lake Cree Nation.

Ovide Mercredi is the former national chief of the Assembly of First Nations as well as the former chief of Misipawistik Cree Nation.

Bram Noble is a professor in the Department of Geography and Planning and Vice-Dean, Research, Scholarly and Artistic Work, in the College of Arts and Science at the University of Saskatchewan.

Melanie O'Gorman is an associate professor in the Department of Economics at the University of Winnipeg.

Agnieszka Pawlowska-Mainville is an associate professor in First Nations studies at the University of Northern British Columbia.

James P. Robson is an associate professor in the School of Environment and Sustainability at the University of Saskatchewan.

Terry Sargeant is the former chair of the Clean Environment Commission during the Keeyask Project hearings.

James A. Schaefer is a professor of biology at Trent University.

Byron Williams is the director of the Manitoba Public Interest Law Centre.